Daily Life through World History in Primary Documents

Daily Life through World History in Primary Documents
Lawrence Morris, General Editor

Volume 1: *The Ancient World*
David Matz

Volume 2: *The Middle Ages and Renaissance*
Lawrence Morris

Volume 3: *The Modern World*
David M. Borgmeyer and Rebecca Ayako Bennette

1 THE ANCIENT WORLD

Daily Life through World History in Primary Documents

Lawrence Morris
GENERAL EDITOR

David Matz
VOLUME EDITOR

GREENWOOD PRESS
Westport, Connecticut • London

Library of Congress Cataloging-in-Publication Data

Daily life through world history in primary documents / Lawrence
Morris, general editor.

    p. cm.

  Includes bibliographical references and index.
  ISBN: 978–0–313–33898–4 (set : alk. paper)
  ISBN: 978–0–313–33899–1 (v. 1 : alk. paper)
  ISBN: 978–0–313–33900–4 (v. 2 : alk. paper)
  ISBN: 978–0–313–33901–1 (v. 3 : alk. paper)
  1. Civilization—History—Sources.   2. Manners and customs—
History—Sources. 3. Social history—Sources.   I. Morris,
Lawrence, 1972–
  CB69.D35   2009
  909—dc22   2008008925

British Library Cataloguing in Publication Data is available.

Library of Congress Catalog Card Number: 2008008925
ISBN: 978–0–313–33898–4 (set)
     978–0–313–33899–1 (vol. 1)
     978–0–313–33900–4 (vol. 2)
     978–0–313–33901–1 (vol. 3)

First published in 2009

Greenwood Press, 88 Post Road West, Westport, CT 06881
An imprint of Greenwood Publishing Group, Inc.
www.greenwood.com

Printed in the United States of America

The paper used in this book complies with the
Permanent Paper Standard issued by the National
Information Standards Organization (Z39.48–1984).

10 9 8 7 6 5 4 3 2

Every reasonable effort has been made to trace the owners of copyrighted materials in this book, but in
some instances this has proven impossible. The author and publisher will be glad to receive information
leading to more complete acknowledgments in subsequent printings of the book and in the meantime
extend their apologies for any omissions.

To my family

CONTENTS

Contents

Contents

PART IV   INTELLECTUAL LIFE

Contents

Contents

PART VII   RECREATIONAL LIFE

Contents

SET INTRODUCTION

What time we leave work; the food we eat for dinner; how we spend our free time—these small, almost mundane details, can shape our lives as powerfully as who is the president or what battles are being fought in a far-distant country. In fact, we often judge major events—wars, legislation, trade deals—by how those events affect our everyday lives. If trade negotiations mean that we can purchase more goods for less money, we may very well support the negotiations: we will be able to eat out more, see more movies, buy more books. If the negotiations mean that we lose our jobs—resulting in skipped meals, bankruptcy, and ulcers caused by stress—we are likely to be much more critical. How an event impacts our daily life frequently determines how we view that event. Daily life, in other words, is very important and always has been.

The study of daily life therefore enables us to examine the cultural norms, concerns, and priorities of societies across time. We learn the vital importance of maritime trade for the citizens of medieval Barcelona, for example, when we examine the detailed law codes by which they carefully regulated the rights and responsibilities of ships' captains and merchants. We understand more deeply the pervasive role of religious ritual in medieval Japan when we read about the exorcisms practiced to combat ailments that we would now consider physical, not spiritual. When we learn about the day-to-day politics of the ancient Roman Republic, we appreciate how radically different life was under the Roman Empire. When we read a letter home from a U.S. soldier fighting in Vietnam, we feel more intimately the pain of separation. By studying daily life, we get a firmer understanding of what it was like to live in a certain era and a certain place. Learning that Constantine I was emperor of Rome in A.D. 313 gives us important information, but learning about the foods prepared by a Roman peasant or how a Roman merchant traveled about on business gives us a better idea of what it was really like to live in Italy during the same time period.

Primary sources, moreover, offer a uniquely valuable way of learning about the past. Primary sources, of course, are documents or artifacts produced by the people under investigation. These sources enable us to listen directly to the voices of the past. A primary source enables us to view the past from the inside, from the point of view of a person alive at the time. Our tour guide to the culture of ancient Egypt is an ancient Egyptian. Primary sources are the ultimate historical authority—there can be no greater expert on ancient Rome than an ancient Roman or on medieval France than a medieval Frenchman or woman or on twentieth-century Africa than a modern African.

Daily Life through World History in Primary Documents, therefore, offers the reader a feast of knowledge. Packed within the covers of this important three-volume set are over 500 documents, each of which offers readers the opportunity to listen to a voice from the past (and sometimes the present) explaining that person's own culture and time. The volumes are organized chronologically as follows:

Volume 1: *The Ancient World* contains almost 300 documents from various ancient cultures, including those of Sumeria, Egypt, Israel, China, India, Greece, and Rome, with its primary focus being upon the daily life of Greece and Rome up to roughly the sack of Rome in the fifth century A.D.

Volume 2: *The Middle Ages and Renaissance* contains almost 130 documents from various European (e.g., Anglo-Saxon England, Renaissance Italy), Asian (e.g., Tang China, medieval Japan, Mogul India), Middle Eastern (e.g., medieval Persia, early Islamic Arabia), and Latin American (e.g., Aztec Mexico, Inca Peru, Mayan Central America) cultures spanning the period from the fifth to the seventeenth centuries.

Volume 3: *The Modern World,* covering the birth of modern democracy in the eighteenth century up through the present day, contains over 100 documents from various world cultures, including Turkey, West Africa, India, the United States, and Russia.

At the edges of these basic divides, there is some overlap between volumes, demonstrating how each era carries on from the preceding one.

Within each volume, the myriad aspects of daily life are grouped under seven overarching categories: Domestic Life, Economic Life; Intellectual Life, Material Life, Political Life, Recreational Life, and Religious Life. These categories, which were also employed by the award-winning *Greenwood Encyclopedia of Daily Life,* allow for quick reference between all three volumes. Browsing Religious Life in all three volumes, for example, will offer a scintillating introduction to and overview of the major spiritual traditions across time. Under these shared categories, each volume then further subgroups the texts in the way most useful for the time period under discussion. Common subcategories include Women, Marriage, Children, Literature, Transportation, Medicine, Housing, Clothing, Law, Reform, Sports, and Rituals. Under "Economic Life" in Volume 2, for example, the subcategories employed highlight the important roles played by urban and rural populations, as well as the well-established practice of slavery and the increasingly important role of international trade and commerce.

The scope of *Daily Life through World History in Primary Documents* is truly global. Within these pages, we see documents from countries with such diverse histories and cultures as Japan, Italy, India, West Africa, Persia, the United States, and Central America. Browsing almost any of the subcategories will offer the reader fascinating voices from non-Western cultures. Each section, however, also includes a solid central focus on the major cultures that have shaped the Western world, including Europe and the Americas. None of these cultures exists in a vacuum, however, nor are they entirely dissimilar. Western and non-Western cultures contextualize each other and comment on the common concerns of human beings around the world. Brief analytical essays at the start of each subcategory outline the documents that follow and draw out important themes that weave throughout the documents, charting a cultural conversation that crosses time and place.

To benefit the most from the primary sources, each individual document also is preceded by an analytical introduction that explains and highlights the main features of that particular document. An author of a primary document, just like authors today, may have a bias, a limited perspective, or missing information that results in a slightly inaccurate portrayal of life in a given culture. The non-specialist reader, moreover, may not be familiar with the items and ideas discussed in a document written a thousand years ago, or in a completely different more contemporary culture. The concise analytical introductions preceding each document mitigate these difficulties by providing an expert evaluation and contextualization of the following document. The combination of primary sources and modern historical analyses of those sources offers the reader a balanced perspective and a solid grounding in the modern the study of daily life.

Part I in each volume offers a detailed historical overview of the period covered. Each volume also contains a chronology of important world events for the period covered, an appendix of brief biographies of document authors or creators, a glossary defining and describing unfamiliar names and terms encountered in the section and document introductions which are also in italics throughout the text for ease of reference, and a bibliography of sources used. Glossary terms in the text appear in italics. Many documents are also illustrated and information can be further accessed through a detailed subject index for the set.

These volumes will be used in many different ways by many different readers, including high school students, college and university undergrads, and interested general readers. Some readers will delve into one volume and browse extensively, gaining an overview of how generations in one era lived their lives. Other readers may be more interested in exploring how one realm of life—political life—for example, has changed from ancient Rome through the present day; those readers will devour the appropriate categories and subcategories from each of the three volumes. Other readers will use the sources to research and support their own written analyses, for assigned essays or for their own independent research. However the reader uses these volumes, I am confident that he or she will enjoy the experience. We have collected an amazing array of intriguing sources that cannot help but capture the interest and the imagination. Enjoy!

SET
ACKNOWLEDGMENTS

Many people have made working on *Daily Life through World History in Primary Documents* rewarding. First of all, the volume editors David Matz, Rebecca Ayako Bennette, and David Borgmeyer have created interesting and illuminating conversations between the plethora of texts included in their volumes—daily life comes alive in their pages. Dr. William McCarthy also helped to get the project rolling in its early stages. All the editors at Greenwood, and most especially Mariah Gumpert and John Wagner, have supported and encouraged us from day one. I thank Joyce Salisbury in particular for first awakening my interest in the study of daily life. Agus, ar ndóigh, gabhaim buíochas ar leith le mo bhean chéile, Amy, agus le mo chlann, a bhí foighneach agus tuisceanach nuair a bhuailinn an doras amach go dtí an oifig arís eile i ndiaidh an dinnéir chun beagáinín tuilleadh a scríobh. Tá cuid díobh féin istigh san obair seo; go gcúití Dia leo é.

CHRONOLOGY

CHRONOLOGY OF SELECTED EVENTS: THE ANCIENT WORLD

c. 3000 B.C.	Sumerian agricultural settlements in Mesopotamia begin to transform into city-states; the Indus Valley Civilization begins to emerge in India
c. 2925	Upper and Lower Egypt are unified
c. 2697	The Yellow Emperor, Huangdi, comes to power in China, and rules for about 100 years
2686–2181	The Old Kingdom flourishes in Egypt
c. 2665–2645	Reign of the Egyptian pharaoh Djoser, for whom the first step pyramid is built at Saqqara
c. 2589–c. 2504	Construction of the great Egyptian pyramids at Giza during the reigns of the fourth Dynasty pharaohs Khufu (c. 2589–2566 B.C.), Khafre (c. 2558–2532 B.C.), and Menkaure (c. 2532–2504 B.C.)
c. 2350	Ptah-hotep, royal vizier, composes his *Maxims*, a compilation of Egyptian didactic literature
c. 2330	The Akkadian king Sargon the Great conquers the Sumerians
2055–1650	The Middle Kingdom flourishes in Egypt
c. 2000	The Minoan Civilization emerges on the island Crete
c. 1750	Promulgation of the Code of Hammurabi, a set of laws issued by Hammurabi, king of Babylon
c. 1648–c. 1540	A Semitic people known as the Hyksos enter the Nile Delta and rule most of Egypt during this period; identified by some scholars as the Hebrews of the Exodus or as the pharaohs who invited the Hebrews into Egypt, the Hyksos introduced new modes of warfare to Egypt, especially use of the chariot
c. 1600	The Mycenaean Civilization, so named because the city of Mycenae was one of its most important centers, emerges on the Greek mainland
1570–1085	The Egyptian New Kingdom
c. 1530–1028	The Shang, or Yin, Dynasty is predominant in China during this period

c. 1500–c. 500	The Vedic period in Indian history, during which the Vedas, the sacred Sanskrit texts of Hinduism, were composed
c. 1352–1336	Reign of the pharaoh Akhenaten, who attempted to compel the Egyptian people to abandon worship of the traditional gods in favor of the one god Aten, who was symbolized by the sun disk
1333–1323	The reign of Tutankhamun, the Egyptian boy-king, who, because of the discovery of his unspoiled tomb in 1922, is best known today as King Tut; during his reign, Egypt returned to the worship of the old gods, abandoning the worship of Aten, which had earlier been instituted by Pharaoh Akhenaten
1286	Battle of Kadesh, in which the Egyptians prevail over the Hittites
c. Thirteenth century	Moses leads the Hebrews from bondage in Egypt
c. 1200	The Trojan War begins between the Greeks and the city of Troy in northwestern Asia Minor; according to Homer's *Iliad*, the war lasted 10 years
c. 1027–256	The Zhou, or Chou, Dynasty rules China; the dynasty's rule sees the further development of Chinese script and the growth of Chinese philosophy
c. 1000	King David comes to power in Israel
c. 970	Solomon succeeds his father David as king of Israel; his reign sees the construction in Jerusalem of a temple where the Ark of the Covenant is kept
c. 930	Following the death of Solomon, the kingdom of Israel splits into two states: Israel in the north ruled eventually from Samaria, and Judah in the south ruled from Jerusalem
776	Traditional founding date of the ancient Greek Olympics
753	Traditional date for the founding of the city of Rome
722	The northern Hebrew kingdom of Israel is conquered by the Assyrians and many of its citizens are carried away into exile, thus becoming known to history as the "lost tribes of Israel"
594	Solon reforms the laws of Athens
586	The Babylonian king Nebuchadnezzar completes the siege of Jerusalem and the destruction of the temple, an event that also marks the beginning of the Jewish Diaspora
c. 566	Birth of Siddhārtha Gautama, known as Buddha, an Indian spiritual teacher and the founder of Buddhism
551	Birth of Confucius, the Chinese thinker and social philosopher
509	Traditional date for the overthrow of the Roman monarchy and the founding of the Roman Republic, which was to last until 27 B.C.
c. 508	Cleisthenes's legal reforms place the Athenian constitution on a democratic footing
490	A Persian army under King Darius invades Greece but is defeated by a smaller mainly Athenian force at the Battle of Marathon

480	The naval component of a second Persian invasion of Greece, led this time by King Xerxes, son of Darius I, is defeated by a Greek fleet at the Battle of Salamis; the Persian army burns Athens after being held up for days at the mountain pass of Thermopylae by a force of 300 Spartans and their allies
479	A Greek army defeats a Persian force at the Battle of Plataea, thereby ending the invasion of Xerxes and the second Persian War
468	Death of the Indian teacher and philosopher Mahavira, "The Great Hero," whose doctrines formed the basis of Indian Jain literature
c. 450	The Twelve Tables, the first codification of Roman law, are published
460–429	The orator and statesman Pericles dominates Athenian political life during this period; many of the great buildings of the Athenian Golden Age are constructed during this time, including the Parthenon
431–404	The Peloponnesian War pits Athens and its allies against Sparta and its allies and ends in the defeat of Athens; the historian Thucydides (c. 460–400 b.c.) spends the last 20 years of his life writing a monumental history of the war
c. 430	Sophocles authors possibly the most famous play in the history of Greek tragedy, *Oedipus the King;* in the fall of 430, Pericles delivers his Funeral Oration, in which he praises the Athenian democracy and claims that Athens is the "School of Greece"
399	Found guilty of corrupting the youth of Athens, the Athenian philosopher Socrates is forced to commit suicide by drinking hemlock
384–322	These dates mark the life spans of two noted Athenians: Demosthenes, the foremost orator of the fourth century b.c., and Aristotle, who was pre-eminent in many fields of inquiry, including philosophy, biology, literature, and political science
338	Philip II of Macedonia defeats the combined forces of Athens and Thebes at the Battle of Chaeronea to establish Macedonian hegemony over Greece
336	Alexander the Great succeeds his assassinated father, Philip II, as king of Macedonia
333	Alexander the Great defeats the main Persian army of Darius III at the Battle Issus, thus beginning the destruction of the Persian Empire, which, after Alexander's death, was succeeded by a number of states ruled by Greek dynasties
331	Alexander the Great founds the Egyptian city of Alexandria, which over the next century evolves into a focal point of learning and creativity, signaling the beginning of the Hellenistic Age; geographers, astronomers, physicians, and mathematicians flourish in Alexandria, which boasts a magnificent library
323	Death of Alexander the Great in Babylon
321–184	The Maurya Dynasty rules most of India

c. 312	Construction begins on the first paved Roman road, the Via Appia, or Appian Way, which runs eventually from Rome to Brundisium in southeastern Italy
c. 273–232	Reign of the emperor Asoka the Great, an aggressive and dynamic ruler of the Maurya Dynasty, who extended his authority over most of India
264–241	The First Punic War, fought between Rome and Carthage, ends in victory for the former, which becomes the dominant naval power in the Mediterranean
221–206	Rule of the Chinese Qin (or Ch'in) Dynasty, from whose name the word *China* derives
218–201	The Second Punic War between Rome and Carthage is noted especially for the invasion of Italy undertaken by the Carthaginian general Hannibal, who defeats several Roman armies and nearly seizes and occupies Rome
216	During the Second Punic War, Hannibal wins the Battle of Cannae, which is considered to be one of the worst military defeats ever suffered by Rome
206 B.C.–220 A.D.	Rule of the Han Dynasty in China
202 B.C.	Fought on African soil, the Battle of Zama, in which a Roman army under Publius Cornelius Scipio defeats a Carthaginian force under Hannibal, ends the Second Punic War with a Roman victory
164–63	An independent Jewish state is ruled from Jerusalem by the Jewish Hasmonean Dynasty
149–146	The Third Punic War between Rome and Carthage results in the complete destruction of Carthage
133	Attempting to pass a land reform bill, the Roman tribune Tiberius Sempronius Gracchus is killed in a riot
121	Death of Gaius Gracchus, brother of Tiberius Gracchus, whose attempted reforms led to his flight from Rome and his death, either by his request or through treachery, at the hands of his slave
100	Birth of Julius Caesar
91–88	Rome defeats a coalition of former allies among the other cities of Italy in what is known as the Social War
82–80	The Roman general Sulla seizes power in Rome as dictator, thereby setting an example of one-man rule that will later help hasten the end of the Roman Republic
73–70	Rome defeats a slave revolt led by the gladiator-slave Spartacus during an uprising known as the Third Servile War
70	Birth of the Roman poet Virgil, who completed his epic poem *Aeneid* shortly before his death in 19 B.C.
63	The noted Roman statesman and lawyer Marcus Tullius Cicero exposes and disrupts the plot of the disappointed office-seeker

	Catiline to overthrow the Roman government in an armed rebellion; Cicero's four speeches against Catiline, delivered in November and December 63, have become classics of Latin literature. Birth of Julius Caesar's grand-nephew Octavian, who becomes the future emperor Augustus
59–54	Caesar, Pompey, and Crassus form and maintain the First Triumvirate to govern the Roman Republic
58–50	Caesar conquers Gaul for Rome
49	Caesar initiates civil war by crossing the Rubicon River and leading his troops into Italy from Gaul; he is opposed by a conservative Senate faction led by his former ally Pompey
44	Julius Caesar is assassinated in the Ides of March conspiracy, which is led by men who oppose his assumption of dictatorial powers in Rome
43	The orator and politician Cicero is killed during the political turmoil that follows upon Caesar's murder; Octavian, Mark Antony, and Lepidus form the Second Triumvirate in opposition to the conservative faction that slew Caesar
42	The civil war initiated by Caesar's murder ends with the defeat of Caesar's assassins by his political heirs, Octavian and Mark Antony
32	Civil war erupts between Octavian, who controls Rome and the western empire, and Antony, who controls the eastern empire
31	The naval Battle of Actium results in the defeat of Mark Antony and Cleopatra by Octavian, who thereafter ends the Roman Republic and initiates the Roman Empire by instituting one-man rule
30	Antony and his lover, Cleopatra, queen of Egypt, who is the former lover of Julius Caesar, commit suicide; Egypt becomes a Roman province
27	Octavian, taking the title Augustus Caesar, becomes sole ruler of Rome, thus initiating the Roman Empire while outwardly retaining the forms and institutions of the Republic
c. 6	Birth of Jesus, the founder of Christianity
A.D. 14	Death of Augustus Caesar, who is succeeded as emperor by his stepson Tiberius
43	The Romans invade Britain under the emperor Claudius (r. A.D. 41–54)
64	The great fire of Rome destroys much of the city; Emperor Nero (r. A.D. 54–68) blames the fire on the Christians, who undergo their first period of state persecution
66–70	Jewish Revolt against Rome culminates in the destruction of the temple in Jerusalem in A.D. 70
79	The eruption of Mount Vesuvius, on August 24 and 25 of this year. The scientist Pliny the Elder is one of the casualties of the eruption. Also in this year, construction begins in Rome on the Flavian Amphitheater, better known as the Coliseum

98–180	The Golden Age of ancient Rome, in which the city is ruled by five effective and conscientious emperors in succession: Nerva; Trajan; Hadrian; Antoninus Pius; Marcus Aurelius. In the words of the historian Edward Gibbon: "If a man were called to fix the period in the history of the world, during which the condition of the human race was most happy and prosperous, he would, without hesitation, name that which elapsed from the death of Domitian [A.D. 98] to the accession of Commodus [A.D. 180]."
122	Construction of Hadrian's Wall begins in northern Britain
280–550	The Gupta Empire rules most of India
303	The emperor Diocletian orders the persecution of Christians
306–337	Reign of Emperor Constantine, who proclaims toleration for Christianity throughout the Roman Empire
476	Deposition of the boy emperor Romulus Augustulus by the Germanic chieftain Odoacer, whose action makes him king of Italy; year is traditionally taken as the ending date of the Roman Empire in the West

Part I
HISTORICAL OVERVIEW

Sumeria

The story of civilization begins with the Sumerians, who settled in Mesopotamia (modern Iraq). They cultivated their once-swampy homeland, creating a thriving agricultural economy. Around 3000 B.C., their agricultural settlements began to be transformed into the following 12 city-states: Adab, Akshak, Bad-tibera, Erech, Kish, Lagash, Larak, Larsa, Nippur, Sippar, Umma, and Ur. The Sumerians were the first civilization to use the city-state form of political and social organization. At the outset, the citizens of the city-states dictated government policy, but, ultimately, monarchies emerged in all 12.

Around 2330 B.C., the Sumerians were conquered by an Akkadian army under the leadership of Sargon the Great. Sargon's vast empire, which overwhelmed the Sumerian city-states, stretched from the Persian Gulf to the Mediterranean Sea. He controlled this sprawling empire by dividing it into smaller administrative units and appointing bureaucrats to supervise each one. After Sargon's death in about 2279 B.C., his empire gradually devolved once more into a series of city-states. Ur, the most prominent of these city-states, became known for the promulgation of one of the earliest law codes.

Around 1900 B.C., the Amorites conquered the Sumerian lands, and the Sumerians, as a distinct cultural entity, faded from the scene. However, the accomplishments of the Sumerians, which included the first practical use of wheels, in both pottery-making and transportation; the first city-states; and, perhaps most importantly, the first system of writing, a collection of symbols carved into clay tablets known as cuneiform, have endured.

China

The early history of China may be studied from the perspective of four of the earliest dynasties: the Shang or Yin, the Chou, the Ch'in, and the Han.

SHANG DYNASTY (C. 1530–1028 B.C.)

Under the Shang Dynasty, the first historic Chinese dynasty, the earliest form of Chinese writing emerged in the form of inscriptions on daggers, earthenware, tortoise shells, and even bones. Monarchy was the predominant form of government, although priests, with their powers of prophecy, also enjoyed great prestige. A wide gulf apparently separated kingly lifestyles from the daily routines of the ordinary people; kings dwelled in ornate palaces, while their subjects passed their days in simple huts and caves. The Shang Dynasty survived for over 500 years, until it was toppled by the Chou Dynasty in about 1027 B.C.

CHOU (ZHŌU) DYNASTY (c. 1027–256 B.C.)

The Chou Dynasty came to power because of the corruption and ineptitude of the last Shang ruler. By contrast, the first two Chou rulers, Wen Wang and his son Wu Wang, were noble and virtuous. Down to about 770 B.C. the dynasty is known as the Western Chou because of the location of the dynastic capital in the northwestern portion of the family's territories. The Western Chou built upon the achievements of the Shang in writing and metallurgy. Chou rulers maintained power through what they termed *the Mandate of Heaven,* wherein the ruler occupied a sort of middle position between heaven and earth. The Chinese of this period attributed the downfall of a ruler or a dynasty to a forfeiture of this mandate through dishonest or ignoble behavior.

Around 770 B.C., barbarian invaders defeated the last Western Chou ruler and moved the capital eastward to Loyang. The dynasty founded by the invaders was hence known as the Eastern Chou, whose rulers were unable to impose the same political and military unity achieved by their predecessors. Nonetheless, the Eastern Chou presided over a sort of Chinese Golden Age sometimes called *The Period of the One Hundred Schools.* During this time, some of the most noteworthy Chinese philosophers flourished, including Kung Fu Tzu (Confucius), out of whose teachings developed the Chinese ethical and philosophical system known as Confucianism; Lao Tzu, the founder of Taoism; and Mo Tzu.

CH'IN DYNASTY (221–206 B.C.)

Although lasting for a mere 15 years, the Ch'in Dynasty had so great an impact on Chinese history that the modern name of the country, *China,* derives from it. The emperor most closely associated with this dynasty is Ch'eng, who took the title Shih Huang Ti, which is variously translated as "The First August Sovereign" or "The First Exalted Emperor." The Ch'in established the first great Chinese empire, with the emperor consolidating administrative authority in his hands by weakening the power of local aristocratic nobles. Under Ch'in rule, a network of highways was constructed and money, the calendar, and weights and measures were standardized. The Ch'in also began a construction of a series of fortifications that eventually became the Great Wall of China.

The Ch'in emperor enforced a Draconian adherence to the accepted laws and legal doctrines; deviation from the prescribed norms meant the death penalty. When Shang Huang Ti died in 210 B.C., the unity that he had brought to China quickly dissolved into rioting and anarchy. The dynasty that was supposedly destined to last 10,000 years outlasted its "first exalted emperor" by only four years.

HAN DYNASTY (202 B.C.–A.D. 220)

Like their predecessors, the goal of the Han rulers was national unification. In this, the Han succeeded to an extent not achieved by previous dynasties. The Han Dynasty saw the expansion of Chinese hegemony into Vietnam and Korea, as well as the establishment of Chinese control over the Silk Road, a trade route that eventually stretched as far as the Roman world in the west. Much of this expansion occurred during the reign of emperor Wu Ti (141–87 B.C.).

The Han Dynasty, like the Eastern Chou before them, inspired a burst of creative activity in many areas. Several noted writers, among them Ssu-ma Ch'ien (first century B.C.) and Pan Ku (A.D. 32–92) produced high quality historical works. The historian Sima Qian's *Records of the Historian* was the exemplar for all future Chinese historians. Around A.D. 100, the first dictionary of Chinese characters was published, the *Shuo Wen,* or *Explanation of Writing.* A comprehensive book on natural history, *Book of the Mountains and Seas,* also appeared during the Han period. Technological advances, including the invention of paper and the development of silk weaving, occurred during this time period. So lasting was the influence of the Han Dynasty that modern Chinese proudly refer to themselves as *Men of Han.*

India

The first important cultural group in Indian history was the Indus Valley Civilization (also known as the Harappan Civilization), which began to flourish sometime after 3000 B.C. Around the middle of the second millennium B.C., various Aryan peoples supplanted the Indus Valley Civilization. During this time, the earliest Indian literary source was compiled, the *Rig Veda,* which is an anthology of religious hymns.

Aryan influence began to wane in the sixth century B.C., when the country was divided into 16 monarchies known collectively as the Mahajanapadas. The most prominent of these was the Kingdom of Magadh in the valley of the Ganges River. Lasting from about 500 to 300 B.C., the period of the 16 kingdoms is regarded as a golden age, when many notable advances occurred, including the development of coinage and the creation of some of the earliest Sanskrit texts. Siddhârtha Gautama, the founder of Buddhism and known to its adherents as the Great Buddha, was born in about 563 B.C., the son of a north Indian ruler.

The Mauryan Kingdom emerged in the third century B.C. under the leadership of one of the most dynamic of Indian monarchs, Asoka the Great, who ruled from 273 to 232 B.C. An aggressive leader, Asoka pushed his conquests as far as the Kingdom of Kalinga on India's eastern shore. As a result of this offensive, Asoka wrote that "150,000 were captured, 100,000 were slain, and many times as many died."

However, after his conversion to Buddhism, he adopted the principle of Ahimsa, "respect for life." He put aside his earlier bellicose inclinations and instead channeled his energies into spreading Buddhism throughout India, as well as into Ceylon and southeast Asia. Asoka's missionaries also came into contact with peoples as far away as north Africa, western Asia, and eastern Europe. Under Asoka's leadership, Buddhism emerged as a prominent world religion.

After Asoka's death, India was not a unified nation but a collection of small, discordant kingdoms subject to attacks from each other and also from foreign invaders. However, unity was restored during the Gupta Period (A.D. 320–540) by the first two Gupta kings, Chandragupta I (A.D. 320–330) and his son Samudragupta (A.D. 330–380), who is sometimes called the "Napoleon of India."

During the Gupta Dynasty, India enjoyed a renaissance in art, literature, science, and other creative endeavors. Kalidas, a famous Sanskrit poet and dramatist, flourished under the Gupta, as did such mathematicians and astronomers as Arybhatta and Varahmihir. Hindu temple architecture also began to take shape under the Gupta. A traveler from China, Fa Hsien, visited India in the early fifth century A.D. and chronicled his observations of the Gupta Dynasty.

Egypt

Egypt boasts a civilization that remained intact for almost 3,000 years, beginning with the unification of Upper and Lower Egypt around the year 2925 B.C. By 2686 B.C., a dynastic tradition had been established, and the history of the Old Kingdom (2686–2181 B.C.) began under the direct and unquestioned control of the pharaoh.

The Old Kingdom is also aptly known as the Pyramid Age, for it was during this time that the construction of those immense tombs began. One of the earliest names associated with pyramid building was Imhotep, a trusted advisor to the pharaoh Djoser. Under Imhotep's direction, a step pyramid (c. 2650 B.C.) was constructed for Djoser; it was the first structure in history in which prepared stone was used throughout.

Pyramid building reached its zenith during the Fourth Dynasty (2613–2494 B.C.), when the famous pyramids of Giza were constructed. The Great Pyramid originally soared to a height of almost 520 feet; over two million limestone blocks were used in its construction. Other Old Kingdom advances included crop irrigation and the invention of a solar calendar similar to the calendar in use today.

The Old Kingdom declined and eventually disappeared after 2181 B.C. After a transitional period lasting over a hundred years, the Middle Kingdom (2055–1650 B.C.) emerged. The Middle Kingdom was marked by a flurry of expansionism, which included the annexation of Nubia (modern Sudan) to the south. This annexation gave the Egyptians access to Nubian gold mines, which increased Middle Kingdom wealth and accelerated its commercial relationships with places such as Palestine, Syria, and Crete.

Around 1700 B.C., Egypt was invaded and occupied by the Hyksos, a people whose origins are unknown, but who may have come from somewhere in the Middle East. The Hyksos ruled Egypt for about a hundred years until their expulsion in 1570 B.C. This expulsion paved the way for the emergence of the Egyptian New Kingdom (1570–1085 B.C.).

Perhaps the most remarkable feature of the New Kingdom was its emphasis on aggressive expansion. The pharaohs of the New Kingdom pushed the boundaries of Egypt to the Euphrates River and also took control of land in Palestine and Syria. Their possession of the Nubian gold mines provided the necessary funding for these ambitious ventures. Commercial interactions with other nations and city-states also increased, coupled with a change in religious belief. For much of their history, the Egyptians had been polytheistic, but the pharaoh Akhenaton (1669–1353 B.C.) introduced the worship of a single god, Aton, who was represented by the sun. Akhenaton's religious views died with him, and the traditional Egyptian religion was revived by his successors, most notably Tutankhamon, whose tomb was discovered intact in the twentieth century. He has become popularly known as King Tut. One other noteworthy New Kingdom event was the exodus of the Israelites from Egypt under the leadership of Moses.

After the reign of Akhenaton, the New Kingdom experienced a slow decline, culminating in its collapse around 1085 B.C. A succession of foreign invaders, including the Libyans, Persians, and, ultimately, in the fourth century B.C., the Greeks, ruled the country. After the conquest of Alexander the Great in 332 B.C., Egypt became fully immersed in Hellenistic culture. Founded by Alexander, the city of *Alexandria* became a center of learning and human creativity. Alexandria could boast of a magnificent library that is thought to have contained over a half million volumes. There were also spectacular advances in medicine, astronomy, and mathematics. The Alexandrian astronomer Aristarchus (c. 310–230 B.C.) argued in favor of a heliocentric solar system almost two millennia before Copernicus and Galileo reached the same conclusion. The geometric proofs of the mathematician Euclid (fl. 300 B.C.) belong to Alexandria's Hellenistic age, while the geographer Eratosthenes (c. 275–194 B.C.) accurately calculated the earth's circumference. In 30 B.C., Egypt came under Roman rule, which lasted until A.D. 395, when control of the country was assumed by Constantinople.

Israel

The earliest Hebrew people, forbears of the Israelites, lived in the land of Canaan. At some point, some of the Hebrews emigrated from Canaan to Egypt seeking a more viable environment for their agricultural production. However, they eventually became the slaves of the Egyptians and sought a way to escape from the clutches of the pharaohs. In the thirteenth century B.C., the Hebrew leader Moses, claiming to be a messenger of God, led the Hebrews from bondage in Egypt. After a long and arduous journey through the desert, they ultimately arrived, again, in Canaan, where they were reunited with the Hebrews who had not emigrated. The Philistines, Aegean Sea islanders who had settled on the southern coasts of Canaan, threatened the security of the newly unified Hebrews, but under the leadership of King Saul, the Philistines were contained.

King David took power among the Hebrews around 1000 B.C. and ushered in a memorable chapter in the history of ancient Israel. King David's armies subjugated the Philistines and subdued other neighboring tribes, including the Moabites and the Ammonites. David established Jerusalem as the capital city of the increasingly powerful and unified Hebrews; he conferred a religious aura on the city by placing the Ark of the Covenant there. The ark was a specially built sacred container within which were placed the tablets containing the Ten Commandments and other sacred objects.

When King David died in 973 B.C., he was succeeded by his son King Solomon. Perhaps the most significant achievement of Solomon's reign was the construction in Jerusalem of a temple where the Ark of the Covenant could be kept. With the help of the seafaring Phoenicians, who lived to the north of Israel, Solomon created a fleet of Hebrew merchant ships that traveled widely on trading expeditions and greatly increased the material prosperity of the kingdom.

After the death of Solomon in 922 B.C., Hebrew unity dissolved into two separate kingdoms: Judah, to the south, and Israel, to the north. The Assyrians invaded and conquered Israel in 722 B.C., dispersing many of the people of the kingdom to other parts of the Assyrian Empire. In 586 B.C., Judah, whose kings ruled from Jerusalem, fell to the Chaldeans, who destroyed Solomon's magnificent temple and exiled many of the kingdom's inhabitants. Many were sent to Babylon, the Chaldean capital, thus initiating a period of almost 50 years that came to be known in Israelite history as the Babylonian Captivity. Shortly after the Persians conquered Babylon in 538 B.C., King Cyrus of Persia allowed the Hebrews to return to Judah, where they retained the right to practice their religion and were allowed to rebuild the temple. The Hebrews remained under Persian rule until the Persian Empire was overthrown by Alexander the Great of the Greek kingdom of Macedonia in the 330s B.C.

Thereafter, the Hebrews or, as they have been commonly called after this period, Jewish people, fell under the rule of the Hellenistic Seleucid kingdom, one of the successor states to Alexander's empire. In 164 B.C., a revolt led by the Maccabees ended Seleucid rule and established an independent Jewish kingdom ruled by the Hasmonean royal dynasty. The Hasmonean kingdom ended in 63 B.C. when Jerusalem and the Jewish state passed under Roman rule. In A.D. 66, the eruption of an ultimately unsuccessful Jewish revolt against the Romans led to the recapture of Jerusalem and the destruction of the temple in A.D. 70. Some 100,000 Jews were killed and another 100,000 were seized as slaves. A second rebellion against Roman rule erupted in A.D. 132 under the leadership of Simon Bar Kokhba, but it was soon put down. The Romans then created a new province, Syria-Palestine, and the region of the old Hebrew kingdoms has been known as Palestine since that time.

Greece

The first important civilization in the Greek world arose not on the Greek mainland but on the Mediterranean island of Crete to the south. Around 2000 B.C., the Minoans—named for the legendary Cretan king Minos—developed a flourishing civilization that featured ornate palaces for the monarchs and their entourages. The palaces had workshops where high-quality vases and other implements were fabricated. The walls were decorated with mural paintings, and the lavatories had running water, baths, and drains. Around 1250 B.C., the Minoan civilization abruptly vanished, perhaps as the result of an earthquake or volcanic eruption, although the exact cause of its demise is unknown.

Coinciding with the decline of the Minoans was the rise of the Mycenaean civilization on the Greek mainland. The Mycenaeans, like the Minoans, built elaborate palaces for their rulers and also developed a system of writing known as Linear B (because the characters appear in straight lines), an early form of Greek. They were also great seafarers, and their merchant ships plied the waters of the Mediterranean from Sicily to the Near East. The city of Mycenae was the capital of *Agamemnon,* the leader of the Greek forces that attacked Troy. Agamemnon's role in the Trojan War is described in detail in Homer's epic poem, *Iliad.* Unfortunately, Mycenaean participation in the Trojan War may have helped hasten the end of its civilization, which collapsed around 1150 B.C.

After the downfall of the Mycenaeans, ancient Greece lapsed into a Dark Age, which lasted until about 800 B.C. At that time, an era of economic expansion, international trade, and overseas colonization emerged. The Greeks established colonies as far east as Asia Minor and as far west as Sicily. The Olympic Games, first held in *Olympia* in 776 B.C., as well as other important athletic/religious festivals, were founded during this period. City-states, or *poleis*, flourished across Greece, and the stage was set for the rise of Athens and other Greek population centers.

Athens eventually became the cultural and economic center of Classical Greece, ultimately evolving into one of the most powerful city-states. One of its earliest identifiable figures was the statesman/philosopher/poet *Solon*, who in 594 B.C. was granted extensive power to reform the laws of Athens. He undertook this awesome responsibility vigorously and comprehensively, drafting or reforming laws and policies in areas such as debt and currency, agriculture, wills, and marriage. So far-reaching was his influence that his name lives on today in the English language to refer to a wise and prudent legislator.

During the sixth century B.C., Athens matured as a city-state. Two notable Athenian politicians book-ended the century—Solon at its beginning and *Cleisthenes* at its end. Around 508 B.C., Cleisthenes took the lead in establishing the beginnings of democracy by spearheading a movement to place governmental power in the Athenian *Assembly,* and by introducing a unique practice called *ostracism,* a method of curtailing the power of overly ambitious politicians. Ostracism worked as follows: Once per year, the Assembly could vote to exile from Athens any one politician for a period of 10 years. Each voter was issued an *ostrakon,* or broken piece of pottery, on which he inscribed the name of the politician he most wished to see exiled. As long as a minimum of 6,000 votes were cast, the individual with the most votes recorded against his name had to undergo the prescribed penalty.

Abuses, however, sometimes occurred. *Aristides,* a fifth-century B.C. politician with so great a reputation for honesty and fairness that he received the sobriquet "the Just," was ostracized in 483 B.C. According to a well-known story, during the voting, an illiterate farmer, who did not known Aristides by sight, marched up to him and asked him to inscribe the name "Aristides" on his ostrakon. Aristides was understandably taken aback; he asked the farmer how Aristides had wronged him and the farmer replied that Aristides had never harmed him in any way, but he was weary of hearing about Aristides the Just all the time. Aristides, honest man that he was, dutifully carved his own name on the potsherd.

In the early fifth century B.C., the Greeks faced a crisis from abroad. The Persians, who had been relentlessly pushing their imperial domains ever further west, invaded Greece in 490 B.C. and again 10 years later in 480 B.C. Both times, the Greeks, under the leadership of Athens, defeated the Persians, even though the Persian king had larger armies and greater resources.

In about 478 B.C., representatives from several hundred Greek poleis met on the tiny island of Delos in the Cyclades archipelago off the eastern coast of Greece. There they form an alliance, known as the Delian League, which was designed to prevent the Persians from attempting a third invasion. Because the Delian League was eventually dominated by Athens, its formation helped set the stage of the golden age of Athenian power.

The groundwork that was laid by Cleisthenes for a democracy in Athens came to full flower in the mid-fifth century B.C. The Athenian Assembly met 40 times per year, not in a comfortable, ornately decorated hall, but out of doors on the side of a rocky hill called the Pnyx. Any male Athenian citizen could attend and participate in Assembly meetings. While the precise number of Athenian citizens at any given time is unknown, there may have been 40,000 in the mid-fifth century, a far greater number than could be comfortably accommodated on the Pnyx. In reality, however, few of the 40,000 likely showed up for Assembly meetings, so overcrowding was seldom, if ever, a problem. In the Assembly, debates and speeches about public policy issues ensued, and attendees could voice their opinions and vote when appropriate.

It has been said that Athenian democracy was noteworthy by virtue of the absence of professional politicians, and this is probably true. However, one area where professional competency was paramount was military leadership. Hence, the generals—*strategoi* (singular *strategos*)—of the Athenian army were elected, 10 per year, for terms of one year. Generals could run for re-election; *Pericles*, perhaps the most famous figure of Athens' Golden Age, was elected strategos 15 consecutive times between 444 and 429 B.C.

The zenith of the Athenian golden age coincided with Pericles's remarkable string of electoral triumphs, and it seems fair to say that he was the driving force that made the golden age possible. During this time, poets and playwrights flourished, notably the famous triad of tragedians—Aeschylus, Sophocles, and Euripides—as well as the comic playwright Aristophanes, and many others, whose works are fragmentary or known only by references to them in works of other authors. Philosophers and historians, such as *Socrates* and Thucydides, also flourished in Periclean Athens. All these writers enjoyed complete freedom of speech. Plutarch, who wrote a biography of Pericles, says that the comic playwrights of the time saddled Pericles with the uncomplimentary nickname *schinocephalus* ("squillhead"), a reference to his misshapen skull. In modern times, such a comment would be at best unseemly, but the unbridled satirists of the fifth century B.C. were bound by no such conventions of nicety or political correctness.

The Athenian golden age was also marked by a flurry of building activity, as Pericles sought to beautify the city with a number of impressive buildings, particularly to serve as tangible examples of Athenian power. Of these structures, the most enduringly famous is the *Parthenon*, a huge temple in honor of the goddess Athena, which was constructed on top of the *Acropolis*, the highest elevation in the city. The Parthenon is about 200 feet long. The exterior supports for its roof are massive Doric columns, each about 34 feet tall, with a diameter of over 6 feet. The building is graced, inside and out, with first-rate sculptural decorations. In the interior stood a colossal statue of Athena, about 40 feet tall, crafted of ivory and gold, and created under the supervision of Athens's most renowned sculptor/artist, *Pheidias*. The entire building was constructed of the most expensive marble, and the bottom-line price tag for the project was an astounding 5,000 talents. (Because a conservative estimate for the dollar value of a talent might be $300,000, the Parthenon, in modern terms, cost at least one and a half *billion* dollars.)

Pericles paid for his ambitious building projects in Athens by siphoning off funds from the Delian League, whose member poleis made annual contributions to the League treasury. This practice was bitterly criticized by League members, but Pericles responded by saying that as long as Athens kept the Persians at bay he had no obligation to provide any justification or explanation to the allies or to rival Athenian politicians for how League funds were spent.

The Athenian golden age ended with the start of the Peloponnesian War (431–404 B.C.), a long and bitter struggle between the two most powerful Greek poleis, Athens and *Sparta*. A long simmering rivalry between the two city-states finally erupted into open war for many reasons, but the two identified by the historian Thucydides (c. 460–c. 400 B.C.) in his monumental work on the conflict were the growing power of Athens and the Spartan fear of that power. The long war finally ended when the victorious Spartans breeched the walls of Athens and occupied the city.

The fourth century B.C. was characterized by the rise and decline of various poleis that were trying, whether consciously or not, to fill the void left by the fall of Athens. Chief among these city-states were Sparta and Thebes. During the century, the city-state model of government gave way to more authoritarian forms, especially when Philip II and his son Alexander, the rulers of the northern kingdom of Macedonia, brought most of Greece under their control in the 330s B.C.

Alexander succeeded Philip on the Macedonian throne in 336 B.C., when Philip was murdered. Only 20 years old, Alexander immediately implemented a plan to invade Persia. Alexander defeated Darius III of Persia at Issus in 333 B.C. He thereafter extended his rule into Egypt and led his army as far east as Afghanistan and India. The result of Alexander's campaigns was a new mingling of eastern and western cultures, encouraged by the king himself, who married a Persian woman and founded over 70 cities, all named Alexandria, throughout his domains. Had he not died prematurely of fever at age 33 in 323 B.C., Alexander might have united all the lands he conquered into a permanent, stable Hellenistic kingdom. As it was, Alexander's empire broke up quickly into a series of successor states ruled by some of his leading commanders. Although Greek literature, philosophy, rhetoric, and language remained as influential forces in the intellectual life of the ancient world, the rising power of Rome gradually emerged as the successor to Greek cultural and political dominance.

Rome

Few Trojans survived the epic conflict with Greek invaders immortalized by the poet Homer in the *Iliad*. According to Roman tradition, one of the survivors, Aeneas, escaped from the burning city of Troy and, with a small band of friends, sailed away as refugees, not knowing where they were headed nor what lay in store for them. After many adventures and setbacks on the high seas, the Trojans eventually landed in central Italy, and, after some resistance from the local inhabitants, established a new homeland. Aeneas, according to this view, was the progenitor of Rome.

A shadowy and poorly attested line of kings ruled for four centuries after Aeneas. Then, some time in the eighth century B.C., came the birth of a pair of twin boys named *Romulus* and Remus. One of them was said to be destined to found a new and great city, but when it could not be determined which of the two it was, both began construction of cities on adjacent hills. According to Roman legend, Remus one day paid a visit to his brother's hill to see how the construction was progressing. Upon seeing that little had been accomplished, Remus began to taunt his brother about the puniness of his fortification walls. Romulus endured this abuse in silence for a short time, but when Remus began to leap back and forth over the unfinished walls, Romulus drew his sword and slew his brother, proclaiming as he did so that a similar fate would await anyone who attempted to breech the walls of his city. Romulus's dictum was never in the future to be taken lightly either by the Romans or by their many foreign enemies. Romulus continued building his new city, which was named Rome in his honor, and became its first king in 753 B.C., the date traditionally taken for the founding of the city. He was succeeded by six more kings, until the last—Tarquinus Superbus—was expelled around 509 B.C., when the monarchy was abolished and replaced with a republic.

In its earliest days, the Roman Republic was divided into two socioeconomic groups: the patricians, who constituted the wealthy nobility, and the plebeians, the common people. A prolonged civil rights struggle characterized the first several centuries of the republic, with the plebeians attempting to gain social, political, and economic equality with the patricians, and the patricians trying to prevent them from doing so. The plebeians eventually prevailed, partly because they outnumbered the patricians, and partly because the patricians needed plebeian soldiers to fight the many expansionist and defensive wars in which the republic was involved.

Among the worst of these conflicts were the Punic Wars (from the Latin word *Punicus* for "Carthaginian"), which pitted Rome against *Carthage,* a north African city of Phoenician origins. A growing rivalry for economic and political control of Sicily, southern Italy, and Spain exploded into the First Punic War (264–241 B.C.), which end with the establishment of Roman hegemony in Sicily. The Second Punic War (218–201 B.C.) was perhaps the most difficult and dangerous conflict in which Rome was ever involved. The brilliant Carthaginian general Hannibal had sworn as oath at the age of nine that he would be the relentless and intractable enemy of the Roman people. As a youth, he accompanied his father, Hamilcar, the leader of the Carthaginian army, to Spain, where the Carthaginians were establishing outposts and military bases. In 221 B.C., when Hannibal was about 26, Hamilcar died, leaving his son to assume command of the army. In 218 B.C., Hannibal blockaded and eventually captured the Spanish coastal town of Saguntum, a nominal Roman ally. Rome declared war on Carthage and the Second Punic War began.

In a bold and unexpected move, Hannibal invaded Italy by marching overland through Spain and southern France before undertaking an arduous October crossing of the Alps. Although the land route was for more difficult and dangerous, especially for the seafaring Carthaginians, Hannibal chose it as the best way to both toughen his men and intimidate the Romans. Hannibal won three decisive victories over the Romans in Italy: at the Trebia River in 218 B.C., at Lake Trasimene in 217 B.C., and at the Battle of Cannae in 216 B.C., with the latter being a particularly disastrous Roman defeat. After Cannae, Hannibal's lifelong desire to destroy Rome seemed about to be realized. Although he marched to the walls of Rome, he had not the strength to take the city. Remaining in Italy for the next 13 years, Hannibal was recalled to Carthage in 203 B.C. In 202 B.C., at Zama in Carthaginian north Africa, the Romans under Scipio Africanus defeated Hannibal for the first and only time during the war. The Third Punic War (149–146 B.C.) was a much briefer conflict that resulted in the complete destruction of Carthage.

The Second Punic War decimated Roman farmland and left in its wake thousands of unemployed and homeless Roman farmers, many of whom had fought as soldiers against Hannibal. No one seriously addressed these pressing economic and social issues until Tiberius Sempronius Gracchus was elected one of the 10 tribunes for the year 133 B.C. As a Roman tribune, Gracchus had the right to introduce legislation, and, having campaigned for office on the issue of land redistribution, he quickly introduction a land reform bill. Much of the farmland in the Italian countryside had been swallowed up into huge holdings known as *latifundia*, which were owned by a comparatively few wealthy aristocrats. Much of this land had been expropriated during or after the Second Punic War, leaving their original owners, who had been away serving in the army, with nothing. Gracchus sought to remedy this situation.

Not surprisingly, the landowners were bitterly opposed to Gracchus's proposal, and they tried every parliamentary trick to stop passage of his bill. However, in the end his land reform measure was enacted into law. Late in 133 B.C., Gracchus, took the unusual step—since the tribunate, like all other elective offices in the republic, was to be held for one year only—of announcing his intention of standing for re-election. This move was more than Gracchus's wealthy foes could tolerate. On election day, Gracchus appeared in the forum with armed guards and wearing mourning clothes, actions that implied that his failure to win re-election would lead to his impeachment and death. During the voting, violence erupted between the factions, and Gracchus's opponents, declaring the he sought to make himself king, invaded the forum. Gracchus was slain in the ensuing disorder.

Some historians see the events of 133 B.C. as the beginning of the end of the Roman Republic, and certainly the activities of ambitious Roman politicians over the next century seem to validate that assessment. The first century B.C. is one of the best documented and most complicated periods in all of ancient history, so it is a daunting task to single out one event, or even series of events, as having the greatest significance on the development of Roman history. But the tenure of the times might be conveniently illustrated by considering the lives and careers of the era's leading figures—Marcus Tullius Cicero and Gaius Julius Caesar.

Cicero (106–43 B.C.) was a statesman, diplomat, politician, and author, but he achieved his greatest fame as a lawyer and orator. His legal career spanned nearly 40 years and included many celebrated cases. His most famous speeches may have been the four he delivered in November and December of 63 B.C., in which he exposed the plot of Lucius Sergius Catilina, or Catiline, to overthrow the Roman government by force. Toward the end of his life, Cicero became increasingly worried about the future of his beloved Roman Republic, and he did not hesitate to lash out at individuals whom he perceived as threats to its survival. His last public speeches, the *Philippics*, were a series of tirades directed, for the most part, at Mark Antony, a public figure for whom Cicero had nothing but contempt. When Mark Antony became part of the triumvirate (three-man coalition) that seized power in Rome shortly after the assassination of Julius Caesar on the Ides of March (March 15) of 44 B.C., he made certain that Cicero's name appeared on the proscription list that the three triumvirs drew up. Cicero was then hunted down and killed in December of 43 B.C.

The century's dominant individual, however, was certainly Julius Caesar (100–44 B.C.). Shrewd, ambitious, ruthless, and brilliant, Caesar was a man who knew what he wanted and who knew how to get it. He served as consul (the most important political office in the republic) in 59 B.C., and, after that, as governor of the province of Gaul (modern France), a post that he held for eight years. Caesar proved to be a very aggressive provincial governor, initiating battles, annexing territories, and capturing prisoners. When he finally returned to Rome in 49 B.C., at the head of a battle-tested army loyal to him, he precipitated a bloody civil war that lasted for four years and ended with the establishment of his own political dominance.

By the end of the civil wars, the Roman Republic had ceased to exist in any meaningful way. In 46 B.C., the Roman Senate granted Caesar the powers of dictator for 10 years and then, 2 years later, gave them to Caesar for life. The biographer Suetonius asserted that Caesar also received many other honors that were deemed inappropriate, including a lifetime consulship; the erection of his statue among those of the early Roman kings; and the establishment of altars, temples, and even a priest of his own religious cult. The seventh month of the year, previously called Quintilis, was renamed Julius in his honor (the current name for the month, July, derives from Julius).

Quixotic defenders of the republic, led by Marcus Junius Brutus and Gaius Cassius Longinus, believed that Caesar had to be stopped; they formed a conspiracy to assassinate him, believing that his plans—whatever they were exactly—could be thwarted in no other way. On March 15, 44 B.C., Caesar self-confidently ignored warnings of plots against his life and entered the Senate, where he was stabbed to death by the conspirators.

Caesar's death began a new round of even bloodier civil wars, which did not end until 31 B.C., when naval forces under the command of Marcus Vipsanius Agrippa and the young Octavian, grand-nephew of Julius Caesar, defeated the fleet of Mark Antony and Queen Cleopatra of Egypt at the Battle of Actium. The subsequent end of the civil war was also effectively the end of the Roman Republic.

By virtue of his victory at Actium, Octavian was unquestioned leader of Rome. In 27 B.C., he received an imposing array of honors from the Senate, including the new name *Augustus*—meaning "the revered one"—which was a term with religious connotations. His mastery of Rome now complete, Augustus shrewdly claimed to be following the customs and traditions of the republic. He sternly denied any aspirations for the kingship, but during his rule the Roman Empire emerged from the ashes of the republic, and Augustus became the first emperor. Augustus so successfully stabilized the Roman government that his 41-year reign saw the establishment of a Pax Romana, a period of relative peace and tranquility that became a Roman golden age of creative expression.

When Augustus died in A.D. 14, at the age of 76, he was succeeded by a line of mainly corrupt or inept emperors that lasted until the accession of Nerva to the imperial throne in A.D. 96. Nerva (A.D. 96–98) and the four emperors who followed him—*Trajan* (A.D. 98–117), Hadrian (A.D. 117–138), Antoninus Pius (A.D. 138–161), and Marcus Aurelius (A.D. 161–180)—were collectively known as the Five Good Emperors because they presided over an unprecedented period of peace and prosperity. Indeed, the famous historian Edward Gibbon described the period as follows: "If a man were to fix the period in the history of the world during which the condition of the human race was most happy and prosperous, he would, without hesitation, name that which elapsed from the death of Domitian to the accession of Commodus" [i.e., the period of the Five Good Emperors].

After the death of Marcus Aurelius in 180, the Roman Empire experienced a gradual decline in its fortune, although it managed to endure for almost another three centuries. Most of the emperors in these years were unremarkable, with a few notable exceptions, such as Aurelian (A.D. 270–275), Diocletian (A.D. 285–313), and Constantine (A.D. 313–337), under whom Christianity was officially recognized. However, the imperial bureaucracy and infrastructure proved strong enough to withstand incompetence at the top until the fifth century A.D., when the empire, particularly in the west, began to break up. In A.D. 476, Germanic tribes captured Rome and overthrew the last Roman emperor, thus effectively ending the Roman Empire in the west. In the east, however, the empire, now ruled from Constantinople, continued to exist until the fifteenth century.

Part II

DOMESTIC LIFE

Families and Households

Not surprisingly, the family unit is a major commonality among ancient civilizations; therefore, much of the primary source material—especially documents pertaining to laws, customs, and traditions—in one way or another reflects ancient family values. Information on marriage customs seems particularly abundant. Many clauses of the Code of Hammurabi (Document 1) pertained to marriage, as did much of the content of the Mosaic law on marriage (Document 2). Strict rules applied in many cases, especially in the matter of the choice of a spouse.

The *polis* of *Sparta* in ancient Greece was an anomalous state in many ways, and such was the case with its marriage customs, as Document 9 indicates. In particular, bachelorhood for men was frowned upon, and severe penalties awaited those who did not marry. Nor were Spartan husbands averse to sharing their wives with other men (Document 13), with the primary aim of begetting strong children. In ancient India, on the other hand, wives were greatly honored, but they also knew their place, which mainly involved cooking and taking care of the household (Document 4). The text of Document 6 reveals that men in ancient Egypt could marry as many wives as they wished, and large families were encouraged. Priests, however, were limited to one wife.

A unique situation prevailed in Athens in the early sixth century B.C. Because the city was in chaos, an extraordinary decision was made to place all legislative authority in the hands of one man, *Solon*, who was given one year to reform all the laws of the city as he saw fit. No limit was set to his powers. His reforms touched virtually all aspects of Athenian public and private life (Document 7), including regulations governing marriages, dowries, rape, adultery, and illegitimate children. Plutarch, conversely, touched upon one of the lighter sides of the marriage equation: why so many guests are invited to—or appear at—wedding receptions (Document 10). The Athenian philosopher *Socrates* claimed that an advantage of having a shrewish wife—as he reputedly did—was that she unintentionally helped prepare him for enduring the pettiness and abuse of his critics in the public arena (Document 8). But the Roman politician Quintus Metellus Numidicus once made a speech in which he wistfully longed for a social state wherein marriage, and women, would be unnecessary (Document 14).

Various aspects of family life in China (Document 3), Egypt (Document 5), and Rome (Documents 11 and 12) round out the material covered in this section. Of particular interest is Document 12, on the responsibilities of a good father, because it pertains to Roman politician Cato the Elder. Cato's public persona was that of a crusty, aggressive, often foul-tempered man; one might conclude that he behaved that way at home also, but such was apparently not the case.

SUMERIA

1. Selections from the Code of Hammurabi

The written evidence for much of Sumerian domestic life is contained in three poorly preserved collections of laws: the reforms of Urukagina, a ruler of Lagash, one of the Sumerian city-states, from about 2400 B.C.; law codes developed by Ur-Nammu, a ruler of Ur, from about 2100 B.C.; and a code of Lipit-Ishtar, the king of Isin, from about 1800 B.C. However, the best-preserved and most complete document from Sumerian/Akkadian times is the eighteenth-century B.C. Code of Hammurabi, a series of some 282 proclamations and decrees issued by the Babylonian king for whom it is named. This law code, in the form of an inscribed stele found in 1901 by French archaeologists, is particularly noteworthy because it is the only known law code that can be dated earlier than the Bible. Reproduced below are some clauses from the code that are pertinent to domestic relations.

137. If a man wishes to separate from a woman who has borne him children, or from his wife who has borne him children, then he shall give that wife her dowry, and a part of the usufruct of field, garden, and property, so that she can rear her children. When she has brought up her children, a portion of all that is given to the children, equal as that of one son, shall be given to her. She may then marry the man of her heart.

141. If a man's wife, who lives in his house, wishes to leave it, plunges into debt, tries to ruin her house, neglects her husband, and is judicially convicted; if her husband offer her release, she may go on her way, and he gives her nothing as a gift of release. If her husband does not wish to release her, and if he take another wife, she shall remain as servant in her husband's house.

142. If a woman quarrel with her husband, and say: "You are not congenial to me," the reasons for her prejudice must be presented. If she is guiltless, and there is no fault on her part, but he leaves and neglects her, then no guilt attached to this woman; she shall take her dowry and go back to her father's house.

152. If after the woman had entered the man's house, both contracted a debt, both must pay the merchant.

168. If a man wishes to put his son out of his house, and declares before the judge: "I want to put my son out," then the judge shall examine his reasons. If the son be guilty of no great fault, for which he can be rightfully put out, the father shall not put him out.

169. If he be guilty of a grave fault, which should rightfully deprive him of the filial relationship, the father shall forgive him the first time; but if he be guilty of a grave fault a second time, the father may deprive his son of all filial relation.

188. If an artisan has undertaken to rear a[n adopted] child and teaches him his craft, he cannot be demanded back.

189. If he has not taught him his craft, this adopted son may return to his father's house.

Source: The Avalon Project at Yale Law School. Translated by L. W. King. http://www.yale.edu/lawweb/avalon/medieval/hamcode.htm.

ISRAEL

2. Jewish Laws on Marriage and Families

In his most highly regarded work, Jewish Antiquities, *the first-century* A.D. *Jewish antiquarian and historian Josephus details some of the provisions of the Mosaic law on marriage and families.*

Let your young men, on reaching the age of wedlock, marry virgins, freeborn and of honest parents. He that will not espouse a virgin must not unite himself to a woman living with another man, corrupting her or wronging her former husband. Female slaves must not be taken in marriage by free men, however strongly some may be constrained to do so by love; such passion must be mastered by regard for decorum and the proprieties of rank. Again, there must be no marriage with a prostitute, since by reason of the abuse of her body, God could not accept her nuptial sacrifices. For so only can your children have spirits that are liberal and uprightly set towards virtue, if they are not the issue of dishonorable marriages or of a union resulting from ignoble passion [i.e., for a slave].

If a man, having betrothed a bride in the belief that she is a virgin, and afterwards finds that she is not so, let him bring a suit and make his own accusation, relying upon what evidence he may have to prove it; and let the woman's defense be undertaken by her father or brother or whosoever, lacking these, be considered her next of kin. If the woman is then declared innocent, let her continue to live with her accuser, who shall have no right to dismiss her, except only if she furnishes him with grave and undeniable reasons for so doing. And for rashly and precipitately brought a calumnious charge against her, let him undergo a double penalty, receiving forty stripes less one, and paying fifty shekels to the father. But should he prove that the young woman has been corrupted, then, if she is one of the people, for not having kept chaste guard over her virginity up to her lawful marriage, let her be stoned. If she is of priestly parentage, let her be burned alive...

Should a man violate a woman who is betrothed to another, if he persuaded her and had obtained her assent to the violation, let him die along with her; for both are guilty alike, he for having persuaded the woman voluntarily to submit to the worst disgrace and to prefer that to honest wedlock, she for being persuaded to lend herself, for pleasure or money, to this outrage. But if he met her alone somewhere and forced her, when no one was nearby to help her, let him die alone. He that violates a virgin who is not yet betrothed shall marry her himself. But if the father of the woman is not willing to give her away to him, he shall pay fifty shekels as compensation for the outrage.

He who desires to be divorced from the wife who is living with him for whatsoever cause—and with mortals, many such may arise—must certify in writing that he will have no further intercourse with her. For thus will the woman obtain the right to consort with another, which thing before then must not be permitted. But if she is maltreated by the other also, or if upon his death her former husband wishes to marry her, she shall not be allowed to return to him.

When a woman is left childless on her husband's death, the husband's brother shall marry her, and shall call the child that shall be born by the name of the deceased, and raise him as heir to the estate; for this will at once be profitable to the public welfare, families not dying out and property remaining with the relatives, and it will moreover bring the women an alleviation of their misfortune to live with the nearest kinsman of their former husbands. But if the brother be unwilling to marry her, let the woman come before the council of elders and testify that, while she desired to remain in this family and to have children, he would not accept her, thereby doing outrage to the memory of his deceased brother. And when the council asks him for what reason he is opposed to the marriage, be his alleged reason slight or serious, the result shall be the same: the wife of his brother shall loose his sandals and spit in his face and declare that he merits this treatment from her for having outraged the memory of the departed. Then let him leave the council of elders to carry this reproach throughout his life, while she shall be free to marry any suitor whom she will…

With regard to those youths who scorn their parents and do not pay them the honor that is due, but whether by reason of disgrace or through witlessness, break out insolently against them, first of all let the parents verbally admonish them, for they have the authority of judges over their sons. Let them tell them that they came together in matrimony not for pleasure's sake, nor to increase their fortunes by uniting their several properties in one, but that they might have children who should tend their old age and who should receive from them everything that they needed…"[W]e raised you up and devoted our utmost care to your upbringing, sparing nothing that appeared profitable for your welfare and training in all that was best. But now—since indulgence must be accorded to the errors of youth—have done with all that scorn of respect towards us and return to saner ways, reflecting that God also is distressed at acts of effrontery to a father, since He is himself Father of the whole human race and regards himself as a partner in the indignity done to those who bear the same title as himself, when they do not obtain from their children what is their due"…If, then, by such means the young men's disrespect is cured, let them be spared further reproach for their sins of ignorance; for thus will be shown the goodness of the lawgiver, while the parents will be happy in seeing neither son nor daughter delivered to punishment. But the youth with whom these words and the lesson in sobriety conveyed by them appear to have no impact, and who makes for himself implacable enemies of the laws by continuous defiance of his parents, let him be led forth by their own hands outside of the city, followed by the multitude, and be stoned to death, and, after remaining for the whole day exposed to the general view, let him be buried at night.

Source: *Josephus*. Volume IV. Translated by H. St. J. Thackeray. Cambridge and London: Loeb Classical Library, 1930.

<hr>

CHINA

<hr>

3. Raising Families in Ancient China

Instructions on raising families form a major part of Chinese culture from the country's earliest times. In the following excerpt from his work, Yan Zhitui (531–590) offers advice on teaching children, and on brotherly and family harmony.

The habits and teaching of our family have always been regular and punctilious. In my childhood, I received good instruction from my parents. With my two elder brothers, I went to greet our parents each morning and evening to ask in winter whether they were warm and in summer whether they were cool; we walked steadily with regular steps, talked calmly with good manners, and moved about with as much dignity and reverence as if we were visiting the awe-inspiring rulers at court. They gave us good advice, asked about our particular interests, criticized our defects, and encouraged our good points—always zealous and sincere . . .

Instructing children: Those of the highest intelligence will develop without being taught; those of great stupidity, even if taught, will amount to nothing; those of medium ability will be ignorant unless taught. The ancient sage kings had rules for prenatal training. Women when pregnant for three months moved from their living quarters to a detached palace where they would not see unwholesome sights nor hear reckless words, and where the tone of music and the flavor of food were controlled by the rules of decorum. These rules were written on jade tablets and kept in a golden box. After the child was born, imperial tutors firmly made clear filial piety, humaneness, the rites, and rightness to guide and train him.

The common people are indulgent and are unable to do this. But as soon as a baby can recognize facial expressions and understand approval and disapproval, training should be begun so that he will do what he is told to do and stop when so ordered. After a few years of this, punishment with the bamboo can be minimized, as parental strictness and dignity mingled with parental love will lead the boys and girls to a feeling of respect and caution and give rise to filial piety. I have noticed about me that where there is merely love without training this result is never achieved. Children eat, drink, speak, and act as they please. Instead of needed prohibitions, they receive praise; instead of urgent reprimands, they receive smiles. Even when children are old enough to learn, such treatment is still regarded as the proper method. Only after the child has formed proud and arrogant habits do they try to control him. But one may whip the child to death and he will still not be respectful, while the growing anger of the parents only increases his resentment . . . A common proverb says, "Train a wife from her first arrival; teach a son in his infancy." How true such sayings are!

Generally, parents' inability to instruct their own children comes not from any inclination just to let them fall into evil ways, but only from parents' being unable to endure the children's looks [of unhappiness] from repeated scoldings, or to bear beating them, lest it do damage to the children's physical being. We should, however, take illness by way of illustration: how can we not use drugs, medicines, acupuncture or cautery to cure it? Should we then view the strictness of reproof and punishment as a form of cruelty to one's own kith and kin? Truly there is no other way to deal with it . . .

In the love of parents for children, it is rare that one succeeds in treating them equally. From antiquity to the present, there are many cases of this failing. It is only natural to love those who are wise and talented, but those who are wayward and dull also deserve sympathy. Partiality in treatment, even when done out of generous motives, turns out badly . . .

When brothers are at odds with each other, then sons and nephews will not love each other, and this in turn will lead to the cousins drifting apart, resulting finally in their servants treating one another as enemies. When this happens, then strangers can step on their faces and trample upon their chests and there will be no one to come to their aid. There are men who are able to make friends with distinguished men of the empire, winning their affection, and yet are unable to show proper respect toward their own elder brothers. How strange that they should succeed with the many and fail with the few! There are others who are able to command troops in the thousands and inspire such loyalty in them that they will die willingly for them, and yet are unable to show kindness toward their own younger brothers. How strange that they should succeed with strangers and fail with their own flesh and blood! . . .

Family governance: . . . if a father is not loving, the son will not be filial; if an elder brother is not friendly, the younger will not be respectful; if the husband is not just, the wife will not be obedient. When the father is kind, but the son refractory, when an elder brother is friendly but the younger arrogant, when a husband is just but a wife overbearing, then indeed they are the bad people of the world; they must be controlled by punishments; teaching them guidance will not change them. If rod and wrath are not used in family discipline, the faults of the son will immediately appear. If punishments are not properly awarded, the people will not know how to act . . .

The burden of daughters on the family is heavy indeed. Yet how else can Heaven give life to the teeming people and ancestors pass on their bodily existence to posterity? Many people today dislike having daughters and mistreat their own flesh and blood. How can they be like this, and still hope for Heaven's blessing? . . .

It is common for women to dote on a son-in-law and to maltreat a daughter-in-law. Doting on a son-in-law gives rise to hatred from brothers; maltreating a daughter-in-law brings on slander from sisters. Thus when these women, whether they act or remain silent, draw criticism from the members of the family, it is the mother who is the real cause of it.

Source: From *Sources of Chinese Tradition*. Volume I. Second edition. Compiled by Theodore de Bary and Irene Bloom. Copyright © 1999 Columbia University Press. Reprinted with permission of the publisher.

INDIA

4. Women, Men, and Marriage in Ancient India

The following directives on marriage, the role of women, and the responsibilities of householders in ancient India come from the Smrti, a class of Hindu sacred texts based on human experience and memory rather than revealed tradition. Although considered less authoritative than the Hindu Vedic literature, the Smrti literature is perhaps more familiar to modern Hindus because it covers matters of law and everyday social conduct.

[From *Asvalayana Grhya Sutra*]. One should first examine the family [of the intended bride], those on the mother's side and on the father's side...One should give his daughter in marriage to a young man endowed with intelligence. One should marry a girl who possesses the characteristics of intelligence, beauty, and good character, and who is free from disease.

[From *Yajnavalkya Smrti*]. A householder should perform every day a Smriti rite on the nuptial fire or on the fire brought in at the time of the partition of ancestral property...

Having attended to the bodily calls, having performed the purificatory rites, and after having first washed the teeth, a...man should offer the morning prayer.

Having offered oblations to the sacred fires, becoming spiritually composed, he should murmur the sacred verses addressed to the sun god.

[From *Manu Smrti*]. Women must be honored and adorned by their fathers, brothers, husbands, and brothers-in-law who desire great good fortune.

Where women, verily, are honored, there the gods rejoice; where, however, they are not honored, there all sacred rites prove fruitless.

Where the female relations live in grief—that family soon perishes completely; where, however, they do no suffer from any grievance, that family always prospers...

Her father protects her in childhood, her husband protects her in youth, her sons protect her in old age—a woman does not deserve independence.

The father who does not give away his daughter in marriage at the proper time is censurable; censurable is the husband who does not approach his wife in due season; and after the husband is dead, the son, verily, is censurable, who does not protect his mother.

Even against the slightest provocations should women be particularly guarded; for unguarded they would bring grief to both the families.

...[H]usbands, though weak, must strive to protect their wives.

His own offspring, character, family, self...does one protect when he protects his wife scrupulously...

The husband should engage his wife in the collection and expenditure of his wealth, in cleanliness...in cooking food for the family, and in looking after the necessities of the household...

Women destined to bear children, enjoying great good fortune, deserving of worship, the resplendent lights of homes on the one hand and divinities of good luck who reside in the houses on the other—between these there is no difference whatsoever.

Source: From *Sources of Indian Tradition*. Volume I. Edited by William Theodore de Bary. Copyright © 1958 Columbia University Press. Reprinted with permission of the publisher.

EGYPT

5. Vizier Ptah-hotep's Advice on Family Life

A vizier—a high ranking political or military advisor—by the name of Ptah-hotep lived in twenty-fourth-century B.C. Egypt during the rule of the Fifth Dynasty. A lengthy series of teachings, on a wide variety of topics, is attributed to him. Reproduced below are some of his precepts on family and domestic life.

If you are a wise man, bring up a son who shall be pleasing to Ptah. If he conforms his conduct to your way and occupies himself with your affairs as is right, do to him all the good you can; he is your son, a person attached to you whom your own self has begotten. Separate not your heart from him…But if he conducts himself ill and transgresses your wish, if he rejects all counsel, if his mouth goes according to the evil word, strike him on the mouth in return. Give orders without hesitation to those who do wrong, to him whose temper is turbulent; and he will not deviate from the straight path, and there will be no obstacle to interrupt the way…

If you desire to excite respect within the house you enter…keep yourself from making advances to a woman, for there is nothing good in so doing…

If you are wise, look after your house; love your wife. Fill her stomach, clothe her back; these are the cares to be bestowed upon her person. Caress her, fulfill her desires during the time of her existence; it is a kindness which does honor to its possessor. Be not brutal; tact will influence her better than violence…Behold to what she aspires, at what she aims, what she regards. It is that which fixes her in your house; if you repel her, it is an abyss. Open your arms for her, respond to her arms; call her, display to her your love…

The merit of one's son is advantageous to the father, and that which he really is, is worth more than the remembrance of his father's rank…

When a son receives the instruction of his father, there is no error at all in his plans. Train your son to be a teachable man whose wisdom is agreeable to the great. Let him direct his mouth according to that which has been said to him; in the docility of a son is discovered his wisdom. His conduct is perfect while error carries away the unteachable. Tomorrow knowledge will support him, while the ignorant will be destroyed.

Source: *Ancient History Sourcebook: The Precepts of Ptah-Hotep,* c. 2200 B.C.E. www.fordham.edu/halsall/ancient/ ptahhotep.html.

6. Egyptian Marriage and Family Customs

Diodorus Siculus, a first-century B.C. Greek historian who was born in Sicily, wrote the following account of Egyptian marriage and family customs in his massive historical work, the Bibliotheca Historica.

In accordance with the marriage customs of the Egyptians, the priests have only one wife, but any other man takes as many as he may determine. And the Egyptians are required to raise all their children in order to increase the population, on the grounds that large numbers are the greatest factor in increasing the prosperity of both country and cities. Nor do they consider any child to be illegitimate, even though he was born of a slave mother. For they have taken the general position

A bas-relief of Ptah-hotep in the tomb of Ptah-hotep and Akhet-hotep, Saqqarah, Egypt. The Art Archive/Gianni Dagli Orti.

that the father is the sole author of procreation and that the mother only supplies the fetus with nourishment and a place to live...

They feed the children in a sort of happy-go-lucky fashion that in its inexpensiveness quite surpasses belief. They serve them with stews made of any stuff that is right at hand and cheap, and give them stalks of the byblos plant as can be roasted in the coals, and the roots and stems of marsh plants, either raw or boiled or baked. And since most of the children are raised without shoes or clothing because of the mildness of the climate, the entire expense incurred by the parents of a child until it comes to maturity is [minimal]. These are the leading reasons why Egypt has such an extraordinarily large population, and it is because of this fact that the country possesses a vast number of great monuments.

Source: *Diodorus of Sicily*. Translated by C. H. Oldfather. London and Cambridge: Loeb Classical Library, 1933.

GREECE

7. Solon Reforms the Domestic Laws of Athens

Almost from its earliest days, ancient Athens was embroiled in civil disputes, lawsuits, discord, and wrangling of all kinds. By the early sixth century B.C., the situation there had become so chaotic that the Athenians took the unusual and drastic step of appointing one man, with carte blanche authority, to rewrite their laws and make any changes to customs and traditions that he saw fit. The man on whom this heavy responsibility fell was Solon, a respected and prosperous citizen with a well-earned reputation for honesty, fairness, and intelligence. He was trusted by all segments and factions of the community. After some initial reluctance, Solon accepted. Writing in the early second century A.D., the Greek essayist and biographer Plutarch provides, in the following excerpt, some insights on Solon's social reforms.

Among his other laws there is a very peculiar and surprising one which ordains that he shall be disenfranchised who, in time of factionalism, takes neither side. He wishes, probably, that a man should not be insensible or indifferent to the common weal, arranging his private affairs securely and glorying in the fact that he has no share in the distempers and distresses of his country, but should rather espouse promptly the better and more righteous cause, share its perils, and give it his aid, instead of waiting in safety to see which cause prevails...

In all other marriages [other than those involving wealthy heiresses], he prohibited dowries; the bride was to bring with her three changes of raiment, household stuff of small value, and nothing else. For he did not wish that marriage should be a matter of profit or price, but that man and wife should dwell together for the delights of love and the getting of children.

Praise is given also to that law of Solon which forbids speaking ill of the dead. For it is piety to regard the deceased as sacred, justice to spare the absent, and good policy to rob hatred of its perpetuity. He also forbade speaking ill of the living in temples, courts of law, public offices, and at festivals; the transgressor must pay three drachmas [about $150] to the person injured, and two more into the public treasury. For never to master one's anger is a mark of intemperance and lack of training; but always to do so is difficult, and for some, impossible...

He was highly esteemed also for his law concerning wills. Before his time, no will could be made, but the entire estate of the deceased must remain in his family. Whereas he, by permitting a man who had no children to give his property to whom he wished, ranked friendship above kinship, and favor above necessity, and made a man's possessions his own property. On the other hand, he did not permit all manner of gifts without restriction or restraint, but only those which were not made under the influence of sickness or drugs, or imprisonment, or when a man was the victim of compulsion or yielded to the persuasions of his wife. He thought, very rightly and properly, that being persuaded into wrong was no better than being forced into it, and he placed deceit and compulsion, gratification and affliction, in one and the same category, believing that both were alike able to pervert a man's reason.

He also subjected the public appearances of the women, their mourning and their festivals, to a law which did away with disorder and license...[Another of his laws] relieved the sons who were born out of wedlock from the necessity of supporting their fathers at all. For he that avoids the honorable state of marriage, clearly takes a woman to himself not for the sake of children, but of pleasure; and he has his reward, in that he robs himself of all right to upbraid his sons for neglecting him, since he has made their very existence a reproach to them.

But in general, Solon's laws concerning women seem very absurd. For instance, he permitted an adulterer caught in the act to be killed; but if a man committed rape upon a free woman, he was merely to be fined a hundred drachmas [about $5,000]; and if he gained his end by persuasion, twenty drachmas [about $1,000]...Still further, no man is allowed to sell a daughter or a sister, unless he finds that she is no longer a virgin.

Source: *Plutarch's Lives.* Volume I. Translated by Bernadotte Perrin. London and Cambridge: Loeb Classical Library, 1914.

8. Socrates's Version of Marital Bliss

Possibly of African birth, the second-century A.D. *Latin writer Aulus Gellius related in his* Noctes Atticae *(Attic Nights) the following brief anecdote of one of ancient Athens's most famous married couples—the philosopher Socrates and his wife Xanthippe. The* Noctes Atticae *is important for the insights it gives into contemporary society and for the excerpts from the lost works of other authors that it preserves.*

Xanthippe, the wife of the philosopher Socrates, is said to have been ill-tempered and quarrelsome to a degree, with a constant flood of feminine tantrums and annoyances day and night. Alcibiades, amazed at this outrageous conduct of hers towards her husband, asked Socrates what earthly reason he had for not showing so shrewish a woman the door. "Because," replied Socrates, "it is by enduring such a person at home that I accustom and train myself to bear more easily away from home the pettiness and injustice of other persons."

In the same vein, Marcus Varro also said in the *Menippean Satire* which he entitled *On the Duty of a Husband:* "A wife's faults must be either put down or put up with. He who puts down her faults, makes his wife more agreeable. He who puts up with them, improves himself."

Source: *The Attic Nights of Aulus Gellius*. Translated by John C. Rolfe. Cambridge and London: Loeb Classical Library, 1927.

9. Unusual Marriage Customs in Sparta

In the following excerpt from his Life of Lycurgus, *the second-century* A.D. *Greek essayist and biographer Plutarch recounts some of the occasionally bizarre marriage customs of the ancient Spartans (see* Lycurgus *and* Sparta *in the Glossary).*

There were incentives to marriage in these things: I mean such things as the appearance of the young women without much clothing in processions and athletic contests, where young men were looking on…Nor was this all. Lycurgus also put a kind of stigma upon confirmed bachelors. They were excluded from the sight of the young men and women at their exercises, and in winter, the magistrates ordered them to march around the marketplace in their tunics only, and as they marched, they sang a certain song about themselves, and its gist was that they were justly punished for disobeying the laws. Besides this, they were deprived of the honor and gracious attentions which the young men habitually paid to their elders. Therefore, there was no one to find fault with what was said to Dercyllidas, even though he was a reputable general. As he entered a group of young men, one of them, who would not offer him his seat, said: "You have fathered no son who will one day offer his seat to me."

For their marriages, the women were carried off by force, not when they were small and unfit for marriage, but when they were fully grown. After the woman was thus carried off, the bridesmaid took her in charge, cut her hair close to the head, put a man's cloak and sandals on her, and laid her down on a pallet, on the floor, alone, in the dark. Then the bridegroom, not overcome with wine nor enfeebled by excesses, but composed and sober, after eating at his public mess table as usual, slipped stealthily into the room where the bridge lay, and bore her in his arms to the marriage bed. Then, after spending a short time with his bride, he went away composedly to his usual quarters, there to sleep with the other young men.

And so he continued to do from that time on, spending his days with his comrades, and sleeping with them at night, but visiting his bride by stealth and with every precaution, full of dread and fear that any of the household might become aware of his visits, his bride also contriving and conspiring with him that they might have stolen moments as the occasion offered. And this they did not for a short time only, but long enough for some of them to become fathers before they had looked upon their own wives by daylight…

After giving marriage such characteristics of reserve and decorum, he nonetheless freed men from the empty and womanish passion of jealous possession…For example, an elderly man with a young wife, if he looked with favor and esteem on some fair and noble young man, might introduce him to her, and adopt her offspring by such a noble father as his own. And again, a worthy man who admired some woman for the fine children that she bore her husband…might enjoy her favors, if her husband would consent, thus…begetting for himself noble sons, who would have the blood of noble men in their veins. For in the first place, Lycurgus did not regard children as the peculiar property of their fathers, but rather as the common property of the state, and therefore would not have his citizens spring from random parentage, but from the best there was. In the second place, he saw much folly and vanity in what other peoples enacted for the regulation of these matters. In the breeding of dogs and horses, they insist on having the best sires which money can buy, but they keep their wives under lock and key, demanding that they have children by none but themselves, even if they are foolish, infirm, or diseased.

The freedom which thus prevailed at that time in marriage relations was aimed at physical and political well-being.

Source: *Plutarch's Lives.* Volume I. Translated by Bernadotte Perrin. London and Cambridge: Loeb Classical Library, 1914.

10. Why So Many Guests Are Invited to Wedding Receptions

In this passage from his Moralia *(translatable as "Matters," relating to mores and customs), a wide-ranging collection of essays and speeches, the Greek biographer Plutarch examines the phenomenon of including so many names on the guest list for a wedding reception.*

At the wedding of my son Autobulus, Sossius Senecio was present in Chaeronea [Plutarch's hometown] as one of our guests. Among many subjects that he brought forward which were particularly appropriate to the occasion, he raised the question of why people invite more guests to wedding dinners than to other parties. It is true, he observed, that those lawgivers who have campaigned most vigorously against extravagance have particularly sought to limit the number of guests at weddings. "But as to the reason for these large numbers," said Senecio, "the only ancient philosopher who had anything to offer was Hecataeus of Abdera, who, in my judgment, said nothing convincing. His point was this: at their marriage, men invite a crowd to the banquet so that there may be many witnesses to testify that the hosts themselves are of good family and that their brides come from good families. On the other hand, the comic poets attack those who celebrate a wedding in a wasteful and ostentatious style, with splendid dinners and great expense, as not putting down a secure foundation, or looking courageously to the future…But to avoid what is all too easy, the appearance of accusing others when I myself have nothing to offer, I will be the first," he said, "to state my view. It is that of all the occasions for a banquet, none is more conspicuous or talked about than a wedding. When we offer sacrifices to the gods, or honor a friend on the eve of a journey, or entertain guests from abroad, it is possible to do so unnoticed by many friends and relatives. But a wedding feast betrays us by the loud marriage cry, the torch, and the shrill pipe…Consequently, since no one is unaware that we are receiving guests and must have invited them, we include all our relatives, acquaintances, and connections of any degree, because we are afraid to leave anyone out."

When we had applauded this, Theon took up the thread with these words: "Let us adopt this theory, for it is quite probable. But add, if you will, a further point, that these particular banquets are not merely friendly entertainments but important family occasions, which solemnize the incorporation of a new set of relatives into the family. What is more important than this, at the union of two houses, each father-in-law regards it as a duty to demonstrate good will to the friends and relatives of the other, and so the guest list is doubled. Besides, many or most of the activities relating to a wedding are in the hands of women, and where women are present, it is necessary that their husbands also should be included."

Source: *Plutarch's Moralia.* Volume VIII. Translated by Paul A. Clement and Herbert B. Hoffleit. London and Cambridge: Loeb Classical Library, 1969.

ROME

11. Parenthood in Ancient Rome

In this passage from his essay "On Mercy," the first-century A.D. *philosopher Seneca offers some thoughts on parenthood, especially father-son relationships.*

The good parent...reprove[s] his children sometimes gently, sometimes with threats...at times...even by stripes. Does any father disinherit a son for his first offense?

Roman relief of family life, from the sarcophagus of Cornelius Statius, second century A.D. The Art Archive/ Musée du Louvre Paris/Gianni Dagli Orti.

Only when great and repeated wrongdoing has overcome his patience, only when what he fears outweighs what he reprimands, does he resort to the decisive pen [i.e. altering his will]. But first he makes many an effort to reclaim a character that is still unformed, though inclined now to the more evil side; when the case is hopeless, he tries extreme measures. No one resorts to the exaction of punishment until he has exhausted all the means of correction. This is the duty of a father…Slow would a father be to sever his own flesh and blood; after severing, he would yearn to restore them, and while severing, he would groan out loud, hesitating long and often. For he comes near to condemning gladly who condemns swiftly, and to punishing unjustly who punishes unduly.

Source: *Seneca: Moral Essays.* Volume I. Translated by John W. Basore. Cambridge and London: Loeb Classical Library, 1928.

12. A Good Father's Responsibilities

Cato the Elder (234–149 B.C.) was the epitome of the stern, disciplined, and stubborn Roman politician and soldier. But despite the renown he won in public life, he considered his role as father and husband to be even more important, as the Greek biographer Plutarch relates in this excerpt from his writings.

He was a good father, a kind husband, and a most capable manager of his own household, since he was far from regarding this side of his affairs as trivial, or allowing it to suffer from neglect. For this reason I think I should give some examples of his conduct in his private life.

He chose his wife for her family rather than her fortune, for he believed that while people of great wealth or high position cherish their own pride and self-esteem, nevertheless women of noble birth are by nature more ashamed of any disgraceful action and so are more obedient to their husbands in everything that is honorable. He used to say that a man who beats his wife or child is laying sacrilegious hands on the most sacred thing in the world. He considered that it was more praiseworthy to be a good husband than a great senator, and also was of the opinion that there was nothing much else to admire in Socrates, except for the fact that he was always gentle and considerate in his dealings with his wife, who was ill-tempered, and his children, who were half-witted.

When his son was born, Cato thought that nothing but the most important business should prevent him from being present when his wife gave the baby its bath and wrapped it in swaddling clothes. His wife suckled the child herself and often did the same for her slaves' children, so as to encourage brotherly feelings in them towards her own son. As soon as the boy was able to learn, his father took charge of his schooling and taught him to read, although he had in the household an educated slave named Chilo, who was a schoolmaster and taught many other boys. However, Cato did not think it right, so he tells us, that his son should be scolded or disciplined by a slave, if he were slow to learn, and still less that he should be indebted to his slave in such a vital matter as his education.

So he took it upon himself to teach the boy, not only his letters, but also the principles of Roman law. He also trained him in athletics, and taught him how to throw the javelin, fight in armor, ride a horse, use his fists in boxing, endure the extremes of heat and cold, and swim across the roughest and most swiftly flowing stretches of the Tiber. He tells us that he composed his history of Rome, writing it out with his own hand and in large characters, so that his son should possess in his own home the means of acquainting himself with the ancient annals and traditions of his country. He also mentions that he was just as careful not to use any indecent expression before his son....

Such was Cato's approach to the noble task of forming and molding his son for the pursuit of virtue. The boy was an exemplary student in his readiness to learn, and his spirit was a match for his natural goodness of disposition.

Source: *The Rise and Fall of Athens: Nine Greek Lives by Plutarch.* Translated by Ian Scott-Kilvert. New York: Penguin Books, 1960. Reproduced by permission of Penguin Books Ltd.

13. A Comparison of Spartan and Roman Marriage and Family Customs

In this passage from his essay comparing the Spartan king Lycurgus with the early Roman king Numa, the Greek biographer Plutarch describes their respective attitudes and policies concerning marriage and families (see also Sparta *in the Glossary).*

With regard to community in marriage and parentage, though both, by a sound policy, inculcated in husbands a freedom from selfish jealousy, still, their methods were not entirely alike. The Roman husband, if he had a sufficient number of children to rear, and another, who lacked children, could persuade him to the step, relinquished his wife to him, having the power of surrendering her entirely, or only for a season. But the Spartan, while his wife remained in his house, and the marriage retained its original rights and obligations, might allow anyone who gained his consent to share his wife for the purpose of getting children by her. And many husbands...would actually invite into their homes men whom they thought most likely to procure them handsome and noble children....

Still further, Numa's watchful care of young maidens was more conducive to feminine decorum; but the treatment of them by Lycurgus, being entirely unconfined and unfeminine, has given occasion to the poets [to ridicule them]. They call them *phainomerides*, "bare-thighed," and revile them as mad for men...

But Numa, while carefully preserving to the matrons that dignified and honorable relation to their husbands which was bestowed upon them by Romulus...nevertheless enjoined great modesty upon them, forbade them all busy intermeddling, taught them sobriety, and accustomed them to be silent. They were to refrain from wine entirely, and were not to speak, even on the most necessary topics, unless their husbands were with them. At any rate, it is said that when a woman once pleaded her own cause in the forum, the senate sent [a delegation] to inquire of an oracle what the event might portend for the city. And for their usual gentleness and readiness to obey, there is strong evidence in the specific mention made of those who were less amenable...the Romans make record of the fact that Spurius Carvilius was the first to divorce his wife, 230 years after the founding of Rome [ca. 523 B.C.], there being no precedent for it. Also, that the wife of Pinarius, Thalaea by name, was the first to quarrel with her own mother-in-law, Gegania, in the reign of Tarquinius Superbus [sixth century B.C.]. In such fitting and proper manner were marriages regulated by their lawgiver....

The Romans...gave their maidens in marriage when they were twelve years old, or even younger. In this way more than any other, it was thought, both their bodies and their dispositions would be pure and undefiled when their husbands took control of them....

For Numa left the bringing up of youths to the wishes or necessities of their fathers. A father might, if he wished, make his son a tiller of the soil, or a shipwright, or might teach him to be a smith or a flute player, as if it were not important that all of them should be trained with one and the same end in view from the outset, and have their dispositions formed alike. But rather, as if they were passengers on a ship, each coming with a different object and purpose, and each therefore uniting with the rest for the common good only in times of peril, through fear of private loss, but otherwise consulting only his own interests...When a wise man had consented to be king over a people newly constituted and pliant to his every wish, what should have been his first care, unless it was the rearing of boys and the training of youths so that there might be no confusing differences in their characters, but that they might be molded and fashioned from the very outset so as to walk harmoniously together in the same path of virtue?

Source: *Plutarch's Lives.* Volume I. Translated by Bernadotte Perrin. London and Cambridge: Loeb Classical Library, 1914.

14. On Living With, and Without, Matrimony

In his Noctes Atticae, *the Roman writer Aulus Gellius relates the following anecdote about a controversial speech on marriage given by a Roman politician named Quintus Metellus Numidicus.*

A number of learned men were listening to the reading of the speech, *On Marriage*, which Metellus Numidicus, an earnest and eloquent man, delivered to the people, urging them to be ready to undertake its obligations. In that speech, these words were written: "If we could get on without a wife, Romans, we would all avoid that annoyance. But since nature has ordained that we can neither live very comfortably with them, nor at all without them, we must consider our lasting well-being rather than for the pleasure of the moment."

It seemed to some of the company that Quintus Metellus...ought not to have admitted the annoyance and constant inconveniences of the married state, and that to do this was not so much to encourage, as to dissuade and deter [people from marrying]. They said that his speech ought rather to have taken just the opposite tone, insisting that as a rule there were no annoyances in marriage, and if after all they seemed sometimes to arise, they were slight, insignificant and easily endured, and were completely forgotten in its greater pleasures and advantages. Furthermore, even these annoyances did not happen in all marriages, or from any fault natural to matrimony, but as the result of the misconduct and injustice of some husbands and wives.

Source: *The Attic Nights of Aulus Gellius.* Volume I. Translated by John C. Rolfe. Cambridge and London: Loeb Classical Library, 1927.

Old Age and Retirement

Ancient sources and writers had a lot to say on the subject of old age and retirement, and much of it was not very optimistic. The ancient world's medical communities seemed to have little or no concept of gerontology, and so the physical ills of old age became magnified. And in a world largely bereft of pensions, whether public or private, comfortable retirement was probably out of reach for many people, assuming, of course, that they lived long enough even to consider retiring.

The downside of old age is revealed by Documents 15 and 16, and most particularly 21. In the last of those three, the aged Greek playwright Sophocles was claimed by his gold-digging sons to be past the age of competence to handle his own affairs, so they attempted to persuade a court of law to declare the old man mentally unfit, thus enabling them to gain control of his financial resources. But Sophocles turned the tables on them by reciting for the court a long choral passage from the play he had just written—at the age of 90!—entitled *Oedipus at Colonus*. His rendition was so passionately emotional that it reportedly brought tears to the eyes of the judges. Not surprisingly, the sons' case was tossed out. The Egyptian octogenarian Ctesicles, unfortunately, had no such literary ability with which to dazzle the court when he complained of abuse and neglect on the part of his daughter and son-in-law (Document 17); the 80-year-old Aurelius Serapion suffered an assault, which he brought to the attention of the legal system, according to Document 18.

Sophocles was not the only spry nonagenarian that we hear of in ancient Greece. The orator Isocrates was composing speeches well into his 90s. His story is recounted in Document 22. Cephalus was yet another old Athenian with a spring in his step (Document 19). Cicero (Document 28) attacks the notion that old age invariably brings with it a diminished capacity for activity, health, and enjoyment of life, while, in Document 20, he offers his views on growing old gracefully.

One's sight sometimes begins to fail in old age (Document 23), and, according to Document 24, old people sometimes were not treated very graciously in Athens. Among the Spartans, however, the opposite was true; when an old man entered the theater one time looking for a place to sit, none of the younger Athenians in the audience would offer him a seat, but when he came to the Spartan section, all of them stood up for him (also Document 24).

In Aristophanes's play *Acharnians*, an elderly character complains about the lack of respect sometimes accorded to old Athenians by the younger generation. Those young people, he complains, conveniently forget about the many contributions made by the old men in their day to the prosperity and freedom that Athens eventually came to enjoy (Document 25).

In Documents 26 and 27, retirement Roman-style is described. Pliny the Younger (26) recounts the very active lifestyle enjoyed by his friend Spurinna, a 78-year-old retiree, while Quintilian (27) describes the ideal retirement for a Roman orator.

INDIA

15. Getting Old Is Not for the Faint-Hearted

Jain literature contains 45 entries, varying in length and content, some in prose, others in poetry, composed over the course of several centuries. The earliest examples of these texts date perhaps to the seventh century B.C.; excerpted below is one of the more pessimistic ones, which dwells on the problems encountered in old age.

He who desires the qualities of things is deluded and falls into the grip of great pain. For he thinks, "I have mother, father, sister, wife, sons, and daughters, daughters-in-law, friends, kin near and remote, and acquaintances. I own various properties, I make profits. I need food and clothes." On account of these things, people are deluded, they worry day and night, they work in season and out of season, they crave for fortune and wealth, they injure and do violence, and they turn their minds again and again to evil deeds. Thus the life of many men is shortened.

For when ear and eye and smell and taste and touch grow weak, a man knows that his life is failing, and after a while, his senses sink into dotage. The kinsfolk with whom he lives first grumble at him, and then he grumbles at them...An old man is fit for neither laughter, nor playing, nor pleasure, nor show. So a man should take to the life of piety, seize the present, be firm, and not let himself be deluded an hour longer, for youth and age and life itself all pass away...

Understanding the nature of all kinds of pain and pleasure, before he sees his life decline, a wise man should know the right moment [for taking up a life of religion]...Before his senses weaken, he should pursue his own true welfare.

Source: From *Sources of Indian Tradition*. Volume I. Edited by William Theodore de Bary. Copyright © 1958 Columbia University Press. Reprinted with permission of the publisher.

EGYPT

16. The Downside of Old Age

In the following passage, the downside of advancing age is described by the twenty-fourth-century B.C. Egyptian vizier Ptah-hotep.

The beginning of the Instruction written by the hereditary noble, the prince, the father of the god [an honorary title, not to be understood literally], the beloved of the god, the judge of the six law courts, the arbiter who causes contentment throughout the entire land, the mayor of the city, the vizier Ptahhotep, under the Majesty of the King of Upper and Lower Egypt, Isesi who lives for ever and eternity. The mayor of the city, the vizier Ptahhotep says:

My Sovereign Lord:
Old age has arrived, infirmity has descended,
Misery has drawn nigh, and weakness increases.

One must take a nap like a child every day,
The eyes are blurred, the ears are deaf,
And vigor wanes because of weariness.
The mouth is silent and no longer speaks;
The memory is gone and cannot recall even yesterday.
The bones ache through frailty,
Pleasure has become repulsive, and all taste has vanished.
What old age does to men is totally despicable.
The nose becomes plugged and cannot breathe;
Even standing and sitting are a bother.
Permit your humble servant to appoint a staff of old age.
Let my son be allowed to succeed to my position.
To that end I will instruct him in the decisions of the judges,
The wisdom of those who have lived in earlier ages,
Those who hearkened to the gods.
So may the same be done for you;
May discord be banished from the people…
Then the Majesty of the god said:
"Before you retire, teach him
about what has been said in the past;
Then he will be an example to the children of the nobles,
When understanding and precision have entered into him.
Instruct him, for no one is born wise."

Source: *The Literature of Ancient Egypt.* Edited by William Kelly Simpson. New Haven, CT: Yale University Press, 2003. Copyright © 2003 by Yale University Press. All rights reserved. Reprinted with permission of the publisher.

17. No Way to Treat One's Father!

In the following document dated 220 B.C., a man by the name of Ctesicles, probably from the town of Crocodilopolis, petitioned Egypt's King Ptolemy Philopator for legal redress from an abusive daughter and her consort.

To King Ptolemy, greeting from Ctesicles. I am being wronged by Dionysius [either his son-in-law, or a friend, of his daughter] and my daughter Nice. For although I had nurtured her, being my own daughter, and educated her, and brought her up to womanhood, when I was stricken with bodily infirmity and my eyesight enfeebled, she would not furnish me with any of the necessities of life. And when I wished to obtain justice from her in Alexandria, she begged my forgiveness and in year 18, she gave me in the temple of Arsinoe Actia a written oath by the king that she would pay me 20 drachmas every month by means of her own bodily labor. If she failed to do so, or transgressed any of the terms of her bond, she was to forfeit to me 500 drachmas, on pain of incurring the consequences of the oath.

Now, however, corrupted by Dionysius, who is a comedian, she is not meeting any of her obligations to me, in contempt of my old age and my present infirmity. I beg you, therefore, O king, not to allow me to be wronged by my daughter and Dionysius the comedian, who has corrupted her, but to order Diophanes the strategus [a local official] to summon them and hear my case. And if my words are true, let Diophanes deal with her corrupter as seems good to him, and compel my daughter, Nice, to yield me my rights... For by this means, I will no longer be wronged, but having sought your protection, O king, I will obtain justice.

Source: *Select Papyri: Non-Literary Papyri. Public Documents.* Volume II. Translated by A. S. Hunt and C. C. Edgar. Cambridge and London: Loeb Classical Library, 1934.

18. No Way to Treat an Old Man!

In the following document from the year A.D. 248, an 84-year-old man from the village of Philadelphia complains of an assault.

To Aurelius Marcianus, centurion, from Aurelius Serapion, son of Pasei, of the village of Philadelphia. There is nothing more dreadful or harder to bear than maltreatment. At the time of life which I have reached, being 80 years old and more, I am serving blamelessly as an Arab archer [local security official]. A sow having escaped from my daughter in the village, and being reported to be at the house of the soldier Julius, I went to him to demand his oath about this matter, and he, laying hands on me, old as I am, in the village in the middle of the day, as if there were no laws, belabored me with blows in the presence of Nepotianus, steward of the most eminent Valerius Titanianus, and of Marcus and Ammonius, Arab archers, so that they, being shocked to see me beaten, separated us and I barely overcame his attempt on my life. I am compelled to present this petition and to request that he be arrested in order that his audacious behavior may receive punishment, and I hold him to account. Farewell.

Serapion, aged about 84 years, with a scar on the right knee.

Source: *Select Papyri: Non-Literary Papyri. Public Documents.* Volume II. Translated by A. S. Hunt and C. C. Edgar. Cambridge and London: Loeb Classical Library, 1934.

GREECE

19. A Spry Old Gentleman

According to Plato in The Republic, *when the Athenian philosopher* Socrates *and his friends paid a visit to the elderly gentleman Cephalus, the following lively discussion on old age ensued.*

So we went with them to Polemarchus's house... and the father of Polemarchus, Cephalus, was at home.

And I thought him much aged, for it was a long time since I had seen him. He was sitting on a sort of couch with cushions, and he had a chaplet on his head, for he had just finished sacrificing in the court. So we went there and sat down beside him, for there were seats there arranged in a circle. As soon as he saw me, Cephalus greeted me and said, "You are not a very frequent visitor, Socrates. You don't often come down to see us. That is not right. For if I were still able to make the journey up to town easily, there would be no need of your coming here, but we would go to visit you. But as it is, you should not space too widely your visits here. I would have you know that, for my part, as the satisfactions of the body decay, in the same measure my desire for the pleasures of good talk and my delight in them increase. Don't refuse, then, but be a friend to my household, and make our house your resort, and consider us to be your very good and close friends."

"Why, yes, Cephalus," I said, "and I enjoy talking with the very aged. To my way of thinking, we have to learn from them, as it were, from wayfarers who have preceded us on a road on which we too, it may be, must some time experience—what it is like—is it rough and hard going or easy and pleasant to travel. And so now I would like to learn from you what you think of this thing, now that your time has come to it, the thing that the poets call the threshold of old age. Is it a hard part of life to bear or what report do you have to make of it?"

"Yes, indeed, Socrates," he said, "I will tell you my own feeling about it. For it often happens that some of us older men of about the same age come together and verify the old proverb of like to like. At these reunions, most of us become nostalgic, longing for the lost joys of youth and recalling to mind the pleasures of wine, women, and feasts, and other things like that, and they lament that the greatest things have been taken from them, and that then, they lived well, and now it is no life at all. And some of them complain of the indignities that friends and family members put upon old age, and then recite a doleful litany of all the miseries for which they blame old age.

"But in my opinion, Socrates, they do not put the blame on the real cause. For if it were the cause, I too should have had the same experience so far as old age is concerned, and so would all others who have come to this time of life. But in fact I have before now met with others who do not feel this way, and in particular I remember hearing Sophocles the poet greeted by a fellow who asked, 'How about your service of Aphrodite, Sophocles? Is your natural force still unabated?' And he replied, 'Quiet! I have very gladly escaped this thing you talk of, as if I had run away from a raging and savage beast of a master.' I thought it a good answer then, and now I think so still more. For certainly, there comes to old age a great peace in such matters and a restful release. When the fierce tensions of the passions and desires relax, then the wisdom of Sophocles is revealed, and we are set free from these many forms of madness. But with respect to these complaints, and in the matter of our relations with family members and friends, there is just one cause, Socrates: not old age, but the character of the man."

Source: *Plato: The Republic.* Translated by Paul Shorey. London and New York: Loeb Classical Library, 1930, pp. 328–329.

20. How to Grow Old Gracefully

In this passage from his essay "On Old Age," the first-century B.C. *Roman orator Cicero cites a number of examples of growing old gracefully among the ancient Greeks, including Plato, Isocrates, and Gorgias of Leontini.*

There is also the tranquil and serene old age of a life spent quietly, amid pure and refining pursuits, such an old age, for example, as we are told was that of Plato, who died, pen in hand, in his 81st year. Or, such as that of Isocrates, who, by his own statement, was 94 when he composed the work entitled *Panathenaicus*, and he lived five years after that. His teacher, Gorgias of Leontini, rounded out 107 years and never rested from his pursuits or his labors. When someone asked him why he chose to remain so long alive, he answered: "I have no reason to complain about old age." A noble answer, and worthy of a scholar.

Source: *Cicero: De Senectute; De Amicitia; De Divinatione.* Translated by William Armistead Falconer. Cambridge and London: Loeb Classical Library, 1923.

21. A Nonagenarian Shows Off His Intellect to Win His Court Case

Cicero then mentions the amazing mental feats performed by the famous Greek playwright Sophocles, who was then a nonagenarian.

And how is it with aged lawyers, pontiffs, augurs, and philosophers? What a multitude of things they remember! Old men retain their mental faculties, provided their interest and application continue. This is true, not only of men in exalted public affairs, but likewise those in the quiet of private life. Sophocles composed tragedies to extreme old age, and when, because of his absorption in literary work, he was thought to be neglecting his business affairs, his sons dragged him into court in order to secure a verdict removing him from the control of his property, on the ground of mental incompetence, under a law similar to ours, whereby it is customary to restrain heads of families from wasting their estates. Thereupon, it is said, the old man read to the jury his play, *Oedipus at Colonus*, which he had just written and was revising, and asked: "Does that poem seem to you to be the work of an imbecile?" When he had finished, he was acquitted by the verdict of the jury. Do you think, then, that old age forced him to abandon his calling, or that it silenced Homer, Hesiod, Simonides, Stesichorus, or Isocrates, and Gorgias (whom I have mentioned already)?...Rather, did not activity in their various pursuits continue with all of them as long as life itself?

Source: *Cicero: De Senectute; De Amicitia; De Divinatione.* Translated by William Armistead Falconer. Cambridge and London: Loeb Classical Library, 1923.

22. Another Spry Nonagenarian

The fourth-century B.C. Athenian orator Isocrates lived well into his 90s, and continued to compose speeches, including the one he describes below, which was entitled "Panathenaicus," and which he began at the age of 94.

When I had written half of it, I was attacked by a malady which it is not decorous to name [some think he may have been referring to dysentery], but which is powerful enough to carry off in the course of three or four days not only older people, but many in the prime of life. I battled against this disease without respite for three years, and I passed every day of that time with such devotion to my work that those who knew of my perseverance, as well as those who learned of it from them, admired me more because of this fortitude than because of the things for which I had been formerly praised. When, however, I had at length given up my work both because of my illness and my age, some of those who were in the habit of visiting me, and who had read again and again the portion of my speech which I had written, begged and urged me not to leave it half-finished or incomplete, but to work on it for a short time and to give my thoughts to what remained to be done. They did not speak as men do who perfunctorily acquit themselves of a duty, but praised extravagantly what I had written, saying about it such things that if any people had heard them who were not my personal friends and kindly disposed towards me, they could not possibly have failed to suppose that my visitors were trying to make a fool of me and that I had lost my wits and was altogether a simpleton if I allowed myself to be persuaded of what they said. Although I had this feeling about the things which they boldly stated, I did allow myself to be persuaded—for why make a long story of it?—to occupy myself with the completion of the speech at a time when I lacked only three years of having lived a century, and when I was in a state of infirmity such that anyone else similarly afflicted, so far from undertaking to write a speech of his own, would not even be willing to listen to one worked out and submitted by someone else.

Source: *Isocrates*. Volume II. Translated by George Norlin. Cambridge and London: Loeb Classical Library, 1929.

23. Near-Sighted Old People

In the following excerpt from his Moralia, *the Greek biographer Plutarch describes how one evening at dinner he and his friends discussed the question of why old people have to hold a script farther away from their eyes to read it.*

Old people place writing far from their eyes to read it, and when the writing is near, they are unable to make it out. Aeschylus suggests this when he says:

> "But you must read it far away,
> For close up you could surely not,
> And you must be a lucid scribe, though old."
> And Sophocles more clearly says the same thing about old people:
> "The sound of talking falls with slow impress,
> And hardly penetrates the stopped-up ear;
> But each man who sees afar, is blind when close."

If, then, the senses of old people respond better to intensity and strength, why is it that in reading they do not endure the impact of light from nearby, but destroy its brightness by moving the book farther away, thereby diluting that brightness with air, as wine is diluted with water?

There were some who replied to this that old people hold the book away from their eyes not to soften the light, but, as it were, to lay hold of and encompass more light and fill with bright air the space between their eyes and the writing. And others agreed with the joined-rays school of thought: inasmuch as a cone of rays extends from each of the eyes, its apex at the eye, its base and foundation encompassing the object viewed, it is probable that each of the cones proceeds separately up to a certain point, but when they have attained a greater distance and merged with each other, they unite their light, and consequently each object viewed appears as one, not two, even though it appears to both eyes at the same time. The reason for this is the simultaneous contact of the cones on the same object, and a union of light which produces single rather than double vision. Since this is so, elderly people who bring writing near their eyes, the rays of vision being not yet fused, contact the writing with each cone separately, and lay weaker hold on it; but those who place the writing farther away, the light now fused and intensified, see the writing with greater exactness, like people who master with both hands together what the cannot with either one...

I...argued that a bright emanation which flows out from the eyes mixes with the light which surrounds objects

Aeschylus, sometimes called the Father of Greek tragedy. © (2008) Jupiterimages Corporation.

and undergoes a fusion with it, so that from the two, one body is formed, compatible through its entirety. Each mingles with the other...one must not be overwhelmed and destroyed by the other, but a single power must be created from both brought together on common ground...Now inasmuch as the stream...or "luminous emanation" is weak and powerless in people past their prime, no mixing and mingling occurs with the light outside, but only the extinction and disintegration of vision, unless by removing the writing to a distance from their eyes, old people destroy the excessive brilliance of the outside light.

Source: *Plutarch's Moralia.* Volume VIII. Translated by Paul A. Clement and Herbert B. Hoffleit. London and Cambridge: Loeb Classical Library, 1969.

24. Rude Athenians, Courteous Spartans

The first-century B.C. *Roman orator Cicero writes below of the respect accorded to old people in Sparta.*

Lysander the Spartan...is reported to have said more than once that in Sparta, old age has its most appropriate home, because nowhere else is so much deference paid to age and nowhere else is it more honored. For example, there is a story that when an old man entered the theater at Athens during the dramatic performances, not one of his countrymen in that huge crowd offered him a place. But when he came to the special seats occupied by the Spartans, and assigned to them because they were ambassadors, all of them arose, it is said, and invited him to sit down. After this action had been greeted by the whole audience with sustained applause, one of the Spartans remarked: "These Athenians know what politeness is, but they won't practice it."

Source: *Cicero: De Senectute, De Amicitia, De Divinatione.* Translated by William Armistead Falconer. Cambridge and London: Loeb Classical Library, 1923.

25. The Old Men Strike Back

In the following passage from the play Acharnians *by the Athenian playwright Aristophanes (c. 445–380 B.C.), an elderly character soliloquizes about the mistreatment of old people in Athens.*

> We think it is high time that someone spoke
> About the way you treat us older folk.
> Time after time our valor's saved the City
> In naval battles. Yet you have no pity
> For our old age, but let the younger sort
> On trumped-up charges haul us into court,
> Young orators who mock us left and right,
> Knowing *our* verbal fire's extinguished quite.
> We stand there leaning on our staffs and pray
> To Lord Poseidon for a storm-free day.
> But mist beclouds our eyes, and we can trace
> Only the dimmest outline of the case.
> The young accuser, scorning others' aid,
> Pelts us with small round phrases deftly made,
> Then calls us up, puts questions with a catch,
> And leaves the accused without a straw to snatch.
> He stammers a few words, but soon it ends,
> And home he goes, convicted to his friends,
> And sobbing says: "The little cash that's mine
> Must go, not on a coffin, but a fine!"

Another elderly gentleman takes up the lament:

> "It's a scandal and a shame to dishonor and defame
> And to laugh at and humiliate in court
> One who's snowy-headed now, but whose sweat
> bedewed his brow
> When the Persian foe at Marathon he fought.
> For at Marathon—ah! Then we were proved courageous men
> As hotly we pursued the fleeing Persian.
> But now it seems the boot's been transferred to the other foot,
> And *we're* persecuted, *we* for mercy plead.

And then when we've had our say, all the jurors vote one way.
They don't care if we are guilty or we ain't.
Why, it's got so bad I guess even Marpsias [unknown reference] would confess
That we have some cause for justified complaint."

The first speaker takes up the refrain:

"…But if on trying old folks you insist,
Then put their names upon a separate list.
If the defendant's old, then don't be ruthless,
But choose a prosecutor who is toothless.
And for the young reserve the subtleties
Of smart young lawyers like Alcibiades.
Then will this just old saw of Athens hold:
'The young should fight the young, the old the old.'"

Source: *Aristophanes: The Acharians; The Clouds; Lysistrata.* Translated by Alan H. Sommerstein. New York: Penguin Books, 1973. Reproduced by permission of Penguin Books Ltd.

ROME

26. An Ideal Retirement

Many ancient Romans looked forward to a life of leisure when their working years were done, but not all of them realized their dreams. In an era when social security was unknown and pensions were rare and usually not generous, a certain amount of careful budgeting was necessary if a working person hoped one day to retire. Still, some prudent Romans enjoyed comfortable retirement lifestyles. The Roman lawyer and writer Pliny the Younger (A.D. 62–114) recounts below the story of a certain Spurinna, who, at the ripe old age of 78, was pursuing what perhaps might have been the ideal retirement.

I never spent my time more agreeably, I think, than I did lately with Spurinna. I was so much pleased with his way of life, that if ever I should arrive at old age, there is no man whom I would sooner choose for my model. I look upon order in human actions, especially at that advanced period, with the same sort of pleasure as I behold the settled course of the heavenly bodies. In youth, indeed, a certain irregularity and agitation is by no means unbecoming; but in age, when business is unseasonable, and ambition indecent, all should be calm and uniform.

Spurinna religiously pursues the above rule of life;…he observes a certain periodical season and method. The first part of the morning he keeps his bed; at eight he calls for his shoes, and walks three miles, in which he enjoys at once contemplation and exercise. Meanwhile, if he has any friends with him in his house, he enters upon some polite and useful topic of conversation; if he is alone, somebody reads to him; and sometimes, too, when he is not, if it is agreeable to his company. When this is over, he reposes himself, and again takes up a book, or else falls into discourse more improving than a book. He afterwards takes the air in his chariot, either with his wife (a lady of exemplary character) or with some friend, a happiness which lately was mine. How agreeable, how noble is the enjoyment of him in that hour of privacy! You would fancy you were hearing some worthy of ancient times, inflaming your breast with the most heroic examples, and instructing your mind with the most exalted precepts, which he yet delivers with such an infusion of his native modesty, that there is not the least appearance of dictating in his conversation. When he has thus taken a tour of seven miles, he gets out of his chariot and walks a mile more, after which he either reposes himself, or retires to his study and pen. For he is an accomplished writer of lyric verse, and that both in Greek and Latin. It is surprising what an ease...runs through his verses, which the moral virtue of the author renders still more acceptable.

When the baths are ready, which in winter is about three o'clock, and in summer about two, he undresses himself; and if there happens to be no wind, he walks about in the sun. After this he puts himself into prolonged and violent motion at playing ball; for by this sort of exercise, he combats the effect of old age. When he has bathed, he throws himself on his couch and waits dinner a little while, and in the meanwhile, some agreeable and entertaining author is read to him. In this, as in all the rest, his friends are at full liberty to partake; or to employ themselves in any other manner more suitable to their taste. You sit down to an elegant yet frugal repast, which is served up in plain and antique plate. He uses likewise dishes of Corinthian bronze, which is his hobby, not his passion. At intervals of the repast, he is frequently entertained with comedians, that even his very pleasures may be seasoned with letters; and though he continues there, even in summer, till the night is somewhat advanced, yet he prolongs the sitting over the wine with so much affability and politeness, that none of his guests ever think it tedious. By this method of living, he has preserved his sight and hearing entire, and his body active and vigorous to his 78th year, without discovering any appearance of old age, but the wisdom.

This is the sort of life which I ardently aspire after; as I purpose to enjoy it, when I shall arrive at those years which will justify a retreat from business. In the meanwhile, I am harassed with a thousand affairs, in which Spurinna is at once my support and my example. For he too, as long as it became him, fulfilled the duties of public life, held the various offices of state, governed provinces, and by indefatigable toil merited the repose he now enjoys. I propose to myself the same course and the same term; and I give it to you under my hand that I do so, in order that, should you see me carried beyond that limit, you may produce this letter against me; and sentence me to repose whenever I can enjoy it without being charged with indolence. Farewell.

Source: *Pliny: Letters*. Translated by William Melmoth, with revisions by W.M.L. Hutchinson. Cambridge and London: Loeb Classical Library, 1915.

27. The Right Time for an Orator to Retire

The first-century A.D. Roman educator and author Quintilian describes in the following excerpt from his writings the ideal retirement for an orator, including some comments on the warning signs that an orator should heed that indicate that the proper time to retire has arrived.

Having practiced these excellences of speaking in courts, councils, assemblies, and the Senate,...our orator will also bring his career to an end in a manner worthy of a good man and of this most revered of professions, not because one can ever have enough of doing good, or because a man endowed with this degree of intellect and capacity should not pray to have as long a time as possible for his glorious work, but because he ought also to take precautions against performing worse than he has performed in the past. The orator depends not only on his knowledge, which increases with the years, but on his voice, lungs, and stamina. If these are broken or impaired by age or illness, he must take care not to fall short of the standards expected of a great orator, to become halting in his speech through fatigue, to realize that his words are no longer listened to, or to look in vain for his former self...

So, before he is ambushed by age, the orator should sound the retreat; he should make for the harbor while his ship is still sound. This done, the fruits of his studies will remain with him undiminished. He will either write a record for posterity, or...offer legal advice to inquirers, compose a treatise on oratory, or give fitting expression to the noblest precepts of morality. Promising young men will frequent his house, as in the old days, and learn the road to true oratory from him as from an oracle. The father of eloquence will educate them, and, like a veteran pilot teach them the coasts and harbors and the signs of the weather, what reason prescribes when the wind is fair and what when it is contrary. His motive will be not only the common duty of humanity, but a love of the work, for no one likes to see the field diminished in which he was once supreme. And what occupation is more honorable than teaching what you know best?...Perhaps indeed one ought to regard this as the happiest time in an orator's life, when, retired and greatly revered, free from envy and far from strife, he has safely secured his reputation, is conscious in his own lifetime of a veneration that commonly comes only after death, and can see what he will mean to future ages.

Source: *Quintilian: The Orator's Education.* Edited and translated by Donald A. Russell. Cambridge and London: Loeb Classical Library, 2001.

28. Old Age Does Not Automatically Equate to a Loss of Vitality

In the following passage, the Roman orator Cicero (106–43 B.C.) refutes the notion that old age inevitably brings lethargy, illness, and disability.

I find four reasons why old age appears to be unhappy. First, that it pulls us away from active pursuits; second, that it weakens the body; third, that it deprives us of almost all physical pleasures; and, fourth, that it is not far removed from death. Let us, if you please, examine each of these reasons separately, and see how much truth they contain.

"Old age pulls us away from active pursuits." From what pursuits? Is it not from those which are followed because of youth and vigor? [Cicero next gives numerous examples from Roman history of elderly but still vigorous statesmen, politicians, and orators.] Those, therefore, who claim that old age is devoid of useful activity have no case, and are like those who would say that the captain does nothing in the sailing of a ship, because, while others are climbing the masts, or running about the gangways, or working at the pumps, he sits quietly in the stern and simply holds the tiller. He may not be doing what younger members of the crew are doing, but what he does is better and much more important. It is not by muscle, speed, or physical dexterity that great things are achieved, but by reflection, force of character, and judgment. In these qualities, old age is usually not only not poorer, but is even richer...

[As for the argument that old age weakens the body]: It may be argued that many old men are so feeble that they can perform no function that duty, or indeed any position life demands. True, but that is not necessarily caused by age. Generally, it is a characteristic of ill health [which also affects young people]. What wonder, then, that the aged are sometimes weak, when even the young cannot escape the same fate? It is our duty to resist old age: to compensate for its defects by a watchful care; to fight against it as we would fight against disease; to adopt a healthy lifestyle; to practice moderate exercise; and to take just enough food and drink to restore our strength and not to overburden the body. Nor are we to give our attention exclusively to the body. Much greater care is due to the mind and soul, for they too, like lamps, grow dim with time, unless we keep them supplied with oil... intellectual activity gives buoyancy to the mind...

We come now to the third alleged disadvantage of old age, and that is, that it is devoid of sensual pleasures. O what a glorious gift, if it does indeed free us from youth's most vicious fault!... The fact that old age feels little longing for sensual pleasures not only is no cause for complaint, but rather is ground for the highest praise. Old age lacks the heavy banquet, the loaded table, and the often-filled cup. Therefore, it also lacks drunkenness, indigestion, and loss of sleep... If reason and wisdom did not enable us to reject pleasure, we should be very grateful to old age for taking away the desire to do what we ought not to do. Carnal pleasure hinders deliberation, is at war with reason, blindfolds the eyes of the mind, and has no fellowship with virtue...

It remains now to consider the fourth reason:... the nearness of death... Wretched indeed is that old man who has not learned in the course of his long life that death should not be feared. Death is clearly negligible, if it utterly annihilates the soul, or even desirable, if it conducts the soul to some place where it is to live forever... What, then, should I fear, if after death I am destined to be either not unhappy, or happy? And yet is there anyone so foolish, even though he is young, as to feel absolutely sure that he will be alive when evening comes? Youth, much more than old age, is subject to the accident of death: the young fall sick more easily, their sufferings are more intense, and they are cured with greater difficulty. Therefore, few arrive at old age... It is in old men that reason and good judgment are found, and had it not been for old men, no state would have existed at all.

Source: *Cicero: De Senectute, De Amicitia, De Divinatione.* Translated by William Armistead Falconer. Cambridge and London: Loeb Classical Library, 1923.

Travel

Travel in the ancient world was generally a dangerous and expensive proposition. This was especially true of overland travel, even after the Romans constructed the world's first network of paved roads; indeed, many of the roads built by the Romans still exist, at least in stages, and some still carry traffic. The Roman poet Horace (65–8 B.C.) describes the annoyances—lack of decent accommodations; bad water; intestinal "issues"; noisy, inebriated fellow-travelers; insects—confronting a traveler on the so-called Queen of Roman Roads, the *Appian Way* (Document 33). Plutarch recounts overland travel problems of a more serious nature—murder and robbery (Document 31). Perhaps these problems could have been avoided altogether had one followed the rather severe travel restrictions proposed by Plato (Document 30), including a requirement that no one under the age of 40 should ever be permitted to travel abroad.

Travel could be undertaken for any number of purposes, as, for example, a trip to *Olympia* to view the Olympic Games (Document 32), a quadrennial event that attracted hundreds of athletes and thousands of spectators from every corner of the Greek world. Some people, like Pliny the Younger, traveled on official business, as his correspondence with the Roman emperor *Trajan* indicates (Documents 34–36). Tourism, then as now, was attractive (Document 29). Occasionally, a sea voyage, with its therapeutic qualities, was recommended by physicians to their ailing patients (Document 37).

EGYPT

29. A Roman Tourist Is Coming!

A papyrus dated 112 B.C. contains instructions, in the form of a letter from one Egyptian official to another, about travel arrangements for a Roman politician who wants to make a trip from Alexandria to the Arsinoite district.

From Hermias...to Asclepiades. Lucius Memmius, a Roman senator who occupies a position of great dignity and honor, is sailing up from Alexandria to the Arsinoite district to see the sights. Let him be received with special magnificence, and take care that at the proper spots the guest chambers be prepared and the landing places to them be completed, and that the gifts [refreshments] be presented to him at the landing place, and that the furniture of the guest chamber...and the conveniences for viewing the Labyrinth [a temple near one of the pyramids], and the offerings and sacrifices be provided. In general, take the greatest pains in everything to see that the visitor is satisfied.

Source: *Select Papyri: Non-literary Papyri: Public Documents.* Volume II. Translated by A. S. Hunt and C. C. Edgar. Cambridge and London: Loeb Classical Library, 1934.

GREECE

30. Plato Suggests Travel Restrictions

The fourth-century B.C. Greek philosopher Plato, in his treatise entitled Laws, *suggests the following fairly severe restrictions for persons traveling outside the boundaries of their city-state.*

In regard, therefore, to the question of going abroad to other lands and places and of the admission of foreigners we must act as follows: First, no man under forty years shall be permitted to go abroad to any place whatsoever; next, no man shall be permitted to go abroad in a private capacity, but in a public capacity permission shall be granted to heralds, embassies, and certain commissions of inspections. Military expeditions in war it would be improper to reckon among official visits abroad. It is right that embassies should be sent to Apollo at Pytho, and Zeus at Olympia, and to Nemea and the Isthmus [of Corinth], to take part in the sacrifices and games in honor of these gods. And it is right also that the ambassadors thus sent should be...as numerous, noble, and good as possible...And these men, when they return home, will teach the youth that the political institutions of other countries are inferior to their own....

If any of the citizens desire to survey the doings of the outside world in a leisurely fashion, no law shall prevent them. For a State that is without experience of bad men and good would never be able (owing to its isolation) to become fully civilized, and perfect, nor would it be able to safeguard its laws...

It is always right for one who dwells in a well-ordered state to go forth on a voyage of inquiry by land and sea, if so be that he himself is incorruptible, so as to confirm thereby such of his native laws as are rightly enacted, and to amend any that are deficient. For without this inspection and inquiry, a State will not permanently remain perfect, nor again if the inspection be badly conducted.

Source: *Plato Laws.* Volume II. Translated by R. G. Bury. London and Cambridge: Loeb Classical Library, 1926.

31. Watch Out for the Wagon-Rollers!

Plutarch describes one of the dangers always faced by overland travelers in the ancient Greek (and Roman) world—murderers and robbers. The following account, from Plutarch's Moralia, *takes place in Megara, a city-state not far from Athens.*

Where did the clan of "Wagon-rollers" in Megara come from?

In the time of the unbridled democracy...a sacred mission of Peloponnesians passed through Megarian territory, on its way to Delphi [site of a famous shrine of the god Apollo] and had encamped, as chance dictated, in their wagons, with their wives and children...beside [a] lake. But the boldest spirits among the Megarians, inflamed with wine, in their insolence and savagery rolled back the wagons and pushed them into the lake, so that many members of the mission were drowned. Now because of the unsettled state of their government, the Megarians took no notice of the crime; but the Amphictyonic Assembly [a league of city-states], since the mission was sacred, took cognizance of the matter and punished some of the guilty men with banishment and others with death. The descendants of these men were called "Wagon-rollers."

Source: *Plutarch's Moralia.* Volume IV. Translated by Frank Cole Babbitt. London and Cambridge: Loeb Classical Library, 1936.

32. Making a Pilgrimage to Olympia

Pilgrimages to Olympia, to view the Olympic Games or to worship there at the shrine of Zeus, were undertaken by many ancient Greeks. In the following excerpt, the historian Xenophon (c. 430–c. 354 B.C.), in his Memorabilia, *recounts one such journey.*

"Have you ever considered, then, which deserves the more stripes, the master or the man?"

When someone was afraid of the journey to Olympia, he said:

"Why do you fear the distance? When you are at home, don't you spend most of the day in walking about? On your way there, you will take a walk before lunch, and another before dinner, and then take a rest. Don't you know that if you put together the walks you take in five or six days, you can easily cover the distance from Athens to Olympia? It is more comfortable, too, to start a day early rather than a day late, since to be forced to make the stages of the journey unduly long is unpleasant; but to take a day extra on the way makes easy going. So it is better to hurry over the start than on the road."

When another said that he was worn out after a long journey, he asked him whether he had carried a load.

"Oh no," said the man; "only my cloak."

"Were you alone, or had you a footman with you?"

"I had."

"Empty-handed, or carrying anything?"

"He carried the rugs and the rest of the baggage, of course."

"And how has he come out of the journey?"

"Better than I, so far as I can tell."

"Well, then, if you had been forced to carry his load, how would you have felt, do you suppose?"

"Bad, of course; or rather, I couldn't have done it."

"Indeed! Do you think that a trained man ought to be so much less capable of work than his slave?"

Source: *Xenophon: Memorabilia and Oeconomicus.* Volume IV. Translated by E. C. Marchant. Cambridge and London: Loeb Classical Library, 1923.

ROME

33. A Trip Down the Appian Way

Overland travel in Roman times was greatly facilitated by the expansive network of paved super highways that the Romans constructed. Perhaps the most famous of these roads was the Via Appia, or Appian Way, extending from Rome to the southern Italian port city of Brundisium, about 360 miles distant. Travel on the roads could be carried out on foot, on the back of a four-footed animal, in a wagon, or in a litter. However, to hear the poet Horace tell it in the following passage from his fifth Satire (Book II), traveling down the Via Appia was anything but a pleasure trip!

Leaving mighty Rome, I found shelter in a modest inn at Aricia, having for a companion Heliodorus the rhetorician, far the most learned of all Greeks. Next came Appii Forum, crammed with boatmen and stingy tavern keepers. This stretch we lazily cut in two, though smarter travelers make it in a single day; the Appian Way is less tiring if taken slowly. Here, owing to the water, for it was villainous, I declare war against my stomach, and wait impatiently while my companions dine.

Already night was beginning to draw her curtain over the earth and to sprinkle the sky with stars. Then slaves loudly rail at the boatmen, boatmen at slaves. "Bring to here!" "You're packing in hundreds!" "Stay, that's enough!" What with collecting fares and harnessing the mule [to pull the boat from shore], a whole hour slips away. Cursed gnats and frogs of the fen drive off sleep, the boatman, soaked in sour wine, singing the while of the girl he left behind, and a passenger taking up the refrain. The passenger at last tires and falls asleep, and the lazy boatman turns his mule out to graze, ties the reins to a stone, and drops snoring on his back. Day was now dawning when we find that our craft was not under way, until one hot-headed fellow jumps out, and with a willow cudgel bangs mule and boatman on the back and head.

At last, by ten o'clock we barely landed, and washed our hands and faces... Then we breakfasted, and crawling on three miles, climbed up to Anxur, perched on her far-gleaming rocks. Here Maecenas [Horace's literary patron] was to meet us, and noble Cocceius, envoys both on business of importance, and old hands at settling feuds... Here I put black ointment on my sore eyes. Meanwhile, Maecenas and Cocceius arrived, and with them Fonteius Capito...

[Next stop]: Fundi, with its [local official] Aufidius Luscus. [We] laugh[ed] at the crazy clerk's cheap trinkets, his bordered robe, broad stripe, and pan of charcoal. Next, tired out, we stopped in the city of the Mamurrae, [where] Murena provid[ed] shelter, and Capito, the larder. Most joyful was the next day's rising, for at Sinuessa, we met up with Plotius, Varius, and Virgil, purest souls earth ever bore, to whom none can be more deeply attached than I am... Nothing, so long as I am in my senses, would I compare to the joy a friend may bring.

The Appian Way was the most important ancient Roman road. It connected Rome to Brundisium, Apulia in southeast Italy. © Pierdelune/Dreamstime.com.

The little house close to the Campanian bridge put a roof over our heads...Next, at Capua [the major city in the district of Campania, south of Rome], our mules laid aside their saddlebags at an early hour. Maecenas went off to play ball, but Virgil and I took a nap; ball playing is hard on the sore-eyed and the dyspeptic. Another stage, and we were taken in at the well-stocked villa of Cocceius....

From there, we traveled straight to Brundisium, where our bustling host was nearly burned out while cooking lean thrushes over the fire. For as the fire slipped out through the old kitchen, the wandering flame hastened to lick the roof. Then you might have seen the hungry guests and the frightened slaves all snatching up the dinner, and all trying to put out the blaze.

From this point, Apulia begins to show to my eyes her familiar hills [Horace hailed from Apulia, in southeastern Italy], and over which we would have never crawled had not a villa near Trivicum taken us in—but not without smoke that brought tears, as green wood, leaves and all, was burning in the stove. Here I, total fool that I was, awaited a faithless girl right up to midnight....

From here, we are whirled in carriages four and twenty miles, to spend the night in a little town I cannot name in verse...Here water, nature's cheapest product, is sold, but the bread is far the best to be had, so that the knowing traveler generally shoulders a load for stages beyond.; for at Canusium...it is gritty, and as to water, the town is no better off....

From there, we came to Rubi, very weary after covering a long stage much marred by the rain. Next day's weather was better, but the road worse, right up to the walls of Barium, a fishing town. Then Gnatia...brought us laughter and mirth in its effort to convince us that frankincense melts without fire at the temple's threshold...Brundisium is the end of a long story and of a long journey.

Source: *Horace: Satires, Epistles, and Ars Poetica.* Translated by H. Rushton Fairclough. Cambridge and London: Loeb Classical Library, 1926.

34. Pliny Reports to Trajan on His Journey to Bithynia

The following three documents (34–36) are excerpts from the correspondence between Pliny the Younger and the emperor Trajan and date from the first decade of the second century A.D. The letters begin with an update to Trajan on the progress Pliny had made en route to Bithynia, in Asia Minor, the province that he had been assigned to govern, and then continue with discussion of Pliny's travel problems.

I feel sure, sir, that you will be interested to hear that I have rounded Cape Malea and arrived at Ephesus [in Greece] with my complete staff, after being delayed by contrary winds. My intention now is to travel on to my province partly by coastal boat and partly by carriage. The intense heat prevents my traveling entirely by road, and the prevailing winds make it impossible to go all the way by sea.

Source: *Pliny: Letters and Panegyricus.* Volume II. Translated by Betty Radice. Cambridge and London: Loeb Classical Library, 1969.

35. Trajan's Reply to Pliny

You did well to send me news, my friend Pliny, for I am very interested to know what sort of journey you are having to your province. You are wise to adapt yourself to local conditions and travel either by boat or carriage.

Source: *Pliny: Letters and Panegyricus*. Volume II. Translated by Betty Radice. Cambridge and London: Loeb Classical Library, 1969.

36. Pliny's Response to Trajan

I kept in excellent health, Sir, throughout my voyage to Ephesus, but I found the intense heat very tiring when I went on to travel by road and developed a touch of fever which kept me at Pergamum [in Greece, north of Ephesus]. Then, when I had resumed my journey by coastal boat, I was further delayed by contrary winds, so that I did not reach Bithynia until September 17th. I had hoped to arrive earlier, but I cannot complain of the delay, as I was in time to celebrate your birthday [September 18th] in my province, and this should be a good omen.

Source: *Pliny: Letters and Panegyricus*. Volume II. Translated by Betty Radice. Cambridge and London: Loeb Classical Library, 1969.

37. You Should Let Them Take You on a Sea Cruise

In the following excerpt from his only extant work, De Medicina, *the first-century* A.D. *Roman physician and encyclopedist Celsus recommends a sea voyage as a possible course of treatment for seriously ill patients.*

If there is more serious illness and a true wasting away [possibly tuberculosis], it is necessary to counter it immediately at the very outset, for when of long standing, it is not readily overcome. If the patient's strength allows it, a long sea voyage is requisite, with a change of air, of such a kind that a denser climate should be sought than that which the patient leaves. Hence, the most suitable is the voyage to Alexandria from Italy...If the patient's weakened condition does not allow this, the best thing for him is to be rocked in a ship without going far away. If anything prevents a sea voyage, the body is to be rocked in a litter, or in some other way.

Source: *Celsus: De Medicina*. Volume I. Translated by W. G. Spencer. London and Cambridge: Loeb Classical Library, 1935.

Making a Living

"Work with work upon work." With those words, the Greek poet Hesiod (Document 41) summed up life on the farm in Greece. But his words probably described the workday generally in the ancient world. Texts from Egypt (Documents 38 and 39) suggest that the life of a scribe might be tolerable, but other occupations seemingly did not have much to recommend them, such as carpenter, cobbler, potter, farmer, artisan, mason, barber, reed cutter, construction worker, weaver, porter, and fisherman, all of which required their practitioners to put in long days of backbreaking labor. In Document 40, the historian Diodorus Siculus noted that in Egypt, craftsmen and other artisans inherited those professions from their parents, and they were forbidden by law to pursue other livelihoods.

The Roman orator Cicero thought that farm work was pleasant enough (Document 43), but he had a distinctly negative attitude toward various other occupations, especially menial jobs involving mostly manual labor (Document 44). The situation was different in Periclean Athens in the fifth century B.C., when *Pericles's* ambitious public works programs created good-paying jobs for all sorts of workers, including carpenters, metal workers, stone cutters, dyers, painters, embroiderers, wagon makers, rope makers, leather workers, road builders, and miners (Document 42). In Document 45, Pliny the Elder addressed the last occupation in that list—mining—calling it dangerous and noting that mining operations were very expensive.

EGYPT

38. Be a Scribe!

The following lugubrious passage from an Eighteenth Dynasty work entitled Instruction of the Scribe Any *lists the various drawbacks and disadvantages of many occupations, with the notable exception of the scribe's profession.*

See for yourself with your own eye. The occupations lie before you.

The washerman's day is going up, going down. All his limbs are weak, [from] whitening his neighbors' clothes every day, from washing their linen.

The maker of pots is smeared with soil, like one whose relations have died. His hands, his feet, are full of clay; he is like one who lives in the bog.

The cobbler mingles with vats. His odor is penetrating. His hands are red with madder, like one who is smeared with blood. He looks behind him for the kite, like one whose flesh is exposed.

The watchman prepares garlands and polishes vase-stands. He spends a night of toil just as one on whom the sun shines.

The merchants travel downstream and upstream. They are as busy as can be, carrying goods from one town to another. They supply him who has wants. But the tax collectors carry off the gold, that most precious of metals.

The ships' crews from every house [of commerce], they receive their loads. They depart from Egypt for Syria, and each man's god is with him. [But] not one of them says: "We shall see Egypt again!"

The carpenter who is in the shipyard carries the timber and stacks it. If he gives the output of yesterday, woe to his limbs! The shipwright stands behind him to tell him evil things.

His outworker who is in the fields, his is the toughest of all the jobs. He spends the day loaded with his tools, tied to his tool-box. When he returns home at night, he is loaded with the tool-box and the timbers, his drinking mug, and his whetstones.

The scribe, he alone, records the output of all of them. Take note of it!

Let me also expound to you the situation of the peasant, that other tough occupation... By day, he attends to his equipment. By day he cuts his farming tools; by night he twists rope. Even his midday hour he spends on farm labor. He equips himself to go to the field as if he were a warrior. The dried field lies before him; he goes out to get his team. When he has been after the herdsman for many days, he gets his team and comes back with it. He makes for it a place in the field. Comes dawn, he goes to make a start and does not find it in its place. He spends three days searching for it; he finds it in the bog. He finds no hides on them; the jackals have chewed them. He comes out, his garment in his hand, to beg for himself a team.

...He spends time cultivating, and the snake is after him. It finishes off the seed as it is cast to the ground. He does not see a green blade. He does three plowings with borrowed grain. His wife has gone down to the merchants and found nothing for barter. Now the scribe lands on the shore. He surveys the harvest. Attendants are behind him with staffs, Nubians with clubs. One says to [him]: "Give grain." "There is none." He is beaten savagely. He is bound, thrown in the well, submerged head down. His wife is bound in his presence. His children are in fetters. His neighbors abandon them and flee. When it's over, there's no grain.

If you have any sense, be a scribe. If you have learned about the peasant, you will not be able to be one. Take note of it!

Source: Lichtheim, Miriam. *Ancient Egyptian Literature, Volume II: The New Kingdom.* Berkeley: University of California Press, 1976.

39. Yes, by All Means Be a Scribe!

Many of the themes put forth in Document 38 are echoed in this set of instructions for a young child named Pepi, who is on his way to school. Pepi is told to take his studies seriously, so that he would not find himself laboring in a menial or dirty job for the rest of his life.

Beginning of the Instruction composed by a man from Sile, Kheti, Duauf's son, for his son, whose name was Pepi... And he said to Pepi:

I have seen defeated, abject men!
You must give yourself whole-heartedly to learning,
discover what will save you from the drudgery of underlings.
Nothing is so valuable as education; it is a bridge over troubled waters.
Just read the end of the *Book of Kemyt,* where you will find these words:
"A scribe in any position whatsoever at the royal palace will never be needy there"...
Let me urge you to love learning more than your mother;
have its perfections enter your mind.
It is more distinguished than any other occupation.
There is nothing like it upon earth!

Good fortune grows for the scribe even from childhood,
and people will respect him.
They will commission him to handle their affairs,
nor will he go about dressed merely in a loincloth.
I do not see carvers sent on missions
or goldsmiths in places where the scribe is sent.
But I have seen the coppersmith at work
at the entrance to his kiln.
His fingers are like crocodile claws,
and he stinks more than the spawn of fish.
Any sort of artisan who takes up tools—
he is as weary as the hoeman
whose fields are full of sticks and troubles for the axe;
only darkness saves him.
He has worked his arms to dropping in his labors,
and it is nightfall when he lights his fire out there.
The mason cutting with his chisel
in all sorts of hard and costly stone—
after he finishes two cubic feet of work,
his arms are dead and he himself is weary.
He sits there until suppertime,
knees cramped and with an aching back.
The barbers barber far into evening,
to earn a bit to swallow, a covering for his shoulders,
taking himself from street to street,
to hunt down any who are ripe for barbering.
He is strong of arm to fill his belly
just like the honeybee at work.
The reed cutter goes down into the marshes
to gather shafts for arrows.
He has worked his arms to dropping in his labors,
bugs and ticks have bitten him to death,
sickness has laid him low;
he fares no better than the damned.
The potter with his earth and clay,
he rises early with the servants.
Weeds and swine hinder his efforts
until he manages to fire his pots.
His clothing is stiff with slime
and his leather apron is in tatters.
The air which enters up his nose
spews directly from his kiln.
He makes a pestle of his feet,
to stamp the clay down flat,
hacking up the courtyards of the houses,
unwelcome in public places.
Let me tell you about the builder of walls:
Life for him is pitiful.
Should he be outdoors in a cutting wind,
he must keep on working in his loincloth.
His apron is mere rags
and the rest-house far behind him.

His arms are dead from wielding the chisel,
and every measurement is wrong.
He eats food with his fingers
and washes once a day.
The carpenter is wretched as he grasps his plan:
the finishing of a chamber, an area in a tomb of six by ten.
A month goes by; its woodwork is torn down, its matting strewn about
and all that was so carefully constructed has been ruined.
As for providing for his own house,
he cannot even feed his children...
The farmer, he complains incessantly,
his cry more raucous than the raven's.
His fingers go about their duties
through all the raging of the storm.
Wearied beyond reward down in the marshes,
he becomes a living wreck.
His storehouse is depleted by the lions,
worse ills from hippopotami are his.
His creatures there lack dwellings
so he must leave them unprotected.
He reaches home exhausted
and the taxman cuts him down.
The mat-maker in his tiny cubicle:
He is more wretched than a woman.
With his knees pressed against his stomach
he can hardly breathe.
If he wastes the day not weaving,
he is beaten with the leather, fifty blows.
He must offer food to the door guard
just to let him see the sun.
The arrow maker is already spent
as he goes into the desert uplands.
What he must pay for donkeys is more costly
than their toil will profit in return.
And costly too his pay to country people
to point him on his way.
When he comes home at evening,
the walking has exhausted him.
The porter who treks to foreign lands
has assigned his meager assets to his children.
Fearful alike of lions and of nomads,
he has his wits about him only in Egypt.
He comes back home all woebegone.
The journey has done him in.
He dresses in a loincloth for his clothing,
and contentment never comes...
The laundry man washing on the riverbank
bows low in the presence of the crocodile god.
"Father, let me go down to the edge of the water!"
clamor his son and daughter.
Oh, there is no profession that satisfies like this,
distinguished above any other calling!

He kneads all sorts of excrement,
with not a limb left clean.
He does the undergarments of a woman...; tears are his,
daylong at the hot washing bowls, or as he heaves the pounding stone.
The tub of dirty water whispers, "Come to me
and let me overflow because of you!"
Let me tell you also of the fisherman.
He is worse off than any other occupation,
as he pursues his work on the River
mingling with the crocodiles.
If he overestimates his harvest,
he is in despair.
He cannot say, "The crocodiles did this!"
It was his own fear that blinded him.
As he goes forth upon the waters of the torrent,
he cries, "This is the very wrath of God!"
There is no occupation without its bosses,
except for the scribe: he *is* the boss.
Now, if you will learn writing,
it will be better
than any of these trades which I have set before you.

Source: From *Ancient Egyptian Literature: An Anthology*. Translated by John L. Foster. Copyright © 2001. By permission of the University of Texas Press.

40. Farmers and Craft Workers in Ancient Egypt

In the following excerpt, the first-century B.C. Greek historian Diodorus Siculus recounts the various duties and responsibilities of rural and urban workers in ancient Egypt.

The farmers rent on moderate terms the arable land held by the king and the priests and the warriors, and spend their entire time in tilling the soil. And since from their infancy, they are brought up in connection with the various tasks of farming, they are far more experienced in such matters than the farmers of any other nation. Out of all mankind, they acquire the most exact knowledge of the nature of the soil, the use of water in irrigation, the times of sowing and reaping, and the harvesting of crops in general, some details of which they have learned from the observations of their ancestors and others in the school of their own experience.

And what has been said applies equally well to the herdsmen, who receive the care of animals from their parents as if by a law of inheritance, and follow a pastoral life all the days of their existence. They have received, it is true, much from their ancestors relative to the best care and feeding of grazing animals, but to this they add not a little by reason of their own interest in such matters. The most astonishing fact is that, by reason of their unusual application to such matter, those who are in charge of poultry and geese, in addition to producing them in the natural way, universally known, raise them by their own hands, by virtue of a skill peculiar to them, in numbers beyond telling. For they do not use the birds for hatching the eggs, but, in bringing this about themselves artificially,

Three scribes at work, painted limestone from the tomb of the official Ty, Saqqara, fifth dynasty, 2450–2325 B.C. The Art Archive/Gianni Dagli Orti.

by their own wit and skill in an astounding manner, they are not surpassed by the operations of nature.

Furthermore, one may also see that the crafts among the Egyptians are very diligently cultivated and brought to their proper development. They are the only people where all the craftsmen are forbidden to follow any other occupation or belong to any other class of citizens than those stipulated by the laws and handed down to them from their parents; the result is that neither ill-will towards a teacher nor political distractions nor any other thing interferes with their interest in their work. Whereas among all other peoples it can be observed that the artisans are distracted in mind by many things, and through the desire to advance themselves do not stick exclusively to their own occupation—some try their hands at agriculture, some dabble in trade, and some cling to two or three crafts, and in states having a democratic form of government, vast numbers of them, trooping to the meetings of the Assembly, ruin the work of government, while they make a profit for themselves at the expense of others who pay their wages, yet among the Egyptians, if any artisan takes part in public affairs or pursues several crafts, he is severely punished.

Source: *Diodorus of Sicily.* Volume I. Translated by C. H. Oldfather. London and Cambridge: Loeb Classical Library, 1933.

GREECE

41. The Farmer's Long Day . . . and Year

"Work with work upon work." With those words, the eighth-century B.C. Greek poet Hesiod summed up the nature of life on the farm in ancient Greece. And farming was un- doubtedly the primary occupation. Since most ancient Greek authors whose work survives were city-dwellers, there is a dearth of primary source material about farm life. Hesiod, who came from an agrarian family, was an exception. His long epic poem, "Works and Days," is filled with advice to farmers, including his brother, Perses, on how to succeed and prosper.

When the Atlas-born Pleiades rise [in May], start the harvest—the plowing, when they set [late October, early November, . . . I bid you take notice of how to clear your debts and how to ward off famine: a house first of all, a woman, and an ox for plowing— the woman one you purchase, not marry, one who can follow with the oxen—and arrange everything well in the house, lest you ask someone else and he refuse and you suffer want, and the season passes by, and the fruit of your work will be diminished. Do not postpone until tomorrow and the next day; for the futilely working man does not fill his granary, nor does the postponer; industry fosters work, and the work-postponing man is always wrestling with calamities.

[In late September], wood that is cut with the iron is least bitten by worms, and its leaves fall to the ground and it ceases putting forth shoots. So at that time be mindful and cut wood, a seasonable work: cut a mortar three feet long, and a pestle three cubits long [four and one-half feet], and an axle seven feet long, for this way things will fit together very well. If you cut a length eight feet long, you could cut a mallet-head from it too... Toil hard to lay up a pair of plows in your house, one of a single piece and one put together, since it is much better this way; if you broke one, you could set the other one upon your oxen... Acquire two oxen, nine years old, male, that have reached the measure of puberty, for their strength has not been drained away yet; they are best at working... Together with these, a strong, forty-year old man should follow with the plow... someone who puts care into his work and will drive a straight furrow, no longer gaping after his age-mates, but keeping his mind on his work. And another man, not a bit younger than him, is better for scattering the weeds and avoiding over-seeding; for a younger man is all aflutter for his age-mates...

When the plowing-time first shows itself to mortals, set out for it, both your slaves and yourself, plowing by dry and by wet in the plowing season, hastening very early, so that your fields will be filled. Turn the soil over in the spring; land left fallow in the summer will not disappoint you; sow the fallow land while the field is still brittle. Fallow land is an averter of death, a soother of children.

Pray to Zeus... and to hallowed Demeter... as you begin plowing at the very start, when you have taken the end of the plow-tail in your hand and have come down with the goad upon the oxen's backs while they draw the yoke-pole by its leather strap. Just a little behind, let another man, slave holding a mattock, make toil for the birds by covering up the seed; for good management is the best for mortal human beings, bad management the worst. In this way the ears of corn will bend towards the ground in their ripeness... You will arrive at bright spring in good shape and will not gape at other people, but some other man will stand in need of you.

Pass by the bronze-worker's bench and his warm lounge in the wintry season, when the cold holds men back from fieldwork but an unhesitating man could greatly foster his household—lest a bad, intractable winter catch you up together with Poverty, and you rub a swollen foot with a skinny hand. A man who does not work, waiting upon an empty hope, in need of the means of life, says many evil things to his spirit. Hope is not good at providing for a man in need who sits in the lounge and does not have enough of the means of life. Point out to the slaves while it is still mid-summer: "It will not always be summer, make huts for yourselves."

As for you, Perses, be mindful of all kinds of work in good season, but above all regarding seafaring. Praise a small boat, but place your load in a big one; for the cargo will be bigger, and your profit will be bigger, profit on profit—if the winds hold back their evil blasts.

Source: *Hesiod: Theogony/Works and Days/Testimonia.* Translated by Glenn W. Most. Cambridge and London: Loeb Classical Library, 2006.

42. An Unrivaled Public Works Program

Even though most ancient Greeks made their livings as farmers, other kinds of employment were also available. In the mid-fifth century B.C., *when the politician/statesman Pericles initiated a massive construction program in Athens, city jobs were plentiful, as Plutarch attests in the following excerpt from his* Life of Pericles.

In his desire that the unwarlike throng of common laborers should neither have no share at all in the public receipts, nor yet get fees for laziness and idleness, he boldly suggested to the people projects for great constructions, and designs for works which would call many arts into play and involve long periods of time, in order that the stay-at-homes, no whit less than the sailors and sentinels and soldiers, might have a pretext for getting a beneficial share of the public wealth. The materials to be used were stone, bronze, ivory, gold, ebony, and cypress-wood; the arts which should elaborate and work up these materials were those of carpenter, moulder, bronze-smith, stone-cutter, dyer, worker in gold and ivory, painter, embroiderer, embosser, to say nothing of the forwarders and furnishers of the material, such as factors, sailors and pilots by sea, and, by land, wagon-makers, trainers of yoked beasts, and drivers. There were also rope-makers, weavers, leather-workers, road-builders, and miners. And since each particular art, like a general with the army under his separate command, kept its own throng of unskilled and untrained laborers in compact array, to be as an instrument unto player and as body unto soul in subordinate service, it came to pass that for every age, almost, and every capacity the city's great abundance was distributed and scattered abroad by such demands.

So then the works arose, no less towering in their grandeur than inimitable in the grace of their outlines, since the workmen eagerly strove to surpass themselves in the beauty of their handicraft.

Source: *Plutarch's Lives.* Volume III. Translated by Bernadotte Perrin. Cambridge and London: Loeb Classical Library, 1916.

ROME

43. Cicero on the Joys of Farming

As with the Greeks, for the ancient Romans, farming was the occupation that employed more workers than any other. In the following passage from his essay "On Old Age," the Roman orator Cicero paints a pleasant picture of the joys of agricultural pursuits.

I come now to the pleasures of agriculture, in which I find incredible delight; they are not one bit checked by old age, and are, it seems to me, in the highest degree suited to the life of the wise man... And yet what I enjoy is not the fruit alone, but I also enjoy the soil itself, its nature and its power...

Why should I mention the origin, cultivation, and growth of the vine? But, that you may know what affords the recreation and delight of my old age, I will say that vine-culture gives me a joy of which I cannot get too much....

Indeed, it is not only the utility of the vine...that gives me joy, but I find joy also in its culture and very nature; in the even-spaced rows of stakes, with strips across the top; in the tying up of the branches; in the propagating of the plants; in the pruning of some branches...and in the leaving of others to grow at will....

Why need I allude to the irrigation, ditching, and frequent hoeing of the soil, whereby its productiveness is so much enhanced? Why need I discuss the advantage of manuring?...Nor does the farmer find joy only in his cornfields, meadows, vine-yards, and woodlands, but also in his garden and orchard, in the rearing of his cattle, in his swarms of bees, and in the infinite variety of flowers. And not only does planting delight him, but grafting also, than which there is nothing in husbandry that is more ingenious....

In those days [that is, in the early days of the Roman Republic, especially the fifth century B.C.], senators...lived on farms—if the story is true that Lucius Quinctius Cincinnatus was at the plow when he was notified of his election to the dictatorship... It was from the farmhouse that Curius and other old men were summoned to the senate...Well, then, was there cause to pity the old age of these men who delighted in the cultivation of the soil? For my part, at least, I am inclined to think that no life can be happier than that of the farmer...Nothing can be more abounding in usefulness or more attractive in appearance than a well-tilled farm.

Source: *Cicero: De Senectute, De Amicitia, De Divinatione.* Translated by William Armistead Falconer. Cambridge and London: Loeb Classical Library, 1923.

44. Cicero on Other, Less Joyful Occupations

In his essay "On Duties," Cicero also describes various other occupations, but not in the flattering terms that he reserved for farm work (see Document 43, above).

Now in regard to trades and other means of livelihood, which ones are to be considered becoming to a gentleman and which ones are not, we have been taught, in general, as follows: First, those means of livelihood are rejected as undesirable, and which incur people's ill-will, as those of tax-gatherers and usurers. Unbecoming to a gentleman, too...are the means of livelihood of all hired workmen whom we pay for mere manual labor, not for artistic skill; for in their case, the very wages they receive is a pledge of their slavery. We must consider inappropriate those also who buy from wholesale merchants to retail immediately; for they would get no profits without a great deal of downright lying; and certainly there is no action that is lower than mis-representation. And all mechanics are engaged in vulgar trades; for no workshop can have anything liberal about it. Least respectable of all are those trades which cater to sensual pleasures...

But the professions in which either a higher degree of intelligence is required or from which no small benefit to society is derived—medicine and architecture, for example, and teaching—these are proper for those whose social position they are appropriate. Trade, if it is on a small scale, is to be considered inappropriate; but if wholesome and on a large scale, importing large quantities from all parts of the world and distributing to many without misrepresentation, it is not to be greatly disparaged. It even seems to deserve the highest respect, if those who are engaged in it [are]...satisfied with the fortunes they have made, and make their way from the port to a country estate, as they have often made it from the sea into port. But of all the occupations by which gain is secured, none is better than agriculture, none more profitable, none more delightful, none more becoming to a freeman.

Source: *Cicero: De Officiis.* Translated by Walter Miller. London and New York: Loeb Classical Library, 1913.

45. There's Gold in Those Hills!

In the following excerpt from his Natural History, *the Roman writer Pliny the Younger describes in some detail the labor—and danger—involved with gold mining.*

Gold in our part of the world...is obtained in three ways: in the detritus of rivers...by sinking shafts...in the fallen debris of mountains. Each of these methods must be described.

People seeking gold begin by getting up *segellum*—that is the name for earth that indicates the presence of gold. This is a pocket of sand, which is washed, and from the sediment left an estimate of the vein is made. Sometimes by a rare piece of luck a pocket is found immediately, on the surface of the earth...

Gold dug up from shafts is called "channeled", or "trenched" gold. It is found sticking to the grit of marble,...sparkling in the folds of the marble. These channels of veins wander to and fro along the sides of the shafts, which gives the gold its name, and the earth is held up by wooden props. The substance dug out is crushed, washed, fired, and ground to a soft powder...

The third method will have outdone the achievements of the Giants. By means of galleries driven for long distances, the mountains are mined by the light of lamps; the spells of work are also measured by lamps, and the miners do not see daylight for many months.

The name for this class of mines is *arrugiae*. Also, cracks give way suddenly and crush the men who have been at work, so that it actually seems less hazardous to try to get pearls and purple fishes out of the depth of the sea, so much more dangerous have we made the earth! Consequently, arches are left at frequent intervals to support the weight of the mountain above. In both kinds of mining, masses of flint are encountered, which are burst apart by means of fire and vinegar, although more often, since this method makes the tunnels suffocating through heat and smoke, they are broken to pieces with crushing machines carrying 150 pounds of iron, and the men carry the stuff out on their shoulders, working night and day, each man passing them on to the next man in the dark, while only those at the end of the line see daylight. If the bed of flint seems too long, the miner follows along the side of it and goes around it. And yet flint is considered to involve comparatively easy work, as there is a kind of earth consisting of a sort of potter's clay mixed with gravel, called *gangadia*, which it is almost impossible to overcome. They attack it with iron wedges and the hammer machines mentioned above, and it is thought to be the hardest thing that exists, except greed for gold, which is the most stubborn of all things.

When the work is completely finished, they cut through the supports of the arched roofs at the top, beginning with the last. A crack gives warning of a crash, and the only person who notices it is the sentinel on a pinnacle of the mountain. By shout and gesture, he gives the order for the workmen to be called out, and he himself at the same moment flies down from his pinnacle. The fractured mountain falls apart in a wide gap, with a crash which it is impossible for human imagination to conceive, and at the same time with an incredibly violent blast of air. The miners gaze as conquerors upon the collapse of Nature. But nevertheless even now, there is no gold so far, nor did they positively know there was any when they began to dig. The mere hope of obtaining their coveted object was a sufficient inducement for encountering such great dangers and expenses.

Source: *Pliny: Natural History.* Volume IX. Translated by H. Rackham. Cambridge and London: Loeb Classical Library, 1952.

Part III

ECONOMIC LIFE

Urban Life

One of the most noteworthy cities in the ancient world was *Alexandria*, Egypt. Its broad and well-planned streets, its magnificent palaces, its two renowned libraries, and its harbor were just a few of the amenities to be found there (Document 4). The Greeks excelled in the realm of city planning; in fact, the first city planner was reputedly a fifth-century B.C. political scientist and legal expert named *Hippodamus* (Documents 5 and 6).

Ancient India seemed to have been so heavily urbanized, if the statement of the historian Arrian is to be believed, that it was impossible to count the cities in India because there were so many (Document 3). City administration was well-organized (Document 2), and there did not seem to be the fear of tax collectors that apparently pervaded some places in China (Document 1).

But of all the urban areas of the ancient world, the Eternal City, Rome, was the most magnificent. From its humble beginnings in about 753 B.C. (Document 7), until its downfall as the capital of the Western Empire in A.D. 476, no other ancient city could match it in terms of power, influence, grandeur, and sheer size. The Romans excelled in civil engineering, and the fruits of their labors were to be seen everywhere in the wide expanses of the city (Documents 10 and 11). Not surprisingly, however, there were extremes: the emperor Nero's ostentatious Golden House on the one hand (Document 9), and poorly constructed slums, with their fire-trap tenement houses, on the other (Document 8).

CHINA

---

1. Life with the Tax Man

During the Chou Dynasty (c. 1100–256 B.C.), tax collectors could make life miserable for the common people of China, and whether they lived in villages or on farms, the "Big Rat" with the upturned palm would be sure to find them and demand their taxes.

(1) Big rat, big rat,
don't eat my millet!
Three years I've served you
but you won't care for me.
I'm going to leave you
and go to that happy land,
happy land, happy land
where I'll find my place.

(3) Big rat, big rat,
don't eat my sprouts!
Three years I've served you
but you give me no comfort.
I'm going to leave you
and go to those happy fields,
happy fields, happy fields,
who will moan there for long?

Source: From *Sources of Chinese Tradition*. Volume I. Second Edition. Compiled by William Theodore de Bary and Irene Bloom. Copyright © 1999 Columbia University Press. Reprinted with permission of the publisher.

INDIA

2. Indian Urban Life

Famous for his 17-volume Geographica, *a descriptive history of peoples and regions known to him, the Greek geographer Strabo (c. 64 B.C.–A.D. 21) wrote the following account of the structures and organization of contemporary Indian urban life.*

Of the [city] officials, some are market commissioners, others are city commissioners, and others are in charge of the soldiers. Among these, the first keep the rivers improved and the land remeasured, as in Egypt, and inspect the closed canals from which the water is distributed into the conduits, in order that all may have an equal use of it. The same men also have charge of the hunters and are authorized to reward or punish those who deserve either. They also collect the taxes and superintend the crafts connected with the land—those of wood-cutters, carpenters, workers in brass, and miners. And they make roads, and...place pillars showing the by-roads and the distances.

The city commissioners are divided into six groups of five each. One group looks after the arts of the craftsmen. Another group entertains strangers, for they assign them lodgings, follow closely their behavior, giving them attendants...and they take care of them when they are sick and bury them when they die. The third group is that of those who scrutinize births and deaths, when and how they take place, both for the sake of taxes and in order that births and deaths, whether better or worse, may not be unknown. The fourth group is that which has to do with sales and barter; and these look after the measures and fruits of the season...The fifth group is that of those who have charge of the works made by artisans and sell these by stamp, the new apart from the old; and the man who mixes them is fined. The sixth and last group is that of those who collect a tenth part of the price of the things sold, and death is the penalty for the man who steals. These are the special duties performed by each group, but they all take care jointly of matters both private and public, and of the repairs of public works, of prices, marketplaces, harbors and temples....

All Indians live a simple life, and especially when they are on expeditions, and neither do they enjoy useless disturbances. And on this account, they behave in an orderly manner.

Source: *The Geography of Strabo.* Volume VII. Translated by Horace Leonard Jones. London and New York: Loeb Classical Library, 1930.

3. Description of Indian Cities

The second-century A.D. *Greek historian, philosopher, and public official, Arrian helped make fashionable a primarily military-based history and is known as one of the most important sources for the campaigns of Alexander the Great, including those in India. In the following excerpt, Arrian provides some information about Indian cities.*

As for the cities of India, it would be impossible to record their number accurately because there are so many. Those on rivers or on the coast are built of wood. If they were built of brick, they could not last long because of the moisture due to rain, and to the fact that the rivers overflow their banks and fill the plains with water. Only where the cities are situated in commanding and lofty places and these are bare, are they built of brick and clay.

The greatest of the Indian cities is called Palimbothra...And Megasthenes says that the length of the city on either side, where it is longest, extends to 80 stades [about 10 miles], its width to 15, and that a ditch has been dug around the city...The wall has 570 towers and 64 gates.

Source: *Arrian.* Volume II. Translated by E. Iliff Robson, with revisions by P. A. Brunt. Cambridge and London: Loeb Classical Library, 1933.

EGYPT

4. The Wonders of Alexandria

Of all the cities in ancient Egypt, probably the most magnificent was Alexandria, home to two of the finest libraries in antiquity, as well as the lighthouse, or Pharos, which was deemed one of the Seven Wonders of the Ancient World. The Greek geographer Strabo offered the following detailed description of life in this cosmopolitan metropolis.

The advantages of the city's site are various, for, first, the place is washed by two seas, on the north by the Egyptian Sea, as it is called, and on the south by Lake Mareia...This is filled by many canals from the Nile, both from above and on the sides, and through these canals the imports are much larger than those from the sea, so that the harbor on the lake was in fact richer than that on the sea...[T]he salubrity of the air is also worthy of remark. And this likewise results from the fact that the land is washed by water on both sides and because of the timeliness of the Nile's risings; for the other cities that are situated on lakes have heavy and stifling air in the heats of summer, because the lakes then become marshy along their edges because of the evaporation caused by the sun's rays, and, accordingly, when so much filth-laden moisture rises, the air inhaled is noisome, and starts pestilential diseases, whereas at Alexandria, at the beginning of summer, the Nile, being full, fills the lake also, and leaves no marshy matter to corrupt the rising vapors. At that time, also, the winds blow from the north and from a vast sea, so that the Alexandrians pass their time most pleasantly in summer.

…The city as a whole is intersected by streets practicable for horse-riding and chariot-driving, and by two that are very broad…And the city contains most beautiful public precincts and also the royal palaces, which constitute one-fourth or even one-third of the whole circuit of the city. For just as each of the kings, from love of splendor, customarily added some adornment to the public monuments, so also

Pharos, the Lighthouse of Alexandria. On top is the sun god Helios pointing a stick to a spheric object, perhaps symbolizing the light of Christ. In the background another colossal statue erected by Pompey at the Serapeion of Alexandria. Sixth century A.D. Gilles M.

he would invest himself with a residence, in addition to those already built, so that now, to quote the words of the poet [Homer], "there is building upon building." All, however, are connected with one another and the harbor, even those that lie outside the harbor. The Museum is also a part of the royal palaces. It has a public walk, an exedra with seats, and a large house, in which is the common mess-hall of the men of learning who share the Museum…

Polybius, who visited the city [second century B.C.], is disgusted with the state of things then existing, and he says that three classes inhabited the city: first, the Egyptian or native stock of people, who were quick-tempered and not inclined to civic life; and, secondly, the mercenary class, who were severe and numerous and intractable…and third, the tribe of the Alexandrians, who were also not distinctly inclined to civil life, and for the same reasons, but still they were better than those others, for even though they were a mixed people, still they were Greeks by origin and mindful of the customs common to the Greeks…

Such, then, if not worse, was the state of affairs under the later kings also. But the Romans have, to the best of their ability, I might say, set most things right, having organized the city.

Source: *The Geography of Strabo.* Volume VIII. Translated by Horace Leonard Jones. London and New York: Loeb Classical Library, 1932.

GREECE

5. The Well-Planned City

In his treatise entitled Politics, *the Greek philosopher Aristotle (384–322 B.C.) provided a survey of the essentials for a well-run and prosperous city. These factors included a favorable location, a strong family structure, a workable set of laws and a constitution, a means for preventing and suppressing civil unrest, an intelligent and engaged citizenry, and a population sufficiently large to ensure that all necessary work is performed. As the following passage indicates, city planning also fell within the purview of Aristotle's work.*

It has been said before that the city should so far as circumstances permit be in communication alike with the mainland, the sea, and the whole of its territory. The site of the city itself we must pray that fortune may place on sloping ground, having regard to four considerations: first, as a thing essential, the consideration of health (for cities whose site slopes east or towards the breezes that blow from the sunrise are more healthy, and in the second degree those that face away from the north wind, for these are milder in winter); and among the remaining considerations, a sloping site is favorable both for political and for military purposes. For military purposes, therefore, the site should be easy to exit for the citizens themselves, and difficult for the enemy to approach and to blockade, and it must possess if possible a plentiful natural supply of pools and springs, but failing this, a mode has been invented of supplying water by means of constructing an abundance of large reservoirs for rain water, so that a supply may never fail the citizens when they are debarred from their territory by war. And since we have to consider the health of the inhabitants, and this depends upon the place being well situated both on healthy ground and with a healthy aspect, and secondly upon using wholesome water supplies, the following matter also must be attended to as of primary importance. Those things which we use for the body in the largest quantity, and most frequently, contribute most to health; and the influence of the water supply and of the air is of this nature. Hence, in wise cities, if all the sources of water are not equally pure and there is not an abundance of suitable springs, the water supplies for drinking must be kept separate from those for other requirements. As to fortified positions, what is expedient is not the same for all forms of constitution alike. For example, a citadel hill is suitable for oligarchy and monarchy, and a level site for democracy. Neither is favorable to an aristocracy, but rather several strong positions. The arrangement of the private dwellings is thought to be more agreeable and more convenient for general purposes if they are laid out in straight streets, after the modern fashion . . . but it is more suitable for security in war if it is on the contrary plan, as cities used to be in ancient times, for their arrangement is difficult for foreign troops to enter and find their way about in when attacking. Hence, it is well to combine the advantages of both plans, . . . and not lay out the whole city in straight streets, but only certain parts and districts, for in this way it will combine security with beauty.

As regards walls, those who state that cities which pretend to valor should not have them hold too old-fashioned a view—and that though they see that the cities that indulge in that form of vanity are refuted by experience. It is true that against an evenly matched foe and one little superior in numbers, it is not honorable to try to secure oneself by the strength of one's fortifications; but as it may possibly happen that the superior numbers of the attackers may be too much for the human courage of a small force, if the city is to survive and not to suffer disaster or insult, the securest fortification of walls must be deemed to be the most warlike, particularly in view of the inventions that have now been made in the direction of precision with missiles and artillery for sieges. To claim not to surround cities with walls is like desiring the country to be easy to invade and stripping it of hilly regions, and similarly not surrounding even private dwellings with house walls on the ground that the inhabitants will be cowardly.

Another point, moreover, that must not be forgotten is that those who have walls around the city can use their cities in both ways, both as walled cities and as open ones, whereas cities not possessing walls cannot be used in both ways. If then this is so, not only must walls be put around a city, but also attention must be paid to them in order that they may be suitable both in regard to the adornment of the city, and in respect to military requirements, especially the new devices recently invented. For just as the attackers of a city are concerned with studying the means by which they can gain the advantage, so also for the defenders some devices have already been invented, and others they must discover and think out; for people do not even start attempting to attack those who are well prepared.

And since the multitude of citizens must be distributed in separate messes, and the city walls must be divided up by guard posts and towers in suitable places, it is clear that these facts themselves call for some of the messes to be organized at these guard posts.

Source: *Aristotle Politics*. Translated by H. Rackham. London and Cambridge: Loeb Classical Library, 1932.

6. Hippodamus: Planner of Cities

Although he does not entirely agree with them, Aristotle also records in the Politics *the ideas of a famous Greek city planner of the fifth century* B.C., *Hippodamus of Miletus.*

Hippodamus, son of Euryphon, a Milesian (who invented the division of cities into blocks... and who also became somewhat eccentric in his general mode of life, owing to a desire for distinction, so that some people thought that he lived too fussily, with a quantity of hair and expensive ornaments, and also a quantity of cheap yet warm clothes, not only in winter, but also in summer, and who wished to be a man of learning in natural science generally), was the first man not engaged in politics who attempted to speak on the subject of the best form of constitution. His system was for a city with a population of 10,000, divided into three classes. He made one class of artisans, one of farmers, and the third the class that fought for the city in wars, and was the armed class. He divided the land into three parts: one sacred, one public, and one private: sacred land to supply the customary offerings to the gods, common land to provide the warrior class with food, and private land to be owned by the farmers. He thought that there are only three divisions of the law, since the matters about which lawsuits take place are three in number: outrage, damage, homicide. He also proposed to establish one supreme court of justice, to which were to be carried up all the cases at law thought to have been decided wrongly, and this court he made to consist of certain selected elders...He proposed a law that those who discovered something of advantage to the city should receive honor, and that the children of those who died in war should have their maintenance from the city, in the belief that this had never yet been provided by law among other people. But as a matter of fact, this law exists at present both at Athens and in other cities.

Source: *Aristotle Politics*. Translated by H. Rackham. London and Cambridge: Loeb Classical Library, 1932.

ROME

7. The Founding of Rome

The legendary founder of Rome was the city's namesake, Romulus. The early second century A.D. *Greek essayist and biographer Plutarch, in the following passage from his biography of Romulus, describes the earliest days of the city.*

[Romulus] set himself to building his city...A circular trench was dug around what is now the Comitium [in the center of the city], and in this were deposited first-fruits of all things, the use of which was sanctioned by custom as good and by nature as necessary. And finally, every man brought a small portion of the soil of his native land, and these were cast in among the first-fruits, and mingled with them...

Then, taking this as a center, they marked out the city in a circle around it. And the founder, having shod a plough with a bronze ploughshare, and having yoked to it a bull and a cow, himself drove a deep furrow around the boundary lines...With this line, they mark out the course of the wall, and it is called, by contraction, "pomerium," that is, "post murum" *behind* or *next to the wall*. And where they intended to put in a gate, there they took the share out of the ground, lifted the plough over, and left a vacant space. And this is the reason why they regard all the wall as sacred except the gates. But if they considered the gates sacred, it would not be possible, without religious rituals, to bring into and send out of the city things which are necessary, and yet unclean.

It is agreed that the city was founded on the 21st of April, and this day the Romans celebrate with a festival, calling it the birthday of their country. And at first, as it is said, they sacrificed no living creature at that festival, but thought that they ought to keep it pure and without stain of blood, since it commemorated the birth of their country. However, even before the founding of the city, they had a pastoral festival on that day, and called it Parilia.

Source: *Plutarch's Lives*. Volume I. Translated by Bernadotte Perrin. London and Cambridge: Loeb Classical Library, 1914.

8. Big-City Blues

Life in the big city could be exciting, or it could be dangerous. The latter view is presented below by the satirical poet Juvenal, writing about Rome in the first century A.D. *As a satirist,*

Juvenal was probably guilty of at least some exaggeration, but there undoubtedly is also a kernel or two of truth in his writing.

Although I'm sad at my old friend's departure [from Rome], yet I praise
His purpose to make his home in abandoned Cumae and raise
The count of citizens of the Sibyl by one. For there
Lies the threshold to Baiae, a welcome resort on a fair
And pleasant shore. I'd even prefer a desert island,
Myself, to downtown Rome. For what place have we seen so vile,
So lonely, that you would not consider that it's much worse
To dread the constant fires and the tumbling houses, the curse
Of our terrible city's countless perils, and the verse
That poets pour out in the month of August in cataracts?...
Umbricius here spoke out: "Since there's no room," he commenced,
"For honest professions in this city, no recompense
For work, since my assets are less today than yesterday
And tomorrow will rub away from what little's left a bit more away,
I've decided to go where Daedalus shed his exhausted wings,
While the gray in my hair is new, while erect though entering
Old age, while some of my life's long thread may still remain
For Lachesis to spin and I can stand on my feet with no cane
In hand. Good bye, my homeland!...
What's there in Rome for me to do? I'm not trained to lie.
I can't praise a book if it's bad, and beg for a copy...
And anyway, what does a poor man's service in Rome afford?
Even if Numa [an early, revered Roman king] himself [were called upon to testify in court],
the first question they ask will be about
His wealth, the last about his character: How many slaves
Does he keep? How much farmland does he own? How many engraved
Dessert plates does he eat from? How big are they? A man's word
Is believed just to the extent of the wealth in his coffers stored.
Though he swear on all the altars from here to Samothrace,
A poor man isn't believed...
Anyway, a poor man's the butt of jokes if his cloak has a rip
Or is dirty, if his toga is slightly soiled, if a strip
Of leather is split in his shoes and gapes, if coarse thread shows
New stitches patching not one but many holes. Of the woes
Of unhappy poverty, none is more difficult to bear
Than that it heaps men with ridicule. Says an usher: How dare
You sit there? Get out of the rows reserved for knights to share,
All of you whose means aren't enough under law! And let sons of pimps,
Born in brothels, take seats...
What son-in-law here was approved on merits
If his money was less than the girl's? What poor man ever inherits
A fortune, or gets appointed as clerk to a magistrate?
Long ago the penniless Romans ought to have staged a great
Mass walkout. It's no easy job for a man to advance
When his talents are blocked by his impoverished circumstance,
But in Rome, it's harder than elsewhere: high rent for tenements,
Fat budgets to feed your slaves' lean bellies, and equal expense
For your own potluck. You're ashamed to eat off earthenware,
But you wouldn't feel so if suddenly set to country fare

Far off...
We buy too much, to impress. It's a common fault hereabout.
We all live in pretentious poverty. Why not speak out?
Everything in Rome has a price...
In cool Praeneste or the verdant hills of Volsinii [pleasant country towns], who
Has ever feared his house would collapse, as we [in Rome] all do?...Here
We live in a city held up for the greater part by mere
Toothpicks, for thus the janitor props the tottering beams
And patches up the old walls at cracks and gaping seams,
And tells the tenants to rest in peace—well said, R.I.P.,
With rafters ready to cave in on their heads! Not for me!
I must live where there are no fires and no alarms in the night.
Below, some tenant already is shouting in fright
For water, and moving his stuff. From your attic room, smoke pours,
But you don't know it; for if the fire starts on the lower floors,
The last one to burn will be the man with nothing to keep
Him from the rain but the roof tiles, beneath which, in a heap,
The soft rock doves lay eggs. The one bed that Codrus [a poor tenant] owned
Was too small for a dwarf, his cupboard boasted six mugs, a lone
Pitcher...made of the same soft stone,
With an old chest of Greek books, whose lovely poems were chewed
By illiterate mice. Poor Codrus had nothing—isn't it true?—
But still he lost the whole nothing. The straw on the camel's back
Is this: although he's stripped of all and begging a snack,
No one will give him a paltry handout, no one a bed,
Or even offer him shelter, a roof above his head.
But let the great house of Asturicus [a rich man] catch and burn,
The matrons mourn, the nobles wear black, the courts adjourn.
Oh, then we bewail the city's disasters and hate its fires!
The palace is still in flames and someone runs up and desires
To give him marble or building funds, another is pleased
To offer shining nude statues, another a masterpiece...And others will give him books,
Bookshelves, a bust of Minerva, or silver in coin or plate...
If you can be torn from the games, you can buy a fine house and stay
In Sora [a country town], or anywhere else for what you now pay
In Rome, to rent a dark hole one year. You'll have a small lawn,
A garden, a shallow well from which water is easily drawn,
With no need of ropes, to wet your tender plants. Live in peace
With a hoe as companion there, grow a truck garden fit to feast
A vegetarian convention. Remote though your farm may be,
It's something to be the lord of one green lizard—and free.
Here most of the sick die off because they get no sleep
(But the sickness is brought on by the undigested heap
Of sour food in their burning stomachs), for what rented flat
Allows you to sleep? Only rich men in this city have that.
There lies the root of the illness—carts rumbling in narrow streets
And cursing drivers stalled in a traffic jam—it defeats
All hope of rest...
When a rich man has a business appointment, the crowd will make
A path for him to be carried above their heads in a rich
Liburnian litter. He reads or scribbles, no matter which,
As he goes along, or into the downy pillows he sinks,

With the litter's curtains closed, and snatches forty winks.
But he gets there before us. Though we hurry, we merely crawl.
We're blocked by a surging mass ahead, a pushing wall
Of people behind. A man jabs me, elbowing through, one socks
A chair pole against me, one cracks my skull with a beam, one knocks
A wine cask against my ear. My legs are caked with splashing
Mud, from all sides the weight of enormous feet comes smashing
On mine, and a soldier stamps his hobnails through to my sole...
Now look at the other and varied perils of the night. What extreme
Height to the lofty roofs from which a piece of a pot
Falls down on my head, how often a broken vessel is shot
From the upper windows, with what a force it strikes and dints
The cobblestones! If you go out to dinner without long since
Having made a will, you'll be thought a fool, reckless of fate
And sudden disaster; for as many sure deaths are lying in wait
In the night as the open windows you pass beneath on the street.
So you hope and plaintively pray they may be content to treat
You to showers of no more than what's in their full slop jars...
But these aren't your only terrors. For you can never restrain
The criminal element. Lock up your house, put bolt and chain
On your shop, but when all's quiet, someone will rob you or he'll
Be a cutthroat perhaps, and do you in quickly with cold steel."

Source: *The Satires of Juvenal.* Translated by Hubert Creekmore. New York: The New American Library, 1963.

9. A Mansion Fit for a... Human Being!

In contrast to the tenements so bitterly described by Juvenal in the previous document, some people in first-century A.D. Rome lived in the lap of luxury, like the emperor Nero. In the following passage, the biographer Suetonius (c. A.D. 70-c. 140) provides an account of Nero's palace in Rome.

He [Nero] made a palace extending all the way from the Palatine to the Esquiline [two of the seven hills of Rome], which at first he called the House of Passage, but when it was burned shortly after its completion and rebuilt, the Golden House. Its size and splendor will be sufficiently indicated by the following details:

Its vestibule was large enough to contain a colossal statue of the emperor, 120 feet high; and it was so extensive that it had a triple colonnade a mile long. There was a pond, too, like a sea, surrounded with buildings to represent cities, besides tracts of country, varied by tilled fields, vineyards, pastures and woods, with great numbers of wild and domestic animals. In the rest of the house all parts were overlaid with gold and adorned with gems and mother-of-pearl. There were dining rooms with fretted ceilings of ivory, whose panels could turn and shower down flowers and were fitted with pipes for sprinkling the guests with perfumes. The main banquet hall was circular and constantly revolved day and night, like the heavens. He had baths supplied with sea water and sulphur water. When the edifice was finished in this style and he dedicated it, he deigned to say nothing more than that he was at last beginning to be housed like a human being.

Source: *Suetonius*. Translated by J. C. Rolfe. Cambridge and London: Loeb Classical Library, 1914.

10. *The Extent of Rome (Part I)*

In the following excerpt from his Natural History, *the Roman writer Pliny the Elder (*A.D. *23–79) describes the size and extent of the city of Rome in the first century* A.D.

In the 826th year after the city's foundation [A.D. 73], the walls of Rome, embracing the seven hills, measured 13.2 miles in circumference. The city itself is divided into 14 districts…A measurement running from the milestone set up at the head of the Roman Forum to each of the city gates gives a total of 20.765 miles in a straight line. But the measurement of all the thoroughfares block by block, from the same milestone to the outermost edge of the buildings…totals a little more than 60 miles. And if one should consider in addition the height of the buildings, he would assuredly form a fitting appraisal and would admit that no city has existed in the whole world that could be compared with Rome in size.

Source: From *Roman Civilization Sourcebook II: The Empire*, by Naphtali Lewis and Meyer Reinhold. Copyright © 1955 Columbia University Press. Reprinted with permission of the publisher.

A woodcut of Pliny the Elder from the Nuremberg Chronicles, compiled by Dr. Hartmann Schedel in 1493. © (2008) Jupiterimages Corporation.

11. *The Extent of Rome (Part II)*

In the following passage, the geographer Strabo (c. 64 B.C.–A.D. *21), writing earlier in the first century* A.D., *amplifies and augments Pliny's remarks in the preceding document regarding the size of the city of Rome.*

If the Greeks had the repute of being most felicitous in the founding of cities, in that they aimed at beauty, strength of position, harbors, and productive soil, the Romans had the best foresight in those matters which the Greeks took but little account of, such as the construction of roads and aqueducts, and of sewers that could wash out the filth of the city into the Tiber…The sewers, vaulted with close-fitting stones, have in some places left room enough for wagons loaded with hay to pass through them. And water is brought into the city through the aqueducts in such quantities that veritable rivers flow through the city and the sewers; and almost every house has cisterns and service pipes and copious fountains...In a word, the early Romans took but little account of the beauty of Rome, because they were occupied with other—greater and more necessary—matters, whereas the later Romans, and particularly those of today and in my time, have not fallen short in this respect either, but have filled the city with many beautiful structures...The Campus Martius [a large, open field in central Rome] contains most of these, and thus, in addition to its natural beauty, it has received still further adornment as the result of foresight. The size of the Campus is awe-inspiring, since it affords space at the same time for chariot races and every other equestrian exercise unhindered by the great multitude of people exercising themselves by playing ball, trundling hoops, and wrestling; and the works of art situated around the Campus Martius, and the ground covered with grass throughout the year, and the crowns of the hills that rise above the river and extend as far as its bed, presenting the appearance of a stage painting—all this affords a spectacle from which it is hard to tear one's self away. And near this Campus is still another, and colonnades around it in very great numbers, and sacred precincts, and three theaters, and an amphitheater, and very costly temples in close succession to one another...And again, if passing on to the Forum, one should see forum after forum ranged alongside it, and basilicas, and temples, and should see also the Capitol and the works of art there and those on the Palatine and in Livia's Promenade, one would easily forget the things outside. Such is Rome.

Source: From *Roman Civilization Sourcebook II: The Empire*, by Naphtali Lewis and Meyer Reinhold. Copyright © 1955 Columbia University Press. Reprinted with permission of the publisher.

Rural Life

Food production is critical to the survival of any civilization. The ancient Indians were particularly adept at raising crops and thereby avoiding famines. The Greek historian Diodorus stated that the reason for their success was the abundance of water, both from the many rivers that crisscrossed the Indian sub-continent and from the frequent rains that fell there (Document 12). Farmers were so revered that even in times of war, when battles were fought near their farms, they were left unharmed to continue their work.

The contrast between rural and urban lifestyles has long been a staple of literature, and, in Document 17, the Roman poet Horace's pleasant poetic discourse on the country and city mouse, that contrast is cleverly and convincingly illustrated. When the farmer came to town in ancient Greece, an event described by the playwright Aristophanes in Document 13, he pined away for his peaceful country home. A grumpier portrayal of country life in Greece is provided in Document 14, an unflattering picture of a rural type, the country bumpkin.

The phenomenon of the gentleman farmer was well known in Roman times, and Pliny the Younger may have been the epitome of the type. He wrote several letters in which he minutely described the features of his comfortable country homes, including the one which is the subject of Document 15. Pliny also helped friends purchase rural property, as is revealed in Document 16.

INDIA

12. The Success of Indian Agriculture

The first-century B.C. *Greek historian Diodorus Siculus explains in the following passage why the ancient Indians were so successful at raising crops and avoiding famines.*

In addition to wheat, there also grows throughout India much millet, which is irrigated by the abundance of running water supplied by the rivers, pulse in large quantities, and of superior quality, rice also and the plant called *bosporus* [a kind of millet], and in addition to these, many more plants which are useful for food, and most of these are native to the country. It also yields many other edible fruits, but to write about them would be a long task.

This is the reason, they say, why a famine has never visited India...Since there are two rainy seasons in the country each year,...it is the general practice to plant the rice and *bosporus,* as well as sesame and millet. And in most years, the Indians are successful in both crops, and they never lose everything, since the fruit of one or the other sowing comes to maturity...Practically all the plains of India enjoy the sweet moisture from the rivers and from the rains which come with astonishing regularity, in a kind of fixed cycle, every year in the summer...

Furthermore, the customs of the Indians contribute towards there never being any lack of food among them. Whereas in the case of all the rest of mankind, their enemies ravage the land and cause it to remain uncultivated, yet among the Indians, the workers of the soil are let alone as sacred and inviolable, and those of them who work near battle lines have no fear of any danger. Although both parties to the war kill one another in their hostilities, yet they leave uninjured those who are engaged in tilling the soil, believing that they are the common benefactors of all, nor do they burn the lands of their enemies, or cut down their orchards.

Source: *Diodorus of Sicily.* Volume II. Translated by C. H. Oldfather. London and Cambridge: Loeb Classical Library, 1935.

GREECE

13. The Farmer Goes to Town

In Aristophanes's (445–380 B.C.*) play* Acharnians, *the main character, a farmer named Dicaeopolis, comes to Athens to participate in a meeting of the Assembly, the main legislative unit of the Athenian democracy. He is the first one to show up for the meeting, so, while waiting for the others to arrive, he soliloquizes about the contrasts between city and country life.*

O city, city! I am always the very first to come to Assembly and take my seat. Then, in my solitude, I sigh, I yawn, I stretch myself, I fiddle, scribble, pluck my beard, do sums, while I gaze off to the countryside and

Aristophanes, referred to as one of the greatest writers of comedy in literary history. Library of Congress.

pine for peace, loathing the city and yearning for my own deme, that never cried "buy coal," "buy vinegar," "buy oil"; it didn't know the word "buy"; no, it produced everything itself, and the Buy Man was out of sight. So now I'm here, all set to shout, interrupt, revile the speakers, if anyone speaks of anything except peace.

Source: *Aristophanes: Acharnians; Knights.* Translated by Jeffrey Henderson. Cambridge and London: Loeb Classical Library, 1998.

14. The Country Bumpkin

The following rather unflattering picture of a rural type is provided by the fourth-century B.C. author Theophrastus, from his Characters.

The farmer is the sort of person who wanders into the assembly drinking wine, and keeps saying that there's no sweeter perfume than thyme, and wears shoes bigger than his feet, and chatters in a loud voice. He won't trust his friends and neighbors, but he confides in his own servants about the most important things. And he explains to his paid farmhands everything that went on in the assembly. He sits down with his clothes hitched up over his knees... And nothing strikes his attention walking down the street, but just let him catch sight of some cow or donkey or goat and he stands and marvels. Snatching a snack out of the larder, he devours it in a startling manner. And the stronger his drink, the better. While no one's looking, he tries to tumble the cook. And he feeds the animals while still eating his own breakfast. He answers the door himself. Taking a coin from someone, he bites it, finds it shortweight, and insists on changing it for another. And if he lends someone his plow, or basket, or sickle, or sack, he lies awake all night worrying about it. Coming into town, he asks everyone he meets: how much is leather? And salt fish? And immediately goes on to say that he's on his way to get his hair cut. And he sings in the bath, and pounds nails into his boots.

Source: Frost, Frank J. *Greek Society.* Third Edition. Lexington, MA: Houghton Mifflin, 1987.

Theophrastus, philosopher of the Peripatetic school, successor to Aristotle at the Lyceum. Library of Congress.

ROME

15. A Roman Gentleman Visits His Country Estate

The Roman writer and public official Pliny the Younger (A.D. 62–114), the nephew of Pliny the Elder, was wealthy enough to enjoy the lifestyle of a country gentleman, and he took advantage of whatever opportunities came his way to do exactly that. In the following excerpts from two letters to his friend Fuscus Salinator, he describes his typical day.

You want to know how I plan the summer days I spend in Tuscany. I wake when I like, usually about sunrise, often earlier but rarely later. My shutters stay closed, for in the stillness and darkness I feel myself surprisingly detached from any distractions and left to myself in freedom. My eyes do not determine the direction of my thinking, but, being unable to see anything, they are guided to visualize my thoughts. If I have anything on hand I work it out in my head, choosing and correcting the wording, and the amount I achieve depends on the ease or difficulty with which my thoughts can be marshaled and kept in my head. Then I call my secretary, the shutters are opened, and I dictate what I have put into shape. He goes out, is recalled, and again dismissed. Three or four hours after I first wake (but I don't keep to fixed times), I go according to the weather, either to the terrace or the covered arcade, work out the rest of my subject, and dictate it. I go for a drive, and spend the time in the same way as when walking or lying down. My powers of concentration do not flag and are in fact refreshed by the change. After a short sleep and another walk, I read a Greek or Latin speech aloud and with emphasis, not so much for the sake of my voice as my digestion, though of course both are strengthened by this.

Then I have another walk, I am oiled, take exercise, and have a bath. If I am dining alone with my wife or with a few friends, a book is read aloud during the meal and afterwards we listen to a comedy or some music. Then I walk again with the members of my household, some of whom are well educated. Thus the evening is prolonged with varied conversation, and, even when the days are at their longest, comes to a satisfying end.

Sometimes I vary this routine, for, if I have spent a long time on my couch or taking a walk, after my siesta and reading, I go out on horseback instead of in a carriage so as to be quicker and take less time. Part of the day is given up to friends who visit me from neighboring towns, and sometimes come to my aid with a welcome interruption when I am tired. Occasionally, I go hunting, but not without my notebooks, so that I will have something to bring home even if I catch nothing. I also give some time to my tenants (they think it should be more) and the boorishness of their complaints gives fresh zest to our literary interests and the more civilized pursuits of town.

Source: *Pliny: Letters and Panegyricus.* Volume II. Translated by Betty Radice. Cambridge and London: Loeb Classical Library, 1969.

16. Buying a Farm

Pliny the Younger wrote a letter to his friend Baebius, on behalf of another friend, the famous biographer Suetonius, who was desirous of purchasing a small farm.

My friend Suetonius has an inclination to purchase a small farm, of which, I am informed, an acquaintance of yours intends to sell. I ask that you would try to see to it that he may buy it on reasonable terms, a circumstance which will add to his satisfaction in obtaining it. An expensive sale price is always disagreeable, especially since it is a reflection upon the purchaser's judgment. There are several circumstances pertaining to this farm which—supposing my friend had no objection to the price—are appealing to him: the convenient distance from Rome, the goodness of the roads, the small size of the building, and the very few acres of land around it, which is just enough to amuse him, but not to overwork him. To a man of the studious inclination that Suetonius is, it is sufficient if he has a small place to relieve the mind and divert the eye, where he can amble around his grounds, traverse his single path, become familiar with his two or three vines, and count his little saplings. I mention these details to let you see how much he will be obliged to me, as I will to you, if you can help him towards the purchase of this little getaway, so agreeable to his taste, upon terms of which he will have no reason to regret. Farewell.

Source: *Pliny: Letters*. Volume I. Translated by William Melmoth, with revisions by W.M.L. Hutchinson. Cambridge and London: Loeb Classical Library, 1915.

17. The Country Mouse and the City Mouse

The sixth entry in Book II of the poet Horace's (65–8 B.C.) Satires nicely contrasts urban and rural lifestyles. It is not too difficult to discern which kind of life Horace prefers!

This was what I had prayed for: a small piece of land
With a garden, a fresh-flowing spring of water at hand
Near the house, and, above and behind, a small forest stand.
But the gods have done much better for me, and more—
It's perfect. I ask nothing else, except to implore,
O son of Maia [the god Mercury], that you make these blessings my own
For the rest of my life. If my property has not grown
By my making a series of deals, neither will it shrink
By my mismanagement. If I'm not one of those who think:
"If only that corner were mine, that lies adjacent
To my strip, cutting in in a manner that's really indecent!"
Or, "if only some luck came my way, like the find which,
Leading the plowman to buried treasure, made him rich
Enough to buy the land he formerly plowed for hire,
Thanks to Hercules!" If what I have is all I desire
And makes me content, then to this one last wish I aspire:
Make my herd grow fat, and everything else I lay claim to,
Except my brains. And, Mercury, still be the same to
Horace as you have been, his great good guardian. To complete
My removal from city streets to mountain retreat,
What else should I do but celebrate it now satirically,
Dwelling, far from town (and far from lyrically),
In my pedestrian style, on how far from that bit of hell
Known as big city life is life in my citadel.
Social climbing can't get me down here, or the lead-weight blows
Of siroccos, or for once and for all plague-laden falls
Lay me out, and enrich the layout in funeral halls.
Instead, I begin this morning by addressing you, Monarch
Of Morning, or more openly, Janus, if you prefer it.
In allegiance to whom men begin all the work of their days—

For so heaven wills it. Be the principal source of my praise.
At Rome, the mornings are different; you rush me right off
To court to vouch for a friend. "Hey there! Get going!
Or some one else will answer this call before you!"
And I *have* to, whether the north wind is raking the land
Or winter drags snow-laden days through diminishing curves.
After saying in court, good and loud, things that may some day
Incriminate me, I fight my way back through the crowd
In the streets, tripping over some slowpoke's toes. "What's up,
You blockhead? What gives?" some stupid assails me. "Oh, Horace,
It's you, is it, racing back home to Maecenas, so full of
The fact that you knock over everything blocking your path!"
Well…the name of Maecenas *is* honey to me, I admit it.
But as soon as I reach the depressing Esquiline Quarter [in Rome],
A hundred conflicting concerns pour down on my head
And stream around me. "Roscius wants you to meet him tomorrow
Before seven in the morning, at Libo's Wall." "Oh, Horace,
The clerks request you to remember to return to the Forum
Today for a big new matter of mutual interest."
"Do have Maecenas affix his seal to these papers."
If I say, "Well, I'll try," he insists, "You can *do* it if you *want* to."
It is now seven years—actually, nearer the eighth—
Since Maecenas began to admit me into his company
Of friends, insofar as a friend is just good company
On a trip, someone to talk to about such subjects as:
"What time is it?"…"Oh, about the [gladiatorial] fight: is the Thracian Bantam
A match for the Sheik?"…"These frosty mornings can nip you
If you don't wrap up." And small-change talk like this,
Which it's perfectly safe to deposit in leaky ears.
And the whole time, daily and hourly, our intimate Horace
Was *envied*. He watched the games from the stands with M.
He played some ball on the Campus, *and* with M.
"Fortune's Favorite Son," they thought in unison.
A hair-raising rumor rolls through the streets from the Rostra [speaker's platform]
And whoever bumps into me seeks my advice. "Dear fellow,
You ought to know, you live so much nearer the gods,
What's up in the Balkans?" "Nothing, as far as I know."
"Oh, you're still making fun of us!" But may the gods undo me
If I've heard a word. "What about the veterans' allotments
Of land Caesar promised? Will they be on the three-cornered isle,
Or Italian soil?" When I swear I know nothing about it,
They marvel at me for being the sole human being
Who knows how to keep an important unfathomable secret.
Amid such lightweight concerns the light of my day
Sputters out, leaving me limp, only able to pray:
Oh, countryside mine, when will I see you again,
Read my favorite classical authors, and then
Get some sleep and get back to my lazy routine of life,
Of pleasure mercifully free from worry and strife?
When shall we dine on beans, Pythagoras' cousins,
And eat, cooked in bacon, country greens in their dozens?
Those nights and feasts of the gods! When friends and I sup

At my home, while the saucy slaves lick up
What's left untouched on the plates. Each guest drains his cup,
Big or small, as it suits him. No Prohibition
To govern his choice except his free disposition
To toss off heroic amounts and keep a clear head,
Or gradually mellow with moderate potions instead.
And then we start talking, not about other men's lives
And property and assets but of things on which wisdom thrives.
Not whether Lepos is really a good dancer or not
But whether happiness comes from the money you've got
Or, rather, derives from virtue. What makes people friends?
Self-interest, or rectitude? This subject lends
Interest to us, the good life and its ends.
From time to time, my good old neighbor, Cervius,
Rattles off an old wives' tale, to make a point.
If someone praises Arellius' wealth, without knowing
What worries it brings, Cervius starts off like this:
"Once upon a time, a country mouse
Welcomed a town mouse in his poor little hole of a house
In the sticks, both host and guest being quite old friends.
The country mouse roughed it, of course; he kept a close eye
On his larder, but not so myopic he couldn't enlarge
His view, with a view to a friend's entertainment. What else?
He was not the mouse to begrudge a friend the choice of chick-peas
Set aside in a special place, or the long grains of oats.
But, eager to conquer the fastidious disdain of a guest
Who tended to turn up his tooth after sampling each dainty,
He brought in by mouth and served, to vary the meal,
A dried grape seed and some half-nibbled pieces of bacon.
The master of the house, stretched out on his couch of chaff
(New chaff), ate spelt and darnel, leaving the best
For his guest to digest. Finally, the city mouse spoke up:
'What pleasure can it be for you, my friend,
Roughing it out here on the edge of a precipitous forest?
Surely you put people and the city ahead of this wildwood?
Take my advice, and my road, with me as your guide.
All earthly creatures, after all, have drawn as their lot
A mortal life. There is no escape from death
For large or small. Therefore, while you still can,
Enjoy a happy career, my good man, live well.
Live mindful of how short life really is.' When these words
Dawned on the yokel, he bounced off happily from home,
And both set out together, according to plan,
Hoping to sneak through the walls of the city by night.
And night was poised, midway across the heavens,
When both set foot in a rich man's house, where crimson
Coverings blazed against ivory couches, and leftovers
From last night's feast were stacked up high in the baskets.
Well, the host then made his rural guest stretch out
On the crimson covers and began dashing madly about,
With his clothes tucked up like a waiter's, serving up dish
After dish and taking a taste, as a proper slave does,

Of each course before serving it. The other mouse meanwhile
Leaned back at ease, delighted with the change in affairs
And with all this good living, and was playing to perfection the part
Of the satisfied guest, when a sudden loud rattling of doors
Shook them both right off of their couches. Frightened, they scampered
Across the whole length of the room, and, even more frightening,
The big house began to ring, at the very same time,
With the barking of colossal hounds. Says the country mouse:
'I have no use for this kind of life. And good-bye!
My woodland and hole, where I'm safe from traps like these,
Will be quite enough, my slim pickings quite food enough.'"

Source: *The Satires and Epistles of Horace.* Translated by Smith Palmer Bovie. Chicago: University of Chicago Press, 1959. Copyright © 1959 by The University of Chicago Press. All rights reserved. Reprinted with permission of the publisher.

Slavery

Slavery was a widespread, if unfortunate, fact of life in the ancient world. Servile docility was a main concern of slave owners, so teaching the slaves obedience was paramount (Document 22). Otherwise, they might attempt to escape, as did two Egyptian slaves, Hermon and Bion (Document 20), perhaps stealing money and property in the process, or, they might even foment a slave revolt (Document 27).

The Greek philosopher Aristotle offered advice on the treatment of slaves (Document 21), with the hoped-for result of producing ideal slaves, ones who were loyal to their masters, who would not shirk hard work, and who would be steady and reliable (Document 25). Slaves were often employed as tutors for the master's children; in those cases, it was particularly important for the slaves to be trustworthy (Document 23). The attitudes of two famous Roman slave owners—Cato the Elder and Marcus Licinius Crassus—are reflected in Documents 28 and 29, respectively.

Undoubtedly, the ultimate goal of most slaves was freedom. Documents 19 and 24 present examples of the conditions under which slaves might be freed, while in Document 26, Pliny the Elder briefly recounts the financial success of a former slave by the name of Gaius Caecilius Isidorus, who had amassed a fortune in both money and property at the time of his death.

ISRAEL/EGYPT

18. *The Enslavement of the Israelites*

The first-century A.D. *Jewish historian Josephus wrote the following account of how the Egyptians came to enslave the Hebrews living in their territory.*

The Egyptians, being a voluptuous people and averse to hard work, slaves to pleasure in general and to a love of money in particular, eventually became bitter towards the Hebrews through envy of their prosperity. Seeing the race of the Israelites flourishing, and that their virtues and willingness to work had already gained them abundant wealth, they believed that their growth in power was to their own detriment. Those benefits which they had received from Joseph, being through the lapse of time forgotten, and the kingdom having now passed to another dynasty, they grossly maltreated the Israelites, and devised for them all manner of hardships. Thus they ordered them to divide the river into numerous canals, to build ramparts for the cities and dikes to hold the waters of the river and to prevent them from forming marshes when they overflowed its banks. And with the constructing of pyramid after pyramid, they exhausted our race, which was being apprenticed to all manner of crafts, and thus immune to toil. For a full 400 years they endured these hardships. It was a contest between them, with the Egyptians striving to kill off the Israelites with hard work, and the Israelites constantly showing themselves superior to their tasks.

Source: *Josephus.* Volume IV. Translated by H. St. J. Thackeray. Cambridge and London: Loeb Classical Library, 1930.

19. Hebrew Slaves of Hebrew Masters

In this passage, Josephus briefly recounts the master/slave relationship when both are Hebrews.

A Hebrew sold to another Hebrew shall serve him for six years; in the seventh, let him go free. But if, having had children by a slave woman at the house of the master who bought him, he, out of love and affection for his own [including his family and his master], desires to continue to serve him, then on the coming of the year of jubilee—which returns every 50 years—let him be liberated, taking his children and wife, also free, along with him.

Source: *Josephus.* Volume IV. Translated by H. St. J. Thackeray. Cambridge and London: Loeb Classical Library, 1930.

EGYPT

20. Hermon and Bion: Escaped Slaves

When slaves escaped, rewards were often offered for their return, as the following papyrus from Alexandria indicates. The year was 156 B.C.

A slave of Aristogenes, son of Chrysippus…ambassador, has escaped in Alexandria, by name Hermon, also called Nilus, by birth a Syrian…about 18 years old, of medium stature, beardless, with good legs, a dimple on the chin, a mole by the left side of the nose, a scar above the left corner of the mouth, tattooed on the right wrist with two barbaric letters. He has taken with him 3 octadrachmas of coined gold, 10 pearls, an iron ring on which an oil flask and strigils are represented, and is wearing a cloak and loincloth. Whoever brings back this slave shall receive 3 talents of copper; if he points him out in a temple, 2 talents; if in the house of a substantial and actionable man, 5 talents. Whoever wishes to give information shall do so to the agents of the strategus.

There is also another who has escaped with him. Bion, a slave of Callicrates, one of the chief stewards at court, short of stature, broad at the shoulders, stout-legged, bright-eyed, who has gone off with an outer garment and a slave's wrap and a woman's dress worth 6 talents 5000 drachmas of copper. Whoever brings back this slave shall receive rewards as for the above-mentioned. Information about this one also is to be given to the agents of the strategus.

Source: *Select Papyri: Non-Literary Papyri. Public Documents*, Volume II. Translated by A. S. Hunt and C. C. Edgar. Cambridge and London: Loeb Classical Library, 1934.

GREECE

Slavery was a fact of life in both ancient Greece and Rome. At least five castes of slaves can be identified in Greek society: (1) state-owned slaves who served the public good as law enforcement officials, or clerks in law courts; (2) privately owned slaves who worked at various crafts and trades; (3) household slaves; (4) slaves employed as agricultural workers; and (5) slaves who worked in the mines, the most hazardous kind of labor.

Most slaves, whether Greek or Roman, were acquired from the ranks of prisoners of war; others became slaves through the marketplace, while still others had the misfortune of being born to slave parents. The exact number of slaves in the Greco-Roman world is difficult to gauge; there may have been 100,000 in any given year in Classical Greece. In Rome, the numbers were far larger, perhaps approaching one to two million people.

21. Treatment of Slaves in Ancient Greece

In his treatise entitled Economics, *the fourth-century* B.C. *Greek philosopher Aristotle outlined the general attitude in ancient Greece toward slaves, especially in terms of the proper ways to treat them.*

Of property, the first and most indispensable kind is that which is also best and most amenable to housecraft; and this is the human chattel. Our first step, therefore, must be to procure good slaves. Of slaves, there are two kinds: those in positions of trust, and the laborers. And since it is a matter of experience that the character of the young can be molded by training, when we need to charge slaves with tasks befitting a free person, we have not only to procure the slaves, but to bring them up [to be trustworthy].

In our dealings with slaves, we must neither allow them to be insolent nor treat them with cruelty. A share of honor should be given to those who are doing more of a freeman's work, and abundance of food to those who are laboring with their hands. And whereas the use of wine renders even free men insolent, so that in many countries, they too refrain from it—as, for instance, the Carthaginians do when they are on military campaigns—it follows that we must either deny wine to slaves altogether, or reserve it for rare occasions.

We may apportion to our slaves (1) work, (2) chastisement, and (3) food. If men are given food, but no chastisement nor any work, they become insolent. If they are made to work, and are chastised, but given insufficient food, such treatment is oppressive, and saps their strength. The remaining alternative, therefore, is to give them work, and a sufficiency of food. Unless we pay men, we cannot control them; and food is a slave's pay.

Slaves, again, are no exception to the rule that men become worse when better conduct is not followed by better treatment, but virtue and vice remain alike unrewarded. Accordingly, we must keep watch over our workers, matching our rewards to what they deserve, whether it be food, clothing, leisure, or chastisement that we are apportioning. Both in theory and in practice, we must take for our model a physician's freedom in prescribing his medicines, observing at the same time that food differs from medicine in that it requires to be constantly administered.

The best laborers will be furnished by those races of mankind which are neither wholly spiritless, nor too aggressive. Each extreme has its vice; the spiritless cannot endure hard labor, and the high-spirited will not readily tolerate control.

Every slave should have before his eyes a definite goal or term of his labor. To set the prize of freedom before him is both just and expedient, since, having a prize to work for, and a time defined for its attainment, he will put his heart into his labors. We should, moreover, take hostages [for our slaves' loyalty] by allowing them to bear children, and avoid the practice of purchasing many slaves of the same nationality... We should also keep festivals and give treats, more on the slaves' account than on that of the freemen, since the free have a fuller share in those enjoyments for the sake of which these institutions exist.

Source: *Aristotle: Metaphysics.* Translated by Hugh Tredennick. *Oeconomica and Magna Moralia.* Translated by G. Cyril Armstrong. London and Cambridge: Loeb Classical Library, 1935.

22. How to Teach Obedience to Slaves

The Greek writer Xenophon (c. 430–c. 354 B.C.), in his "Oeconomicus," a Socratic dialogue covering mainly household management and agriculture, weighs in below on the subject of appropriate treatment of slaves.

Well, now, Socrates, other creatures learn obedience in two ways—by being punished when they try to disobey, and by being rewarded when they try to serve you. Colts, for example, learn to obey the horsebreaker by getting something they like when they are obedient, and suffering inconvenience when they are disobedient, until they carry out the horsebreaker's intentions. Puppies, again, are much inferior to humans in intelligence and power of expression, and yet they learn to run in circles and turn somersaults and do many other tricks in the same way. For when they obey, they get something they want, and when they are careless, they are punished. And humans can be made more obedient by word of mouth alone, by being shown that it is good for them to obey.

But in dealing with slaves, the training thought suitable for wild animals is also a very effective way of teaching obedience. For you will do much with them by filling their bellies with the food they hanker after. Those of an ambitious disposition are also spurred on by praise, some natures being hungry for praise as others for meat and drink. Now these are precisely the things that I do myself with a view to making humans more obedient...I [also] have other ways of helping them on. For the clothes that I must provide for my work-people and the shoes are not all alike. Some are better than others, some worse, in order that I may reward the better servant with the superior articles, and give the inferior things to the less deserving. For I think it is very disheartening to good servants, Socrates, when they see that they do all the work, and others who are not willing to work hard and run risks when necessary, get the same as they. For my part, then, I don't choose to put the deserving on a level with the worthless, and when I know that my bailiffs have distributed the best things to the most deserving, I commend them. And if I see that flattery or any other futile service wins special favor, I don't overlook it, but reprimand the bailiff, and try to show him, Socrates, that such favoritism is not even in his own interest.

Source: *Xenophon: Memorabilia and Oeconomicus.* Translated by E. C. Marchant. Cambridge and London: Loeb Classical Library, 1923.

23. Ideal and Inappropriate Slaves to Associate with and Instruct Children

Slaves were sometimes employed as both companions and tutors for the children of their masters, but the second-century A.D. Greek biographer Plutarch urges in the following passage that care be taken in selecting these slaves.

There is another point which should not be omitted, that in choosing the younger slaves, who are to be the servants and companions of young masters, those should be sought out who are, first and foremost, sound in character, who are also Greeks, and distinct of speech, so that the children will not be contaminated by barbarians and persons of low character, and so take on some of their commonness. The proverb makers say, and quite to the point, "If you live with a lame man, you will learn to limp."

When the children become old enough to be put under the care of attendants, then especially great care must be taken in the appointment of these, so as not to entrust one's children inadvertently to slaves taken in war or to barbarians or to those who are unstable. Nowadays, the common practice of many persons is more than ridiculous, for they appoint some of their trustworthy slaves to manage their farms, others they make masters of their ships, others their shops, others they make house stewards, and some even money lenders. But any slave whom they find to be a wine tippler and a glutton, and useless for any kind of business, to him they bring their children and put them in his charge. But the good attendant ought to be a man of such nature as was Phoenix, the attendance of Achilles.

Source: *Plutarch's Moralia.* Volume I. Translated by Frank Cole Babbitt. London and Cambridge: Loeb Classical Library, 1927.

ROME

24. Freedom for Tiro

In Roman society, the two great categories of slaves were city and country slaves, with the former being the more desirable; life on the farm could be challenging and difficult for slave laborers. City slaves were often well educated, or skilled at a particular trade, and, in consequence, were generally treated more kindly by their masters than were their counterparts in the country. A good example is seen in a congratulatory letter written to the orator Cicero by his brother Quintus, upon hearing the news that Cicero had manumitted his longtime slave and secretary, Tiro.

I have just heard about Tiro. He ought never to have been a slave, and now you have decided that he should be our friend instead. My delight at the news is matched only by the longing I have to see you all, your children and my own boy. After reading your letter and Tiro's, I jumped with joy. Thank you for what you have done. And many congratulations. The loyalty which I receive from [my slave] Statius is a sheer delight to me; so how much you will gain, in the same way, from Tiro—and more, because Tiro is a scholar, a conversationalist, a humane man, and these are qualities which count for more than material values. I have innumerable reasons for loving you, but this tops them all, especially because, as was right, you wrote to send me the news. I read your letter, and it was you all over.

Source: Balsdon, J.P.V.D. *Life and Leisure in Ancient Rome.* Translated by J.P.V.D. Balsdon. New York: Phoenix Press, 1969.

25. The Ideal Country Slave

The agricultural writings of several Roman authors survive to the present day. In their treatises on farm management, they not surprisingly include the treatment of slaves as one of the topics. One of these authors, Marcus Terentius Varro (116–27 B.C.), offered the following as his view of the ideal country slave.

Slaves ought to be neither cowed nor high-spirited. They ought to be supervised by men who know how to read and write, and who have some education, who are dependable and older than the hands whom I have mentioned; for they will be more respectful to these, than to overseers who are younger. Furthermore, it is especially important that the foremen be men who are experienced in farm operations. For the foreman must not only give orders but also take part in the work, so that his subordinates may follow his example, and also understand that there is a good reason for his being over them—the fact that he is superior to them in knowledge. They are not to be allowed to control their men with whips rather than with words, if only you can achieve the same result.

Avoid having too many slaves of the same nation, for this is a fertile source of domestic quarrels. The foremen are to be made more zealous by rewards, and care must be taken that they have a bit of property of their own, and spouses from among their fellow slaves to bear them children. For by this means, they are made more steady, and more attached to the place. Thus, it is on account of such relationships that slave families of Epirus have the best reputation and bring the highest prices. The good will of the foremen should be won by treating them with some degree of consideration, and those of the hands who excel the others should also be consulted as to the work to be done. When this is done, they are less inclined to think that they are looked down upon, and rather think that they are held in some esteem by the master. They are made to take more interest in their work by being treated more liberally in respect either to food, or to more clothing, or exemption from work, or permission to graze some cattle of their own on the farm, or other things of this kind. So that, if some unusually heavy task is imposed, or punishment inflicted on them in some way, their loyalty and kindly feeling to the master may be restored by the consolation derived from such measures.

With regard to the number of slaves required, Cato [another agricultural writer] has in view two bases of calculation: the size of the place, and the nature of the crop grown. Writing of olive-yards and vineyards, he gives two formulas. The first is one in which he shows how an olive-yard of 300 acres should be equipped. On a place of this size, he says that the following thirteen slaves should be kept: an overseer, a house-keeper, five laborers, three teamsters, one muleteer, one swineherd, one shepherd. The second he gives for a vineyard of 120 acres, on which he says should be kept the following fifteen slaves: an overseer, a housekeeper, ten laborers, a teamster, a muleteer, a swineherd.

Source: *Marcus Terentius Varro: On Agriculture.* Translated by William Davis Hooper, with revisions by Harrison Boyd Ash. Cambridge and London: Loeb Classical Library, 1934.

26. Rags-to-Riches Stories

The first-century A.D. naturalist Pliny the Elder, in discussing some of the wealthiest men in Roman history, noted that sometimes, even former slaves could amass great riches.

[W]e have known...of many liberated slaves who have been wealthier [than Marcus Licinius Crassus, a Roman noted for his great wealth], and three not long before our own days [in the first century A.D.]...namely Callistus, Pallas, and Narcissus...[T]here is also Gaius Caecilius Isidorus, a former slave of Gaius Caecilius, who [in 8 B.C.] executed a will dated January 27 in which he declared that in spite of heavy losses in the civil war, he nevertheless left 4,116 slaves, 3,600 pairs of oxen, 257,000 head of other cattle, and 60 million sesterces in cash [a substantial fortune], and he gave instructions for 1,100,000 to be spent on his funeral.

Source: *Pliny: Natural History.* Volume IX. Translated by H. Rackham. Cambridge and London: Loeb Classical Library, 1968.

27. A Slave Revolt

*One disadvantage of the concentration of large numbers of slaves is the ever-present danger
of a slave rebellion, especially if the slaves feel unduly mistreated. As the first-century* B.C.
*Greek historian Diodorus Siculus relates in the following passage, such an event occurred
in Sicily around 135* B.C.

The Italians who were engaged in agriculture purchased great numbers of slaves, all
of whom they marked with brands, but failed to provide them with sufficient food, and
by oppressive work, wore them out...

Not only in the exercise of political power should prominent people be considerate towards those of low estate, but so also in private life they should—if they are
sensible—treat their slaves gently. Heavy-handed arrogance leads states into civil strife
and factionalism between citizens, and in individual households it paves the way for
plots of slaves against masters and for terrible uprisings and conspiracies against the
whole state... Anyone whom fortune has set in low estate willingly yields to his superiors in point of gentility and esteem, but if he is deprived of due consideration, he comes
to regard those who harshly lord it over him with bitter hatred.

There was a certain Damophilus, a native of Enna [in Sicily], a man of great wealth
but arrogant in manner who, since he had under cultivation a great area of land and
owned many herds of cattle, emulated not only the luxurious lifestyles of the Italian
landowners in Sicily, but also the inhumanity and severity which they exhibited towards their troops of slaves... Purchasing a large number of slaves, he treated them out-
rageously, marking with branding irons the bodies of people who in their own countries
had been free, but who through capture in war had come to know the fate of a slave.
Some of these he put in chains and thrust into slave pens; others he designated to act as
his herdsmen, but neglected to provide them with suitable clothing or food...

Because of his arbitrary and savage temperament, not a day passed that this same
Damophilus did not torment some of his slaves without just cause. His wife Metallis,
who delighted no less in these arrogant punishments, treated her maidservants cruelly,
as well as many other slaves who fell into her clutches. And because of the inhumane
punishments received from them both, the slaves were filled with rage against their
masters, and believing that they could encounter nothing worse than their present
misfortunes, they began to form conspiracies to revolt and to murder their masters.

Approaching Eunus [a charismatic and mystical man, who eventually became the
leader of the revolt], who lived not far away, they asked whether their plan had the approval of the gods. He... stated clearly that the gods favored their revolt, provided that
they did not delay, but implemented the plan immediately, seeing that it was decreed
by fate that Enna, the citadel of the whole island, should be their land. Having heard
this, and believing that Providence was assisting them in their objective, they were so
enthusiastic for revolt that there was no delay in implementing their plans. Therefore,
they immediately set free those in chains, and collecting the others who lived nearby,
they assembled about 400 men at a field not far from Enna. After making a mutual
agreement and exchanging pledges sworn by night over sacrificial victims, they armed
themselves in such ways as the occasion allowed. But they were all equipped with the

best of weapons, fury, which was bent on the destruction of their arrogant masters. Their leader was Eunus. With cries of encouragement to one another, they broke into the city about midnight, and killed many.

There was in Sicily a daughter of Damophilus, a girl of marriageable age, remarkable for her simplicity of manner and her kindness of heart. It was always her practice to do all she could to comfort the slaves who were beaten by her parents, and since she also took the part of any who had been chained, she was wondrously loved by one and all for her kindness. So now at this time, since her past favors enlisted in her service the mercy of those to whom she had shown kindness, no one was so bold as to lay violent hands upon the girl…And selecting suitable men from their number, among them Hermeias, her warmest champion, they escorted her to the home of certain family members in Catana.

Although the rebellious slaves were enraged against the whole household of their masters, and resorted to unrelenting abuse and vengeance, there were yet some indications that it was not from innate savagery but rather because of the inhumane treatment they had themselves received that they now ran wild when they began to avenge themselves on their persecutors.

Even among slaves, human nature needs no instructor in regard to a just repayment, whether of gratitude or of revenge.

Source: *Diodorus of Sicily.* Volume XII. Translated by Francis R. Walton. London and Cambridge: Loeb Classical Library, 1967.

Cato the Elder, a second century B.C. Roman politician, general, and writer noted for his austere way of life and rigid principles. Library of Congress.

28. A Slave Owner's Philosophy: Cato the Elder

The Roman statesman Cato the Elder (234–149 B.C.) owned a large number of slaves, and he had some very firmly entrenched ideas about how to manage them all. In the following excerpts, the biographer Plutarch provides some instances of these ideas.

Cato possessed a large number of slaves, whom he usually bought from among the prisoners captured in war, but it was his practice to choose those who, like puppies or colts, were young enough to be trained and taught their duties. None of them ever entered any house but his own, unless they were sent on an errand by Cato or his wife, and if they were asked what Cato was doing, the reply was always that they did not know. It was a rule of his establishment that a slave must either be doing something about the house, or else be asleep. He much preferred the slaves who slept well, because he believed that they were more even-tempered than the wakeful ones, and that those who had had enough sleep produced better results at any task than those who were short of it. And as he was convinced that slaves were led into mischief more often on account of love affairs than for any other reason, he made it a rule that the men could sleep with the women slaves of the establishment for a fixed price, but must have nothing to do with any others.

At the beginning of his career, when he was a poor man and was frequently on active service, he never complained of anything that he ate, and he used to say that it was ignoble to find fault with a servant for the food that he prepared. But in later life, when he had become more prosperous, he used to invite his friends and colleagues to dinner, and immediately after the meal he would beat with a leather thong any of the slaves who had been careless in preparing or serving it. He constantly contrived to provoke quarrels and dissensions among his slaves, and if they ever arrived at an understanding with one another, he became alarmed and suspicious. If ever any of his slaves was suspected of committing a capital offense, he gave the culprit a formal trial in the presence of the rest, and if he was found guilty, he had him put to death...

He would also lend money to any of his slaves who wished it. They used these sums to buy young slaves, and after training them and teaching them a trade for a year at Cato's expense, they would sell them again. Often Cato would keep these boys for himself, and he would then credit to the slave the price offered by the highest bidder.

Source: *The Rise and Fall of Athens: Nine Greek Lives by Plutarch.* Translated by Ian Scott-Kilvert. New York: Penguin Books, 1960. Reproduced by permission of Penguin Books Ltd.

29. A Slave Owner's Philosophy: Marcus Licinius Crassus

Marcus Licinius Crassus (c. 112–53 B.C.) was noted for his great wealth, and, therefore, he owned a large number of slaves, as Plutarch describes below.

Crassus observed how frequent and everyday occurrences in Rome were fire and the collapse of buildings, owing to their size and their close proximity to each other. He therefore bought slaves who were architects and builders, and then, when he had more than 500 of them, he would buy up houses that were either on fire themselves or near the scene of the fire. The owners of these properties, in the terror and uncertainty of the moment, would let them go for next to nothing. In this way, most of Rome came into his possession. Yet although he owned so many workmen, he built no houses for himself except the one in which he lived. He used to say that people who were fond of building needed no enemies; they would ruin themselves by themselves.

He owned countless silver mines, large areas of valuable land, and laborers to work it for him, yet all this, one may say, was nothing compared with the value of his slaves. There were great numbers of them and they were of the highest quality—readers, secretaries, silversmiths, stewards, waiters. He used to direct their education himself and take part in it by giving them personal instructions. Altogether his view was that the chief duty of a master is to care for his slaves who are, in fact, the living tools for the management of a household. And in this he was right if, as he used to say, he believed that the slaves should do the work, but he should direct the slaves. For we observe that the management of a household is a financial activity in so far as it deals with lifeless things, but it becomes a political activity in so far as it deals with human beings.

Source: *Fall of the Roman Republic: Six Lives by Plutarch.* Translated by Rex Warner. Baltimore: Penguin Books, 1958.

Trade and Commerce

National and international commerce abounded in the ancient world. Greek and Roman traders penetrated as far as the Black Sea, and even to India, seeking goods and products not available in their part of the world (Document 30). The result was that both Athens and Rome became thriving commercial centers (Documents 33, 34, 35, and 37).

But none of this commercial activity could have occurred without a unit of exchange. The Greek philosopher Aristotle (Document 31) explained how the use of coined money developed. Once individual entrepreneurs learned the "tricks of the trade," they often used this knowledge to establish monopolies. Aristotle recounted the accomplishments of two of these businessmen, also in Document 31. Successful business managers are described in Document 32.

High finance and global markets did not complete the picture of trade and commerce in the ancient world, however. Mundane transactions such as buying a previously owned horse were undoubtedly common occurrences (Document 36).

EGYPT/INDIA

30. A Rather Lengthy Business Trip

Greek and Roman literature featured a genre of travel writing called the periplous *(literally "voyage around"), a description of a sea voyage of some distance, in which the ship stayed close to the coastline. Authors of the various* periploi *usually included information about cities observed during the voyage; mountains, rivers, and other topographical matters; distance estimates from one port to another; trading, commerce, and trade goods; and many other related topics.*

One of the most important of these travelogues is the first-century A.D. Periplous Maris Erythraei *(Voyage Around the Red Sea), by an unknown author. It contains much information about the trading contacts between the classical Greek and Roman world, and Egypt, Arabia, the Middle East, and India.*

Of the designated ports on the Erythraean [Red] Sea, and the market towns around it, the first is the Egyptian port of Mussel Harbor. To those sailing down from that place, on the right hand, after 1,800 stadia [about 225 miles], there is Berenice [in Egypt]. The harbors of both are at the boundary of Egypt, and are bays opening from the Erythraean Sea.

...Adulis [is] a port established by law, lying at the inner end of a bay that runs in toward the south. Before the harbor lies the so-called Mountain Island, about 200 stadia [about 25 miles] seaward from the very head of the bay, with the shores of the mainland close to it on both sides. Ships bound for this port now anchor here because of attacks from the land. They used formerly to anchor at the very head of the bay, by an island called Diodorus, close to the shore, which could be reached on foot from the land, by which means the barbarous natives attacked the island. Opposite Mountain Island, on the mainland 20 stadia [about two and one-half miles] from the shore, lies Adulis, a fair-sized village, from which there is a three days' journey to Coloe, an inland town and the first market for ivory. From that place to the city of the people called Auxumites there is a five days' journey more; to that place, all the ivory is brought from the country beyond the Nile, through the district called Cyeneum, and thence to Adulis. Practically the whole number of elephants and rhinoceros that are killed live in the places inland, although at rare intervals they are hunted on the seacoast, even near Adulis. Before the harbor of that market town, out at sea on the right hand, there lie a great many little sandy islands called Alalaei, yielding tortoise shell, which is brought to market there by the Fish-Eaters...

There are imported into these places [in Africa, south of Egypt] undressed cloth made in Egypt for the Berbers; robes from Arsinoe; cloaks of poor quality dyed in colors; double-fringed linen mantles; many articles of flint glass, and others of murrhine, made in Diospolis; and brass, which is used for ornament and in cut pieces instead of coin; sheets of soft copper, used for cooking utensils and cut up for bracelets and anklets for the women; iron, which is made into spears used against the elephants and other wild beasts, and in their wars. Besides these, small axes are imported, and adzes and swords; copper drinking cups, round and large; a little coin for those coming into the market; wine of Laodicea and Italy, not much; olive oil, not much; for the king, gold and silver plate made after the fashion of the country; and for clothing, military cloaks, and thin coats of skin, of no great value. Likewise from the district of Ariaca across this sea, there are imported Indian iron, and steel, and Indian cotton cloth; the broad cloth called monache and that called sagmatogene, and girdles, and coats of skin and mallow-colored cloth, and a few muslins, and colored lac. There are exported from these places ivory, and tortoise shell and rhinoceros horn. The most from Egypt is brought to this market from the month of January to September...but seasonably, they put to sea about the month of September.

From this place, the Arabian Gulf trends toward the east and becomes narrowest just before the Gulf of Avalites. After about 4,000 stadia [about 500 miles], for those sailing eastward along the same coast, there are other Berber market towns, known as the "far-side" ports; lying at intervals one after the other, without harbors but having roadsteads where ships can anchor and lie in good weather. The first is called Avalites; to this place, the voyage from Arabia to the far side coast is the shortest. Here there is a small market town called Avalites, which must be reached by boats and rafts. There are imported into this place flint glass, assorted; juice of sour grapes from Diospolis; dressed cloth, assorted, made for the Berbers; wheat, wine, and a little tin. There are exported from the same place, and sometimes by the Berbers themselves, crossing on rafts...spices, a little ivory, tortoise shell, and a very little myrrh, but better than the rest. And the Berbers who live in the place are very unruly.

After Avalites, there is another market town, better than this, called Malao...The anchorage is an open roadstead, sheltered by a spit running out from the east. Here the natives are more peaceable. There are imported into this place the things already mentioned, and many tunics, cloaks from Arsinoe, dressed and dyed; drinking cups, sheets of soft copper in small quantity, iron, and gold and silver coin, not much. There are exported from these places myrrh, a little frankincense...the harder cinnamon, duaca, Indian copal and macir, which are imported into Arabia; and slaves, but rarely.

Two days' sail, or three, beyond Malao is the market town of Mundus, where the ships lie at anchor more safely behind a projecting island close to the shore. There are imported into this place the things previously set forth, and from it likewise are exported the merchandise already stated, and the incense called mocrotu. And the traders living here are more quarrelsome.

Beyond Mundus, sailing toward the east, after another two days' sail, or three, you reach Mosyllum, on a beach, with a bad anchorage. There are imported here the same things already mentioned, also silver plate, a very little iron, and glass. There are shipped from the place a great quantity of cinnamon (so that this market town requires ships of larger size), and fragrant gums, spices, a little tortoise shell, and mocrotu... frankincense... ivory and myrrh in small quantities...

Beyond Tabae, after 400 stadia [about 50 miles], there is the village of Pano [in modern Somalia]. And then, after sailing 400 stadia along a promontory, toward which place the current also draws you, there is another market town called Opone, into which the same things are imported as those already mentioned, and in it the greatest quantity of cinnamon is produced...and slaves of the better sort, which are brought to Egypt in increasing numbers; and a great quantity of tortoise shell, better than that found elsewhere.

The voyage to all these farside market towns is made from Egypt about the month of July...And ships are customarily fitted out from the places across this sea...bringing to these farside market towns the products of their own places: wheat, rice, clarified butter, sesame oil, cotton cloth...and girdles, and honey...Some make the voyage especially to these market towns, and others exchange their cargoes while sailing along the coast. This country is not subject to a king, but each market town is ruled by its separate chief.

...Arabia in its length border[s] a great distance on the Erythraean Sea. Different tribes inhabit the country, differing in their speech, some partially, and some altogether. The land next to the sea is similarly dotted here and there with caves of the Fish-Eaters, but the country inland is peopled by rascally men speaking two languages, who live in villages and nomadic camps, by whom those sailing off the middle course are plundered, and those surviving shipwrecks are taken for slaves...Navigation is dangerous along this whole coast of Arabia, which is without harbors, with bad anchorages, foul, inaccessible because of breakers and rocks, and terrible in every way. Therefore, we hold our course down the middle of the gulf and pass on as fast as possible by the country of Arabia until we come to the Burnt Island, directly below which there are regions of peaceful people, nomadic, pasturers of cattle, sheep, and camels....

There are imported into this place [Arabia] from Egypt a little wheat and wine...clothing in the Arabian style, plain and common and most of it spurious; and copper and tin and coral and storax and other things...and for the king, usually wrought gold and silver plate, also horses, images, and thin clothing of fine quality. And there are exported from this place native produce, frankincense and aloes, and the rest of the things that enter into the trade of other ports...

...There is an island...called Dioscorida [near modern Yemen], and [it] is very large, but desert and marshy, having rivers in it and crocodiles and many snakes and great lizards, of which the flesh is eaten and the fat melted and used instead of olive oil. The island yields no fruit, neither vine nor grain. The inhabitants are few, and they live on the coast toward the north...They are foreigners, a mixture of Arabs and Indians and

Greeks, who have emigrated to carry on trade there. The island produces the true sea tortoise, and the land tortoise, and the white tortoise which is very numerous, and preferred for its large shells; and the mountain tortoise, which is largest of all and has the thickest shell, of which the worthless specimens cannot be cut apart on the under side, because they are even too hard. But those of value are cut apart, and the shells made whole into caskets and small plates and cake dishes and that sort of ware. There is also produced in this island cinnabar, that called Indian, which is collected in drops from the trees...

Beyond the gulf of Baraca is that of Barygaza and the coast of the country of Ariaca [India], which is the beginning of the kingdom of Nambanus and of all India...It is a fertile country, yielding wheat and rice and sesame oil and clarified butter, cotton and the Indian cloths made from it, or the coarser sorts. Very many cattle are pastured there, and the men are of great stature and black in color. The metropolis of this country is Minnagara, from which much cotton cloth is brought down to Barygaza. In these places there remain, even to the present time, signs of the expedition of Alexander, such as ancient shrines, walls of forts, and great wells...

For this reason [strong tides and currents], entrance and departure of vessels [to and from Barygaza] is very dangerous to those who are inexperienced or who come to this market town for the first time. For the rush of waters at the incoming tide is irresistible, and the anchors cannot hold against it, so that large ships are caught up by the force of it, turned broadside on through the speed of the current, and so driven on the shoals and wrecked. And smaller boats are overturned. And those that have been turned aside among the channels by the receding waters at the ebb, are left on their sides, and if not held on an even keel by props, the flood tide comes upon them suddenly and under the first head of the current they are filled with water...

Inland from this place and to the east, is the city called Ozene, formerly a royal capital. From this place are brought down all things needed for the welfare of the country about Barygaza, and many things for our trade: agate and carnelian, Indian muslins and mallow cloth, and much ordinary cloth...There are imported into this market town wine, Italian preferred, also Laodicean and Arabian; copper, tin, and lead; coral and topaz; thin clothing and inferior sorts of all kinds; bright colored girdles a cubit wide; storax; sweet clover, flint glass; realgar; antimony; gold and silver coin, on which there is a profit when exchanged for the money of the country; and ointment, but not very costly and not much. And for the king there are brought into those places very costly vessels of silver, singing boys, beautiful maidens for the harem, fine wines, thin clothing of the finest weaves, and the choicest ointments. There are exported from these places spikenard, costus, bdellium, ivory, agate, and carnelian, lycium, cotton cloth of all kinds, silk cloth, mallow cloth, yarn, long pepper and such other things as are brought here from the various market towns. Those bound for this market town from Egypt make the voyage favorably about the month of July...

The regions beyond these places are either difficult of access because of their excessive winters and great cold, or else cannot be sought out because of some divine influence of the gods.

Source: *Ancient History Sourcebook: The Periplus of the Erythraean Sea. Travel and Trade in the Indian Ocean by a Merchant of the First Century.* Translated and edited by W. H. Schoff. London, Bombay & Calcutta: n.p., 1912. http://www.fordham.edu/halsall/ancient/periplus.html.

GREECE

31. The Beginnings of Trade, Commerce, and Money

The fourth-century B.C. Greek philosopher Aristotle traces below the origins of trade and commerce, and the eventual necessity of coined money to replace commodity trading.

But there is another kind of acquisition that is specifically called wealth-getting, and that is rightly so called; and to this kind, it is due that there is thought to be no limit to riches and property...One of [the methods of acquiring things] is natural, the other is not natural, but carried on rather by means of certain acquired skill or art. We may take our starting point for its study from the following consideration: With every article of property, there is a double way of using it. Both uses are related to the article itself, but not related to it in the same manner; one is peculiar to the thing, and the other is not peculiar to it. Take, for example, a shoe. There is its wear as a shoe, and there is its use as an article of exchange. Both are ways of using a shoe, inasmuch as even he that trades a shoe for money or food with the customer that wants a shoe uses it as a shoe, although not for the use proper to a shoe, since shoes have not come into existence for the purpose of trade.

And the same also holds true about the other articles of property, for all of them have a use in exchange related to them, which began in the first instance from the natural order of things, because people had more than enough of some things, and less than enough of others. This consideration also shows that the art of trade is not by nature a part of the art of wealth acquisition, because the practice of trade was necessary only so far as to satisfy human needs. In the primary association, therefore—I mean the household—there is no function for trade, but it only arises after the association has become more numerous. For the members of the primitive household used to share commodities that were all their own, whereas on the contrary, a group divided into several households participated also in a number of commodities belonging to their neighbors, according to their needs for which they were forced to make their interchanges by way of trading, as many barbarian tribes still do. These tribes do not go beyond exchanging actual commodities for actual commodities, for example giving and taking wine for corn, and so with the various other things of the sort. Exchange on these lines, therefore, is not contrary to nature, nor is it any branch of the art of wealth acquisition, for it existed for the replenishment of natural self-sufficiency. But out of it, the art of business arose in due course.

When people had come to supply themselves more from abroad by importing things which they lacked and exporting those of which they had a surplus, the employment of money necessarily came to be devised. The necessities of life are not in every case readily portable, so for the purpose of exchange of goods, people made a mutual compact to give and accept some substance of such a sort as being itself a useful commodity that was easy to handle in use for general life, iron, for instance, silver and other metals, at the first stage defined merely by size and weight, but finally also by impressing a stamp on it, in order that this might relieve them of having to measure it, the stamp having been put on as a token of the amount. So when currency had been now invented as an outcome of the necessary interchange of goods, there came into existence the other form of wealth acquisition, which at first no doubt was carried on in a simple form, but later became more highly organized as experience discovered the sources and methods of exchange that would result in the most profit. From this arises the idea that the art of wealth acquisition deals especially with money, and that its function is to be able to discern from what source a large supply can be procured, as this art is supposed to create wealth and riches. Indeed, wealth is often assumed to consist of a quantity of money, because money is the thing with which business and trade are employed.

In the following passage, Aristotle goes on to describe some examples of individuals who used their knowledge and intuition to create monopolies.

Thales [of Miletus, a philosopher, and one of the famed Seven Sages of Greek philosophy], so the story goes, because of his poverty was taunted with the uselessness of philosophy. But from his knowledge of astronomy, he had observed while it was still winter that there was going to be a large crop of olives, so he raised a small sum of money and paid deposits for all of the olive presses in Miletus and Chios, which he acquired at a low price because there were no other buyers. When the season arrived, there was a sudden demand for a number of presses all at the same time, and by renting them out on what terms he liked, he earned a large sum of money, in the process proving that it is easy for philosophers to be rich if they choose, but this is not what they care about. Thales, then, is reputed to have thus displayed his wisdom, but as a matter of fact, this strategy of taking an opportunity to secure a monopoly is a universal principle of business.

Even some governments employ this plan of attack as a method of raising revenue when short of funds; they introduce a monopoly of marketable goods. There was a man in Sicily who used a sum of money deposited with him to buy up all the iron from the iron foundries, and afterwards when the dealers came from the trading centers, he was the only seller, although he did not greatly raise the price, but all the same, he made a profit of 100 talents on his capital of 50. When Dionysius [tyrant of Syracuse (405–367 B.C.)] found out about this, he ordered the man to take his money with him, but clear out of Syracuse on the spot, since he was inventing a means of profit which was detrimental to the tyrant's own business affairs. Yet this strategy really is the same as the discovery of Thales, for both men alike contrived to secure themselves a monopoly. An understanding of these strategies is also useful for statesmen, because many states need financial aid and sources of revenue like those just described, just as a household may, but to a greater degree. Therefore, some statesmen even devote their political activity exclusively to finance.

Source: *Aristotle: Politics.* Translated by H. Rackham. London and Cambridge: Loeb Classical Library, 1932.

32. How to Succeed in Business

In the following passage from his essay on management entitled "Oeconomicus," the fourth-century B.C. writer Xenophon sets forth some of the principles that a successful manager should possess and put into practice.

In private industries, the person in authority—bailiff or manager—who can make the workers enthused, industrious, and persevering, he is the one who gives a lift to the business and swells the profit. But if the appearance of the master in the field, of the one who has the fullest power to punish the bad and reward the hardworking employees, makes no striking impression on the men at work, I for one cannot envy him. But if at the sight of him, they get busy, and a spirit of determination of rivalry and eagerness to excel falls on every workman, then I would say that this man has a touch of the kingly nature in him. And this, in my judgment, is the greatest thing in every operation that makes any demand on the labor of workers, and therefore in agriculture.

To acquire these powers, a person needs education. He must possess great natural gifts, and above all, he must be a genius [in the sense of being divinely inspired]. For I consider this gift to be not altogether human, but divine, this power to win willing obedience; it is manifestly a gift of the gods.

Source: *Xenophon: Scripta Minora.* Volume VII. Translated by E. C. Marchant. London and Cambridge: Loeb Classical Library, 1925.

33. The World's Produce Flows to Athens: Thucydides

Athens was a leading commercial center of ancient Greece, especially in the fifth century B.C., *when, as the historian Thucydides attests in the following excerpt, all manner of goods and commodities passed through its port city of* Piraeus.

And our city [Athens] is so great that all the products of the earth flow in upon us, and ours is the happy lot to gather in the good fruits of our own soil with no more home-felt security of enjoyment than we do those of other lands.

Source: *Thucydides.* Translated by Charles Forster Smith. Cambridge and London: Loeb Classical Library, 1919.

34. The World's Produce Flows to Athens: Isocrates

The fourth-century B.C. *orator Isocrates, in this excerpt from his speech "Panegyricus," also describes the abundance of trade that flowed into Athens.*

Again, since the different populations did not in any case possess a country that was self-sufficient, each lacking in some things and producing others in excess of their needs, and since they were greatly at a loss where they should dispose of their surplus and whence they should import what they lacked, in these difficulties also our city [Athens] came to the rescue. For she established the Piraeus as a market in the center of Greece—a market of such abundance that the

Thucydides, one of the greatest ancient Greek historians and author of the *History of the Peloponnesian War*. Library of Congress.

articles which it is difficult to get, one here, one there, from the rest of the world, all these it is easy to procure from Athens.

Source: *Isocrates*. Translated by George Norlin. London and New York: Loeb Classical Library, 1928.

35. Athens as a Commercial Center

In this passage from his essay entitled "Ways and Means," the fourth-century B.C. writer Xenophon extols the virtues of Athens as a hub of commercial activity.

I will now say something about the unrivaled amenities and advantages of our city [Athens] as a commercial center.

In the first place, I presume, Athens possesses the finest and safest accommodations for shipping, since vessels can anchor here and ride safe at their moorings in spite of bad weather. Moreover, at most other ports, merchants are compelled to ship a return cargo, because the local currency has no circulation in other states. But at Athens, they have the opportunity of exchanging their cargo and exporting very many classes of goods that are in demand or, if they do not want to ship a return cargo of goods, it is sound business to export silver, because wherever they sell it, they are sure to make a profit on the capital invested.

Isocrates, an anti-Sophist who firmly believed the Greek city-states must unite. Library of Congress.

If prizes were offered to the magistrates of the market [at Piraeus, Athens's port city] for just and prompt settlement of disputes, so that sailings were not delayed, the effect would be that a far larger number of merchants would trade with us and with much greater satisfaction. It would also be an excellent plan to reserve front seats in the theater for merchants and shipowners, and to offer them hospitality occasionally, when the high quality of their ships and merchandise entitles them to be considered benefactors of the state. With the prospect of these honors before them, they would look on us as friends and hasten to visit us to win the honor as well as the profit.

The rise in the number of residents and visitors would, of course, lead to a corresponding expansion of our imports and exports, of sales, rents, and customs...

When funds were sufficient, it would be a fine plan to build more lodging houses for shipowners near the harbors, and convenient places of exchange for merchants, and also hotels to accommodate visitors. And if houses and shops were put up both in the Piraeus and in the city for retail traders, they would be an ornament to the state, and at the same time the source of a considerable revenue...

As for the silver mines, I believe that if a proper system of working were introduced, a vast amount of money would be obtained from them apart from our other sources of revenue. I want to point out the possibilities of these mines to those who do not know. Once you realize the possibilities, you will be in a better position to consider how the mines should be managed.

We all agree that the mines have been worked for many generations. At any rate, no one even attempts to date the beginning of mining operations. And yet, although digging and the removal of the silver ore have been carried on for so long a time, note how small is the size of the dumps compared with the virgin and silver-laden hills. And it is continually being found that, so far from shrinking, the silver-yielding area extends further and further.

As long as the maximum number of workmen was employed in them, no one ever lacked a job; in fact, there were always more jobs than the laborers could deal with. And even at the present day, no owner of slaves employed in the mines reduces the number of his men. On the contrary, every master obtains as many more as he can. The fact is, I imagine, that when there are few diggers and searchers, the amount of metal recovered is small, and when there are many, the total of ore discovered is multiplied. Hence, of all the industries with which I am acquainted, this is the only one in which expansion of business causes no jealousy.

In addition to all this, every farmer can tell just how many yoke of oxen are enough for the farm and how many workers. To put more on the land than the requisite number is counted as a loss. In mining operations, on the contrary, everyone tells you that he is short of labor. Mining, in fact, is quite different from other industries. An increase in the number of coppersmiths, for example, produces a fall in the price of copper work, and the coppersmiths retire from business. The same thing happens in the iron trade. When corn and wine are abundant, the crops are cheap, and the profit from growing them disappears, so that many farmers give up farming and set themselves up as merchants or shopkeepers or moneylenders. But an increase in the amount of silver ore discovered and of the metal won is accompanied by an increase in the number of persons who take up this industry. Nor is silver like furniture, of which a homeowner never buys more when once he has gotten enough for his house. No one ever yet owned so much silver as to want no more. If a person finds himself with a huge amount of it, he takes as much pleasure in burying the surplus as in using it.

Source: *Xenophon: Scripta Minora*. Volume VII. Translated by E. C. Marchant. London and Cambridge: Loeb Classical Library, 1925.

36. In the Market for a Good Used Horse?

In this excerpt from his treatise entitled The Art of Horsemanship, *Xenophon takes up the issue of buying a previously owned horse.*

In case the intention is to buy a horse already ridden, we will write out some notes that the buyer must thoroughly master if he is not to be cheated over his purchase.

First, then, he must not fail to ascertain the age. A horse that has shed all his milk teeth does not afford much ground for pleasing expectations, and is not so easily got rid of.

If he is clearly a youngster, one must notice further how he receives the bit in his mouth and the harness about his ears. This may be best noticed if the buyer sees the bridle put on and taken off again.

Next, attention must be paid to his behavior when he receives the rider on his back. Many horses will not readily accept a thing if they know beforehand that, if they accept it, they will be forced to work.

Another thing to observe is whether when mounted, he is willing to leave the other horses, or whether in passing standing horses he does not bolt towards them. Some too, as a result of bad training, run away from the riding ground to the paths that lead home...

It is likewise necessary to know whether, when going at full speed, he can be pulled up sharp, and whether he turns readily. And it is well to make sure whether he is equally willing to obey when roused by a blow. A disobedient servant and a disobedient army are, of course, useless. And a disobedient horse is not only useless, but often behaves just like a traitor...

To sum up: the horse that is sound in his feet, gentle and fairly fast, has the will and the strength to stand work and, above all, is obedient, is the horse that will give the least trouble and the greatest measure of safety to his rider in warfare. But those that need a lot of driving on account of their laziness, or a lot of coaxing and attention on account of their high spirit, make constant demands on the rider's hands and rob him of confidence in moments of danger.

Source: *Xenophon: Scripta Minora*. Volume VII. Translated by E. C. Marchant. London and Cambridge: Loeb Classical Library, 1925.

ROME

37. All Roads... and Shipping Lanes... and Trade Routes Lead to Rome

All roads led to Rome, so the saying went, as did all shipping lanes, and all trade routes, or so it seemed. The second-century A.D. philosopher Aelius Aristides comments on that topic in this passage from his essay "To Rome."

Around [the Mediterranean] lie the continents far and wide, pouring an endless flow of goods to you [Rome]. There is brought from every land and sea whatever is brought forth by the seasons and is produced by all countries, rivers, lakes, and the skills of Greeks and foreigners. So that anyone who wants to behold all these products must either journey through the whole world to see them, or else come to this city. For whatever is raised or manufactured by each people is assuredly always here to overflowing. So many merchants arrive here with cargoes from all over, at every season, and with each return of the harvest, that the city seems like a common warehouse of the world. One can see so many cargoes from India, or, if you wish, from Arabia, that one may surmise that the trees there have been left permanently bare, and that those people must come here to beg for their own goods whenever they need anything. Clothing from Babylonia and the luxuries from the barbarian lands beyond arrive in much greater volume and more easily than if one had to sail from Naxos or Cythnos to Athens, transporting any of their products. Egypt, Sicily, and the civilized part of

Africa are your farms. The arrival and departure of ships never ceases, so that it is astounding that the sea—not to mention the harbor—suffices for the merchants...And all things converge here, trade, seafaring, agriculture, metallurgy, all the skills which exist and have existed, anything that is begotten and grows. Whatever cannot be seen here belongs completely to the category of nonexistent things.

Source: From *Roman Civilization Sourcebook II: The Empire*, by Naphtali Lewis and Meyer Reinhold. Copyright © 1955 Columbia University Press. Reprinted with permission of the publisher.

Part IV

INTELLECTUAL LIFE

Education

The great civilizations of the world customarily place a high priority on education. In ancient Egypt, priests taught select students reading, writing, arithmetic, and geometry, but most children received a more superficial education (Documents 1 and 2). The ancient Greeks, at least in Athens, taught their children the "three R's" (reading, writing, and arithmetic), supplemented by history, literature, music, drawing, and athletic training (Documents 3 and 4). In *Sparta*, however, there were different emphases. At the age of seven, young boys were taken from their parents and raised in state-run schools, like military barracks, where the curriculum consisted mostly of subjects and exercises related to military training. Scant attention was paid to reading and writing (Document 5).

Often, children in both Greece and Rome did not attend formal schools but rather were home-schooled, being taught by nurses, educated slaves, private tutors, or even by the parents themselves. Hence, it would come as no surprise that advice on choosing teachers was a common topic in many writings. The Greek biographer Plutarch (Document 6) exhorted parents to make careful choices, and not to worry about the expense involved—better to pay more for an experienced and effective teacher than to pay a bargain basement fee for one who is incompetent. The Roman historian Tacitus echoed that idea, lamenting the fact that children were often taught by "some silly little Greek serving-maid, with a male slave, who may be anyone, to help her" (Document 9). The Roman writer Quintilian subscribed to the notion that every child had the innate ability to learn: "That there are any [children] who gain nothing from education, I absolutely deny" (Document 7). Quintilian also expressed the opinion (Document 8) that children should be taught to read as soon as possible, and that waiting until the customary age of seven was doing a disservice to young minds that were capable of learning to read long before reaching that age.

Perhaps one reason that formal schools were in short supply was the cost that they would entail. Few communities were apparently as fortunate as the northern Italian town of Comum, whose local school was handsomely endowed by Pliny the Younger (Document 10).

EGYPT

1. The Scribal Profession: Learn It!

The unknown author of the following excerpt from the Twentieth Dynasty Papyrus Lansing upbraids a young student who has the potential to become an excellent scribe, but who refuses to take instruction.

Young fellow, how conceited you are! You do not listen when I speak. Your heart is denser than a great obelisk, a hundred cubits high, ten cubits thick...

So also a cow is bought this year, and it plows the following year. It learns to listen to the herdsman; it only lacks words. Horses brought from the field, they forget their mothers. Yoked they go up and down on all his majesty's errands. They become like those that bore them, that stand in the stable. They do their utmost, for fear of a beating.

But though I beat you with every kind of stick, you do not listen. If I knew another way of doing it, I would do it for you, that you might listen. You are a person fit for writing, though you have not yet known a woman. Your heart discerns, your fingers are skilled, your mouth is apt for reciting...

You are busy coming and going, and don't think of writing. You resist listening to me; you neglect my teachings.

You are worse than the goose of the shore, that is busy with mischief. It spends the summer destroying the dates, the winter destroying the seed-grain. It spends the balance of the year in pursuit of the cultivators. It does not let seed be cast to the ground without snatching it in its fall. One cannot catch it by snaring. One does not offer it in the temple. The evil, sharp-eyed bird that does no work!

You are worse than the desert antelope that lives by running. It spends no day in plowing. Never at all does it tread on the threshing floor. It lives on the oxen's labor, without entering among them. But though I spend the day telling you "Write!," it seems like a plague to you. Writing is very pleasant!...

I spend the day instructing you. You do not listen! Your heart is like an <empty> room. My teachings are not in it...

The marsh thicket is before you each day, as a nestling is after its mother. You follow the path of pleasure; you make friends with revelers. You have made your home in the brewery, as one who thirsts for beer. You sit in the parlor with an idler. You hold the writings in contempt...Do not do these things! What are they for? They are of no use. Take note of it!

Source: Lichtheim, Miriam. *Ancient Egyptian Literature: A Book of Readings. Volume II: The New Kingdom.* Berkeley: University of California Press, 1976.

2. The Two-Track Egyptian Curriculum

According to the first-century B.C. Greek historian Diodorus Siculus, the Egyptian educational curriculum of the first century B.C. included the following subjects:

In the education of their sons, the priests teach them two kinds of writing, that which is called "sacred" and that which is used in the more general instruction. Geometry and arithmetic are given special attention. For the river, by changing the face of the country each year in many ways, causes many and varied disputes between neighbors over their boundary lines, and these disputes cannot be easily resolved with any exactness unless a geometer works out the truth scientifically by the application of his experience. And arithmetic is useful with reference to the business affairs connected with making a living and also in applying the principles of geometry, and likewise is also of no small assistance to students of astrology...

As to the general mass of the Egyptians, they are instructed from their childhood by their fathers or relatives in the practices appropriate to [their] manner of life...But as for reading and writing, the Egyptians at large give their children only a superficial instruction in them, and not all do this, but for the most part, only those who are engaged in the crafts. In wrestling and music, however, it is not customary among them to receive any instruction at all. They believe that from the daily exercises in wrestling, their young men will gain, not health, but a vigor that is only temporary and in fact dangerous, while they consider music to be not only useless, but even harmful, since it makes the spirits of the listeners effeminate.

Source: *Diodorus of Sicily.* Volume I. Translated by C. H. Oldfather. London and Cambridge: Loeb Classical Library, 1933.

GREECE

3. The Curriculum from Childhood through Adolescence

A rhetorician and satirist born in the Roman province of Syria, Lucian (A.D. c. 120–c. 200) wrote in Greek. In the following excerpt from his writings, Lucian, speaking through the words of the famous sixth-century B.C. Athenian lawgiver Solon, explains the principles of the ancient Athenian educational system.

We entrust the early upbringing of children to mothers, nurses and tutors, to train and rear them with liberal teachings. But when at length they become able to understand what it right, when modesty, shame, fear and ambition spring up in them, and when at length their bodies seem well-fitted for hard work as they get more muscular and become more strongly compacted, then we take them in hand and teach them, not only prescribing for them certain disciplines and exercises for the mind, but in certain other ways acclimatizing their bodies to hard work. We have not thought it sufficient for each person to be as he was born, either in mind or in body, but we want education and disciplines for them by which their good traits may be much improved, and their bad traits changed for the better. We take farmers as an example, who shelter and enclose their plants while they are small and young, so that they may not be injured by the breeze. But when the stalk at last begins to thicken, they prune away the excessive growth and expose them to the winds to be shaken and tossed, in that way making them more productive.

We fan into flame their minds with music and arithmetic at first, and we teach them to write and read their letters. As they progress, we recite for them sayings of wise men, deeds of long ago times, and helpful fictions, which we have put into meter to help them remember them better. Hearing of certain feats of arms and famous events, little by little they become envious, and are motivated to imitate them, in order that they, too, may be praised and admired by future generations. Both Hesiod and Homer have composed poetry of that sort for us.

Source: *Lucian*. Volume IV. Translated by A. M. Harmon. London and New York: Loeb Classical Library, 1925.

4. Aristotle's Vision of Education

In this passage from his Politics, *the fourth-century* B.C. *Greek philosopher Aristotle offers some thoughts on the importance of education, and the kinds of forms it could take.*

No one will doubt that the legislator should direct his attention above all to the education of youth; for the neglect of education does harm to the [state's] constitution. The citizen should be molded to suit the form of government under which he lives...

Again, for the exercise of any faculty or art, a previous training and habituation are required... And since the whole city has one end, it is manifest that education should be one and the same for all, and that it should be public, and not private—not as at present, when everyone looks after his own children separately, and gives them separate instruction of the sort which he thinks best. The training in things which are of common interest should be the same for all. Neither must we suppose that any one of the citizens belongs to himself, for they all belong to the state... In particular... the Spartans are to be praised, because they take the greatest pains about their children, and make education the business of the state.

That education should be regulated by law and should be an affair of the state is not to be denied, but what should be the character of this public education, and how young persons should be educated, are questions which remain to be considered. As things are, there is disagreement about the subjects. For people by no means agree about the things to be taught, whether we look to virtue or the best life. Neither is it clear whether education is more concerned with intellectual or with moral virtue. The existing practice is perplexing; no one knows on what principle we should proceed—should the useful in life, or should virtue, or should the higher knowledge, be the aim of our training? All three opinions have been considered... There can be no doubt that children should be taught those useful things which are really necessary, but not all useful things; for occupations are divided into liberal and illiberal; and to young children should be imparted only such kinds of knowledge as will be useful to them... Any occupation, art, or science, which makes the body or soul or mind of the freeman less fit for the practice or exercise of virtue, is vulgar...

The customary branches of education are in number four; they are: (1) reading and writing, (2) gymnastic exercises, (3) music, to which is sometimes added (4) drawing.

Of these, reading and writing and drawing are regarded as useful for the purposes of life in a variety of ways, and gymnastic exercises are thought to infuse courage. Concerning music, a doubt may be raised—in our own day, most people cultivate it for the sake of pleasure, but originally it was included in education, because nature itself, as has been often said, requires that we should be able, not only to work well, but to use leisure well. For, as I must repeat once again, the first principle of all action is leisure. Both are required, but leisure is better than occupation...

It is clear, then, that there are branches of learning and education which we must study merely with a view to leisure spent in intellectual activity, and these are to be valued for their own sake, whereas those kinds of knowledge which are useful in business are to be deemed necessary, and exist for the sake of other things. And therefore our forbears included music in education, not because of its necessity or utility, for it is not necessary nor indeed useful in the same manner as reading and writing, which are useful in money making, in the management of a household, in the acquisition of knowledge and in political life, nor like drawing, useful for a more correct judgment of the works of artists, nor again like gymnastics, which gives health and strength, for neither of these is to be gained from music. There remains, then, the use of music for intellectual enjoyment in leisure, which is evidently the reason of its introduction, this being one of the ways in which it is thought that a free person should pass his leisure...

A fifteenth-century painting of the famous philosopher Aristotle, by Justus van Gent. © (2008) Jupiterimages Corporation.

It is evident, then, that there is a sort of education in which parents should train their children, not as being useful or necessary, but because it is liberal or noble...This much we are now in a position to say, that the ancients witness to us; for their opinion may be gathered from the fact that music is one of the received and traditional branches of education. Further, it is clear that children should be instructed in some useful things, for example, in reading and writing, not only for their usefulness, but also because many other sorts of knowledge are acquired through them. With a similar view, they may be taught drawing, not to prevent their making mistakes in their own purchases, or in order that they may not be imposed upon in the buying or selling of articles, but perhaps rather because it makes them judges of the beauty of the human form. To be always seeking after the useful is not appropriate to free and exalted souls.

Source: ROSS, ARISTOTLE SELECTIONS, 1st, © 1976. Reproduced by permission of Pearson Education, Inc., Upper Saddle River, New Jersey.

5. The Differing Spartan Vision of Education

The Spartans had their own ideas on education, as the Greek biographer Plutarch (A.D. *c. 45–c. 120*) *shows in this passage from his biography of* Lycurgus, *Sparta's legendary seventh-century* B.C. *lawgiver.*

Lycurgus would not put the sons of Spartans under the supervision of purchased or hired tutors, nor was it lawful for every father to raise or train his son as he pleased, but as soon as they were seven years old, Lycurgus ordered them all to be taken by the state and enrolled in companies, where they were put under the same discipline and training, and so became accustomed to share one another's sports and studies. The boy who excelled in judgment and was the most courageous in fighting, was made captain of his company. All the rest kept their eyes on him, obeying his orders, and submitting to his punishments, so that their boyish training was a practice of obedience...

Of reading and writing, they learned only enough to serve their turn. All the rest of their training was calculated to make them obey commands well, endure hardships, and conquer in battle.

Source: *Plutarch's Lives*. Volume I. Translated by Bernadotte Perrin. London and Cambridge: Loeb Classical Library, 1914.

6. *Choosing a Teacher*

In this excerpt from his Moralia, *Plutarch offers parents advice for choosing a teacher for their children, a decision not to be taken lightly.*

I come now to a point which is more important and more serious than anything I have said so far. Teachers must be sought for the children who are free from scandal in their lives, who are unimpeachable in their manners, and in experience the very best that may be found. To receive a proper education is the source and root of all goodness. As farmers place stakes beside the young plants, so do competent teachers with all care set their instruction and encouragement beside the young, in order that their characters may grow to be upright.

Nowadays, there are some parents who deserve utter contempt, who, before examining prospective teachers, either because of ignorance or sometimes because of inexperience, hand over their children to untried and untrustworthy men. And this is not so ridiculous if their action is due to inexperience, but there is another case which is absurd to the highest degree. What is this? Sometimes, even with knowledge and with information from others, who tell them of the inexperience and even of the depravity of certain teachers, they nevertheless entrust their children to them. Some yield to the flatteries of those who would please them, and there are those who do it as a favor to insistent friends. Their action resembles that of a person who, if he were afflicted with bodily disease, would reject that man who by his knowledge might save his life and, as a favor to a friend, would prefer one who by his inexperience might cause his death. Or another example, that of a person who would dismiss a most excellent ship's captain, and accept the very worst, because of a friend's insistence. Heaven help us! Do parents...think more of gratifying those who ask favors than they think of the education of their children?

And did not Socrates often say, very fittingly, that if it were in any way possible, one should go up to the highest part of the city and cry out loud: "Citizens, where is your course taking you, who give all possible attention to the acquisition of money, but give small thought to your children to whom you are to leave it?" To this I would like to add that such parents act nearly as one would act who should give thought to his shoe but pay no regard to his foot. Many parents, however, go so far in their devotion to money as well as in animosity to their children that in order to avoid paying a larger fee, they select as teachers for their children individuals who are not worth any wage at all…Hence Aristippus, not inelegantly, but very cleverly, criticized a father who lacked both mind and sense, for when this man asked him what fee he would require for teaching his child, Aristippus replied, "A thousand drachmas." When the other exclaimed, "Great heavens! What an excessive demand! I can buy a slave for a thousand," Aristippus replied, "Then you will have two slaves, your son and the one you buy."

In general, is it not ridiculous for people to accustom children to take their food with their right hand and if one puts out his left, to scold him, and yet take no forethought that their children will hear right and proper words of instruction?

Source: *Plutarch's Moralia.* Volume I. Translated by Frank Cole Babbitt. London and Cambridge: Loeb Classical Library, 1927.

ROME

7. Quintilian's Prescription for Educating a Child

The ancient Romans had a high regard for formal training and education, especially for a young person who might one day embark upon a career in public service, including oratory. The educator/philosopher Quintilian (A.D. c. 35–c. 100), in this excerpt from his Institutes of Oratory, *offers his thoughts on the kind of educational experience most appropriate for a child who might one day grow up to be the next Demosthenes or Cicero.*

There is one point which I must emphasize before I begin, which is this. Without natural gifts, technical rules are useless. Consequently, the student who is devoid of talent will derive no more profit from this work than barren soil from a treatise on agriculture. There are, it is true, other natural aids, such as the possession of a good voice and robust lungs, sound health, powers of endurance and grace, and if these are possessed only to a moderate extent, they may be improved by methodical training. In some cases, however, these gifts are lacking to such an extent that their absence is fatal to all such advantages as talent and study can confer while, similarly, they are of no profit in themselves unless cultivated by skillful teaching, persistent study, and extensive practice in writing, reading, and speaking.

I would, therefore, have a father conceive the highest hopes of his son from the moment of his birth. If he does so, he will be more careful about the groundwork of his education. For there is absolutely no foundation for the complaint that but few men have the power to take in the knowledge that is imparted to them, and that the majority are so slow of understanding that education is a waste of time and labor. On the contrary, you will find that most are quick to reason and ready to learn. Reasoning comes as naturally to human beings as flying to birds, speed to horses and ferocity to beasts of prey; our minds are endowed by nature with such activity and sagacity that the soul is believed to proceed from heaven. Those who are dull and unteachable are as abnormal as prodigious births and monstrosities, and are but few in number. A proof of what I say is to be found in the fact that boys commonly show promise of many accomplishments, and when such promise dies away as they grow up, this is plainly due not to the failure of natural gifts, but to the lack of the requisite care.

But, it will be urged, there are degrees of talent. Undoubtedly, I reply, and there will be a corresponding variation in actual accomplishment. But that there are any who gain nothing from education, I absolutely deny. The man who shares this conviction must, as soon as he becomes a father, devote the utmost care to fostering the promise shown by the son whom he destines to become an orator.

Above all, see that the child's nurse speaks correctly. The ideal…would be that she should be a philosopher. Failing that…the best should be chosen, as far as possible. No doubt the most important point is that they should be of good character, but they should speak correctly as well. It is the nurse that the child first hears, and her words that he will first attempt to imitate. And we are by nature most tenacious of childish impressions, just as the flavor first absorbed by vessels when new persists, and the color imparted by dyes to the primitive whiteness of wool is indelible.

Further, it is the worst impressions that are most durable. For, while what is good readily deteriorates, you will never turn vice into virtue. Do not, therefore, allow the child to become accustomed, even in infancy, to a style of speech which he will subsequently have to unlearn.

As regards parents, I should like to see them as highly educated as possible, and I do not restrict this remark to fathers alone. We are told that the eloquence of the Gracchi [brothers Tiberius and Gaius Gracchus, noted second century B.C. politicians and orators] owed much to their mother Cornelia, whose letters even today testify to the cultivation of her style. [The examples of two daughters of noted orators are cited next.] Laelia, the daughter of Gaius Laelius, is said to have reproduced the elegance of her father's language in her own speech, while the oration delivered before the triumvirs by Hortensia, the daughter of Quintus Hortensius, is still read and not merely as a compliment to her sex. And even those who have not had the fortune to receive a good education should not for that reason devote less care to their child's education, but should, on the contrary, show all the greater diligence in other matters where they can be of service to their children…

If any of my readers regards me as somewhat exacting in my demands, I would ask that reader to reflect that it is no easy task to create an orator, even though his education be carried out under the most favorable circumstances, and that further and greater difficulties are still before us. For continuous application, the very best of teachers, and a variety of experiences are necessary. Therefore, the rules which we lay down for the education of our pupil must be of the best. If anyone refuses to be guided by them, the fault will lie not with the method, but with the individual. Still, if it should prove impossible to secure the ideal nurse, the ideal companions, or the ideal *paedagogus* [literally, "child-leader," a trusted slave who escorted children to and from school], I would insist that there should be one person at any rate attached to the child who has some knowledge of speaking, and who will, if any incorrect expression should be used by the nurse or *paedagogus* in the presence of the child under their charge, at once correct the error and prevent its becoming a habit. But it must be clearly understood that this is only a remedy, and that the ideal course is that indicated above.

Source: *The Institutio Oratoria of Quintilian.* Translated by H. E. Butler. Cambridge and London: Loeb Classical Library, 1920.

8. At What Age Should a Child Be Taught to Read?

In this later passage from his Institutes of Oratory *(see also Document 7, above), Quintilian addresses the subject of the ideal age when children should be taught to read.*

Some believe that children should not be taught to read till they are seven years old, that being the earliest age at which they can derive profit from instruction and endure the strain of learning. Most of the them attribute this view to Hesiod,…[and] other authorities, among them Eratosthenes, give the same advice. Those, however, who argue that that a child's mind should not be allowed to lie fallow for a moment are wiser…Since children are capable of moral training [at an early age], should they not be capable of literary education?…Still, those who disagree with me seem in taking this line to spare the teacher rather than the student. What better occupation can a child have as soon as he is able to speak? And he must be kept occupied somehow or other. Or why should we despise the profit to be gained before the age of seven, small though it may be? Although the knowledge absorbed in the previous years may be slight, yet the child will be learning something more advanced during that year, in which he would otherwise have been occupied with something more elementary. Such progress each successive year increases the total, and the time gained during childhood is clear profit to the period of youth…Let us not, therefore, waste the earliest years. There is all the less excuse for this, since the elements of literary training are solely a question of memory, which not only exists even in small children, but is especially retentive at that age.

Source: *The Institutio Oratoria of Quintilian.* Translated by H. E. Butler. Cambridge and London: Loeb Classical Library, 1920.

9. An Orator's Education

The Roman historian Tacitus (A.D. c. 55–c. 117), who wrote an essay on oratory entitled, appropriately enough, "A Dialogue on Oratory," discusses, in this passage from the essay, the proper education for the would-be orator.

I pass by the first rudiments of education, though even these are taken too lightly. It is in the reading of authors, and in gaining a knowledge of the past, and in making acquaintance with things and persons and occasions that too little solid work is done. Recourse is had instead to the so-called rhetoricians...

Well, then, in the good old days, the young man who was destined for the oratory of the bar, after receiving the rudiments of a sound training at home and storing his mind with liberal culture, was taken by his father, or his relations, and placed under the care of some orator who held a leading position at Rome. The youth had to get the habit of following his patron about, of escorting him in public, of supporting him at all his appearances as a speaker, whether in the law courts or on the platform, hearing also his word-combats at first hand, standing by him in his duelings, and learning, as it were, to fight in the fighting line. It was a method that secured at once for the young students a considerable amount of experience, great self-possession, and a goodly store of sound judgment. For they carried on their studies in the light of open day, and amid the very shock of battle, under conditions in which any stupid or ill-advised statement brings prompt retribution in the shape of the judge's disapproval, taunting criticism from the opponent—yes, and from your own supporters, expressions of dissatisfaction.

So it was a genuine and unadulterated eloquence that they were initiated in from the very first. And though they attached themselves to a single speaker, yet they got to know all the contemporary members of the bar in a great variety of both civil and criminal cases. Moreover, a public meeting gave them the opportunity of noting marked divergences of taste, so that they could easily detect what commended itself in the case of each individual speaker...

Nowadays, on the other hand, our children are handed over at their birth to some silly little Greek serving-maid, with a male slave, who may be anyone, to help her—quite frequently the most worthless member of the whole establishment, incompetent for any serious service. It is from the foolish tittle-tattle of such persons that the children receive their earliest impressions, while their minds are still pliant and unformed. And there is not a soul in the whole house who cares a jot what he says or does in the presence of his baby master. Yes, and the parents themselves make no effort to train their little ones in goodness and self-control. They grow up in an atmosphere of laxity and pertness, in which they come gradually to lose all sense of shame, and all respect both for themselves and for other people.

Again, there are the peculiar and characteristic vices of this metropolis of ours, taken on, as it seems to me, almost in the mother's womb: the passion for play actors, and the mania for gladiatorial shows and horseracing. And when the mind is engrossed in such occupations, what room is left over for higher pursuits? How few are to be found whose home talk runs to any other subjects than these? What else do we overhear our younger men talking about whenever we enter their lecture halls? And the teachers are just as bad. With them, too, such topics supply material for gossip with their classes more frequently than any others.

Source: *Tacitus: Dialogus, Agricola, Germania*. Translated by Sir W. Peterson, revised by M. Winterbottom. Cambridge and London: Loeb Classical Library, 1914.

10. Pliny the Younger Endows a School

The Roman writer Pliny the Younger (A.D. 62–114) was shocked to learn that children in his hometown of Comum had to travel to Milan, about 25 miles away, for schooling. In this letter to his friend, the historian Cornelius Tacitus (A.D. c. 55–c. 117), Pliny describes what he decided to do about the situation.

Having recently been to my hometown, a young boy, son of one of my fellow townsmen, paid me a visit. "Do you go to school?" I asked him. "Yes," he said. "And where?" He told me, "At Milan." "And why not here?" "Because," said his father, who was present, and had in fact brought the boy with him, "we have no teachers." "How is that?" I said. "Surely it must concern you who are fathers"—and very opportunely several in the group were so—"that your children should receive their education here, rather than anywhere else. Where can they be placed more agreeably than in their own town, or maintained in more modest habits and at less expense than at home and under the eye of their parents? By a general contribution, you could procure teachers on very favorable terms, if you would only apply towards their salaries what you now spend on your children's room, board and travel expenses, and whatever else must be paid for when traveling, which means paying for everything. I, who have as yet no children myself, am ready to give a third part of any sum you would think proper to raise for this purpose, for the benefit of our country, whom I regard as a daughter or a parent. I would take upon myself the whole expense, were I not concerned that my endowment might be abused at some future time, and be perverted for private ends, as I have observed to be the case in several places where teachers are hired by the local authorities. The one way to prevent this kind of mismanagement is to leave the choice of the teachers entirely up to the discretion of the parents, who will be so much more careful to determine properly, since they will be obligated to share the expense of maintaining them. Although they may be careless in disposing of someone else's wealth, they will certainly be cautious about how they apply their own, and will see to it that no teachers except those who deserve it will receive my money, when they must at the same time receive theirs, too."

"Let my example, then, encourage you to unite enthusiastically in the plan, and be assured that the greater the sum my share will amount to, the more agreeable it will be to me. You can undertake nothing more advantageous to your children, nor more acceptable to your country. By this means, they will receive their education where they were born, and be accustomed from infancy to live in and love their hometown. I hope that you can hire teachers of such distinguished abilities that neighboring towns will be glad to obtain their learning here, and just as now you send your children to another town for education, maybe out-of-towners will in the future flock here for their instruction.

"I thought it proper to explain this whole matter to you, so that you might better understand how agreeable it would be to me, if you perform the task which I request. I ask you, therefore, with all the seriousness a matter of so much importance deserves, to look out among the great numbers of men of letters which your reputation brings to you, teachers whom we may approach for this purpose. But it must be understood that I cannot make a binding agreement with any of them. I would leave it entirely up to the parents to judge and choose as they see fit. The only share that I pretend to claim is that of contributing my interest and my money. If anyone therefore is found who relies on his own talents, he may go there, on this condition: that that reliance is all he can count upon, as far as I am concerned. Farewell."

Source: *Pliny: Letters.* Volume I. Translated by William Melmoth, with revisions by W.M.L. Hutchinson. Cambridge and London: Loeb Classical Library, 1915.

Respect for Writing, Language, and Literature

All ancient cultures respected the power of the written word, and, by extension, the people sufficiently gifted to express themselves in writing. Poetry was highly prized in India (Document 11) and in Greece, although the philosopher Plato thought that poetic topics should be limited to "hymns to the gods and paeans in praise of good citizens" (Document 13). The scribal profession was highly valued in ancient Egypt because of its prestige and because it freed its practitioners from the burdens of manual labor (Document 12). An ancient Greek style manual offers hints and suggestions about syntax and word usage, including the creation of neologisms (Document 15).

Possibly one of the most difficult literary genres was history, at least if the ancient historians are to be believed. The Greek historian Polybius, among others, described the frustrations that await authors of historical texts (Document 16). The Roman orator Cicero did a survey of Greek historians. Not surprisingly, perhaps, he ranked Herodotus and Thucydides as two of the best, with Xenophon not far behind (Document 14).

The name of the Roman architect Vitruvius is generally not connected with literary criticism, but in *De Architectura*, his treatise on architecture, he included a short commentary on the contributions of writers to a society, remarking that even though writers are more important than champion athletes, it was the athletes who almost always received far more public acclaim (Document 18). And Cicero, who greatly respected Greek and Roman literature, selected a rather unusual and irregular venue in which to make a strong case for its importance—the middle of a courtroom speech on a case involving Roman citizenship (Document 17).

INDIA

11. The Delights of Poetry

The "treasury" of Sanskrit poetry compiled by the eleventh-century Buddhist abbot Vidya-kara includes a selection in praise of poets; the following excerpt from that selection contains some generous accolades for the poetic art.

Vagura was well versed in the path of speech
trod by former master poets.
Yogesvara knew how to make words blossom
when he wrote of the Reva and the Vindhyas,
of Pulindra and of Pamara girls,

and of a message carried by the monsoon wind.
Would you drink elixir with your ear
or fashion phrases which the wise approve;
would you reach the height of learning
or the farther shore of the stream of sentiments;
would you eat the sweetest fruit that the tree of life can give?
Then, brother, hear the nectar-dripping speech
of the poet Rajasekhara...
These phrases of Murari are like a trough beside a well;
the well: the nectar of Valmiki's verse,
deep and delicious from its praise
of a dynasty so brilliant as was Rama's.
Out upon those literary styles
that pain one with exertion!
Out on fruitless speech, in which does not appear
the nectareous delight produced by Vallana,
whose verses are a dancing ground for sentiments of love,
a moonrise for the high tide of our tears,
a cause of pride's annihilation
in all his literary rivals...
What delights is when the soul of what one says
appears not in the words themselves
but in the way the words are put together;
this, rather than a flavor that is obvious;
just as a woman's breast excites us
when but a glimpse of it is seen
as her silken garment flutters in the wind;
this, rather than the breast laid bare...
Your words are such that there is none
but lies in the common road of thought,
nor do you take a word in another sense
than what runs on the highway of our speech.
How different is the frigidly contrived
and arbitrary joining of the word and sense
by which these other cursed poets
exhaust our minds.
Supreme stands Kalidasa,
an ornament for the throats of poets,
who, having reaped the field of simile
with the sickle of his mind,
has left all other poets to glean.
Kalidasa and the rest were poets,
poets too are we;
a mountain and an atom
are both substances...
When a special nectar, made up of the workings
of word and meaning, with its delightful current bathes
the minds of men of taste, we have true poetry;
but the finest subtlety therein
is that which bursts upon our inner sense
although not designated by the words.
The words of a good poet

even before one proves their excellence
pour sweetness in the ear.
A jasmine garland
attracts the eye
before one knows its scent...
It took me a long time
to fathom, as it were,
the deep, sweet flood
of Kalidasa's muse...
Valmiki dammed the sea with rocks
put into place by monkeys,
and Vyasa filled it with the arrows shot by Partha;
yet neither is suspected of hyperbole.
On the other hand, I weigh both word and sense
and yet the public sneers and scorns my work.
O reputation, I salute thee!...
No one rides before, no one comes behind
and the path bears no fresh prints.
How now, am I alone? Ah yes, I see:
the path which the ancients opened up by now is overgrown
and the other, that broad and easy road, I've surely left...
Those who scorn me in this world
have doubtless special wisdom,
so my writings are not made for them;
but are rather with the thought that some day will be born,
since time is endless and the world is wide,
one whose nature is the same as mine...
As long as the left side of Siva's body
is graced with woman's breast,
as long as Visnu's arms are busy
in clasping Laksmi's neck;
as long as Brahma's hands keep moving
to the accents of his Vedic hymns:
so long may last the verses of good poets,
sweet potion for the conch shell of the ear!

Source: Reprinted by permission of the publisher from SANSKRIT POETRY FROM VIDYAKARA'S "TREASURY," by Daniel H. H. Ingalls, pp. 314–317, Cambridge, Mass.: The Belknap Press of Harvard University, Copyright © 1965, 1968 by the President and Fellows of Harvard College.

EGYPT

12. The Scribal Profession: Be One!

In the following passage, the unknown author of the Papyrus Lansing, *which dates to the Twentieth Dynasty (1190–1077 B.C.), praises the noble pursuits and activities of scribes.*

Love writing, shun dancing; then you become a worthy official. Do not long for the marsh thicket. Turn your back on throw stick and chase. By day write with your fingers; recite by night. Befriend the scroll, the palette. It pleases more than wine. Writing for him who knows it is better than all other professions. It pleases more than bread and beer, more than clothing and ointment. It is worth more than an inheritance in Egypt, than a tomb in the west...

The scribe of the army and commander of the cattle of the houses of Amun, Nebmare-nakht, speaks to the scribe Wenemdiamun, as follows: Be a scribe! Your body will be sleek; your hand will be soft. You will not flicker like a flame, like one whose body is feeble. For there is not the bone of a man in you. You are tall and thin. If you lifted a load to carry it, you would stagger, your legs would tremble. You are lacking in strength; you are weak in all your limbs; you are poor in body.

Set your sight on being a scribe; a fine profession that suits you. You call for one; a thousand answer you. You stride freely on the road. You will not be like a hired ox. You are in front of others.

...I instruct...you [to] become one whom the king trusts; to make you gain entrance to treasury and granary. To make you receive the ship-load at the gate of the granary. To make you issue the offerings on feast days. You are dressed in fine clothes; you own horses. Your boat is on the river; you are supplied with attendants. You stride about inspecting. A mansion is built in your town. You have a powerful office, given you by the king. Male and female slaves are about you. Those who are in the fields grasp your hand, on plots that you have made. Look, I make you into a staff of life! Put the writings in your heart, and you will be protected from all kinds of toil. You will become a worthy official.

Do you not recall the (fate of) the unskilled man? His name is not known. He is ever burdened <like an ass carrying> in front of the scribe who knows what he is about.

Writing is more enjoyable than enjoying a basket of...beans; more enjoyable than a mother's giving birth, when her heart knows no distaste. She is constant in nursing her son; her breast is in his mouth every day. Happy is the heart [o]> him who writes; he is young each day.

Source: Lichtheim, Miriam. *Ancient Egyptian Literature: A Book of Readings. Volume II: The New Kingdom.* Berkeley: University of California Press, 1976.

GREECE

13. The Place of Poetry in Plato's Ideal Republic

In this excerpt from his famous book on the ideal state, The Republic, *the Greek philosopher Plato (428–347 B.C.) discusses the role of literature, especially poetry.*

"And so, Glaucon," I continued, "when you meet people who admire Homer as the educator of Greece, and who say that in social and educational matters, we should study him and model our lives on his advice, you must feel kindly towards them as good men within their limits, and you may agree with them that Homer is the best of poets and the first of tragedians. But you will know that the only poetry that should be allowed in a state is hymns to the gods and paeans in praise of good citizens; once you go beyond

Plato, often referred to as one of the greatest philosophers of all time. © (2008) Jupiterimages Corporation.

that and admit the sweet lyric or epic muse, pleasure and pain become your rulers instead of law and the principles commonly accepted as best."

Source: *Plato: The Republic.* Translated by H.D.P. Lee. Baltimore: Penguin Books, 1955.

14. A Ciceronian Survey of Greek Historians

In this passage from his treatise on oratory, the first-century B.C. *Roman orator Cicero evaluates the Greek writers of history, and notes that none of them ever achieved prominence as orators.*

Not one of us Romans seeks after eloquence, except for the purpose of a career as a lawyer and as a public speaker, whereas in Greece, the most eloquent were strangers to forensic advocacy, and applied themselves chiefly to reputable studies in general, and particularly to writing history. Indeed, even of the renowned Herodotus, who first imparted distinction to such work, we have heard that he was in no way concerned with lawsuits, and yet his eloquence is of such quality as to afford intense pleasure, to me at any rate, so far as I can comprehend what is written in Greek.

After his day, Thucydides, in my judgment, easily surpassed all others in dexterity of composition. So abounding is he in fullness of material that in the number of his ideas, he practically equals the number of his words, and furthermore, he is so exact and clear in expression that you cannot tell whether it be the narrative that gains illumination from the style, or the diction from the thought. Yet even of him, although he was a man of public affairs, we are not told that he was numbered among forensic speakers. And it is related that when writing the volumes in question, he was far away from civic life, having in fact been driven into exile, as generally happened at Athens to anyone of excellence.

He was succeeded by Philistus of Syracuse who...spent his leisure in writing history and, to my thinking, was above all else an imitator of Thucydides. Afterwards, however, from what I may call that most famous factory of rhetoricians [i.e., Athens], there arose a pair of outstanding talent in Theopompus and Ephorus, who applied themselves to historical writings at the insistence of their teacher, Isocrates. They never handled lawsuits at all.

And at length historians appeared who had begun as philosophers, first Xenophon, that notable follower of Socrates, afterwards Callisthenes, Aristotle's disciple and Alexander's friend, the latter approaching the rhetorical school in method, while his predecessor adopted a gentler kind of tone, lacking the characteristic vigor of oratory and possibly less animated, but in my view, at any rate, somewhat more pleasing. Timaeus, the most recently born of all these, but as well as I can judge, by far the best informed, the most amply endowed in wealth of material and range of thought, and a man whose very style had some polish, brought to authorship abounding eloquence, but no experience of public speaking.

Source: *Cicero: De Oratore.* Volume I. Translated by E. W. Sutton, with revisions by H. Rackham. Cambridge and London: Loeb Classical Library, 1942.

15. An Ancient Style Manual

A (likely) third-century B.C. *treatise entitled* On Style, *by an author named Demetrius, is a manual on the proper writing of prose. In the following excerpt, the author provides examples of good writing from the annals of Greek literature.*

We all remember in a special degree, and are stirred by, words that come first and the words that come last, whereas those that come between them have less effect upon us, as though they were obscured or hidden among the others. This is clearly seen in Thucydides, whose verbal dignity is almost in every instance due to the long syllables used in his rhythms. It may indeed be said that, while the stateliness of that writer has many sides, it is this marshalling of words which, alone or chiefly, secures his greatest elevation...Composition makes style impressive in the same way as a rugged word does. Instances of rugged words are "shrieking" in place of "crying," and "bursting" in place of "charging." Thucydides uses all expressions of this kind, assimilating the words to the composition, and the composition to the words.

Words should be ordered in the following way. First should be placed those that are not especially vivid; in the second or last place should come those that are distinctly so. In this way, what comes first will strike the ear as vivid, and what follows as more vivid still. Failing this, we shall seem to have lost vigor, and, so to speak, to have lapsed from strength to weakness. An illustration will be found in a passage of Plato: "when a man allows music to play upon him and to flood his soul through his ears." Here the second expression is far more vivid than the first. And farther on he says: "but when he ceases not to flood it, or even throws a spell over it, thereupon he causes it to melt and waste away." The word "waste" is more striking than the word "melt," and approaches more nearly to poetry. If Plato had reversed the order, the verb "melt," coming later, would have appeared too weak...

Homer impresses his readers greatly by his employment of words resembling inarticulate sounds, and by their novelty above all. He is not making use of existing words, but of words then coming into existence. Moreover, the creation of a fresh word on the model of words already in use is regarded as a kind of poetic gift. As a word maker, Homer seems, in fact, to resemble those who first gave things their names...

Impressiveness may result from verbal repetitions, such as those of Xenophon, who says: "the chariots rushed, some of them right through the ranks of friends, some right through the ranks of foes." Such a sentence is far more striking than if Xenophon had put it in this way: "right through the ranks both of friends and foes."...

When Sappho sings of beauty, she does so in lines that are themselves beautiful and sweet. So too when she sings of love, and springtime, and the halcyon. Every lovely word is interwoven with the texture of her poetry. And some are of her own invention.

Source: *Demetrius: On Style*. Translated by W. Rhys Roberts. London and New York: Loeb Classical Library, 1927.

16. The Frustrations and Rewards of Writing History

In the course of his book on Roman history, the Greek historian Polybius (c. 205–123 B.C.) tries to explain to his readers the difficulties faced by historians as they endeavor to create a work that is both readable and accurate, with due attention paid to chronology.

Now that I have arrived at a place that is suitable both chronologically and historically, I will shift the scene to Asia, and turning to the doings there during this same Olympiad [218 B.C.] will again confine my narrative to that field... I am perfectly aware that at the date I chose for breaking off my narrative of events in Greece, this war [in Asia] was on the point of being decided and coming to an end, but I deliberately resolved to make a break here in this history and open a fresh chapter for the following reasons. I am confident that I have provided my readers with sufficient information to prevent them from going wrong about the dates of particular events by my parallel recapitulations of general history, in which I state in what year of this Olympiad and contemporaneously with what events in Greece each episode elsewhere began and ended. But in order that my narrative may be easy to follow and clear, I think it most essential as regards this Olympiad not to interweave the histories of different countries, but to keep them as separate and distinct as possible until, upon reaching the next and subsequent Olympiads, I can begin to narrate the events of each year in chronological order. Since my plan is to write the history not of certain particular matters, but of what happened all over the world, and indeed... I have undertaken, I may say, a vaster task than any of my predecessors, it is my duty to pay particular attention to the matter of arrangement and treatment, so that both as a whole and in all its details, my work may have the quality of clarity.

I will therefore on the present occasion also go back a little,... to take some generally recognized and accepted starting point for my narrative, the most necessary thing to provide for. For the ancients, saying that the beginning is half of the whole [i.e., the importance of engaging the reader from the outset], advised that in all matters, the greatest care should be taken to make a good beginning. One may indeed confidently affirm that the beginning is not merely half of the whole, but reaches as far as the end.

How is it possible to begin a thing well without having present in one's mind the completion of the project, and without knowing its scope, its relation to other things, and the object for which one undertakes it? And again, how is it possible to sum up events properly without referring to their beginnings, and understand how and why the final solution was brought about? So we should think that beginnings not only reach half way, but reach to the end, and both writers and readers of a general history should pay the greatest attention to them. And I will attempt to do this.

I am well aware that several other writers make the same boast as I do, that they write general history and have undertaken a vaster task than any predecessor...I will avoid criticizing at length or mentioning by name any of the others, but will simply say this much, that certain writers of my own time, after giving an account of the war between Rome and Carthage in three or four pages, claim that they write universal history [while neglecting important details of that event]...But some of those who write about it, after giving a more superficial sketch of it even than those worthy citizens who jot down occasional scribblings of events on the walls of their houses, claim to have included in their work all events in Greece and abroad. This is because it is a very simple matter to engage by words in the greatest undertakings, but by no means easy to attain actual excellence in anything. Promise, therefore, is open to anyone and is the common property of all, one may say, who have nothing beyond a little audacity, while performance is rare and falls to few in this life.

I have been led into making these remarks by the arrogance of those authors who extol themselves and their own writings, and I will now return to the subject which I proposed to deal with.

Source: *Polybius: The Histories*. Volume III. Translated by W. R. Paton. London and New York: Loeb Classical Library, 1923.

ROME

17. *Cicero Argues the Case of the Importance of Literature*

One of the best expressions of Roman respect for literature is to be found, oddly enough, in the text of one of Cicero's court cases. In 62 B.C., the famous lawyer and orator defended the claim to Roman citizenship of the Greek poet Archias. In the course of his address to the jury, Cicero paid tribute to the importance of literature and scholarship to the overall strength of any city, including Rome.

You will be no doubt asking me, Gratius [the prosecutor], why I feel such an affection for this man Archias. The answer is that he provides my mind with refreshment after this din of the courts; he soothes my ears to rest when they are wearied by angry disputes. How could I find material, do you suppose, for the speeches I make every day on such a variety of subjects, unless I steeped my mind in learning? How could I endure the constant strains if I could not distract myself from them by this means? Yes, I confess that I am devoted to the study of literature. If people have buried themselves in books, if they have used nothing they have read for the benefit of their fellow citizens, if they have never displayed the fruits of such reading before the public eye, well, let them by all means be ashamed of the occupation. But why, gentlemen, should I feel any shame? Seeing that not once throughout all these years have I allowed myself to be prevented from helping anyone in the hour of need because I wanted a rest...

I cannot therefore, I submit, be justly rebuked or censured if the time which others spend in advancing their own personal affairs, taking vacations and attending games, indulging in pleasures of various kinds or even enjoying mental relaxation and bodily recreation, the time they spend on protracted parties and gambling and playing ball, proves in my case to have been taken up with returning over and over again to these literary pursuits. And I have all the more right to engage in such studies because they improve my capacity as a speaker; and this, for what it is worth, has unfailingly remained at the disposal of my friends whenever prosecutions have placed them in danger. Even if some may regard my ability as nothing very great, at least I realize the source from which the best part of it has come. For unless I had convinced myself from my earliest years, on the basis of lessons derived from all I had read, that nothing in life is really worth having except moral decency and reputable behavior, and that for their sake, all physical tortures and all perils of death and banishment must be held of little account, I should never have been able to speak up for the safety of you all in so many arduous clashes, or to endure these attacks which dissolute rogues launch against me every day. The whole of literature, philosophy, and history is full of examples which teach this lesson—but which would have been plunged into utter darkness if the written word had not been available to illuminate them. Just think of the number of vividly drawn pictures of valiant men of the past that Greek and Latin writers have preserved for our benefit, not for mere inspection only, but for imitation as well. Throughout my public activities, I have never ceased to keep these great figures before my eyes, and have modeled myself heart and soul on the contemplation of their excellence.

It might be objected that these great men, whose noble deeds have been handed down in the literary record, were not themselves by any means thoroughly well versed in the learning which I praise so highly. Certainly, it would be difficult to make a categorical assertion that they were...Nevertheless, I do also maintain that, when noble and elevated natural gifts are supplemented and shaped by the influence of theoretical knowledge, the result is then something truly remarkable and unique...[Many of the most outstanding individuals in Roman history] would certainly never have spent their time on literary studies if these had not helped them to understand what a better life could be, and how to bring that ideal into effect for themselves.

And yet let us leave aside for a moment any practical advantage that literary studies may bring. For even if their aim were pure enjoyment and nothing else, you would still, I am sure, feel obliged to agree that no other activity of the mind could possibly have such a broadening and enlightening effect. For there is no other occupation on earth which is so appropriate to every time and every age and every place. Reading stimulates the young and diverts the old, increases one's satisfaction when things are going well, and when they are going badly provides refuge and solace. It is a delight in the home; it can be fitted in with public life; throughout the night, on journeys, in the country, it is a companion which never lets me down...

A Roman wallpainting of Cicero speaking to the Senate, by nineteenth-century artist Cesare Maccari. Scala/Art Resource, NY.

We have it on eminent and learned authority that, whereas other arts need to be based upon study and rules and principles, poets depend entirely on their own inborn gifts and are stimulated by some internal force, a sort of divine spark within the depths of their own souls...Even the most barbarous of races never treated the name of poet with disrespect. How imperative, therefore, it is that you yourselves, with all your noble culture should regard it as holy indeed! The very rocks and deserts echo the poet's song. Many is the time when ferocious beasts have been enchanted and arrested in their tracks as these strains come to their ears. Shall we, then, who have been nurtured on everything that is fine, remain unmoved at a poet's voice?...

Archias is a Greek poet. But it would be entirely wrong to suppose that Greek poetry ranks lower than Latin in value. For Greek literature is read in almost every country in the world, whereas Latin is understood only within its own boundaries...Our deeds, it is true, extend to all the regions of the earth. But the effect of this should be to inspire us with the determination that every country where the strong arm of Rome has carried its weapons should also be given an opportunity to learn of our illustrious achievements. For literary commemoration is a most potent factor in enhancing a country's prestige. And to those who risk their lives for the sake of glory, such literature is a vigorous incentive, stimulating them to risk fearful perils and perform noble endeavors.

Source: *Cicero's Pro Archia Poeta,* from *Selected Political Speeches of Cicero.* Translated by Michael Grant. New York: Penguin Books, 1977. Reproduced by permission of Penguin Books Ltd.

18. Another Case for Literature

As an architect, Vitruvius (fl. first century B.C.) might not seem to be a likely source when it comes to praising literature, but in Book IX of his treatise on architecture, he does exactly that.

Famous athletes who win victories at Olympia, Corinth, and Nemea, have been assigned such great distinctions by the ancestors of the Greeks that they not only receive praise publicly at the games, as they stand with palm and crown, but also, when they go back victorious to their own people, they ride triumphantly with their four-horse chariots into their native cities, and enjoy a pension for life from the state. When I observe this, I am surprised that similar or even greater distinctions are not granted to those authors who confer infinite benefits to mankind throughout the ages. This is the more worthy of note, in that while athletes make their own bodies stronger, authors not only cultivate their own perceptions, but by the information in their books, they prepare the minds of all to acquire knowledge, and thus stimulate their talents.

In what respect could Milo of Croton benefit mankind because he was undefeated [in Olympic wrestling] or others who won victories of the same kind, except that in their lifetime they enjoyed fame among their fellow citizens? But the daily teachings of Pythagoras, Democritus, Plato, Aristotle and other thinkers, elaborated as they were by unbroken application, furnish ever-fresh and flowering harvests, not only to their fellow citizens, but also to all mankind. Those who from the earliest years are fulfilled with an abundance of knowledge acquire the best habits of thought, institute civilized manners, equal rights, laws without which no state can be secure. Since, therefore, such advantages have been conferred upon individuals and communities by wise writers, not only do I think that palms and crowns should be awarded to them, but that triumphs also should be decreed and that they should be canonized in the mansions of the gods.

Source: *Vitruvius: On Architecture*. Volume II. Translated by Frank Granger. Cambridge and London: Loeb Classical Library, 1934.

Health and Medicine

In some ways, ancient ideas about health and medicine seem startlingly modern, and, in other ways, hopelessly naïve. The documents in this section offer a mixture of both kinds of attitudes.

Perhaps the most famous medical writing from ancient times is the physician's code of ethics, the Hippocratic Oath (Document 23). Hippocrates and his associates gathered data from many case studies (Document 24) as they strove to enlarge their understanding of disease and how to treat it. In a similar vein, the *Edwin Smith Surgical Papyrus* from ancient Egypt, the earliest known scientific document in the history of the Western world, reads like a millennia-old medical textbook (Document 22). Other Egyptian medical practices, including the prohibition of payments of fees by patients to their physicians (who received their financial support from the government) are recounted in Document 21. Several clauses in the Code of Hammurabi (Document 19) specify penalties for medical malpractice.

The classic Chinese view of medicine, or of the entire universe for that matter, was the principle of Yin and Yang, co-existing opposite forces of nature. The way in which this principle applied to medicine is described in the *Yellow Emperor's Classic of Medicine* (Document 20).

Most terrifying of all may have been the contagious plagues for which there was neither known cause nor effective treatment. One such plague swept through Athens at the outset of the Peloponnesian War around 430 B.C. (Document 26). Less lethal, but still bothersome, was the common cold, manifested by coughing spells. Cures are suggested in Document 29. In some cases, gold may have had curative properties (Document 30). Or, a patient might hope for a miraculous healing (Document 25).

The hypochondriacal Roman emperor *Augustus* (63 B.C.-14 A.D.) suffered throughout his life from various nagging illnesses, but still managed to live to the age of 76 (Document 31). Perhaps he drank too much water from lead cups or jugs, or water that had flowed into his residences through lead pipes. Interestingly, the Romans knew of the dangerous properties of lead, as the architect Vitruvius explains in Document 32. The best way, then as now, to avoid illness is to maintain a healthy lifestyle, as suggested by the Roman medical writer Celsus, author of a history of medicine (Documents 27 and 28).

SUMERIA

19. Medical Strictures from the Code of Hammurabi

The following clauses from the eighteenth-century B.C. Code of Hammurabi pertain to medical practice, and, in some cases, malpractice.

215. If a physician makes a large incision with an operating knife and cures it, or if he opens a tumor [over the eye] with an operating knife, and saves the eye, he shall receive ten shekels in money.

216. If the patient is a freed man, he receives five shekels.

217. If he is the slave of someone, his owner shall give the physician two shekels.

218. If a physician makes a large incision with the operating knife, and kills the patient, or opens a tumor with the operating knife, and cuts out the eye, his hands shall be cut off.

219. If a physician makes a large incision in the slave of a freed man, and kills him, he shall replace the slave with another slave.

220. If he had opened a tumor with the operating knife, and put out his eye, he shall pay half his value.

Source: *The Code of Hammurabi.* Translated by L. W. King. The Avalon Project at Yale Law School: http://www.yale.edu/lawweb/avalon/medieval/hamcode.htm.

CHINA

20. The Principle of Yin and Yang

The Yellow Emperor's Classic of Medicine *serves as the basis for medical knowledge and practice in ancient China. Authorship is unknown. Tradition states that the document was written in the third millennium B.C. by a legendary figure known only as the Yellow Emperor. Although it may have had its origins in the earliest days of ancient China, the work probably appeared in written form no earlier than the Han Dynasty (c. 206 B.C.–A.D. 220).*

The Yellow Emperor said: "The principle of Yin and Yang is the foundation of the entire universe. It underlies everything in creation. It brings about the development of parenthood; it is the root and source of life and death; it is found within the temples of the gods. In order to treat and cure diseases, one must search for their origins.

"Heaven was created by the concentration of Yang, the force of light; Earth was created by Yin, the force of darkness. Yang stands for peace and serenity; Yin stands for confusion and turmoil. Yang stands for destruction; Yin stands for conservation. Yang brings about disintegration; Yin gives shape to things...

"The pure and lucid element of light is manifested in the upper orifices, and the turbid element of darkness is manifested in the lower orifices. Yang, the element of light, originates in the pores. Yin, the element of darkness, moves within the five viscera. Yang, the lucid force of light, truly is represented by the four extremities; and Yin, the turbid force of darkness, stores the power of the six treasures of nature. Water is an embodiment of Yin, as fire is an embodiment of Yang. Yang creates the air, while Yin creates the senses, which belong to the physical body. When the physical body dies, the spirit is restored to the air, its natural environment. The spirit receives its nourishment through the air, and the body receives its nourishment through the senses...

"If Yang is overly powerful, then Yin may be too weak. If Yin is particularly strong, then Yang is apt to be defective. If the male force is overwhelming, then there will be excessive heat. If the female force is overwhelming, then there will be excessive cold. Exposure to repeated and severe cold will lead to fever. Exposure to repeated and severe heat will induce chills. Cold injures the body, while heat injures the spirit. When the spirit is hurt, severe pain will ensue. When the body is hurt, there will be swelling. Thus, when severe pain occurs first and swelling comes on later, one may infer that a disharmony in the spirit has done harm to the body. Likewise, when swelling appears first and severe pain is felt later on, one can say that a dysfunction in the body has injured the spirit... Yin and Yang should be respected to an equal extent."...

The Yellow Emperor asked: "Is there any alternative to the law of Yin and Yang?"

Ch'i Po answered: "When Yang is the stronger, the body is hot, the pores are closed, and people begin to pant. They become boisterous and coarse and do not perspire. They become feverish, their mouths are dry and sore, their stomachs feel tight, and they die of constipation. When Yang is the stronger, people can endure winter, but not summer. When Yin is the stronger, the body is cold and covered with perspiration. People realize they are ill; they tremble and feel chilly. When they feel chilled, their spirits become rebellious. Their stomachs can no longer digest food and they die. When Yin is the stronger, people can endure summer but not winter. Thus Yin and Yang alternate. Their ebbs and surges vary, and so does the character of their diseases."...

The Yellow Emperor asked: "Can anything be done to harmonize and adjust these two principles of nature?"

Ch'i Po answered: "If one has the ability to know the seven injuries and the eight advantages, one can bring the two principles into harmony. If one does not know how to use this knowledge, his life will be doomed to early decay. By the age of 40, the Yin force in the body has been reduced to one-half of its natural vigor, and an individual's youthful prowess has deteriorated. By the age of 50, the body has grown heavy. The ears no longer hear well. The eyes no longer see clearly. By the age of 60, the life-producing power of Yin has declined to a very low level...

"Those who seek wisdom beyond the natural limits will retain good hearing and clear vision. Their bodies will remain light and strong. Although they grow old in years, they will stay able-bodied and vigorous and be capable of governing to great advantage. For this reason the ancient sages did not rush into the affairs of the world. In their pleasures and joys, they were dignified and tranquil. They did what they thought best and did not bend their will or ambition to the achievement of empty ends. Thus their allotted span of life was without limit, like that of Heaven and Earth. This is the way the ancient sages controlled and conducted themselves...

"By observing myself, I learn about others, and their diseases become apparent to me. By observing the external symptoms, I gather knowledge about the internal diseases. One should watch for things out of the ordinary. One should observe minute and trifling things, and treat them as if they were big and important. When they are treated, the danger they pose will be dissipated. Experts in examining patients judge their general appearance; they feel their pulse and determine whether it is Yin or Yang that causes the disease...To determine whether Yin or Yang predominates, one must be able to distinguish a light pulse of low tension from a hard, pounding one. With a disease of Yang, Yin predominates. With a disease of Yin, Yang predominates. When one is filled with vigor and strength, Yin and Yang are in proper harmony."

Source: Reprinted with permission of The Free Press, a division of Simon & Schuster Adult Publishing Group, from *Chinese Civilization and Society: A Sourcebook*, edited by Patricia Buckley Ebrey. Copyright © 1981 by The Free Press. All rights reserved.

EGYPT

21. Egyptian Medical Practices

The first-century B.C. *Greek historian Diodorus Siculus describes Egyptian medical practices in the following excerpt from his writings.*

In order to prevent sicknesses, [the Egyptians] look after the health of their bodies by means of drenches, fastings, and emetics, sometimes every day and sometimes at intervals of three or four days. They say that the larger part of the food taken into the body is superfluous, and it is from this superfluous part that diseases arise. Consequently, the treatment just mentioned, by removing the beginnings of disease, would be most likely to produce health.

On their military campaigns and their journeys in the country, they all receive treatment without the payment of any private fee, because the physicians' salaries come from public funds, and they administer their treatments in accordance with a written law which was composed in ancient times by many famous physicians. If they follow the rules of this law as they read them in the sacred book and yet are unable to save their patient, they are absolved from any charge and go unpunished. However, if they go contrary to the law's prescriptions in any respect, they must submit to a trial, with death as the penalty, the lawgiver believing that few physicians would ever show themselves wiser than the method of treatment which had been closely followed for a long period and had been originally prescribed by the ablest practitioners.

Source: *Diodorus of Sicily.* Volume I. Translated by C. H. Oldfather. London and Cambridge: Loeb Classical Library, 1933.

22. Treatments for Fractured Skulls and Broken Collarbones

The earliest known scientific document in the history of the Western world is the Edwin Smith Surgical Papyrus, *written sometime during the Old Kingdom in Egypt. The following excerpts from the* Papyrus *deal with treating head wounds and broken clavicles.*

Case 1: A wound in the head penetrating to the bone.

Examination: If you examine a man having a wound in his head, penetrating to the bone of his skull, but not having a gash, you should palpate the wound. Should you find his skull uninjured, not having a perforation, a split, or a smash in it:

Diagnosis: You should say regarding him: "One having a wound in his head, while his wound does not have two lips [...] nor a gash, although it penetrates to the bone of his head. An ailment which I will treat."

Treatment: You should bind it with fresh meat the first day and treat afterward with grease, honey, and lint every day until he recovers...

Case 4: A gaping wound in the head penetrating to the bone and splitting the skull.

Examination: If you examine a man having a gaping wound in his head, penetrating to the bone, and splitting his skull, you should palpate his wound. Should you find something disturbing therein under your fingers, and he shudders exceedingly, while the swelling which is over it protrudes, he discharges blood from both his nostrils and from both his ears, he suffers with stiffness in his neck, so that he is unable to look at his two shoulders and his chest:

Diagnosis: You should say regarding him: "One having a gaping wound in his head, penetrating to the bone, and splitting his skull; while he discharges blood from both his nostrils and from both his ears, and he suffers with stiffness in his neck. An ailment with which I will contend."

Treatment: When you find that the skull of that man is split, you should not bind him, but moor him at his mooring stakes [i.e., put him on his customary diet] until the period of his injury passes by. His treatment is sitting. Make for him two supports of brick, until you know he has reached a decisive point. You should apply grease to his head, and soften his neck and both his shoulders. You should do likewise for every man whom you find having a split skull...

Case 35: A fracture of the clavicle.

Examination: If you examine a man having a break in his collarbone, and you should find his collarbone short and separated from its fellow:

Diagnosis: You should say concerning him: "One having a break in his collarbone. An ailment which I will treat."

Treatment: You should place him prostrate on his back, with something folded between his two shoulder blades. You should spread out with his two shoulders in order to stretch apart his collarbone until that break falls into its place. You should make for him two splints of linen, and you should apply one of them both on the inside of his upper arm and the other on the under side of his upper arm. You should bind it...and treat it afterward with honey every day, until he recovers.

Source: *Readings in Ancient History From Gilgamesh to Diocletian.* Bailkey, Nels, *Readings in Ancient History.* Copyright © 1969 by Houghton Mifflin Company. Reprinted with permission.

GREECE

23. The Hippocratic Oath

Widely believed to have been written by the Greek physician Hippocrates in the fourth century B.C., *the Hippocratic Oath, the oath traditionally taken by physicians as a promise of ethical practice, is perhaps the most renowned medical document from the ancient world.*

I swear by Apollo Physician, by Asclepius, by Health, by Panacea and by all the gods and goddesses, making them my witnesses, that I will carry out, according to my ability and judgment, this oath and this indenture. To hold my teacher in this art equal to my own parents; to make him partner in my livelihood; when he is in need of money, to share mine with him; to consider his family as my own brothers, and to teach them this art, if they want to learn it, without fee or indenture; to impart precept, oral instruction, and all other instruction to my own sons, the sons of my teacher, and to indentured pupils who have taken the physician's oath, but to nobody else. I will use treatment to help the sick according to my ability and judgment, but never with a view to injury and wrongdoing. Neither will I administer a poison to anybody when asked to do so, nor will I suggest such a course. Similarly, I will not give to a woman a device to cause abortion. But I will keep pure and holy both my life and my art. I will not use the knife, not even on sufferers from stone, but I will give place to such as are craftsmen therein. Into whatever houses I enter, I will enter to help the sick, and I will abstain from all intentional wrongdoing and harm, especially from abusing the bodies of man or woman, slave or free. And whatever I will see or hear in the course of my profession, as well as outside my profession in my dealings with others, if it be what should not be disseminated, I will never divulge, holding such things to be holy secrets. Now if I carry out this oath, and do not break it, may I gain forever a reputation from all others for my life and for my art; but if I transgress it and break my oath, may the opposite befall me.

Some additional excerpts from the Hippocratic corpus:

And I believe that of all the powers, none hold less sway in the body than cold and heat. My reasons are these. So long as the hot and cold in the body are mixed up together, they cause no pain. For the hot is tempered and moderated by the cold, and the cold by the hot. But when either is entirely separated from the other, then it causes pain. And at that season, when cold comes upon a man and causes him some pain, for that very reason internal heat first is present quickly and spontaneously, without needing any help or preparation. The result is the same, whether the patient is diseased or in good health. For instance, if a man in health will cool his body in winter, either by a cold bath, or in any other way, the more he cools it (provided that his body is not entirely frozen) the more he becomes hotter than before when he puts his clothes on and enters his shelter. Again, if he will make himself thoroughly hot by means of either a hot bath or a large fire, and afterwards wear the same clothes and stay in the same place as he did when chilled, he feels far colder and besides more shivery than before. Or if a man fans himself because of the stifling heat and makes coolness for himself, on ceasing to do this in this way, he will feel ten times the stifling heat felt by one who does nothing of the sort.

Now the following is much stronger evidence still. All who go afoot through snow or great cold, and become over-chilled in feet, hands or head, suffer at night very severely from burning and tingling when they come into a warm place and wrap up. In some cases, blisters arise like those caused by burning in fire. But it is not until they are warmed that they experience these symptoms. So ready is cold to pass into heat, and heat into cold. I could give a multitude of other proofs. But in the case of sick people, is it not those who have suffered from shivering in whom breaks out the most acute fever? And not only is it not powerful, but after awhile does it not subside, generally without doing harm all the time it remains, hot as it is? And passing through all the body it ends in most cases in the feet, where the shivering and chill were the most violent and lasted unusually long. Again, when the fever disappears with the breaking out of the perspiration, it cools the patient, so that he is far colder than if he had never been attacked at all. What important or serious consequence, therefore, could come from that thing on which quickly supervenes in this way its exact opposite, spontaneously annulling its effect? Or what need has it of elaborate treatment?

Source: *Hippocrates*. Translated by W.H.S. Jones. Cambridge and London: Loeb Classical Library, 1923.

24. Case Studies from the Writings of Hippocrates

This section of the work entitled Epidemics *by the fourth-century* B.C. *Greek physician Hippocrates contains a number of case studies.*

Book I, Case 10. The man of Clazomenae, who lay sick by the well of Phrynichides, was seized with fever. Pain at the beginning in head, neck, and loins, followed immediately by deafness. No sleep; seized with acute fever; hypochondrium swollen, but not very much; distension; tongue dry.

Fourth day. Delirium at night.

Fifth day. Painful.

Sixth day. All symptoms exacerbated.

About the eleventh day, slight improvement. From the beginning to the fourteenth day, there were from the bowels thin discharges, copious, of a watery biliousness; they were well supported by the patient. Then the bowels were constipated. Urine throughout thin, but of good color. It had much cloud spread through it, which did not settle in a sediment. About the sixteenth day, the urine was a little thicker, and had a slight sediment. The patient became a little easier, and was more rational.

Seventeenth day. Urine thin again; painful swelling by both ears. No sleep; wandering; pain in the legs.

Twentieth day. A crisis left the patient free from fever; no sweating; quite rational. About the twenty-seventh day, violent pain in the right hip, which quickly ceased. The swellings by the ears neither subsided nor suppurated, but continued painful. About the thirty-first day, diarrhea with copious, watery discharges and signs of dysentery. Urine thick; the swellings by the ears subsided.

Fortieth day. Pain in the right eye; sight rather impaired; recovery.

Book III, Case 10. In Abdera, Nicodemus after sexual indulgence and drunkenness was seized with fever. At the beginning, he had nausea and heart pain; thirst; tongue parched; urine thin and black.

Second day. The fever increased; shivering; nausea; no sleep; bilious yellow vomits; urine the same; a quiet night; sleep.

Third day. All symptoms less severe; relief. But about sunset, he was again somewhat uncomfortable; painful night.

Fourth day. Rigor; much fever; pains everywhere; urine thin, with floating substance in it; the night, on the other hand, was quiet.

Fifth day. All symptoms present, but relieved.

Sixth day. Same pains everywhere; substance floating in urine; much delirium.

Seventh day. Relief.

Eighth day. All the other symptoms less severe.

Tenth day and following days. The pains were present, but all less severe. The exacerbations and the pains in the case of this patient tended throughout to occur on the even days.

Twentieth day. Urine white, having consistency; no sediment on standing. Copious sweating; seemed to lose his fever, but towards evening, grew hot again, with pains in the same parts; shivering; thirst; slight delirium.

Twenty-fourth day. Much white urine, with much sediment. Hot sweating all over; the fever passed away in a crisis.

Source: *Hippocrates.* Translated by W.H.S. Jones. Cambridge and London: Loeb Classical Library, 1923.

Hippocrates, the "father of medicine," in recognition of his lasting contributions to the field, as the founder of the Hippocratic school of medicine. © (2008) Jupiterimages Corporation.

25. A Miraculous Healing

Construction accidents were probably fairly common in the ancient world. In the following passage, the Greek biographer Plutarch relates a story about the miraculous recovery of a worker who took a nasty spill during the construction of the Propylaea (gates to the Athenian Acropolis) in the fifth century B.C.

The Propylaea, or portals of the Acropolis, of which Mnesicles was the architect, were finished in the space of five years. While they were being built, a miraculous incident took place, which suggested that the goddess Athena herself, so far from standing aloof, was taking a hand and helping to complete the work. One of the workmen, the most active and energetic among them, slipped and fell from a great height.

He lay for some time severely injured, and the doctors could hold out no hope that he would recover. Pericles was greatly distressed at this, but the goddess appeared to him in a dream and ordered a course of treatment, which he applied, with the result that the man was easily and quickly healed. It was to commemorate this that Pericles set up the bronze statue of Athena the Healer near the altar dedicated to that goddess.

Source: *The Rise and Fall of Athens: Nine Greek Lives by Plutarch.* Translated by Ian Scott-Kilvert. New York: Penguin Books, 1960. Reproduced by permission of Penguin Books Ltd.

26. The Great Plague of Athens

In the early days of the Peloponnesian War (c. 430 B.C.*), a deadly plague swept through Athens; its cause and cure were unknown. One of its victims was the famous orator and statesman* Pericles. *The Greek historian Thucydides, in this excerpt from his history of the war, describes the symptoms of the disease.*

There seemed to be no reason for the attacks. People in perfect health suddenly began to have burning feelings in the head. Their eyes became red and inflamed; inside their mouths, there was bleeding from the throat and tongue, and the breath became unnatural and unpleasant. The next symptoms were sneezing and hoarseness of voice, and before long the pain settled on the chest and was accompanied by coughing. Next the stomach was affected with stomach aches and with vomitings of every kind of bile that has been given a name by the medical profession...In most cases, there were attacks of ineffectual retching, producing violent spasms...Inside there was a feeling of burning, so that people could not bear the touch even of the lightest linen clothing, but wanted to be completely naked, and indeed most of all would have liked to plunge into cold water. Many of the sick who were uncared for actually did so, plunging into the water tanks in an effort to relieve a thirst which was unquenchable, for it was just the same with them whether they drank much or little. Then all the time they were afflicted with insomnia, and the desperate feeling of not being able to keep still.

Source: *History of the Peloponnesian War by Thucydides,* translated by Rex Warner, with an introduction and notes by M. I. Finley. Penguin Classics 1954, revised edition 1972. Translation copyright © Rex Warner, 1954. Introduction and Appendices copyright © M. I. Finley, 1972. Reproduced by permission of Penguin Books Ltd. and Curtis Brown Group, Ltd., London, on behalf of the Estate of Rex Brown.

ROME

27. A History of Ancient Medicine

The name most often associated with the history and practice of medicine in ancient Rome is Celsus, to whom the work On Medicine *is attributed. Little is known of his life; he may have been born around 25* B.C. *In this passage from the introductory section of his work, Celsus provides a long explication of the history of ancient medicine.*

Just as agriculture promises nourishment to healthy bodies, so does the Art of Medicine promise health to the sick. Nowhere is this Art lacking, for the most uncivilized nations have had knowledge of herbs, and other things to hand for the aiding of wounds and diseases. This Art, however, has been cultivated among the Greeks much more than in other nations—not, however, even among them from their first beginnings, but only for a few generations before ours. Hence, Aesculapius is celebrated as the most ancient authority, and because he cultivated this science, as yet rude and vulgar, with a little more than common refinement, he was numbered among the gods. After him, his two sons, Podalirius and Machaon, ... gave no inconsiderable help to their comrades [in the Trojan War]. Homer stated, however, not that they gave any aid in the pestilence or in the various sorts of diseases, but only that they relieved wounds by the knife and by medicaments. Hence it appears that by them those parts only of the Art were attempted, and that they were the oldest. From the same author, it can be learned that diseases were then ascribed to the anger of the immortal gods, and from them, help used to be sought. And it is probable that with no aids against bad health, nonetheless health was generally good because of good habits, which neither indolence more luxury had vitiated, since it is these two which have afflicted the bodies of human beings, first in Greece, and later among us. And hence this complex Art of Medicine, not needed in former times, nor among other nations even now, scarcely protracts the lives of a few of us to the verge of old age ...

At first, the science of healing was held to be a part of philosophy, so that treatment of disease and contemplation of the nature of things began through the same authorities ... Hence, we find that many who professed philosophy became expert in medicine, the most famous being Pythagoras, Empedocles and Democritus. But it was, as some believe, a student of the last, Hippocrates of Cos, a man first and foremost worthy to be remembered, notable both for professional skill and for eloquence, who separated this branch of learning from the study of philosophy.

Source: *Celsus: De Medicina.* Translated by W. G. Spencer. London and Cambridge: Loeb Classical Library, 1935.

28. Health Maintenance

In this excerpt from Book I of On Medicine, *the Roman physician Celsus offers some thoughts about how to maintain good health.*

A person in health, who is both vigorous and his own master, should be under no obligatory rules, and have no need, either for a medical attendant, or for a rubber and anointer. His kind of life should afford him variety; he should sometimes be in the country, sometimes in town, and more often on the farm. He should sail, hunt, rest sometimes, but more often exercise. For while inaction weakens the body, work strengthens it; the former brings on premature old age, whereas the latter prolongs youth.

It is well also at times to go to the bath, and at times to make use of cold waters; to sometimes undergo anointment with oils, sometimes to neglect that same; to avoid no kind of food in common use; to attend at times a banquet, and at other times to avoid banquets; to eat more than sufficient at one time, at another, no more; to eat food twice rather than once a day, and always as much as one wants, provided one digests it...

People in poor health, however, among whom are a large portion of townspeople, and almost all those who are fond of reading and studying, need to take greater precautions, so that a health care regimen may re-establish what the character of their constitution or of their study detracts. Anyone, therefore, of these who has digested well may safely arise early; if too little, he must go to sleep again; he who has not digested, should lie up altogether, and neither work, nor exercise, nor attend to business...

He should also live in a house that is light and airy in summer, sunny in winter, and avoid the midday sun, the morning and evening chill, and also exhalations from rivers and marshes. And he should not often go outside when the sky is cloudy but when the sun may break through... lest he should be affected alternately by cold and heat...

On waking, one should lie still for while, then, except in the winter, bathe the face freely with cold water. When the days are long, a nap should be taken before the midday meal, when short, after it. In winter, it is best to rest in bed the whole night long. If there must be study by lamplight, it should not be done immediately after eating, but after digestion. He who has been engaged in business affairs during the day... ought to reserve some portion of the day for the care of the body. The primary care in this respect is exercise, which should always precede eating...

Useful exercises are: reading aloud, drill, handball, running, walking. But walking is not by any means most useful on the level, since walking up and down hills varies the movement of the body...It is better to walk in the open air rather than under cover, better, when the head allows it, in the sun than in the shade, better under the shade of a wall or of trees than under a roof; better a straight than a winding walk. But the exercise ought to come to an end with sweating, or at any rate fatigue, which should be well this side of exhaustion...The proper sequel to exercise is: at times an anointing, whether in the sun or in front of a fire; at times a bath, which should be in a chamber as lofty, well lighted, and spacious as possible...There is need of a short rest afterwards.

Source: *Celsus: De Medicina*. Translated by W. G. Spencer. London and Cambridge: Loeb Classical Library, 1935.

29. Cures for the Common Cough

In this passage from Book IV of On Medicine, *the Roman physician Celsus suggests some cures for coughing.*

Coughing is generally caused by ulceration of the throat. This is incurred in many ways, and so, when the throat is healed, the cough is ended. Nevertheless, at times cough is a trouble by itself, and when it has become chronic, is difficult to get rid of. Sometimes the cough is dry, sometimes it excites phlegm. Hyssop should be taken every other day; the patient should run while holding the breath, but not where there is dust. He should practice reading loudly, which may at first be impeded by the cough, but later overcomes it. Next, walking, and then manual exercises also, and the chest should be rubbed for a long while. After such exercises, he should eat three ounces of very juicy figs, cooked over charcoal. Besides the above, when the cough is moist, smart rubbings with some kind of heating substance are good, provided that the head, too, is briskly rubbed when dry. In addition, cups are applied to the chest, mustard put on the outside over the throat until there is slight excoriation, and a drink taken, composed of mint, almonds, and starch. First of all, dry bread should be eaten, and then any kind of bland food. But if the cough is dry and very troublesome, it is relieved by taking a cup of dry wine, provided that this is done only three or four times at rather long intervals. Further, there is need to swallow a little of the best laser [gum resin], to take juice of leeks or horehound, to such a squill, to sip vinegar of squills, or at any rate sharp vinegar, or two cupfuls of wine with a bruised clove of garlic. In every case of cough, it is useful to travel, take a long sea voyage, live at the seaside, swim, sometimes to eat bland food, such as mallows or nettle-tops, sometimes bitter food; milk cooked with garlic; gruels to which laser has been added, or in which leeks have been boiled to pieces; a raw egg to which sulphur has been added; at first warm water to drink, then, in turn, one day water, the next day wine.

Source: *Celsus: De Medicina.* Translated by W. G. Spencer. London and Cambridge: Loeb Classical Library, 1935.

30. *The Medicinal Properties of Gold*

Gold is generally not thought of in terms of its usefulness as a cure for various physical ailments, but in this excerpt the first-century A.D. Roman writer Pliny the Elder offers some examples to the contrary.

Gold is effective as a remedy in a variety of ways, and is used as an amulet for wounded people and for infants, to render less harmful poisonous charms that may be directed against them... As a remedy, it is smeared on, then washed off and sprinkled on the persons you wish to cure. Gold is also heated twice its weight of salt, and three times its weight of copper pyrites, and again with two portions of salt and one of the stone they call *schiston,* "splitable." Treated in this way, it draws poison out; when the other substances have been burned up with it in an earthenware crucible, it remains pure and uncorrupted itself. The ash remaining is kept in an earthenware jar, and eruptions on the face may well be cleansed away by being smeared with this lotion from the jar. It also cures fistulas and...hemorrhoids. With the addition of ground pumice stone, it relieves putrid and foul smelling sores, while boiled down in honey and git [member of the buttercup family], and applied as a liniment to the navel, it acts as a mild laxative. According to Marcus Varro, gold is a cure for warts.

Source: *Pliny: Natural History.* Volume IX. Translated by H. Rackham. Cambridge and London: Loeb Classical Library, 1952.

31. The Ills of the Emperor Augustus

The Roman emperor Augustus (63 B.C.-A.D. 14), who may have been a borderline hypochondriac, suffered from a number of ailments, as the biographer Suetonius (A.D. c. 70–c. 140) relates in this excerpt from his biography of the emperor.

He was not very strong in his left hip, thigh and leg, and even limped slightly at times. But he strengthened them by treatment with sand and reeds [apparently some sort of topical application]. He sometimes found the forefinger of his right hand so weak, when it was numb and shrunken with the cold, that he could hardly use it for writing…He complained of his bladder, too, and was relieved of the pain only after passing stones in his urine.

In the course of his life, he suffered from several severe and dangerous illnesses, especially after the subjugation of Cantabria [23 B.C.], when he was in such a desperate plight from abscesses of the liver that he was forced to submit to an unprecedented and hazardous course of treatment. Since hot fomentations gave him no relief, he was led by the advice of his physician, Antonius Musa, to try cold ones. He also experienced some disorders which recurred every year at definite times. He was commonly ailing just before his birthday, and at the beginning of spring, he was troubled with an enlargement of the diaphragm, and when the wind was from the south, with catarrh. Hence, his constitution was so weakened that he could not readily endure either cold or heat.

Source: *Suetonius.* Volume I. Translated by John C. Rolfe. Cambridge and London: Loeb Classical Library, 1913.

32. Don't Drink the Water (If It Comes Via Lead Pipes)

The ancient Romans knew that lead water pipes and drinking cups could be dangerous to one's health, as the first-century B.C. architect Vitruvius points out in this excerpt from his writings.

Water supplied by earthenware pipes has these advantages. First, if any fault occurs in the work, anybody can repair it. Also, water is much more wholesome from earthenware pipes than from lead pipes. It seems to be made injurious by lead, because white lead is produced by it, and this is said to be harmful to the human body. Thus, if what is produced by anything is injurious, it is not doubtful that the thing is not wholesome in itself.

We can take examples by the workers in lead who have complexions affected by pallor. For when, in casting, the lead receives the current of air, the fumes from it occupy the members of the body, and burning them, rob the limbs of the virtues of the blood. Therefore, it seems that water should not be brought in lead pipes if we desire to have it healthy for drinking. Our daily meals may show that the flavor from earthenware pipes is better, because everybody, even when they pile up their dining tables with silver vessels, for all that, uses earthenware to preserve the flavor of water.

Source: *Vitruvius: On Architecture*. Volume II. Translated by Frank Granger. Cambridge and London: Loeb Classical Library, 1934.

Oratory

Well-honed oratorical skills were a sine qua non for ancient political, military, and religious leaders, just as for their counterparts in the modern world, whether in public settings (Document 33), or in the courtroom (Document 34). Accomplished Greek orators like *Pericles* and *Demosthenes* obviously understood the keys to oratorical success (Document 35), but philosophers too, like *Socrates*, could expound upon the essentials of effective oratory (Document 36). It is not surprising that the name of Demosthenes often surfaces when the subject of Greek oratory is discussed (Document 38), nor is it unusual for his name to be linked to the greatest Roman orator, Cicero (Document 37). Cicero wrote several detailed treatises about the art of oratory (Document 40), and yet the entire subject could be summed up in just a few words: "instruct, delight, and move," the orator's three goals (Document 42).

ISRAEL

33. Moses Uses the Power of Oratory to Avoid a Stoning

When Moses led the Jewish people out of bondage in Egypt, the journey turned out to be long and difficult, with many hardships. At one point, the Israelites were so incensed with their condition, and what they viewed as Moses's failure of leadership, that they were ready to stone him. It took all of Moses's powers of oratory to prevent that from happening, as the first-century A.D. Jewish historian Josephus relates in this passage from his book Jewish Antiquities.

They viewed their general [Moses] with indignation and were eager to stone him, as the man answerable for their instant distress.

But he, before this mob so excited and embittered against him, confident in God and in the consciousness of his own care for his countrymen, advanced into their midst and, as they clamored upon him and still held the stones in their hands, he, with that winning presence of his and that extraordinary influence in addressing a crowd, began to pacify their wrath. He exhorted them not, with present discomforts engrossing all their thoughts, to forget the benefits of the past, nor because they suffered now to banish from their minds the favors and bounties, so great and unlooked for, which they had received from God. Rather, they ought to expect relief also from their present straits to come from God's solicitude, for it was probably to test their manhood, to see what fortitude they possessed, what memory of past services, and whether their thoughts would not revert to those services because of the troubles now in their path, that He was testing them with these trials of the moment. But now they were convicted of failure, both in endurance and in recollection of benefits received, by showing at once such contempt of God and of His purpose, in accordance with which they had left Egypt, and such demeanor towards himself, God's minister, although he had never proved false to them in anything that he had said, or in any order that he had given them at God's command.

He then enumerated everything, how the Egyptians had been destroyed in attempting to detain them by force in opposition to the will of God, how the same river had for those become bloody and undrinkable while remaining for themselves drinkable and sweet, how through the waters of the sea retiring far before them they had departed by a new road, finding in it salvation for themselves while seeing their enemies perish, how, when they lacked arms, God had abundantly provided them even with these. He further recounted all the other occasions on which, when they seemed on the verge of destruction, God had delivered them by ways unlooked for, such as lay within His power.

So they should not despair even now of His providence, but should await it without anger, not thinking that His help was late in coming, even if it did not come immediately and before they had some experience of discomfort, but rather believing that it was not from negligence that God delayed in this way, but to test their manhood and their delight in liberty...He added that, if he feared anything, it was not so much for his own safety—for it would be no misfortune to him to be unjustly done to death—as for them, lest in flinging those stones at him they should be thought to be pronouncing sentence upon God. Thus he calmed them, restraining that impulse to stone him, and moving them to repent of their intended action.

Source: *Josephus: Jewish Antiquities.* Volume IV. Translated by H. St. J. Thackeray. Cambridge and London: Loeb Classical Library, 1930.

EGYPT

34. Courtroom Oratory

The maxims of the twenty-fourth-century B.C. vizier Ptah-hotep provide advice and information about a wide variety of topics. In the following excerpt, the vizier advises his son, Ptah-hotep the Younger, on courtroom oratory.

The beginning of the wise maxims spoken by...the Vizier Ptahhotep, to teach the ignorant about knowledge and about the principles of good conduct, things such as are profitable to him who will listen, but a source of sorrow to him who disregards them. Thus he spoke to his son, Ptahhotep the Younger:

Do not be haughty because of your knowledge
But take counsel with the unlearned man as well as with the learned,

For no one has ever attained perfection of competence,
And there is no craftsman who has acquired (full) mastery.
Good advice is rarer than emeralds,
But yet it may be found even among women at the grindstones.
If you come up against an aggressive adversary (in court),
One who has influence and is more excellent than you,
Lower your arms and bend your back,
For if you stand up to him, he will not give in to you.
By not opposing him in his vehemence.
The result will be that he will be called boorish,
And your control of temper will have equaled his babble.
If you come up against an aggressive adversary,
Your equal, one who is of your own social standing,
You will prove yourself more upright than he by remaining silent,
While he speaks vengefully.
The deliberation by the judges will be somber,
But your name will be vindicated in the decision of the magistrates.
If you come up against an aggressive adversary,
A man of low standing, one who is not your equal,
Do not assail him in accordance with his lowly estate.
Leave him be, and he will confound himself.
Do not answer him in order to vent your frustration.
Do not alleviate your anger at the expense of your adversary.
Wretched is he who persecutes one who is inept.
Things will turn out in accordance with your will,
And you will defeat him through the censure of the magistrates.

Source: *The Literature of Ancient Egypt: An Anthology of Stories, Instructions, Stelae, Autobiographies, and Poetry.* Third Edition. Edited by William Kelly Simpson. New Haven, CT: Yale University Press, 2003. Copyright © 2003 by Yale University Press. All rights reserved. Reprinted with permission of the publisher.

GREECE

35. The Keys to Success for an Orator

In this excerpt from The Art of Rhetoric, *the Greek philosopher Aristotle (384–322 B.C.) describes the essential characteristics of a successful orator.*

Now the proofs furnished by the speech are of three kinds. The first depends upon the moral character of the speaker, the second upon putting the hearer into a certain frame of mind, the third upon the speech itself, in so far as it proves or seems to prove.

The orator persuades by moral character when his speech is delivered in such a manner as to render him worthy of confidence. For we feel confidence in a greater degree and more readily in persons of worth in regard to everything in general, but where there is no certainty and there is room for doubt, our confidence is absolute. But this confidence must be due to the speech itself, not to any preconceived idea of the speaker's character. For it is not the case, as some writers of rhetorical treatises [claim]…that the worth of the orator in no way contributes to his powers of persuasion. On the contrary, moral character, so to say, constitutes the most effective means of proof. The orator persuades by means of his hearers, when they are roused to emotion by his speech. For the judgments we deliver are not the same when we are influenced by joy or sorrow, love or hate. And it is to this alone, as we have said, the present day writers of treatises endeavor to devote their attention...Lastly, persuasion is produced by the speech itself, when we establish the true or apparently true from the means of persuasion applicable to each individual subject.

Source: *Aristotle: The "Art" of Rhetoric.* Translated by John Henry Freese. London and New York: Loeb Classical Library, 1926.

36. Socrates Discusses the Essentials of Effective Oratory

In this passage from his dialogue entitled Phaedrus, *the Greek philosopher Plato (428–347 B.C.) reports the words of his mentor Socrates (469–399 B.C.) on the topic of oratory.*

Since it is the function of speech to lead souls by persuasion, he who is to be a rhetorician must know the various forms of soul. Now, they are so and so many, and of such and such kinds; therefore, people also are of different kinds, and we must classify these. Then, there are various classes of speeches, to one of which every speech belongs. So people of a certain sort are easily persuaded by speeches of a certain sort for a certain reason to actions or beliefs of a certain sort, and people of another sort cannot be so persuaded. The student of rhetoric must, accordingly, acquire a proper knowledge of these classes and then be able to follow them accurately with his senses when he sees them in the practical affairs of life. Otherwise, he can never have any profit from the lectures he may have heard. But when he has learned to tell what sort of person is influenced by what sort of speech, and is able, if he comes upon such a person, to recognize him and to convince himself that this is the man and this now actually before him is the nature spoken of in a certain lecture, to which he now must make a practical application of a certain kind of speech in a certain way to persuade his hearer to a certain action or belief—when he has acquired all this, and has added to it a knowledge of the times for speaking and for keeping silence, and has also distinguished the favorable occasions for brief speech or pitiful speech or intensity and all the classes of speech which he has learned, then, and not till then, will his art be fully and completely finished.

Source: *Plato: Euthyphro, Apology, Crito, Phaedo, Phaedrus.* Translated by Harold North Fowler. London and New York: Loeb Classical Library, 1914.

37. A Comparison of Two Oratorical Heavyweights: Demosthenes and Cicero

In this excerpt from the introductory sections of Plutarch's biography of the famous fourth-century B.C. Athenian orator Demosthenes, he compares Demosthenes with the first-century B.C. Roman orator Cicero, who is the consensus choice among historians as the greatest orator in Roman history.

In the case of Demosthenes and Cicero, then, it would seem that the Deity originally fashioned them on the same plan, implanting in their natures many similarities, such as their love of distinction, their love of freedom in their political activities, and their lack of courage for wars and dangers, and uniting in them also many similarities of fortune. For in my opinion, two other orators could not be found who, from small and obscure beginnings, became great and powerful; who came into conflict with kings and tyrants; who each lost a daughter; who were banished from their native cities and returned with honor.

Source: *Plutarch's Lives.* Volume VII. Translated by Bernadotte Perrin. London and Cambridge: Loeb Classical Library, 1919.

38. How Demosthenes Became Interested in Oratory

In this excerpt, the Greek biographer Plutarch recounts how the fourth-century B.C. Athenian Demosthenes became interested in the art of oratory.

The origin of his eager desire to be an orator...was as follows. Callistratus the orator was going to make a plea in court...and the trial was eagerly awaited, not only because of the ability of the orator, who was then at the very height of his reputation, but also because of the circumstances of the case...Accordingly, when Demosthenes heard the teachers and tutors agreeing among themselves to be present at the trial, with great importunity he persuaded his own tutor to take him to the hearing. This tutor...succeeded in procuring a place where the boy could sit unseen and listen to what was said. Callistratus won his case and was extravagantly admired, and Demosthenes conceived a desire to emulate his fame, seeing him escorted by the multitude and congratulated by all. But he had a more wondering appreciation of the power of his oratory...Therefore, bidding farewell to his other studies and to the usual pursuits of boyhood, he practiced laboriously in declamation, with the idea that he, too, was to be an orator...

When Demosthenes came of age he began to bring suits against his guardians, and to write speeches attacking them [because they had swindled him out of much of his property and inheritance]. They devised many evasions and new trials, but Demosthenes, after practicing in these exercises...not without toil and danger, won his cause, although he was able to recover not even a small fraction of his patrimony. However, he acquired sufficient skill and confidence in speaking, and got a taste of the distinction and power that go with forensic contests, and he therefore came forward and engaged in public matters...So Demosthenes, after applying himself to oratory in the first place for the sake of recovering his private property, by this means acquired ability and power in speaking, and at last in public business...

And yet, when he first addressed the people, he was interrupted by their shouting, and laughed at for his inexperience, since his speeches seemed to them to be confus[ing]...and immoderately tortured by formal arguments. He had also, as it would appear, a certain weakness of voice and indistinctness of speech and shortness of breath which disturbed the sense of what he said by disjoining his sentences...

At another time…when he had been rebuffed by the people and was going home disconcerted and in great distress, Satyrus the actor, who was a good friend of his, followed after, and went indoors with him. Demosthenes complained to him that although he was the hardest-working of all the orators, and had almost used up the strength of his body in this profession, he had no popularity among the people, whereas debauchees, sailors, and illiterate speakers were listened to…while he himself was ignored. "You are right, Demosthenes," said Satyrus, "but I will quickly remedy the cause of all this, if you will consent to recite off-hand for me some narrative speech from Euripides or Sophocles." Demosthenes did so, whereupon Satyrus, taking up the same speech after him, gave it such a form and recited it with such appropriate sentiment and disposition that it appeared to Demosthenes to be quite another.

Persuaded now how much ornament and grace action lends to oratory, he considered it of little or no use to an orator to practice speaking if he neglected the delivery and disposition of his words. After this, we are told, he built a subterranean study…and into this he would descend every day without exception in order to form his action and cultivate his voice, and he would often remain there even for two or three months, shaving one side of his head in order that shame might keep him from going abroad, even though he greatly wished to do so.

Nor was this all, but he would make his interviews, conversations, and business with those outside the foundation and the starting point for hard work. For as soon as he left his associates, he would go down into his study, and there he would go over his transactions with them in due order, and the arguments used in defense of each course…Consequently, it was thought that he was not a man of good natural talent, but that his ability and power were the products of hard work…Demosthenes was rarely heard to speak on the spur of the moment, but although the people often called upon him by name as he sat in the assembly, he would not come forward unless he had given thought to the question and was prepared to speak on it…

For his bodily deficiencies, he adopted exercises…The indistinctness and lisping in his speech he used to correct and drive away by stuffing pebbles in his mouth and then reciting speeches. He used to exercise his voice by speaking while running or going up steep places, and by reciting speeches or verses in a single breath. Moreover, he had in his house a large mirror, and in front of this, he used to stand and go through his oratorical exercises.

Source: *Plutarch's Lives*. Volume VII. Translated by Bernadotte Perrin. London and Cambridge: Loeb Classical Library, 1919.

ROME

39. A Historian Writes about Oratory

The Romans, like the Greeks, had a high regard for oratorical skills, and, indeed, it would be impossible for a politician who lacked such skills to succeed in either society. Not surprisingly, then, Roman literature abounds with writings about the art of oratory. The Roman historian Tacitus (A.D. c. 55–c. 117) covers the subject in this passage from his "A Dialogue on Oratory."

At Rome, so long as the constitution was unsettled, so long as the country kept wearing itself out with factions and dissensions and disagreements, so long as there was no peace in the forum, no harmony in the senate, no restraint in the courts of law, no respect for authority, no sense of propriety on the part of the officers of the state, the growth of eloquence was doubtless sturdier, just as untilled soil produces certain vegetation in greater luxuriance...

In the same way, what little our orators have left them of the old forensic activities goes to show that our civil condition is still far from being ideally perfect. Does anyone ever call us lawyers to his aid unless he is either a criminal or in distress? Does any country town ever ask for our protection except under pressure either from an aggressive neighbor or from internal strife? Are we ever retained for a province except where robbery and oppression have been at work? Yet surely it would be better to have no grievances than to need to seek redress. If a community could be found in which nobody ever did anything wrong, orators would be just as superfluous among saints as are doctors among those that need no physician. Just as the healing art, I repeat, is very little in demand and makes very little progress in countries where people enjoy good health and strong constitutions, so oratory has less prestige and smaller consideration where people are well behaved and ready to obey their rulers.

What is the use of long arguments in the senate, when good citizens agree so quickly? What is the use of one harangue after another on public platforms, when it is not the ignorant multitude that decides a political issue, but a monarch who is the incarnation of wisdom? What is the use of taking a prosecution on one's own shoulders when misdeeds are so few and so trivial, or of making oneself unpopular by a defense of inordinate length, when the defendant can count on a gracious judge meeting him halfway? Believe me, my friends, you who have all the eloquence that the times require. If you had lived in bygone days, or if the orators who rouse our admiration had lived today; if some deity, I say, had suddenly made you change places in your lives and epochs, you would have attained to their brilliant reputation for eloquence just as surely as they would show your restraint and self-control. As things are, since it is impossible for anybody to enjoy at one and the same time great renown and great repose, let everyone make the most of the blessings his own times afford without disparaging any other age.

Source: *Tacitus: Dialogus, Agricola, Germania.* Translated by Sir W. Peterson, revised by M. Winterbottom. Cambridge and London: Loeb Classical Library, 1914.

40. The Orator Nonpareil Discusses His Art

In this excerpt from his book Concerning the Orator, *the first-century* B.C. *Roman orator Cicero provides some information about the requirements that must be fulfilled to become a successful orator.*

An engraving of the Roman historian Tacitus. Library of Congress.

To begin with, a knowledge of very many matters must be grasped, without which oratory is nothing but an empty and ridiculous swirl of verbiage. And the distinctive style has to be formed, not only by the choice of words, but also by the arrangement of the same. And all the mental emotions, with which nature has endowed the human race, are to be intimately understood, because it is in calming or kindling the feelings of the audience that the full power and science of oratory are to be brought into play. To this there should be added a certain humor, flashes of wit, the culture befitting a gentleman, and readiness and terseness alike in repelling and in delivering the attack, the whole being combined with a delicate charm and urbanity.

Further, the complete history of the past and a store of precedents must be retained in the memory, nor may a knowledge of statute law and our national law in general be omitted. And why should I go on to describe the speaker's delivery? That needs to be controlled by bodily carriage, gesture, play of features and changing intonation of voice; and how important that is wholly by itself, the actor's trivial art and the stage proclaim. For there, although all are laboring to regulate the expression, the voice, and the movements of the body, everyone knows how few actors there are, or ever have been, whom we could bear to watch! What need to speak of that universal treasure house, the memory? Unless this faculty be placed in charge of the ideas and phrases which have been thought out and well weighed, even though as conceived by the orator they were of the highest excellence, we know that they will all be wasted...

And indeed in my opinion, no one can be an orator complete in all points of merit, who has not attained a knowledge of all important subjects and arts. For it is from knowledge that oratory must derive its beauty and fullness, and unless there is such knowledge, well-grasped and comprehended by the speaker, there must be something empty and almost childish in the utterance.

Source: *Cicero: De Oratore.* Volume I. Translated by E. W. Sutton and H. Rackham. Cambridge and London: Loeb Classical Library, 1942.

41. Isaeus Has No Equal

In this letter to his friend Nepos, the Roman writer Pliny the Younger (A.D. 62–114) extols the oratorical skills of the rhetorician Isaeus.

We had received very favorable accounts of Isaeus, before his arrival here, but he is superior to all that was reported of him. He possesses the utmost ease and abundance of expression, and although always extemporaneous, his speeches have all the propriety and elegance of the most carefully prepared and elaborate composition...His prefatory remarks are terse, easy, and harmonious, and when the occasion requires it, serious and majestic. He proposes several questions for discussion, gives his audience liberty to request any they please, and sometimes even to name what side of the argument he should take up. Immediately, he rises up, assumes his gown, and begins.

He handles almost every point with equal readiness. Profound ideas occur to him as he proceeds. His language—how admirable that is! So choice, so refined! These unprepared speeches plainly show that he is very conversant with the best authors, and very accustomed to writing his own compositions. He begins his subject with great propriety. His narration is clear, his arguments ingenious, his logic forcible, and his rhetoric sublime. In short, he instructs, entertains, and moves his audience all at the same time, and each in so high a degree, that you are at a loss to determine in which of those talents he most excels. He abounds in logical reasoning and syllogisms, the latter of a formal exactness, not very easy to attain even in writing. His memory is so extraordinary that he can recollect what he has said before extemporaneously, word for word. He has acquired this wonderful talent by great application and practice. His whole time is so devoted to subjects of this nature, that he thinks, hears, and talks of nothing else.

Although he is over 63 years of age, he still chooses to continue to be a mere teacher of rhetoric; no class abounds with men of more worth, simplicity, and integrity. We who are conversant with the real contentions of the legal profession unavoidably come into contact with a good deal of negative behaviors, however contrary to our natural inclinations. But the lecture room, the auditorium, the mock trial offer an employment as unoffending as it is enjoyable, particularly so for those who are advanced in years. Nothing can give more happiness at that period of life than to enjoy what were the most pleasing entertainments of our youth.

Therefore, I look upon Isaeus not only as the most eloquent, but also the most happy of men, as I will consider you the most insensible, if you appear to slight his acquaintance. Let me prevail upon you, then, to come to Rome, if not on my account, or any other, at least for the pleasure of hearing this extraordinary person... You will tell me, perhaps, that you have authors in your own library equally eloquent. I don't deny it. And those authors you may turn to at any time, but you cannot always have an opportunity of hearing Isaeus. Besides, as the common saying has it, the spoken word has a much greater effect. There is something in the voice, the countenance, the bearing, and the gesture of the speaker that combine to create an impression on the mind, deeper than can even vigorous writings. This at least was the opinion of [the Athenian orator] Aeschines who, having read to the Rhodians a speech of Demosthenes which they loudly applauded: "But how," he said, "would you have been affected, had you heard the wild beast's own roar!" Aeschines, if we may believe Demosthenes, had great energy of elocution but, you see, he had to confess that it would have been a considerable advantage to the oration if it had been pronounced by the author himself.

What I aim at by this is to persuade you to come and hear Isaeus. And let me again invite you to do so, if for no other reason than at least you may have the pleasure to say that you once heard him. Farewell.

Source: *Pliny: Letters.* Volume I. Translated by William Melmoth, with revisions by W.M.L. Hutchinson. Cambridge and London: Loeb Classical Library, 1915.

42. "Instruct, Delight, Move": The Orator's Three Goals

Who better than the great first-century B.C. *orator Cicero to summarize the importance of the oratorical art? He does so in this excerpt from his essay "On the Best Kind of Orators."*

The supreme orator, then, is the one whose speech instructs, delights, and moves the minds of his audience. The orator is duty bound to instruct; giving pleasure is a free gift to the audience, but to move them is indispensable.

Source: *Cicero: De Inventione; De Optimo Genere Oratorum.* Translated by H. M. Hubbell. Cambridge and London: Loeb Classical Library, 1949.

Part V
MATERIAL LIFE

Food and Drink

No matter what the time period or which civilization is under consideration, the two biggest questions surrounding the issue of food and drink are these: what can (and cannot) be consumed, and with whom? Literary references to the ancients' preferred cuisines abound, so it seems clear that this was an important issue in their lives.

Prohibited foods seem to be mentioned almost as frequently as desirable foods. The Israelites faced many restrictions on their dietary intake (Document 1), even though food and drink were of great concern on their flight from Egypt (Document 2), while in India (Document 4), the eating of meat was frowned upon. Many of the Pythagorean philosophers in ancient Greece observed dietary restrictions, but, contrary to some stories, they *did* enjoy eating beans (Document 13). Some ancient authors suggested moderation in food consumption (Documents 10, 12, 16) or even fasting (Document 26), while others advised against excessive drinking (Document 15). The Greek philosopher Aristotle went so far as to recommend that water from melted snow should be avoided (Document 14).

The food and drink of priests, kings, and emperors was widely reported (Documents 7, 9, 24, 28), while lavish repasts thrown by wealthy individuals are the subject of Documents 17 and 18. The staples of the Egyptian diet, like bread and fish, are revealed in Documents 5 and 6, whereas some Romans went beyond the basics to feast on delicacies such as cranes, peacocks, lampreys, and swordfish (Document 29). As for onions, Egyptian priests avoided them (Document 6), but the Athenian philosopher *Socrates* and his friends enjoyed them (Document 11).

The success, or lack thereof, of a dinner party often depended on the generosity and temperament of the host or hosts, and their ability to create the proper dining ambience. The details of such parties are recorded in Documents 19, 20, 21, and 25. In Document 22, the Roman writer Pliny the Younger complained about an invited guest who failed to appear for dinner. In every case, however, the servants who prepared and served the dinner should be treated kindly (Document 23).

Possibly the most unique document pertaining to food and its preparation comes from a cookbook written by the Roman author Apicius (Document 27). A perusal of its pages describes and reveals Roman haute cuisine at its finest.

ISRAEL

1. Clean and Unclean Foods

In the book of Deuteronomy, the Israelites are given the following specific instructions from God, through Moses, about the foods that they may and may not eat.

Don't eat any disgusting animals. You may eat the meat of cattle, sheep, and goats; wild sheep and goats and gazelles, antelopes and all kinds of deer. It is all right to eat meat from any animals that have divided hoofs and also chew the cud.

But don't eat camels, rabbits, and rock badgers. These animals chew the cud but do not have divided hoofs. You must treat them as unclean. And don't eat pork, since pigs have divided hoofs, but they do not chew their cud. Don't even touch a dead pig!

You can eat any fish that has fins and scales. But there are other creatures that live in the water, and if they do not have fins and scales, you must not eat them. Treat them as unclean.

You can eat any clean bird. But don't eat the meat of any of the following birds: eagles, vultures, falcons, kites, ravens, ostriches, cormorants, storks, herons, and hoopoes. You must not eat bats. Swarming insects are unclean, so don't eat them. However, you are allowed to eat certain kinds of winged insects.

You belong to the LORD your God, so if you happen to find a dead animal, don't eat its meat. You may give it to foreigners who live in your town or sell it to foreigners who are visiting your town.

Don't boil a young goat in its mother's milk.

Source: Scripture taken from *The Holy Bible: Contemporary English Version.* © 1995 by American Bible Society.

2. Food and Drink on the Flight from Egypt

The first-century A.D. Jewish historian Josephus relates in the following passage how God, through Moses, met the Hebrews' need for food and water on their exodus from Egypt.

God thereon promised to take care of them and to provide the resources which they craved. Having received this response from God, Moses descended to the multitude. And they, on seeing him all radiant at the divine promises, passed from dejection to a more optimistic mood, while he, standing in their midst, told them that he had come to bring them from God deliverance from their present predicament. And not long after that, a flock of quails—a species of bird abundant, above all others, in the Arabian gulf—came flying over this stretch of sea, and, both tired from their flight and accustomed more than other birds to skim the ground, settled in the Hebrews' camp. And they, collecting them as the food provided for them by God, satisfied their hunger, while Moses addressed his thankful prayers to God...

Immediately after this first supply of food, God sent down to them a second. While Moses raised his hands in prayer, a dew descended and, as this congealed about his hands, Moses, surmising that this too was a nutriment come to them from God, tasted it and was delighted. The multitude, in their ignorance, took this for snow and attributed the phenomenon to the season of the year, but he instructed them that this heaven-descending dew was not as they supposed, but was sent for their salvation and sustenance, and tasting it, he ordered them thus to convince themselves. They, then, imitating their leader, were delighted with what they ate, for it had the sweet and delicious taste of honey...and they fell to collecting it with the greatest enthusiasm. Orders, however, were issued to all to collect each day [a moderate amount], since this food would never fail them. This was to ensure that the weak would not be prevented from obtaining some, should their stronger brethren use their strength to amass a larger harvest...

It is a mainstay to dwellers in these parts against their dearth of other provisions, and to this very day all that region is watered by a rain like to that which them, as a favor to Moses, the Deity sent down for human's sustenance. The Hebrews call this food *manna*...So they continued to rejoice in their heaven-sent gift, living on this food for forty years, all the time they were in the desert.

Upon their departure, when they reached Raphidin, in extreme agony from thirst—for having on the earlier days found some scanty springs, they then found themselves in an absolutely waterless region—they were in great distress and again vented their anger on Moses. But he, shunning for a while the onset of the crowd, began to pray, beseeching God, as He had given meat to them in their need, so now to provide drink for them, for their gratitude for the meat would perish if there were nothing to drink. Nor did God long defer this gift, but promised Moses that He would provide a spring with abundant water where they had not looked for it. He then ordered him to strike with his staff the rock which stood there before their eyes, and from it, they would receive a plenteous supply of what they needed. Moreover, He would see to it that this water would appear for them without work or effort.

Having received this response from God, Moses now approached the people... When he arrived, he told them that God would deliver them from this distress, and had even promised to save them in an unexpected way: a river was to flow for them out of the rock. They were very distraught at this news, aghast at the thought of being forced, exhausted as they were with thirst and travel, to split the rock. But Moses struck it with his staff, whereupon it opened and there gushed out an abundant stream of the clearest water. Amazed at this marvelous occurrence, the mere sight of which already quenched their thirst, they drank and found the current sweet and delicious and all that was to be looked for in a gift from God.

Source: *Josephus.* Volume IV. Translated by H. St. J. Thackeray. Cambridge and London: Loeb Classical Library, 1930.

CHINA

3. A Cook Who Took Care of His Carving Knife

Laozi may have been a philosopher, or perhaps the word Laozi is a generic term for a consortium of philosophers, who flourished perhaps around the fourth century B.C. *in China.*

In any event, the teachings of Laozi include the following story of a cook named Ding, and the way in which he performed his duties.

Your life has a limit, but knowledge has none. If you use what is limited to pursue what has no limit, you will be in danger. If you understand this and still strive for knowledge, you will be in danger for certain! If you do good, stay away from fame. If you do evil, stay away from punishments. Follow the middle, go by what is constant, and you can stay in one piece, keep yourself alive, look after your parents, and live out your years.

Cook Ding was cutting up an ox for Lord Wenhui. At every touch of his hand, every heave of his shoulder, every move of his feet, every thrust of his knee—zip, zoop! He slithered the knife along with a zing, and all was in perfect rhythm...

"Ah, this is marvelous!" said Lord Wenhui. "Imagine skill reaching such heights!"

Cook Ding laid down his knife and replied: "What I care about is the Way, which goes beyond skill. When I first began cutting up oxen, all I could see was the ox itself. After three years, I no longer saw the whole ox. And now—now I go at it by spirit, and don't look with my eyes. Perception and understanding have come to a stop and spirit moves where it wants. I go along with the natural makeup, strike in the big hollows, guide the knife through the big openings, and follow things as they are. So I never touch the smallest ligament or tendon, much less a main joint.

"A good cook changes his knife once a year—because he cuts. A mediocre cook changes his knife once a month—because he hacks. I've had this knife of mine for 19 years, and I've cut up thousands of oxen with it, and yet the blade is as good as though it had just come from the grindstone. There are spaces between the joints, and the blade of the knife has really no thickness. If you insert what has no thickness into such spaces, then there's plenty of room, more than enough for the blade to play about it. That's why after 19 years, the blade of my knife is still as good as when it first came from the grindstone.

"However, when I come to a complicated place, I size up the difficulties, tell myself to watch out and be careful, keep my eyes on what I'm doing, work very slowly, and move the knife with the greatest subtlety, until—flop! The whole thing comes apart like a clod of earth crumbling to the ground. I stand there holding the knife and look all around me, completely satisfied and reluctant to move on, and then I wipe off the knife and put it away."

"Excellent!" said Lord Wenhui. "I have heard the words of Cook Ding and learned how to care for life!"

Source: From *Sources of Chinese Tradition*. Volume I. Second edition. Compiled by William Theodore de Bary and Irene Bloom. Copyright © 1999 Columbia University Press. Reprinted with permission of the publisher.

A full-length stone engraving of Laozi, c. 700–750. Interphoto Pressebildagentur/ Alamy.

INDIA

4. Do Not Eat Meat

In this passage from the Lankavatara Sutra, *a Buddhist religious text from perhaps the fourth century* B.C., *the bodhisattva, or disciple of Buddha, is cautioned not to eat meat.*

Here in this long journey of birth-and-death, there is no living being who...has not at some time been your mother or father, brother or sister, son or daughter...So how can the *bodhisattva*, who wishes to treat all beings as though they were himself,...eat the flesh of any living being...Therefore, wherever living beings evolve, people should feel toward them as to their own kin, and, looking on all beings as their only child, should refrain from eating meat...

The *bodhisattva*...desirous of cultivating the virtue of love, should not eat meat, in order that he does not cause terror to living beings. Dogs, when they see, even at a distance, an outcaste...who likes eating meat, are terrified with fear, and think, "They are the dealers of death, they will kill us!" Even the tiny animals in earth and air and water, who have a very keen sense of smell, will detect at a distance the odor of the demons in meat-eaters, and will run away as fast as they can from the death which threatens them...

Moreover, the meat-eater sleeps in sorrow and wakes in sorrow. All his dreams are nightmares, and they make his hair stand on end...Things other than human sap his vitality. Often he is struck with terror, and trembles without cause...He knows no measure in his eating, and there is no flavor, digestibility, or nourishment in his food. His bowels are filled with worms and other creatures, which are the cause of leprosy. And he ceases to think of resisting diseases...

It is not true...that meat is right and proper for the disciple when the animal was not killed by himself or by his orders, and when it was not killed specially for him...Pressed by a desire for the taste of meat, people may string together their sophistries in defense of meat-eating...and declare that the Lord permitted meat as legitimate food, that it occurs in the list of permitted foods, and that he himself ate it. But...it is nowhere allowed in the sutras as a...legitimate food...All meat-eating in any form or manner and in any circumstances is prohibited, unconditionally, once and for all.

Source: From *Sources of Indian Tradition*. Volume I. Edited by William Theodore de Bary. Copyright © 1958 Columbia University Press. Reprinted with permission of the publisher.

EGYPT

5. The Staples of the Egyptian Diet According to Herodotus

In the following passage from his Histories, *the fifth-century* B.C. *Greek historian Herodotus comments on Egyptian cuisine.*

[The Egyptians are]...next to the Libyans, the healthiest people in the world. I should put this down myself to the absence of changes in climate; for change, and especially change of weather, is the prime cause of disease. They eat loaves made from spelt—*cyllestes* is their word for them—and drink a wine made from barley, as they have no vines in their country. Some kinds of fish they eat raw, either dried in the sun, or salted; quails, too, they eat raw, and ducks and various small birds, after pickling

The Greek researcher and storyteller Herodotus of Halicarnassus (fifth century B.C.) was said to be the world's first historian. Library of Congress.

them in brine. Other sorts of birds and fish, apart from those which they consider sacred, they either roast or boil.

Source: *Herodotus: The Histories.* Translated by Aubrey de Selincourt. Baltimore: Penguin Books, 1954. Reproduced by permission of Penguin Books Ltd.

6. The Staples of the Egyptian Diet According to Plutarch

In this excerpt from his long essay on the Egyptian deities Isis and Osiris, the Greek biographer and essayist Plutarch (A.D. c. 45–c. 120) discusses Egyptian dietary habits.

As for sea fish, all Egyptians do not abstain from all of them, but from some kinds only. For example, the inhabitants of Oxyrhynchus abstain from those that are caught with a hook; for inasmuch as they revere the fish called oxyrhynchus (the pike), they are afraid that the hook may be unclean, since a pike may have been caught with it. The people of Syene abstain from the phagrus (the sea bream), because this fish is reputed to appear with the oncoming of the Nile, and to be a self-sent messenger which, when it is seen, declares to a glad people the rise of the river.

The priests, however, abstain from all fish. And on the ninth day of the first month, when every one of the other Egyptians eats a broiled fish in front of the outer door of his house, the priests do not even taste the fish, but burn them up in front of their doors. For this practice, they have two reasons, one of which is religious and curious, and I will discuss it at another time . . . The other is obvious and commonplace, in that it declares that fish is an unnecessary and superfluous food, and confirms the words of Homer who, in his poetry, represents neither the Phaeacians, who lived amid a refined luxury, nor the Ithacans, who lived on an island, as making any use of fish, nor did even the companions of Odysseus, while on such a long voyage and in the midst of the sea, until they had come to the extremity of want.

In sum, these people consider the sea to be derived from infected matter, and to lie outside the confines of the world and not to be a part of it or an element, but a corrupt and pestilential residuum of a foreign nature . . .

The priests keep themselves clear of the onion and hate it and are careful to avoid it, because it is the only plant that naturally thrives and flourishes in the waning of the moon. It is suitable neither for fasting nor festival, because in the one case, it causes thirst, and in the other, tears for those who eat it. In like manner, they consider the pig to be an unclean animal, because it is reputed to be most inclined to mate in the waning of the moon, and because the bodies of those who drink its milk break out with leprosy and scabrous itching.

Source: *Plutarch's Moralia.* Volume V. Translated by Frank Cole Babbitt. Cambridge and London: Loeb Classical Library, 1936.

7. Royal Repasts

According to the flowing excerpt from the writings of the first-century B.C. *Greek historian Diodorus Siculus, Egyptian kings, like Egyptian priests, had a restricted diet.*

It was the custom for kings to eat delicate food, eating no other meat than veal and duck, and drinking only a prescribed amount of wine, which was not enough to make them unreasonably full or drunken. And, speaking generally, their whole diet was ordered with such moderation that it had the appearance of having been drawn up, not by a lawgiver, but by the most skilled of their physicians, with only their health in view.

Source: *Diodorus of Sicily.* Volume I. Translated by C. H. Oldfather. London and Cambridge: Loeb Classical Library, 1933.

8. Pumpkin Purveyors Prevent Me from Paying My Taxes

In the following document, a third-century B.C. *lentil cook in the Egyptian town of Philadelphia requests some tax relief from a local official because of some unexpected competition.*

To Philiscus, greeting from Harentotes, lentil cook of Philadelphia. I give the product of 35 *artabae* [about 1,400 liters] per month, and I do my best to pay the tax every month in order that you may have no complaint against me. Now the people in town are roasting pumpkins. For that reason, then, nobody buys lentils from me at the present time. I beg and beseech you, then, if you think fit, to be allowed more time, just as has been done in Crocodilopolis, for paying the tax to the king. In the morning, right away they sit down beside the lentils, selling their pumpkins, and give me no chance to sell my lentils.

Source: *Select Papyri: Non-Literary Papyri; Public Documents.* Volume II. Translated by A. S. Hunt and C. C. Edgar. Cambridge and London: Loeb Classical Library, 1934.

GREECE

9. Alexander the Great's Daily Meal Routine

*In his biography of Alexander the Great, the Greek biographer Plutarch (*A.D. *c. 45–c. 120) provides the following details about Alexander's eating and drinking habits.*

He had the most complete mastery over his appetite...When, in the kindness of her heart [referring to a queen whom he knew], she used to send him, every day, many fancy dishes and sweets, and finally offered him bakers and cooks reputed to be very skillful, he said that he wanted none of them, for he had better cooks who had been given to him by his tutor, Leonidas: For his breakfast, namely, a night march, and for his supper, a light breakfast...

He was less addicted to wine than was generally believed. The belief arose from the great amount of time he would spend over each cup, more in talking than in drinking...After he had taken quarters for the night...he would inquire of his chief cooks and bakers whether the arrangements for his supper had been made. When it was late and already dark, he would begin his supper, reclining on a couch, and his care and moderation at the dinner table were remarkable...over the wine, as I have said, he would sit long, for the sake of conversation...After the drinking was over, he would take a bath and sleep, often until mid-day, and sometimes he would actually spend the entire day in sleep.

In the matter of delicacies, too, he was master of his appetite, so that often, when the rarest fruits or fish were brought to him from the seacoast, he would distribute them to each of his friends until he was the only one for whom nothing remained. His suppers, however, were always magnificent, and the outlay on them increased with his successes.

Source: *Plutarch's Lives*. Volume VII. Translated by Bernadotte Perrin. London and Cambridge: Loeb Classical Library, 1919.

10. Avoid Superfluous Food

In this excerpt from his Moralia, *the Greek biographer Plutarch (A.D. c. 45–c. 120) comments on the dangers of overeating.*

Just as the scents of flowers are weak by themselves, whereas when they are mixed with oil, they acquire strength and intensity, so a great mass of food to start with provides substance and body, as it were, for the causes and sources of disease that come from the outside. Without such material, none of these things would cause any trouble, but they would readily fade away and be dissipated, if clear blood and an unpolluted spirit are at hand to meet the disturbance. But in a mass of superfluous food a sort of turbulent sediment is stirred up, which makes everything foul and hard to manage, and hard to get rid of. Therefore, we must not act like those much-admired ship captains who, because of greed, take on a big cargo, but then are continually engaged in baling out the sea water. So we must not stuff and overload our body, and afterwards employ purgatives and injections, but rather keep it trim all the time.

Source: *Plutarch's Moralia*. Volume II. Translated by Frank Cole Babbitt. London and New York: Loeb Classical Library, 1928.

11. The Joy of Eating Onions

In the following excerpt, the Greek historian Xenophon (c. 430–c. 354 B.C.) describes a Greek banquet in which the diners discuss the properties of the onion.

And beside this, I know something else, which you may test immediately. For Homer says somewhere: "An onion, too, a relish for the drink." Now if someone will bring an onion, you will receive this benefit, at any rate, without delay, for you will get more pleasure out of your drinking.

"Gentlemen," said Charmides, "Niceratus is intent on going home smelling of onions to make his wife believe that no one would even have conceived the thought of kissing him."

"Undoubtedly," said Socrates. "But we run the risk of getting a different sort of reputation, one that will bring us ridicule. For though the onion seems to be in the truest sense a relish, since it adds to our enjoyment not only of food, but also of drink, yet if we eat it not only with our dinner, but after it as well, take care that someone does not say of us that [during our banquet], we were merely indulging our appetites."

"Heaven forbid, Socrates!" was the reply. "I grant that when a man is setting out for battle, it is well for him to nibble an onion, just as some people give their fighting birds a feed of garlic before pitting them together in the ring. As for us, however, our plans perhaps look more to getting a kiss from someone than to fighting."

Source: *Xenophon: Symposium and Apology.* Translated by O. J. Todd. Cambridge and London: Loeb Classical Library, 1923.

12. A Sensible Diet

As a medical writer, the fourth-century B.C. *Greek physician Hippocrates recognized the important of diet in maintaining good health.*

For the art of medicine would never have been discovered to begin with, nor would any medical research have been conducted...if sick people had profited by the same mode of living and regimen as the food, drink, and mode of living of people in health...To trace the matter yet further back, I assert that not even the mode of living and nourishment enjoyed at the present time by healthy people would have been discovered, had a person been satisfied with the same food and drink as satisfy an ox, a horse, and every animal except humans; for example, the products of the earth: fruits, wood, and grass. For on these, animals are nourished, grow, and live without pain, having no need at all of any other kind of living. In my opinion, to begin with, humans also used this sort of nourishment...the ancients seem to me to have sought for nourishment that which harmonized with their constitution, and to have discovered that which we use now. So from wheat, after steeping it, winnowing, grinding and sifting, kneading, baking, they produced bread, and from barley, they produced cake. Experimenting with food, they boiled or baked, after mixing, many other things, combining the strong and uncompounded with the weaker components, so as to adapt all to the constitution and power of humans, thinking that from foods which, being too strong, the human constitution cannot assimilate when eaten, will come pain, disease and death, while from such as can be assimilated will come nourishment, growth and health... [This] discovery was a great one, implying much investigation and skill. At any rate, even in the present day, those who study gymnastics and athletic exercises are constantly making some fresh discovery by investigating on the same method what food and what drink are best assimilated and make a person grow stronger.

Source: *Hippocrates.* Translated by W.H.S. Jones. Cambridge and London: Loeb Classical Library, 1923.

13. *The Pythagoreans Did Like Beans*

The second-century A.D. *Roman author Aulus Gellius, in this passage from his* Attic Nights, *debunks the notion that the sixth-century* B.C. *Greek philosopher* Pythagoras *excluded meat and beans from his diet.*

An erroneous belief of long standing has established itself and become current, that the philosopher Pythagoras did not eat meat, and also that he abstained from eating beans. In accordance with that belief, the poet Callimachus wrote:
I tell you too, as did Pythagoras,
Withhold your hands from beans, a hurtful food.
Also, as the result of the same belief, Cicero wrote these words in the first book of his work *On Divination:* "Plato therefore bids us go to our sleep in such bodily condition that there may be nothing to cause delusion and disturbance in our minds. It is thought to be for that reason, too, that the Pythagoreans were forbidden to eat beans, a food that produces great flatulency, which is disturbing to those who seek mental calm."
So then, Cicero. But Aristoxenus the musician, a man thoroughly versed in early literature, a pupil of the philosopher Aristotle, in the book *On Pythagoras* which he has left us, says that Pythagoras ate no vegetable more often than beans, since that food gently loosened the bowels and relieved them. I add Aristoxenus' own words: "Pythagoras among vegetables especially recommended the bean, saying that it was both digestible and loosening; and therefore, he most frequently ate it."
Aristoxenus also relates that Pythagoras ate very young pigs and tender kids. This fact he seems to have learned from his close friend Xenophilus the Pythagorean and from some other older men, who lived not long after the time of Pythagoras. And the same information about animal food is given by the poet Alexis, in the comedy entitled *The Pythagorean Bluestocking.* Furthermore, the reason for the mistaken idea about abstaining from beans seems to be, that in a poem of Empedocles, who was a follower of Pythagoras, this line is found:
"O wretches, utter wretches, from beans withhold your hands…" Plutarch, too, a man of weight in scientific matters, in the first book of his work *On Homer,* wrote that Aristotle gave the same account of the Pythagoreans, namely that except for a few parts of the flesh, they did not abstain from eating meat.

Source: *The Attic Nights of Aulus Gellius.* Volumes I and III. Translated by John C. Rolfe. Cambridge and London: Loeb Classical Library, 1927.

14. *Don't Drink Snow-Melt Water*

In this excerpt from his Attic Nights *(see also Document 13, above), the Roman author Aulus Gellius (*A.D. *c. 125–c. 180) references some passages from the fourth-century* B.C. *Greek philosopher Aristotle, about the unhealthiness of drinking water from melted snow.*

In the hottest season of the year, with some companions and friends of mine who were students of eloquence or of philosophy, I had withdrawn to the country place of a rich friend at Tibur. There was with us a good man...well trained, and especially devoted to [the writings of] Aristotle. When we drank a good deal of water made of melted snow, he tried to restrain us, and rather severely scolded us. He cited for us the authority of famous physicians, and in particular of the philosopher Aristotle...who declared that snow water was indeed helpful to grain and trees, but was a very unwholesome drink for human beings, and that it gradually produced wasting diseases in the body, which made their appearance only after a long time.

This advice he gave us repeatedly, in a spirit of prudence and good will. But when the drinking of snow water went on without interruption, from the library of Tibur, which...was well supplied with books, he pulled out a volume of Aristotle and brought it to us, saying, "At least believe the words of the wisest of men, and stop ruining your health."

In that book it was written that water from snow was very bad to drink, as was also that water which was more solidly and completely congealed, which the Greeks call *krystallos*, or "clear ice"; and the following reason was there given for this: "That when water is hardened by the cold air and congeals, it necessarily follows that evaporation takes place and that a kind of very thin vapor, so to speak, is forced from it and comes out of it. But its lightest part," he said, "is that which is evaporated. What remains is heavier and less clean and wholesome, and this part, beaten upon by the throbbing of the air, takes on the form and color of white foam. But that some more wholesome part is forced out and evaporated from the snow is shown by the fact that it becomes less than it was before it congealed."

I have taken a few of Aristotle's own words from that book, and I quote them: "Why is the water made from snow or ice unwholesome? Because from all water that is frozen, the lightest and thinnest part evaporates. And the proof of this is that when it melts after being frozen, its volume is less than before. But since the most wholesome part is gone, it necessarily follows that what is left is less wholesome."

After I read this, we decided to pay honor to the learned Aristotle. And so I for my part immediately declared war upon snow and swore hatred against it, while the others made truces with it on various terms.

Source: *The Attic Nights of Aulus Gellius.* Volumes I and III. Translated by John C. Rolfe. Cambridge and London: Loeb Classical Library, 1927.

15. Plato Did Not Approve of Excessive Drinking

In another passage from his Attic Nights *(see Documents 13 and 14, above), Aulus Gellius (A.D. c. 125–c. 180) relates a story about a man who drank to excess at parties in the mistaken belief that the Greek philosopher Plato (428–347 B.C.) approved of such behavior.*

A man from the island of Crete, who was living in Athens, gave out that he was a Platonic philosopher, and desired to pass himself off as one. He was, however, a man of no worth, a trifler, boastful of his command of Grecian eloquence, besides having a passion for wine which made him a laughing stock. At the parties which it was the custom of us young men to hold at Athens at the beginning of each week, as soon as we had finished eating and an instructive and pleasant conversation had begun, this fellow, having called for silence that he might be heard, began to speak, and using a cheap and disordered rabble of words after his usual fashion, urged all to drink. He declared that he did this in accordance with the opinion of Plato, maintaining that Plato in his work *On the Laws* had written most eloquently in praise of drunkenness, and had decided that it was beneficial to good and strong men. And at the same time, while he was speaking like this, he drenched such wits as he had with frequent and huge beakers of wine, saying that it was a kind of kindling wood and tinder to the intellect and the faculties, if mind and body were inflamed with wine.

However, Plato, in the first and second books of his work *On the Laws* did not, as that fool thought, praise that shameful intoxication which generally undermines and weakens people's minds.

Source: *The Attic Nights of Aulus Gellius*. Volume III. Translated by John C. Rolfe. Cambridge and London: Loeb Classical Library, 1927.

16. How to Avoid Over-Indulgence at Parties and Banquets

The Greek biographer and essayist Plutarch (A.D. c. 45–c. 120) knew that people tend to eat and drink to excess at banquets, so in this excerpt from his Moralia *he offers some advice on avoiding this kind of unhealthy over-indulgence.*

Something was said to the effect that, while less expensive things are always more healthful for the body, we ought especially to guard against excess in eating and drinking, and against all self-indulgence when we have immediately on hand some festival or a visit from friends, or when we are expecting an entertainment of some king or high official, with its unavoidable social engagements. And so we should, as it were, make our body trim in fair weather, and buoyant against the oncoming wind and wave. It is indeed a hard task, in the midst of good friends and good cheer, to keep to moderation and one's habits, and at the same time to avoid the extreme disagreeableness which makes one appear annoying and boring to the whole group.

Therefore, to avoid adding fire to fire—as the proverb has it—and gorging to gorging, and strong drink to strong drink, we ought with all seriousness to imitate the polite joke of Philip. It goes like this: a man had invited Philip to dinner in the country, assuming that he had only a few friends with him, but when later the host saw Philip bringing a large contingent of people, and since the host had not made preparations for such a crowd, he was much disconcerted. Philip, becoming aware of the situation, sent word privately to each of his friends to "leave room for cake." Following the advice, and looking for more to come, they ate sparingly of what was before them, and so there was plenty of food for everyone. In this manner, then, we ought to prepare ourselves in anticipation of our obligatory round of social engagements by keeping room in the body for elaborate dishes and pastry and, may I say it, for indulgence in strong drink also, by bringing to these things a fresh and willing appetite.

Source: *Plutarch's Moralia.* Volume II. Translated by Frank Cole Babbitt. London and New York: Loeb Classical Library, 1928.

ROME

17. Mark Antony's Lavish Dinner

The Egyptian queen Cleopatra (69–30 B.C.) knew how to throw a dinner party, especially when the guest of honor was the Roman soldier and politician Mark Antony (83–30 B.C.). The Greek author Athenaeus, who wrote at the end of the second century A.D., provides the particulars of one banquet in the following excerpt from his Deipnosophistae.

Socrates of Rhodes...describes the banquet given by Cleopatra, the last queen of Egypt, who married the Roman general, Antony...His words are: "Meeting Antony in Cilicia, Cleopatra arranged in his honor a royal banquet, in which the service was entirely of gold and jeweled vessels made with exquisite art. Even the walls, says Socrates, were hung with tapestries made of purple and gold threads. And having spread twelve dining couches, Cleopatra invited Antony and his chosen friends. He was overwhelmed with the richness of the display, but she quietly smiled and said that all these things were a present for him. She also invited him to come and dine with her again the next day, with his friends and his officers. On this occasion, she provided an even more sumptuous banquet by far, so that she caused the vessels which had been used on the

first occasion to appear paltry. And once more, she presented him with these also. As for the officers, each was allowed to take away the couch on which he had reclined. Even the sideboards, as well as the spreads for the couches, were divided among them. And when they departed, she furnished litters for the guests of high rank, with bearers, while for the rest she provided horses...with silver-plated harnesses, and for all she sent along Ethiopian slaves to carry the torches. On the fourth day, she distributed fees, amounting to a talent, for the purchase of roses, and the floors of the dining rooms were strewn with them to a depth of 18 inches, in net-like festoons spread everywhere.

Source: *Athenaeus: The Deipnosophists.* Volume II. Translated by Charles Burton Gulick. London and New York: Loeb Classical Library, 1928.

Cleopatra's Banquet, by the eighteenth-century artist Tiepolo Giambattista. Cameraphoto/ Art Resource, NY.

18. Trimalchio's Lavish Dinner

The ancient Romans loved to eat, and there is plenty of evidence to illustrate their fondness for eating and drinking. Possibly the most famous Roman dinner party was the one thrown in the first century A.D. by the fictional Trimalchio, a principle character in the Latin novel entitled Satyricon, which was written by the Roman satirist Petronius (A.D. c. 27–65). As the following excerpt from the novel shows, Trimalchio was boastful, arrogant, officious, irritating, and misinformed on many subjects . . . but rich. And he knew how to put on a spread!

Now that the guests were all in their places, the *hors d'oeuvres* were served, and very sumptuous they were. Trimalchio alone was still absent, and the place of honor—reserved for the host in the modern fashion—stood empty. But I was speaking of the *hors d'oeuvres*. On a large tray stood a donkey made of rare Corinthian bronze; on the donkey's back were two panniers, one holding green olives, the other, black. Flanking the donkey were two side dishes, both engraved with Trimalchio's name and the weight of the silver, while in dishes shaped to resemble little bridges there were dormice, all dipped in honey and rolled in poppyseed. Nearby, on a silver grill, piping hot, lay small sausages, while beneath the grill, black damsons and red pomegranates had been sliced up and arranged so as to give the effect of flames playing over charcoal . . .

We, meanwhile, were still occupied with the *hors d'oeuvres* when a tray was carried in and set down before us. On it lay a basket, and in it a hen, carved from wood, with wings outspread as though sitting on her eggs. Then two slaves came forward and, to a loud flourish from the orchestra, began rummaging in the straw and pulling out peahen's eggs, which they divided among the guests. Trimalchio gave the whole performance his closest attention. "Friends," he said, "I ordered peahen eggs to be set under that hen, but I'm half afraid they may have hatched already. Still, let's see if we can suck them." We were handed spoons—weighing at least half a pound apiece—and cracked open the eggs, which turned out to be baked from rich pastry. To tell the truth, I had almost tossed my share away, thinking the eggs were really addled. But I heard one of the guests, obviously a veteran of these dinners, say, "I wonder what little surprise we've got in here." So I cracked the shell with my hand, and found inside a fine fat oriole, nicely seasoned with pepper . . .

The [next] course . . . failed to measure up to our expectations of our host, but it was so unusual that it took everybody's attention. Spaced around a circular tray were the twelve signs of the zodiac, and over each sign, the chef had put the most appropriate food. Thus, over the sign of Aries were chickpeas, over Taurus a slice of beef, a pair of testicles and kidneys over Gemini, a wreath of flowers over Cancer, over Leo an African fig, virgin sowbelly on Virgo, over Libra a pair of scales with a tartlet in one pan and a cheesecake in the other, over Scorpio a crawfish, a lobster on Capricorn, on Aquarius a goose, and two mullets over the sign of the Fishes. The centerpiece was a clod of turf with the grass still green on top and the whole thing surmounted by a fat honeycomb. Meanwhile, bread in a silver chafing dish was being handed around by a slave with long hair who was shrilling in an atrocious voice some song from the pantomime called *Asafoetida*. With some reluctance, we began to attack this wretched fare, but Trimalchio kept urging us, "Eat up, gentlemen, eat up!"

Suddenly, the orchestra gave another flourish and four slaves came dancing in and whisked off the top of the tray. Underneath, in still another tray, lay fat capons and sowbellies and a hare decked out with wings to look like a little Pegasus. At the corners of the tray stood four little gravy boats, all shaped like the satyr Marsyas, with...a spicy hot gravy dripping down over several large fish swimming about in the lagoon of the tray. The slaves burst out clapping, we clapped too, and turned with gusto to these new delights. Trimalchio, enormously pleased with the success of his little *tour de force*, roared for a slave to come and carve. The carver appeared instantly and went to work, thrusting with his knife like a gladiator practicing to the accompaniment of a water-organ. But all the time Trimalchio kept mumbling in a low voice, "Carver, carver, carver, carver." I suspected that this chant was somehow connected with a trick, so I asked my neighbor, an old hand at these party surprises. "Look," he said, "you see that slave who's carving? Well, he's called Carver, so every time Trimalchio says 'Carver', he's also saying 'Carve 'er!', and giving him orders to carve"...

...Servants came with a tray on which we saw a wild sow of absolutely enormous size. Perched rakishly on the sow's head was the cap of freedom which newly freed slaves wear in token of their liberty, and from her tusks hung two baskets woven from palm leaves. One was filled with dry Egyptian dates, the other held sweet Syrian dates. Clustered around her teats were little suckling pigs made of hard pastry, gifts for the guests to take home as it turned out, but intended to show that ours was a brood-sow. The slave who stepped up to carve, however, was not our old friend Carver who had cut up the capons, but a huge fellow with a big beard, a coarse hunting cape thrown over his shoulders, and his legs bound up in cross-gaiters. He whipped out his knife and gave a savage slash at the sow's flanks. Under the blow, the flesh parted, the wound burst open and dozens of thrushes came whirring out! But bird-catchers with limed twigs were standing by, and before long they had snared all the birds as they thrashed wildly around the room. Trimalchio ordered that a thrush be given to each guest, adding for good measure, 'Well, that old porker liked her acorns juicy all right.' Then servants stepped forward, removed the baskets hanging from the sow's nose, and divided the dry and sweet dates out equally among the guests...

He [Trimalchio] was still chattering away when the servants came in with an immense hog on a tray almost the size of the table. We were, of course, astounded at the chef's speed and swore it would have taken longer to roast an ordinary chicken, all the more since the pig looked even bigger than the one served to us earlier. Meanwhile, Trimalchio had been scrutinizing the pig very closely and suddenly roared, 'What! What's this? By god, this hog hasn't even been gutted! Get that cook in here on the double!'

Looking very miserable, the poor cook came shuffling up to the table and admitted that he had forgotten to gut the pig.

"You *forgot?*" bellowed Trimalchio. "*You forgot to gut a pig?*" And I suppose you think that's the same thing as merely forgetting to add salt and pepper. Strip that man!"

The cook was promptly stripped and stood there stark naked between two bodyguards, utterly forlorn. The guests, to a man, however, interceded for the chef. "Accidents happen," they said, "please don't whip him. If he ever does it again, we promise we won't say a word for him." My own reaction was anger, savage and unrelenting. I could barely restrain myself and leaning over, I whispered to Agamemnon [one of the other dinner guests], "Did you ever hear of anything worse? Who could forget to gut a pig? By god, you wouldn't catch me letting him off, not if it was just a fish he'd forgotten to clean."

Not so Trimalchio, however. He sat there, a great grin widening across his face, and said: "Well, since your memory's so bad, you can gut the pig here in front of us all." The cook was handed back his clothes, drew out his knife with a shaking hand and then slashed at the pig's belly with crisscross cuts. The slits widened out under the pressure from inside, and suddenly out poured, not the pig's bowels and guts, but link upon link of tumbling sausages and blood puddings.

Source: From THE SATYRICON by Petronius, translated by William Arrowsmith, copyright © 1959, renewed © 1987 by William Arrowsmith. Used by permission of Dutton Signet, a division of Penguin Group (USA) Inc.

19. Horace's Refined Dinner

In contrast to the excesses of Trimalchio's dinner party (see Document 18, above), the Roman poet Horace (65–8 B.C.), in this excerpt from the second satire of Book II of his Satires, *recommends a somewhat less luxurious eating regimen.*

When hard work and toil has knocked the daintiness out of you, when you are thirsty and hungry, refuse, if you can, plain food. Refuse to drink any mead, unless the honey is from Hymettus, and the wine from Falernum. How do you think this comes about? The chief pleasure lies, not in the costly dinner, but in yourself. So earn your sauce with hard exercise. The man who is bloated and pale from excess will find no comfort in oysters or trout or foreign grouse.

Yet, if a peacock is served for dinner, I will hardly root out your longing to tickle your palate with it rather than with a pullet. You are deceived by the peacock's vain appearance, because the rare bird costs gold and makes a brave show with the picture of its outspread tail—as though that had anything to do with the case! Do you eat the feathers you so admire? Does the bird look as fine when cooked? Yet, though in their meat they are on a par, to think that you crave the one rather than the other, duped by the difference in appearance! . . .

Now learn what and how great are the blessings that simple living brings with it. First of all, good health. For how harmful to a person a variety of dishes is, you may realize if you recall that plain food which agreed with you in other days. But as soon as you mix boiled and roast, shell fish and thrushes, the sweet will turn to bile, and the thick phlegm will cause intestine feud. Do you see how pale the guests are as they arise from this smorgasbord? Furthermore, clogged with yesterday's excess, the body drags down with itself the mind as well.

Source: *Horace: Satires, Epistles, and Ars Poetica.* Translated by H. Rushton Fairclough. Cambridge and London: Loeb Classical Library, 1926.

20. The Dinner Party Thrown by Nasidienus Rufus

In this passage from Book II of Satire VIII (see also Document 19, above), the Roman poet Horace (65–8 B.C.) describes a dinner party given by a certain Nasidienus Rufus.

Horace: How did you like your dinner with the rich Nasidienus? Yesterday, when I tried to get you as my own guest, I was told you had been dining there since midday.

Fundanius: So much so that never in my life did I have a better time.

Horace: Tell me, if you don't mind, what was the first dish to appease an angry appetite?

Fundanius: First, there was a wild boar. It was caught when a gentle south wind was blowing, as the father of the feast kept telling us. Around it were pungent turnips, lettuces, radishes—such things as whet a jaded appetite—skirret, fish-pickle, and Coan lees. When these were removed, a high-girt slave wiped the maple-wood table with a purple napkin, while a second swept up the scraps and anything that could offend the guests...

Horace:...Who, Fundanius, were those at dinner, with whom you had so fine a time? I am eager to know.

Fundanius: Myself at the top, then next to me Viscus of Thurii, and below, if I remember, Varius. Then Vibidius and Servilius Balatro, the two moochers. Above our host was Nomentanus; below him, Porcius, who made us laugh by swallowing whole cheesecakes in one bite. Nomentanus was there to see that if anything might escape our notice, he would point it out with his forefinger. For the rest of the guests—we, I mean—eat fowl, oysters, and fish, which had a flavor far different from any we knew, as, for instance, was made clear at once, after he had handed me the livers of a plaice and a turbot, a dish I had never tasted before. After this he informed me that the honey apples were red because they were picked in the light of a waning moon. What difference that would make, you could better learn from him...

Then is brought in a lamprey, outstretched on a platter, with shrimps swimming all around it. Upon seeing this, the master said: "This was caught before spawning. If it were taken later, its flesh would have been poorer. The ingredients of the sauce are these: oil from Venafrum of the first pressing; roe from the juices of the Spanish mackerel; [Italian] wine five years old, poured in while it is on the boil...white pepper, and vinegar"...

Then follow servants, bearing on a huge charger the limbs of a crane sprinkled with much salt and meal, and the liver of a white goose fattened on rich figs, and hares' limbs torn off, as being more dainty than if eaten with the loins. Then we saw blackbirds served with the breast burned, and pigeons without the rumps—real dainties...But off we ran, taking our revenge on [our host] by tasting nothing at all, as though the things were...more deadly than African serpents.

Source: *Horace: Satires, Epistles, and Ars Poetica.* Translated by H. Rushton Fairclough. Cambridge and London: Loeb Classical Library, 1926.

21. Horace Invites His Friend Torquatus to Dinner

The Roman poet Horace (65–8 B.C.) enjoyed entertaining friends at dinner, but certainly never on the lavish scale of a Trimalchio (see Document 18, above). He once issued the following dinner invitation to his friend Torquatus (see also Documents 19 and 20, above).

Torquatus, you're expected at my house this evening at sunset,
That is, if you think you can stretch out your legs comfortably
On the old-fashioned couches that Archias designed for me,
And can put up with a modest meal served on plain plates.
The wine we'll drink is Second Consulate Taurian [i.e., from the second consulship of Titus
    Statilius Taurus, 26 B.C.],
Poured off at Villa Petrinum, near Sinuessa,
Below the salt flats of Minturnae. Or have you a better
Vintage to offer? If so, send it round with your slave.
If not, you'll have to take your orders from me.
My hearth has been gleaming for days now, just for your sake,
My furniture cleaned up and set right. Drop everything,
Those airy ambitions, that drive to make still more money,
Your defense of Moschus on that poisoning charge.
Tomorrow [September 22] is Caesar's birthday. We're all excused, to sleep late,
To stretch the summer night with copious talk.
What is my fortune for, if I can't make use of it?
Someone who, out of regard for his heir, is stingy,
And much too hard on himself, sits next to a madman.
So I will begin the rites, the scattering of flowers...
I take it upon myself to vouch for the following,
And do so gladly: that no tattered linen of mine,
No dirty napkin, will make you turn up your nose
In disgust; that pitchers and plates reflect your image
Like mirrors; that no one is present who will gossip outside
About what is said among faithful friends, so that equals
May be intimate with equals. I'll invite Septicius
And Butra to meet you, and add Sabinus to the list,
Unless a prior engagement or a slyer girl
Detains him. There are places enough for a few of your shades,
But when goats get too close together, the air's a bit thick.
You've only to write back how many you want us to be,
Then drop everything: the client you're supposed to see,
Your business. Sneak out the back. Come to my dinner party!

22. Stiffed for Dinner!

The Roman writer Pliny the Younger (A.D. 62–114) dropped the following note to his friend Septicius Clarus, who was supposed to join him for dinner, but who never showed up.

How did it happen, my friend, that you did not keep your appointment the other night to have dinner with me? Now take notice: the court is in session, and you will fully reimburse me the expense I laid out to treat you, which, let me tell you, was no small sum. I want you to know that I had prepared a lettuce and three snails apiece, along with two eggs, barley water, some sweet wine and snow—I most certainly will charge the snow to your account, as it was spoiled in the serving. Besides all these curious dishes, there were olives, beets, gourds, shallots, and a hundred other delicacies, equally sumptuous.

Likewise, you would have been entertained either with an interlude, the rehearsal of a poem, or a piece of music, as you like best, or—such was my generosity—with all three. But the oysters, chitterlings, seas urchins, and Spanish dancers, of a certain, I know not who, were, it seems, more to your taste. However, I'll have my revenge; you can count on it. What kind of revenge will be a secret for now. In good truth, it was not kind of me to humble a friend—I almost said yourself, and upon second thought, I do say so. How pleasantly would we have spent the evening, in laughing, joking, and friendship! You can get a better dinner at many other places, I'm sure. But you can be treated nowhere, believe me, with more unrestrained cheerfulness, forthrightness, and freedom. Please give it a try. And if you do not forever after prefer my dinner parties to any others, then never dine with me again. Farewell.

Source: *Pliny's Letters*. Volume I. Translated by William Melmoth, with revisions by W.M.L. Hutchinson. Cambridge and London: Loeb Classical Library, 1915.

23. *Treat the Help Kindly*

The Roman philosopher Seneca (4 B.C.–A.D. 65) was no Trimalchio *either (see Document 18, above), when it came to dinner etiquette. Unlike Trimalchio, Seneca believed that servants and slaves, who prepared and served the food, always deserved to be treated respectfully.*

I smile at those who think it degrading for a man to share a meal with his slave. But why should they think it degrading? It is only because a purse-proud etiquette surrounds a householder at his dinner with a mob of standing slaves. The master eats more than he can hold, and with monstrous greed loads his belly until it is stretched and at length ceases to do the work of a belly, so that he is at greater pains to discharge all the food than he was to stuff it down. All this time, the poor slaves may not move their lips, even to speak...

When we recline at a banquet, one slave mops up the disgorged food, another crouches beneath the table and gathers up the leftovers of the tipsy guests. Another carves the priceless game birds. With unerring strokes and skilled hand, he cuts the choice morsels along the breast or the rump. Poor fellow, to live only for the purpose of cutting fat capons correctly, unless the other man is still more unhappy than he, who teaches this art for pleasure's sake, rather than he who learns it because he must.

Another, who serves the wine, must dress like a woman and wrestle with his advancing years... Another, whose duty it is to put a valuation on the guests, must stick to his task, unlucky man, and watch to see whose flattery and whose immodesty, whether of appetite or of language, is to get them an invitation for tomorrow. Think also of the poor purveyors of food, who note their masters' tastes with delicate skill, who know what special flavors will sharpen their appetite, what will please their eyes, what new combinations will rouse their cloyed stomachs, what food will excite their disgust through sheer superabundance, and what will stir them to hunger on that particular day.

The master cannot bear to dine with slaves like these. He would think it beneath his dignity to associate with his slave at the same table! God forbid!

Source: *Seneca: Ad Lucilium Epistulae Morales.* Volume I. Translated by Richard M. Gummere. Cambridge and London: Loeb Classical Library, 1917.

24. The Emperor Augustus's Meal Routines

The dining and entertaining habits of the emperor Augustus (reigned 27 B.C.–A.D. 14) were hardly sumptuous, according to this excerpt from the writings of the Roman biographer Suetonius (A.D. c. 70–c. 140).

He gave dinner parties constantly and always formally, with great regard to the rank and personality of his guests…He would sometimes come to table late on these occasions and leave early, allowing his guests to begin to dine before he took his place, and keep their places after he went out. He served a dinner of three courses or of six when he was most lavish, without needless extravagance but with the greatest good fellowship. For he drew into the general conversation those who were silent or chatted under their breath, and introduced music and actors, or even strolling players from the circus, and especially story tellers…

He was a light eater…and as a rule ate plain food. He particularly liked coarse bread, small fishes, hand-made moist cheese, and green figs of the second crop. And he would eat even before dinner, wherever and whenever he felt hungry. I quote word for word from some of his letters: "I ate a little bread and some dates in my carriage." And again: "As I was on my way home…in my litter, I devoured an ounce of bread and a few berries from a cluster of hard-fleshed grapes." Once more: "Not even a Jew…fasts so scrupulously on the Sabbaths as I have today. For it was not until after the first hour of the night that I ate two mouthfuls of bread in the bath before I began to be anointed." Because of this irregularity, he sometimes ate alone either before a dinner party or after it was over, touching nothing while it was in progress.

He was by nature most sparing also in his use of wine. [The historian] Cornelius Nepos writes that in camp before Mutina [during a military campaign], it was his habit to drink not more than three times at dinner. Afterwards, when he indulged most freely, he never exceeded a pint, or if he did, he used to throw it up. He…rarely drank before dinner. Instead, he would eat a bit of bread soaked in cold water, a slice of cucumber, a sprig of young lettuce, or an apple with a tart flavor, either fresh or cold.

Source: *Suetonius.* Translated by J. C. Rolfe. Cambridge and London: Loeb Classical Library, 1913.

25. A Pompous Host

The Roman writer Pliny the Younger (A.D. 62–114), never one to hobnob with the rich and famous (at least according to his statement in the following letter), nevertheless accepted a dinner invitation from a self-important host, with predictable results.

[A letter] to Avitus:

It would be a long and trivial story, were I to recount in too much detail by what accident I—who am not fond at all of polite society—had dinner recently with a person who in his own opinion lives in splendor combined with fiscal prudence, but according to my opinion, in a distasteful but expensive manner. Some very elegant dishes were served up to himself and a few more of the dinner guests, while those which were placed before the rest were cheap and paltry. He had apportioned in three pitchers three different sorts of wine, but you are not to suppose it was that the guests might take their choice. On the contrary, they were not allowed to choose at all. One was for himself and me; the next for his friends of a lower order—you must know that he measures out his friendship according to the degrees of quality—and the third for his own freedmen and mine.

Someone who sat next to me noticed this, and asked me if I approved of it. "Not at all," I told him. "Tell me, then," he said, "what do you do [when you host a dinner party under similar circumstances]?" "My practice," I replied, "is to give all my guests the same food and drink, because when I send out dinner invitations, it's for dinner, not for a property assessment. Every person whom I have placed on an equal plane with myself by inviting him to dinner, I treat as an equal in every way." "Even freedmen?" he asked. "Even them," I replied, "for on these occasions, I do not regard them as freedmen, but as pleasant dinner companions." "This must put you to great expense," he said. I assured him not at all; and on his asking how that could be, I said, "You must understand that my freedmen don't drink the same wine I do—but I drink what they do."

And certainly, if a man is wise enough to moderate his own gluttony, he will not find it so very burdensome a thing to entertain all his visitors in general as he does himself. Restrain and, so to speak, humble that failing, if you seriously wish to spend your money wisely. You will find your own temperance a much better method of saving expenses than insults to other people.

What is my point in all this, you ask? Why to hinder a young man of your excellent disposition from being imposed upon by the self-indulgence which prevails at some men's dinner parties, under the guise of frugality. And whenever any foolishness of this nature falls within my observation, I will, as a result of that kind feeling which I bear you, point it out to you as an example which you should avoid. Remember, therefore, that nothing is more to be avoided than this modern conjunction of self-indulgence and stinginess, qualities which are exceedingly distasteful even when existing separately, but still more distasteful when they meet together in the same person. Farewell.

Source: *Pliny's Letters.* Volume I. Translated by William Melmoth, with revisions by W.M.L. Hutchinson. Cambridge and London: Loeb Classical Library, 1915.

26. The Benefits of Fasting

On the other hand, some Romans occasionally fasted, or at least subsisted on very little food, as the philosopher Seneca (4 B.C.–A.D. 65) describes, and even recommends, in the following passage from one of his Epistles.

I am so firmly determined to test the constancy of your mind that, drawing from the teachings of great men, I will give you also a lesson: Set aside a certain number of days, during which you will be content with the scantiest and cheapest food, with coarse and rough clothing, saying to yourself all the while: "Is this the condition that I feared?" It is precisely in times of immunity from care that the soul should toughen itself beforehand for occasions of greater stress, and it is while Fortune is kind that it should fortify itself against her violence...

You need not suppose that I mean meals [of complete deprivation]. Let the dish be a real one, and the coarse cloak. Let the bread be hard and grimy. Endure all this for three or four days at a time, sometimes for more, so that it may be a test of yourself instead of a mere hobby. Then, I assure you, my dear Lucilius, you will leap for joy when filled with a penny's worth of food, and you will understand that a person's peace of mind does not depend on Fortune. For, even when angry, she grants enough for our needs.

There is no reason, however, why you should think that you are doing anything great. For you will merely be doing what many thousands of slaves and many thousands of poor men are doing every day. But you may credit yourself with this item: that you will not be doing it under compulsion, and that it will be as easy for you to endure it permanently as to make the experiment from time to time...

Even Epicurus, the teacher of pleasure, used to observe stated intervals, during which he satisfied his hunger in scanty fashion. He wished to see whether he thereby fell short of full and complete happiness, and if so, by what amount he fell short...Do you think that there can be fullness on such food? Yes, and there is pleasure also—not that shifty and fleeting pleasure...but a pleasure that is steadfast and sure. For although water, barley meal, and crusts of barley bread are not a cheerful diet, yet it is the highest kind of pleasure to be able to derive pleasure from this sort of food, and to have reduced one's needs to that modicum which no unfairness of Fortune can snatch away. Even prison food is more generous, and those who have been set apart for capital punishment are not so poorly fed by the man who is to execute them. Therefore, what a noble soul one must have, to descend of one's own free will to a diet which even those who have been sentenced to death have not to fear! This is indeed forestalling the spear-thrusts of Fortune.

So begin, my dear Lucilius, to follow the custom of these people, and set apart certain days on which you will withdraw from your business, and make yourself at home with the scantiest food. Establish business relations with poverty.

Source: *Seneca: Ad Lucilium Epistulae Morales*. Volume I. Translated by Richard M. Gummere. Cambridge and London: Loeb Classical Library, 1917.

27. A Roman Cookbook

A Roman gourmet by the name of Apicius, who lived in the first century A.D., compiled a book of recipes, a sort of Roman cookbook. Below are some recipes from Apicius's work.

Honey refresher for travelers:

The wayfarer's honey refresher (so called because it gives endurance and strength to pedestrians), with which travelers are refreshed by the wayside, is made in this manner: Flavor honey with ground pepper and skim. In the moment of serving, put honey in a cup, as much as is desired to obtain the right degree of sweetness, and mix with spiced wine, not more than a needed quantity; also, add some wine to the spiced honey to facilitate its flow and the mixing.

To keep grapes:

Take perfect grapes from the vines, place them in a vessel, and pour rain water over them that has been boiled down one third of its volume. The vessel must be pitched and sealed with plaster, and must be kept in a cool place to which the sun has no access. Treated in this manner, the grapes will be fresh whenever you need them. You can also serve this water as honey mead to the sick.

Also, if you cover the grapes with barley, you will find them sound and uninjured.

Supreme style cooked peas:

Cook the peas with oil and a piece of sow's belly. Put in a sauce pan broth, leek heads, green coriander, and put on the fire to be cooked. Of tid-bits [i.e., finely-chopped meats or seasonings] cut little dice. Similarly cook thrushes or other small [game] birds, or take sliced chicken and diced brain, properly cooked. Further cook, in the available liquor or broth, Lucanian sausage and bacon; cook leeks in water. Crush a pint of toasted pignolia nuts. Also crush pepper, lovage, origany, and ginger, dilute with the broth of pork, tie. Take a square baking dish, suitable for turning over; oil it well. Sprinkle [on the bottom] a layer of crushed nuts, upon which put some peas, fully covering the bottom of the squash dish. On top of this, arrange slices of the bacon, leeks, and sliced Lucanian sausage. Again cover with a layer of peas and alternate all the rest of the available edibles in the manner described until the dish is filled, concluding at last with a layer of peas, utilizing everything. Bake this dish in the oven, or put it into a slow fire [covering it with live coals], so that it may be baked thoroughly. [Next make a sauce of the following]: Put yolks of hard-boiled eggs in the mortar with white pepper, nuts, honey, white wine, and a little broth. Mix, and put it into a sauce pan to be cooked. When [the sauce is] done, turn out the peas into a large [silver dish], and mask them with this sauce, which is called white sauce.

Crane or duck with turnips:

Take out [entrails]. Clean, wash, and dress [the bird], and parboil it in water with salt and dill. Next, prepare turnips, and cook them in water, which is to be squeezed out. Take them out of the pot and wash them again, and put into a sauce pan the duck, with oil, broth, a bunch of leeks, and coriander. The turnips, cut into small pieces: these put on top of the [duck], in order to finish cooking. When half done, to give it color, add reduced must. The sauce is prepared separately: pepper, cumin, coriander, laser root moistened with vinegar and diluted with its own broth [of the fowl]. Bring this to a boiling point, thicken with roux. [In a deep dish, arrange the duck]; on top of the turnips [strain the sauce over it]. Sprinkle with pepper and serve.

Pig's paunch.

Clean the paunch of a suckling pig well with salt and vinegar, and presently wash with water. Then fill it with the following dressing: pieces of pork pounded in the mortar, three brains—the nerves removed—mix with raw eggs, add nuts, whole pepper, and sauce to taste. Crush pepper, lovage, silphium, anise, ginger, a little rue; fill the paunch with it, not too much, though, leaving plenty of room for expansion, so that it does not burst while being cooked. Put it in a pot with boiling water, retire and prick with a needle so that it does not burst. When half done, take it out and hang it into the smoke to take on color. Now boil it over again and finish it leisurely. Next take the broth, some pure wine, and a little oil, open the paunch with a small knife. Sprinkle with the broth and lovage; place the pig near the fire to heat it, turn it around in bran [or bread crumbs], immerse it in brine, and finish [the outer crust to a golden brown].

Spiced hare:

[The well-prepared hare]: Cook in wine, broth, water, with a little mustard [seed], dill, and leeks with the roots. When all is done, season with pepper, satury, round onions, Damascus plums, wine, broth, reduced wine and a little oil; tie with roux, let boil a little longer, [baste], so that the hare is penetrated by the flavor, and serve it on a platter masked with sauce.

Source: *Apicius: Cookery and Dining in Imperial Rome*. Translated by Joseph Dommers Vehling. New York: Dover Publications, Inc., 1936.

28. Priestly Banquets

In this excerpt from his Saturnalia, *the fifth-century* A.D. *writer Macrobius describes a banquet enjoyed by Roman priests of what he calls "early times."*

You must understand that extravagant profusion was found among the highest dignitaries, for I would remind you of a pontifical banquet of early times...There were served, for the preliminary service, sea urchins, unlimited raw oysters, scallops, cockles, thrushes on asparagus, fattened fowls, a dish of oysters and scallops, acorn fish (both black and white), then another service of cockles, mussels, sea nettles, figpeckers, haunches of venison and boar, fattened fowls cooked in pastry, more figpeckers, murex, and purple fish. For the main dishes were served sow's udders, boar's head, stewed fish, stewed sow's udders, ducks, boiled teal, hares, fattened fowls roasted, creamed wheat, and rolls of Picenum.

With a pontiff's table loaded with all those delicacies, one would suppose that no charge of extravagance would thereafter any longer lie. But is it not enough to make one blush even to speak of the kinds of food indulged in?

Macrobius describes the many varieties of figs:

The dried figs...suggest that we should make a list of the varieties of fig:...the African fig, the white fig, the reed fig, the donkey fig, the black fig, the marsh fig, the Augustan fig, the fig that yields two crops, the Carian fig, the white and black Chalcidic fig, the white and black Chian fig, the white and black Calpurnian fig, the gourd-shaped fig, the hard-skinned fig, the fig of Herculaneum, the Livian fig, the Lydian fig, the small Lydian fig, the Marsic fig, the dark Numidian fig, the Pompeian fig, the early-ripening fig, and the black Tellanian fig.

Source: From *Macrobius: The Saturnalia*. Translated by Percival Vaughan Davies. Copyright © 1969 Columbia University Press. Reprinted with permission of the publisher.

29. Exotic Foods, Gluttonous Romans

In this passage from his Attic Nights, *Aulus Gellius* (A.D. c. 125–c. 180) *references a poem by the grammarian Marcus Terentius Varro (116–27 B.C.), about the gluttonous tendencies of some of his fellow Romans, and their love of exotic foods.*

Marcus Varro, in the satire which he entitled *On Edibles*, in verses written with great charm and cleverness, discusses exquisite elegance in banquets and foods. He has set forth and described in poetry the greater number of things of that kind which such gluttons seek out on land and sea.

As for the verses themselves, he who has leisure may find and read them in the book which I have mentioned. So far as my memory goes, these are the varieties and names of the foods surpassing all others, which is bottomless gullet has hunted out and which Varro has assailed in his satire, with the places where they are found: a peacock from Samos, a woodcock from Phrygia, cranes of Media, a young goat from Ambracia, a young tuna from Chalcedon, a lamprey from Tartessus, codfish from Pessinus, oysters from Tarentum, cockles from Sicily, a swordfish from Rhodes, pike from Cilicia, nuts from Thasos, dates from Egypt, acorns from Spain.

But this tireless gluttony, which is ever wandering about and seeking for flavors, and this eager quest of dainties from all quarters, we shall consider deserving of the greater detestation, if we recall the verses of Euripides of which the philosopher Chrysippus made frequent use, to the effect that gastronomic delicacies were sought and desired not because of the necessary uses of life, but because of a spirit of luxury that disdains what is easily attainable.

Source: *The Attic Nights of Aulus Gellius*. Volume II. Translated by John C. Rolfe. Cambridge and London: Loeb Classical Library, 1927.

Houses and Furniture

When the Greek hero Odysseus finally returned home to his island kingdom of Ithaca after a 20-year absence—10 years spent fighting in the Trojan War, and another 10 on the voyage home—one of the ways in which he revealed and confirmed his identity was by describing how he built a special bed for himself and his wife—one of the bedposts was fashioned from a living olive tree trunk (Document 30). The furniture preferred by the Roman emperor *Augustus*, however, was not nearly as unique as that; simplicity was the watchword for his houses and their furnishings (Document 33).

Houses owned by wealthy Romans could be quite ornate and extensive, as revealed in a letter written by Pliny the Younger about one of his country estates (Document 34), and often these upscale houses were equipped with very expensive furnishings (Document 35). Greek style houses are described in Document 31. A house, whether small, moderately sized, or large, required good household management, a topic addressed in Document 32.

GREECE

---

30. Odysseus's Unique Bed

When he was a young man, Odysseus, the hero of the Odyssey *by the legendary Greek poet Homer, built a special bed for himself and his wife Penelope. The bed was unique because one of the bedposts was fashioned from a living olive tree trunk.*

An old trunk of olive
grew like a pillar on the building plot,
and I laid out our bedroom round that tree,
lifted up the stone walls, built the walls and roof,
gave it a doorway and smooth-fitting doors.
Then I lopped off the silvery leaves and branches,
hewed and shaped that stump from the roots up
into a bedpost, drilled it, let it serve
as model for the rest. I planed them all,
inlaid them all with silver, gold and ivory,
and stretched a bed between—a pliant web
of oxhide thongs dyed crimson.

Source: Excerpts from THE ODYSSEY by Homer, translated by Robert Fitzgerald. Copyright © 1961, 1963 by Robert Fitzgerald. Copyright renewed 1989 by Benedict R. C. Fitzgerald, on behalf of the Fitzgerald children. Reprinted by permission of Farrar, Straus and Giroux, LLC.

31. Ancient Greek House Building Styles

Although he was a Roman architect, Vitruvius (fl. first century B.C.*) in his book on architecture, devotes a lengthy section, which is excerpted below, to Greek homes.*

The Greeks…do not build as we do. But as you enter, they make passages of scanty width with stables on one side, and the porter's rooms on the other, and these immediately adjoin the inner entrance. The space between the two entrances is called, in Greek, *thyroron*. You then enter the peristyle. This has colonnades on three sides. On the side which looks southward, there are two piers at a fair distance apart, on which beams are laid. The space behind is recessed two-thirds of the distance between the piers…

As we pass in, there is the Great Hall, in which the ladies sit with the spinning women. Right and left of the recess are the bedchambers, of which one is called the *thalamus*, the other the *amphithalamus*. Around the colonnades are the ordinary dining rooms, the bedrooms, and the servants' rooms. This part of the building is called the women's quarter, *gynaeconitis*.

Next to this is a larger block of buildings with more splendid peristyles…In these halls, men's banquets are held, for it was not customary for women to join men at dinner. These peristyles are called the men's block, for in them men meet without interruption from the women. Moreover, on the right and left, lodges are situated with their own entrances, dining rooms, and bedrooms, so that guests on their arrival may be received into the guest houses and not in the peristyles. When the Greeks were more luxurious and in circumstances more opulent, they provided for visitors on their arrival, dining rooms, bedrooms, and storerooms with supplies. On the first day, they invited them to dinner; afterwards, they sent poultry, eggs, vegetables, fruit, and other country produce.

Source: *Vitruvius: On Architecture*. Volume II. Translated by Frank Granger. Cambridge and London: Loeb Classical Library, 1934.

32. Managing the Household

The Oeconomicus of the Greek writer Xenophon (c. 430–354 B.C.) is a practical manual on household management. One of the topics addressed by the author is the proper arrangement and organization of household possessions. The setting of the following excerpt is a conversation between the fifth-century B.C. Athenian philosopher Socrates, and a friend of his named Ischomachus.

"Now," [said Ischomachus], "after seeing [the perfect ordering and organization of a ship's cargo], I told my wife: 'Considering that sailors aboard a merchant vessel, even though it be a little one, find room for things and keep order, though tossed violently to and fro, and find what they want to get, though terror-stricken, it would be downright carelessness on our part if we, who have large storerooms in our house to keep everything separate and whose house rests on solid ground, fail to find a good and handy place for everything. Would it not be sheer stupidity on our part?

"How good it is to keep one's stock of utensils in order, and how easy to find a suitable place in a house to put each set in, I have already said. And what a beautiful sight is afforded by boots of all sorts and conditions arranged in rows! How beautiful it is to see cloaks of all sorts and conditions kept separate, or blankets, or bronze vessels, or table furniture! Yes, no serious person will smile when I claim that there is beauty in the order even of pots and pans set out in neat array, however much it may move the laughter of a wit. There is nothing, in short, that does not gain in beauty when set out in order. For each set looks like a troop of utensils, and the space between the sets is beautiful to see, when each set is kept clear of it, just as a troop of dancers about the altar is a beautiful spectacle in itself, and even the free space looks beautiful and unencumbered...

"Such is the gist of the conversation I think I remember having with her about the arrangement of utensils and their use."

"And what was the result?" I asked. "Did you think, Ischomachus, that your wife paid any attention to the lessons you tried so hard to teach her?"

"Why, she promised to live up to them, and she was evidently pleased beyond measure to feel that she had found a solution to her difficulties, and she begged me to lose no time in arranging things as I had suggested."

"And how did you arrange things for her, Ischomachus?" I asked.

"Why, I decided first to show her the possibilities of our house. For it contains few elaborate decorations, Socrates. But the rooms are designed simply with the object of providing as convenient receptacles as possible for the things that are to fill them, and thus each room invited just what was suited to it. Thus the storeroom, by the security of its position, called for the most valuable blankets and utensils, the dry-covered rooms for the corn, the cool ones for the wine, the well-lit for those works of art and vessels that need light. I showed her decorated living rooms for the family that are cool in summer and warm in winter. I showed her that the whole house fronts south, so that it was obvious that it is sunny in winter and shady in summer. I showed her the women's quarters too, separated by a bolted door from the men's, so that nothing which ought not to be moved may be taken out...

"And now that we had completed the list, we immediately set about [sorting and organizing the furniture]. We began by collecting the vessels we use in sacrificing. After that, we put together the women's holiday finery, and the men's holiday and war garb, blankets in the women's quarters, blankets in the men's quarters, women's shoes, men's shoes. Another category consisted of arms, and three others of implements for spinning, for bread making, or for cooking; others, again, of the things required for washing, at the kneading-trough, and for table use. All these we divided into two sets, things in constant use and things reserved for festivities. We also put by themselves the things consumed month by month, and set apart the supplies calculated to last for a year. This plan makes it easier to tell how they will last to the end of the time.

"When we had divided all the portable property...we arranged everything in its proper place. After that, we showed the servants who have to use them where to keep the utensils they require daily, for baking, cooking, spinning, and so forth; handed them over to their care and ordered them to see that they were safe and sound. The things that we use only for festivals or entertainments, or on rare occasions, we handed over to the housekeeper, and after showing her their places and counting and making a written list of all the items, we told her to give them out to the right servants, to remember what she gave to each of them, and when receiving them back, to put everything in the place from which she took it...

"When all this was done, Socrates, I told my wife that all these measures were futile, unless she saw to it herself that our arrangement was strictly adhered to in every detail. I explained that in well-ordered cities, the citizens are not satisfied with passing good laws; they go further, and choose guardians of the laws, who act as overseers, commending the law-abiding and punishing law-breakers. So I encouraged my wife to consider herself a guardian of the laws of our household. And just as the commander of a garrison inspects his guards, so must she inspect the household goods whenever she thought it well to do so...She was to make sure that everything was in good condition. Like a queen, she must reward the worthy with praise and honor, so far as in her lay, and not spare criticism and punishment when they were called for.

"Moreover, I taught her that she should not be upset that I assigned heavier duties to her than to the servants in respect to our possessions. Servants, I pointed out, carry, tend, and guard their master's property, and only in this sense have a share in it. They have no right to use anything except by the owner's permission. But everything belongs to the master, to use as he wishes. Therefore, I explained, the one who gains most by the preservation of the goods and loses most by their destruction, is the one who is bound to take most care of them."

"Well, now, Ischomachus," said I, "was your wife inclined to pay attention to your words?"

"Why, Socrates," he replied, "she just told me that I was mistaken if I supposed that I was laying a hard task on her in telling her that she must take care of our things. It would have been harder, she said, had I required her to neglect her own possessions, than to have the duty of attending to her own personal blessings. The fact is…just as it naturally comes easier to a good woman to care for her own children than to neglect them, so, I imagine, a good woman finds it pleasanter to look after her own possessions than to neglect them."

Source: *Xenophon: Memorabilia and Oeconomicus*. Translated by E. C. Marchant. Cambridge and London: Loeb Classical Library, 1923.

ROME

33. The Furniture Preferred by the Emperor Augustus

Unlike some of the later Roman emperors, the emperor Augustus (reigned 27 B.C.–A.D. 14) preferred a rather simple lifestyle when it came to houses and furniture, as the Roman biographer Suetonius (A.D. c. 70–c. 140) explains in this excerpt from his writings.

It is generally agreed that he was most temperate and without even the suspicion of any fault. He lived at first near the Roman Forum… [and] afterwards on the Palatine [Hill], but in [a] modest dwelling…which was remarkable neither for size nor elegance, having but short colonnades…and rooms without any marble decorations or handsome pavements. For more than 40 years, too, he used the same bedroom in winter and summer; although he found the city unfavorable to his health in the winter, yet he continued to winter there. If ever he planned to do anything in private or without interruption, he had a retired place at the top of the house, which he called… "technyphion" [little workshop]. In this he used to take refuge, or else in the villa of one of his freedmen in the suburbs; but whenever he was not well, he slept at Maecenas' house. When not in Rome, he went most frequently to places by the sea and the islands off Campania [central Italy], or to the towns near Rome, such as Lanuvium, Praeneste, or Tibur… He disliked large and sumptuous country palaces, actually razing to the ground one which his granddaughter Julia built on a lavish scale. His own villas, which were modest enough, he decorated not so much with handsome statues and pictures, as with terraces, groves, and objects noteworthy for their antiquity and rarity…

The simplicity of his furniture and household goods may be seen from couches and tables still in existence [during Suetonius's time, a century or so after Augustus's death], many of which are scarcely fine enough for a private citizen. They say that he always slept on a low and plainly furnished bed.

Source: *Suetonius*. Translated by J. C. Rolfe. Cambridge and London: Loeb Classical Library, 1913.

34. Pliny's Tuscan Villa

The politician and diplomat Pliny the Younger (A.D. 62–114) owned several country homes, which he described with great detail in letters to friends. An example of his description of his Tuscan villa is found in the following excerpt.

The exposure of the main part of the house is full south; thus, it seems to invite the sun... into a wide and proportionably long portico, containing many divisions, one of which is an atrium... In front of the portico is a terrace divided into a great number of geometrical figures, and bounded with a box-hedge...

At the extremity of the portico stands a grand dining room, which through its folding doors looks upon one end of the terrace; while beyond there is a very extensive view over the meadows up into the country. From the windows, you see on the one hand the side of the terrace and such parts of the house which project forward; on the other, with the woods enclosing the adjacent hippodrome. Opposite almost to the center of the portico stands a suite of apartments... which encompasses a small court, shaded by four plane trees, in the midst of which a fountain rises, from whence the water running over the edges of a marble basin gently refreshes the surrounding plane trees and the ground underneath them. This suite contains a bedroom free from every kind of noise, and which the light itself cannot penetrate, together with my ordinary dining room that I use when I have none but close friends with me. This looks out over the little court which I just now described, and also upon the portico... There is besides another room, which, being situated close to the nearest plane tree, enjoys constant shade;... its sides are covered with marble up to the cornice. On the frieze above a foliage is painted, with birds perched among the branches, which has an effect altogether as agreeable as that of the marble. In this room is place a little fountain, that, playing through several small pipes into a vase, produces a most pleasing murmur.

From a wing of the portico, you enter into a very spacious chamber opposite to the grand dining room, which, from some of its windows, has a view of the terrace, and from others of the meadow, while those in the front dominate an ornamental basin just beneath them, which entertains both the eye and the ear; for the water falling from a great height foams around its marble receptacle. This room is extremely warm in winter, being much exposed to the sun, and on a cloudy day the hot air from an adjoining stove very well supplies the absence of the sun.

From here, you pass through a spacious and pleasant dressing room into the cold-bath room, in which is a large, gloomy bath. But if you prefer to swim more at large, or in warmer water, there is a pool for that purpose in the courtyard, and near it a reservoir from which you may be supplied with cold water to brace yourself again, if you should perceive that you are too much relaxed by the warm. Contiguous to the cold bath is a lukewarm one, which enjoys the kindly warmth of the sun, but not so intensely as that of the hot bath, which projects from the house...

Over the dressing room is built the ball court, which is large enough to allow several different kinds of games being played at once, each with its own circle of spectators. Not far from the baths is a staircase which leads to a gallery, and to three apartments on the way. One of these looks out upon the little court with the four plane trees around it; another has a view of the meadows; the third abuts upon the vineyard... At one end of the gallery... is a chamber that overlooks the hippodrome... adjoining is a room which has a full exposure to the sun, especially in winter. From there runs an apartment that connects the hippodrome with the house.

Such are the villa's beauties and conveniences on the front. On the side is a summer gallery which stands high, and has not only a view of the vineyard, but seems almost to touch it. Midway, it contains a dining room cooled by the wholesome breezes which come from the Apennine valleys; the back windows, which are extremely large, let in, as it were, the vineyards, as do the folding doors…Along that side of this dining room where there are no windows, runs a private staircase for the greater convenience of serving at entertainments. At the farther end is a chamber from which the eye is entertained with a view of the vineyards, and, what is equally agreeable, of the gallery. Underneath this room is a gallery resembling a crypt, which in the midst of summer heat retains its pent-up chilliness, and, enjoying its own atmosphere, neither admits nor wants the refreshment of external breezes.

…At the upper end [of the portico] is a semi-circular bench of white marble, shaded with a vine which is trained upon four small pillars of Carystian marble. Water gushing through several little pipes from under this bench, as if it were pressed out by the weight of the persons who sit on it, falls into a stone cistern underneath; from there, it is received into a fine marble basin, so artfully designed that it is always full, without ever overflowing. When I eat here, the tray of *hors d'oeuvres* and larger dishes are placed around the edge, while the smaller ones swim about in the form of little ships and water fowl. Opposite this is a fountain which is incessantly emptying and filling, for the water, which it throws up a great height, falling back again into it, is by means of connected openings returned as fast as it is received…

Many other luxuries and amenities are described next.

I have now informed you why I prefer my Tuscan villa to those which I possess at Tusculum, Tibur, and Praeneste. Besides the advantages already mentioned, I there enjoy a securer, as it is a more profound leisure. I never need to put on full dress; nobody calls from next door on urgent business. All is calm and composed which contributes no less than its clear air and unclouded sky to the healthfulness of the spot.

Source: *Pliny: Letters.* Volume I. Translated by William Melmoth, with revisions by W.M.L. Hutchinson. Cambridge and London: Loeb Classical Library, 1915.

35. *Silver Furniture and Dinner Dishware*

In this excerpt from his Natural History, *Pliny the Elder* (A.D. 23–79) *provides some examples of the overuse of silver in Roman furniture and dishes.*

While we know that ladies' bedsteads have for a long time now been entirely covered with silver plating, so for just as long have banqueting couches also been covered. It is recorded that Carvilius Pollio…was the first person who had silver put on these latter…in the Corinthian style. In this latter style, he also had bedsteads made of gold, and not long afterwards, silver bedsteads were made…

In fact it was shortly before this period [of the dictator Sulla, in the early first century B.C.] that silver dishes were made weighing 100 pounds, and it is well known that there were at that date over 150 of those at Rome, and that many people were sentenced to outlawry because of them, by the schemes of people who coveted them…Our generation has gone one better. Under the emperor Claudius [reigned A.D. 41–54], his slave Drusillanus…possessed a silver dish weighing 500 pounds, for the manufacture of which a workshop had first been specially built, and eight others of 250 pounds went with it as side dishes. How many of his fellow slaves, I ask, were to bring them in or who were to dine off them?

[The historian] Cornelius Nepos records that before the victory won by Sulla [82 B.C.] there were only two silver dining couches at Rome, and that silver began to be used for decorating sideboards within his own recollection. And Fenestella, who died towards the end of the principate of Tiberius [reigned A.D. 14–37], says that tortoiseshell sideboards also came into fashion at that time, but a little before his day, they had been solid round structures of wood, and not much larger than tables, but that even in his boyhood, they began to be made square and of planks morticed together and veneered either with maple or citrus wood, while later silver was laid on at the corners and along the lines marking the joins, and when he was a young man they were called "drums," and then also the dishes for which the old name had been *magides* came to be called basins from their resemblance to the scales of a balance…

But what is the point of collecting these instances [of ostentatious use of silver], when our soldiers' sword hilts are made of chased silver, even ivory not being thought good enough, and when their scabbards jingle with little silver chains, and their belts with silver tabs? Nowadays, our schools for pages just at the point of adolescence wear silver badges as a safeguard, and women use silver to wash in and scorn baths not made of silver, and the same substance does service both for our food and for our baser needs. If only Fabricius [third-century B.C. austere Roman office-holder, who died in poverty] could see these displays of luxury—women's bathrooms with floors of silver, leaving nowhere to set your feet—if only Fabricius, who forbade courageous generals to possess more than a dish and a salt cellar of silver, could see how nowadays the rewards of bravery are made from the utensils of luxury, or else are broken up to make them! Alas for our present lifestyles; Fabricius makes us blush!

Source: *Pliny: Natural History.* Volume IX. Translated by H. Rackham. Cambridge and London: Loeb Classical Library, 1952.

Clothing

As was the case with food and dinners, housing, and household furnishings, some people in the ancient world, like the high priest in Israel (Document 37), the flamboyant *Trimalchio* (Document 45), or the Roman emperor *Caligula* (Document 46), wore expensive, fancy clothing. Wealthy Roman women were partial to pricey jewelry (Document 48). On the other hand, the emperor *Augustus* preferred a more modest wardrobe, clothes more suited for the average citizen than for a powerful leader (Document 42), and the philosopher Seneca argued in favor of frugality in clothing, as well as in food and furniture (Document 44). Roman orators were often in the public eye, and so their clothing, while not ornate, had to follow certain expectations commensurate with their profession (Document 43). Others, like Roman senators, were also expected to dress appropriately when in public (Document 47). Some Romans were influenced in their clothing choices by fashions from abroad, especially from Greece (Document 41).

Extremes in temperature might dictate clothing styles, as in India (Document 38), where loose fitting, brightly colored linen clothing was the norm. Linen clothing was also preferred in Egypt (Document 39). Regardless of the color, style, or fabric, all clothing required laundering at one time or another, and for that onerous task, laundry advice is presented in Document 40.

SUMERIA

36. Babylonian Clothing

The fifth-century B.C. *Greek historian Herodotus provides a description of Babylonian clothing in the following excerpt from his* Histories.

The dress of the Babylonians consists of a linen tunic reaching to the feet, with a woolen one over it, and a short white cloak on top. They have their own fashion in shoes, which resemble the slippers one sees in Boeotia [a district in Greece]. They grow their hair long, wear turbans, and perfume themselves all over. Everyone owns a seal and a walking stick specially made for him, with a device carved on the top of it, an apple or a rose or lily or eagle or something of the sort. For it is not the custom to have a stick without some such ornament.

Source: *Herodotus: The Histories.* Translated by Aubrey de Selincourt. Baltimore: Penguin Books, 1954. Reproduced by permission of Penguin Books Ltd.

ISRAEL

37. The High Priest's Wardrobe

In the thirty-ninth chapter of the book of Exodus, there appears the following detailed description of the attire of Aaron, the high priest.

Beautiful priestly clothes were made of blue, purple, and red wool for Aaron to wear when he performed his duties in the holy place. This was done exactly as the LORD had commanded Moses.

The entire priestly vest was made of fine linen, woven with blue, purple, and red wool. Thin sheets of gold were hammered out and cut into threads that were skillfully woven into the vest. It had two shoulder straps to support it and a sash that fastened around the waist. Onyx stones were placed in gold settings, and each one was engraved with the name of one of Israel's sons. Then these were attached to the shoulder straps of the vest, so the LORD would never forget his people. Everything was done exactly as the LORD had commanded Moses.

A neo-Babylonian limestone relief of King Marduk of Babylon (with a bouquet) greets scribe Ibni-Ishtar, ninth century B.C. Uruk. The Art Archive/Musée du Louvre Paris/ Gianni Dagli Orti.

The breastpiece was made with the same materials and designs as the priestly vest. It was nine inches square and folded double with four rows of three precious stones: A carnelian, a chrysolite, and an emerald were in the first row; a turquoise, a sapphire, and a diamond were in the second row; a jacinth, an agate, and an amethyst were in the third row; and a beryl, an onyx, and a jasper were in the fourth row. They were mounted in a delicate gold setting, and on each of them was engraved the name of one of the twelve tribes of Israel.

Two gold rings were attached to the upper front corners of the breastpiece and fastened with two braided gold chains to gold settings on the shoulder straps. Two other gold rings were attached to the lower inside corners next to the vest, and two more near the bottom of the shoulder straps, right above the sash. To keep the breastpiece in place, a blue cord was used to tie the two lower rings on the breastpiece to those on the vest. These things were done exactly as the LORD had commanded Moses.

The priestly robe was made of blue wool with an opening in the center for the head. The material around the collar was bound so as to keep it from unraveling. Along the hem of the robe were woven pomegranates of blue, purple, and red wool, with a bell of pure gold between each of them. This robe was to be worn by Aaron when he performed his duties.

Everything that Aaron and his sons wore was made of fine linen woven with blue, purple, and red wool, including their robes and turbans, their fancy caps and underwear, and even their sashes that were embroidered with needlework.

"Dedicated to the LORD" was engraved on a narrow strip of pure gold, which was fastened to Aaron's turban. These things were done exactly as the LORD had commanded Moses.

Source: *The Holy Bible: Contemporary English Version.* Translator(s) not stated. New York: American Bible Society, 1995.

INDIA

38. Comfortable Clothing in a Hot Climate

The second-century A.D. *Greek historian Arrian, in this excerpt from his book* Indica, *provides some information about the typical clothing of the inhabitants of India.*

The Indians wear linen garments, according to Nearchus [another historian] . . . This linen is brighter in color than any other, or else people's own blackness makes it look brighter. They wear a linen tunic down to the middle of the calf, one garment thrown about their shoulders, and another wound around their heads. Some wear ivory earrings, but only if they are very rich. Nearchus says that they dye their beards, but with various colors; some make them look as white as possible, others are dark-blue, crimson, purple, or grass-green. All the respectable Indians use sunshades against the summer heat. They have sandals of white skin, and these are elaborately fashioned; and the heels of their sandals are of different colors, and high to make them look taller.

Source: *Arrian.* Volume II. Translated by P. A. Brunt. Cambridge and London: Loeb Classical Library, 1933.

EGYPT/GREECE

39. Linen Clothing

In this passage from his Histories, *the fifth-century* B.C. *Greek historian Herodotus provides a brief description of Egyptian clothing.*

The clothes they wear consist of a linen tunic with a fringe hanging around the legs (called in their language *calasiris*), and a white woolen garment on top of it. It is, however, contrary to religious usage to be buried in a woolen garment, or to wear wool in a temple.

Source: *Herodotus: The Histories.* Translated by Aubrey de Selincourt. Baltimore: Penguin Books, 1954. Reproduced by permission of Penguin Books Ltd.

40. Laundry Advice

*One of the topics of conversation that came up at a dinner party attended by the Greek biographer Plutarch (*A.D. *c. 45–c. 120) dealt with the best and most efficient ways to wash clothing. The following excerpt is from Plutarch's* Moralia.

When we were being entertained at the house of Mestrius Florus [a close friend of Plutarch], Theon [one of the other guests] raised the question . . . why [the philosopher] Chrysippus never gave an explanation for any of the strange and extraordinary things he mentions . . . Themistocles [another guest] answered: . . . "What business have you, sir, to raise a question about these matters? If you have become inquisitive and speculative in the matter of explanations, do not camp so far away from your own province, but tell us for what reason Homer has described Nausicaa [a princess in the *Odyssey*] doing her washing in the river instead of the sea, although the latter was nearby and quite likely was warmer, clearer, and more cleansing."

"But," said Theon, "this problem you propose to us Aristotle long ago solved by considering the earthy matter in sea water. Much coarse, earthy matter is scattered in the sea. Being mixed with the water, this matter is responsible for the saltiness, and because of it, sea water also supports swimmers better and floats heavy objects, while fresh water lets them sink, because it is light and unsubstantial. The latter is unmixed and pure, and so because of its light consistency, it soaks into cloth and, as it passes through, dissolves stains more readily than sea water. Don't you think what Aristotle says is plausible?"

"Plausible," I said, "but not true. I observe that people frequently thicken their water with ash, or soda, or, if these are not at hand, with a powdery solid. The earthy matter, it would seem, is more easily able by its roughness to wash out dirt, while the water alone because of its lightness and weakness does not do this with equal efficiency. Therefore, it is not the coarseness of sea water that prevents this action, nor is sea water a less efficient cleanser because of its acridness, for this quality cleans out and opens up the mesh of the cloth and sweeps away the dirt. But since everything oily is hard to wash and makes a stain, and the sea is oily, this would surely be the reason for its not cleaning efficiently. That the sea is oily, Aristotle himself has said. Salt contains fat, and so it makes lamps burn better, and sea water itself, when it is sprinkled into flames, flashes up with them. Among waters, it is particularly sea water that is flammable and, in my view, this is the reason why it is also the warmest.

"What is more, the phenomenon can also be explained in another manner. Since cleansing is the aim of washing, and what dries quickest appears cleanest, the washing liquid must depart with the dirt... The sun easily evaporates fresh water because of its lightness, but salt water dries up with difficulty, since its coarseness holds it in the mesh of the cloth."

Another time, another conversation, but a similar topic:

"[Olive oil] resists evaporation and does not easily disappear. When a garment happens to be soaked with water, it dries easily, but an oil stain requires more than ordinary effort to remove. Oil stains enter deepest into the fabric because the refinement and liquidity of oil is greatest. As Aristotle says, wine is also more difficult to remove from cloth when mixed, because it is then of finer grain and settles more deeply into the pores."

Source: *Plutarch's Moralia.* Volume VIII. Translated by Paul A. Clement and Herbert B. Hoffleit. London and Cambridge: Loeb Classical Library, 1969.

GREECE/ROME

41. Greek Clothing Styles Invade Rome

In this passage from his Attic Nights, *the Roman writer Aulus Gellius* (A.D. c. 125–c. 180) *discusses Greek influence on Roman attire.*

For a man to wear tunics coming below the arms and as far as the wrists, and almost to the fingers, was considered inappropriate in Rome, and all the surrounding areas.

Such tunics our countrymen called by the Greek name *chiridotae* (long-sleeved), and they thought that a long and full-flowing garment was appropriate only for women to wear, to hide their arms and legs from sight. But Roman men at first wore the toga alone without tunics; later, they had close, short tunics ending below the shoulders, the kind which the Greeks call *exomides* (sleeveless). Habituated to this older fashion, Publius Africanus...a man gifted with all worthy arts and every virtue, among many other things with which he reproached Publius Sulpicius Gallus...included this also, that he wore tunics which covered his whole hands...

Virgil, too, attacks tunics of this kind as effeminate and shameful, saying: "Sleeves have their tunics, and their turbans, ribbons."

[The historian] Quintus Ennius also seems to have spoken scornfully of "the tunic-clad men" of the Carthaginians.

Source: *The Attic Nights of Aulus Gellius.* Volume II. Translated by John C. Rolfe. Cambridge and London: Loeb Classical Library, 1927.

ROME

42. An Emperor's Modest Attire

As emperor of Rome, Augustus (reigned 27 B.C.–A.D. 14) probably could have afforded the finest clothing that money could buy. But he was content with less ostentatious finery, as the biographer Suetonius (A.D. c. 70–c. 140) notes in this excerpt from his writings.

Except on special occasions, he wore common clothes for the house, made by his sister, wife, daughter, or granddaughters. His togas were neither close nor full, his purple stripe [on the toga] neither narrow nor broad, and his shoes somewhat high-soled, to make him look taller than he really was. But he always kept his shoes and clothing to wear in public ready in his room for sudden and unexpected occasions...

In winter he protected himself with four tunics and a heavy toga, besides an undershirt, a woolen chest protector, and wraps for his thighs and shins, while in summer he slept with the doors of his bedroom open, often in the open court near a fountain, besides having someone to fan him. Yet he could not endure the sun even in winter, and never walked in the open air without wearing a broad-brimmed hat, even at home.

Source: *Suetonius.* Translated by J. C. Rolfe. Cambridge and London: Loeb Classical Library, 1913.

43. The Well-Dressed Roman Orator

The Roman philosopher and orator Quintilian (A.D. c. 35–c. 100) provides a lengthy and detailed description of the appropriate clothing for an orator in this passage from his Institutio Oratoria.

With regard to dress, there is no special clothing peculiar to the orator, but his dress comes more under the public eye than that of other people. It should, therefore, be distinguished and manly, as, indeed, it ought to be with all prominent individuals. For excessive care with regard to the cut of the toga, the style of the shoes, or the arrangement of the hair, is just as reprehensible as excessive carelessness. There are also details of dress which are altered to some extent by successive changes in fashion. The ancients, for example, wore no folds, and their successors wore them very short. Consequently it follows that in view of the fact that their arms were, like those of the Greeks, covered by the garment, they must have employed a different form of gesture...from that which is now in use.

However, I am speaking of our own day. The speaker who has not the right to wear the broad stripe [indicating senatorial status] will wear his girdle in such a way that the front edges of the tunic fall a little below his knees, while the edges in rear reach to the middle of the backs of his legs. For only women draw them lower, and only centurions higher. If we wear the purple [i.e., senatorial] stripe, it requires little care to see that it falls becomingly; negligence in this respect sometimes generates criticism. Among those who wear the broad stripe, it is the fashion to let it hang somewhat lower than in garments that are restricted by the girdle. The toga itself should, in my opinion, be round, and cut to fit; otherwise, there are a number of ways in which it may be unshapely. Its front edge should by preference reach to the middle of the shin, while the back should be higher in proportion as the girdle is higher behind than in front. The fold is most becoming if it falls to a point a little above the lower edge of the tunic, and should certainly never fall below it. The other fold, which passes obliquely like a belt under the right shoulder and over the left, should neither be too tight nor too loose. The portion of the toga which is last to be arranged should fall rather low, since it will sit better in this way and be kept in its place.

A portion of the tunic also should be drawn back in order that it may not fall over the arm when we are arguing a case, and the fold should be thrown over the shoulder, while it will not be unbecoming if the edge is turned back. On the other hand, we should not cover the shoulder and the whole of the throat; otherwise, our clothing will be unduly narrowed and will lose the impressive effect produced by breadth at the chest. The left arm should only be raised so far as to form a right angle at the elbow, while the edge of the toga should fall in equal lengths on either side.

The hand should not be overloaded with rings, which should under no circumstances encroach upon the middle joint of the finger... The ancients used to let the toga fall to the heels, as the Greeks are in the habit of doing with the cloak; Plotius and Nigidius [first-century B.C. intellectuals] both recommend this in the books which they wrote about gesture as practiced in their own day... [Pliny the Elder] asserts that Cicero was in the habit of wearing his toga in such a fashion to conceal his varicose veins, despite the fact that this fashion is to be seen in the statues of persons who lived after Cicero's day. Regarding the short cloak, bandages used to protect the legs, mufflers, and coverings for the ears, nothing short of ill-health can excuse their use.

But such attention to clothing is only possible at the beginning of a speech, since [as the speech continues]...the fold will slip down from the shoulder quite naturally and as if it were of its own accord…The left hand may be employed to pluck the toga from the throat and the upper portion of the chest, for by now the whole body will be hot. And just as at this point the voice becomes more vehement and more varied in its utterance, so the clothing begins to assume something of a combative pose. Consequently, although to wrap the toga around the left hand or to pull it about us as a girdle would be almost a symptom of madness, while to throw back the fold from its bottom over the right shoulder would be a foppish and effeminate gesture, and there are yet worse effects than these, there is, at any rate, no reason why we should not place the looser portions of the fold under the left arm, since it gives the impression of vigor and freedom not ill-suited to the warmth and energy of our action.

When, however, our speech draws near its close, more especially if fortune shows herself kind, practically everything is appropriate. We may stream with sweat, show signs of fatigue, and let our clothing fall in careless disorder, and the toga slip loose from us on every side…On the other hand, if the toga falls down at the beginning of our speech, or when we have only proceeded a little way, the failure to replace it is a sign of indifference, or laziness, or sheer ignorance of the way in which clothes should be worn.

Source: *The Institutio Oratoria of Quintilian.* Translated by H. E. Butler. Cambridge and London: Loeb Classical Library, 1922.

44. Frugality in Clothing, Furniture, and Food

The first-century A.D. *philosopher Seneca, in this excerpt from his essay entitled "On Tranquility of Mind," heaps praise upon the frugal life when it comes to clothing, food, and household furnishings.*

I am possessed by the very greatest love of frugality, I must confess. I do not like a couch made up for display, nor clothing brought forth from a chest, or pressed by weights and a thousand mangles to make it glossy, but homely and cheap, that is neither preserved nor to be put on with anxious care. The food that I like is neither prepared nor watched by a household of slaves; it does not need to be ordered many days before, nor to be served by many hands, but is easy to get and abundant. There is nothing far-fetched or costly about it. Nowhere will there be any lack of it, it is burdensome neither to the purse nor to the body, nor will it return by the way it entered.

The silver [eating utensils] is my country-bred father's heavy plate, bearing no stamp of the maker's name, and the table is not notable for the variety of its markings or known to the town from the many fashionable owners through whose hands it has passed, but one that stands for use, and will neither cause the eyes of any guest to linger upon it with pleasure, nor fire them with envy.

Source: *Seneca: Moral Essays.* Volume II. Translated by John W. Basore. Cambridge and London: Loeb Classical Library, 1932.

45. Trimalchio's Fancy Wardrobe

On the other hand, Trimalchio, *a character in the Latin novel* Satyricon *by Petronius (A.D. c. 27–65), was hardly interested in the frugal lifestyle, especially when clothing was involved, as this excerpt from the novel indicates (see also Document 18, above).*

Suddenly the trumpets blazed a fanfare and Trimalchio was carried in, propped up on piles of miniature pillows in such a comic way that some of us couldn't resist impolitely smiling. His head, cropped close in a recognizable slave cut, protruded from a cloak of blazing scarlet; his neck, heavily swathed already in bundles of clothing, was wrapped in a large napkin bounded by an incongruous senatorial purple stripe with little tassels dangling down here and there. On the little finger of his left hand, he sported an immense gilt ring; the ring on the last joint of his fourth finger looked to be solid gold of the kind the lesser nobility wear, but was actually, I think, an imitation, pricked out with small steel stars. Nor does this exhaust the inventory of his trinkets. At least he rather ostentatiously bared his arm to show us a large gold bracelet and an ivory circlet with a shiny metal plate.

Source: From THE SATYRICON by Petronius, translated by William Arrowsmith, copyright © 1959, renewed © 1987 by William Arrowsmith. Used by permission of Dutton Signet, a division of Penguin Group (USA) Inc.

46. An Emperor's Immodest Attire

The Roman emperor Caligula (reigned A.D. 37–41), always one given to excess, wore an assortment of clothing, depending on the occasion, as the Roman biographer Suetonius (A.D. c. 70–c. 140) relates in this excerpt from his writings.

In his clothing, his shoes, and the rest of his attire, he did not follow the usage of his country and his fellow citizens . . . nor even, in fact, that of an ordinary mortal. He often appeared in public in embroidered cloaks covered with precious stones, with a long-sleeved tunic and bracelets, sometimes in silk and in a woman's robe. Sometimes he wore slippers or buskins, sometimes boots, such as the emperor's bodyguards wear, and at times in the low shoes which are worn by women. Often, he exhibited himself with a golden beard, holding in his hand a thunderbolt, a trident, or a caduceus, emblems of the gods . . . he frequently wore the clothing of a triumphant general, even before his campaigns, and sometimes the breastplate of Alexander the Great, which he had taken from his sarcophagus.

Source: *Suetonius.* Volume I. Translated by John C. Rolfe. Cambridge and London: Loeb Classical Library, 1913.

47. School Clothes

In this passage from his Attic Nights, *the Roman writer Aulus Gellius (A.D. c. 125–c. 180) relates a story about a teacher who had high standards when it came to proper attire for his students, present and past.*

Titus Castricius, a teacher of the art of rhetoric, who held the first rank at Rome as a declaimer and an instructor, a man of the greatest influence and dignity, was highly regarded also by the deified [emperor] Hadrian for his character and his learning. Once when I happened to be with him (for he was my teacher), and he had seen some students of his who were senators, wearing tunics and cloaks on a holiday, and with sandals on their feet, he said: "For my part, I would have preferred to see you in your togas, or if that was too much trouble, at least with girdles and mantles. But if this present attire of yours is now pardonable from long custom, yet it is not at all appropriate for you, who are senators of the Roman people, to go through the streets of the city in sandals, nor is this less criminal in you that it was in one [Mark Antony] whom Cicero once criticized for such attire." This, and some other things on the same subject, Castricius said in my hearing with true Roman austerity.

Source: *The Attic Nights of Aulus Gellius.* Volume II. Translated by John C. Rolfe. Cambridge and London: Loeb Classical Library, 1927.

48. Upscale Adornments

Wealthy Roman women sometimes went all out in the fashion department, as the writer Pliny the Elder (A.D. 23–79) relates in this excerpt from his Natural History.

I have seen Lollia Paulina, who became the consort of Gaius, not at some considerable or solemn ceremonial celebration, but actually at an ordinary betrothal banquet, covered with emeralds and pearls interlaced alternately and shining all over her head, hair, ears, neck, and fingers, the sum total amounting to the value of 40,000,000 sesterces [an outlandish sum of money], she herself being ready at a moment's notice to give documentary proof of her ownership of them. Nor had they been presents from an extravagant emperor, but ancestral possessions, acquired in fact with the spoil of the provinces...

There have been two pearls that were the largest in the whole of history, and both were owned by Cleopatra, the last of the queens of Egypt...

...This article [a pearl] is an almost everlasting piece of property. It passes to its owner's heir, it is offered for public sale like some landed estate, whereas every hour of use wears away robes of scarlet and purple, which the same mother, namely luxury, had made almost as costly as pearls.

Source: *Pliny: Natural History.* Volume III. Translated by H. Rackham. London and Cambridge: Loeb Classical Library, 1940.

Part VI

POLITICAL LIFE

Government

Most governments of the ancient world were characterized by one-man rule, as Documents 1–3, and 5 indicate. But civil servants of various descriptions were also needed for kingdoms to function efficiently. In Document 4, the duties of an Egyptian government inspector are recounted. He was particularly responsible for seeing that crops and livestock were being tended properly.

The world's first fully functioning democracy evolved in Athens in the fifth century B.C. At the heart of the Athenian democracy was the *Assembly*, where all important public issues were debated, and policy decisions were made. Membership was open to all Athenian citizens, no matter how uninformed or apathetic they might be; no election or other selection process was employed. Assembly members enjoyed complete freedom of speech. They felt no hesitation whatsoever at making statements that in today's climate of political correctness would not be tolerated. This democracy had its critics (Document 6), and its proponents (Document 7).

The historian Polybius, who was Greek by birth but who lived in Rome for about 20 years during the second century B.C., greatly admired the Roman form of government, especially its system of checks and balances. His thoughts appear in Document 8.

CHINA

1. *"Govern the State by Correctness"*

Laozi was a Chinese philosopher and political scientist (or, according to some historians, a consortium of writers), who lived sometime between the sixth and fourth centuries B.C. Below are various selections from the thoughts of Laozi on the proper ways to govern.

Govern the state by correctness;
Deploy the army by deception;
Acquire the empire by taking no action.
How do I know this is so? By this.
The more prohibitions there are in the world,

The poorer are the people.
The more sharp weapons people have,
The more disorder is fomented in the family and state.
The more adroit and clever men are,
The more deceptive things are brought forth.
The more laws and ordinances are promulgated,
The more thieves and robbers there are.
Therefore the sage says: I do nothing.
And the people are transformed by themselves.
I value tranquility,
And the people become correct by themselves.
I take no action,
And the people become prosperous by themselves.
I have no desires,
And the people of themselves become like uncarved wood.
Governing a large state is like cooking a small fish.
By using the Way to manage the empire,
Spiritual forces lose their potency.
Not that they lose their potency,
But that their potency does not harm people,
Not only does their potency not harm people,
But the sage also does not harm people.
The two do not harm one another,
So that virtue accumulates in both and returns [to the people]…
Let the state be small and the people be few.
There may be ten or even a hundred times as many implements.
But they should not be used.
Let the people, regarding death as a weighty matter, not travel far.
Though they have boats and carriages, none shall ride in them.
Though they have armor and weapons, none shall display them.
Let the people return once more to the use of knotted ropes [for record-keeping].
Let them savor their food and find beauty in their clothing,
peace in their dwellings, and joy in their customs.
Though neighboring states are within sight of one another,
And the sound of roosters and dogs is audible from one to the other,
People will reach old age and death and yet not visit one another [because there is nothing that they want from each other].

Source: From *Sources of Chinese Tradition*. Volume I. Second edition. Compiled by William Theodore de Bary and Irene Bloom. Copyright © 1999 Columbia University Press. Reprinted with permission of the publisher.

INDIA

2. The Kings of India

Arrian, a Greek historian born around A.D. 95, wrote a treatise on India in which he included a history of early Indian kings. Below is a brief excerpt from that history.

When departing from India, after setting all this in order, Dionysus made Spatembas king of the land, one of his companions who was most expert in Bacchic rites. When Spatembas died, Budyas, his son, reigned in the stead. The father was king of India

52 years, and the son 20. His son Cradeuas came to the throne and his descendants mostly received the kingdom in succession, son succeeding father. If the succession failed, then Indian kings were appointed for merit...From Dionysus to Sandracottus, the Indians counted 153 kings.

Source: *Arrian*. Translated by E. Iliff Robson, with revisions by P. A. Brunt. Cambridge and London: Loeb Classical Library, 1933.

EGYPT

3. How the Kings of Egypt Governed

In the following excerpt from his writings, Diodorus Siculus, a first-century B.C. Greek historian born in Sicily provides an overview of how Egyptian kings governed their country.

Strange as it may appear that the king did not have the entire control of his daily meals, far more remarkable still was the fact that the kings were not allowed to render any legal decisions or transact any business at random or to punish anyone through malice or in anger or for any other unjust reason, but only in accordance with the established laws relative to each offense. And in following the dictates of custom in these matters, so far were they from being indignant or taking offense...that, on the contrary, they actually believed that they led a most happy life, because they reasoned that other men, in thoughtlessly following their natural passions, commit many acts which bring them injuries and perils, and that often some who realize that they are about to commit a sin nevertheless engage in unseemly acts when overpowered by love or hatred or some other emotion, while they, on the other hand, by virtue of their having cultivated a manner of life which had been chosen before all others by the most prudent of all men, fell into the fewest mistakes.

And since kings followed so righteous a course in dealing with their subjects, the people manifested a good will towards their rulers which surpassed even the affection they had for their own family members. Not only the priests, but all the inhabitants of Egypt were less concerned for their wives and children and their other cherished possessions than for the safety of their kings. Consequently, during most of the time covered by the reigns of the kings of whom we have a record, they maintained an orderly civil government, and continued to enjoy a most happy life, so long as the system of laws described was in force. And more than that, they conquered more nations and achieved greater wealth than any other people, and adorned their lands with monuments and buildings never to be surpassed, and their cities with costly dedications of every description.

Source: *Diodorus of Sicily*. Volume I. Translated by C. H. Oldfather. London and Cambridge: Loeb Classical Library, 1933.

4. The Duties of a Government Inspector

This passage from a third-century B.C. papyrus contains information about the responsibilities of an Egyptian government official—the oeconomus—during his inspection tours of the government-owned lands and weaving establishments of his district.

In your tours of inspection, try in going from place to place to cheer everybody up and to give them greater confidence. Not only should you do this by words but also, if any of them [especially the peasant farmers] complain to the village scribes...about any matter concerning agricultural work, you should make an inquiry and put a stop to such doings as far as possible.

When the sowing has been completed, it would be no bad thing if you were to make a careful round of inspection, for in this way, you will get an accurate view of the sprouting of the crops and will easily notice the lands which are badly sown or are not sown at all, and you will therefore know those who have neglected their duty and will become aware if any have used the seed for other purposes.

You must regard it as one of your most important duties to see that the district be sown with the kinds of crops prescribed by the sowing schedule. And if there are any who are hard pressed by their rents or are completely exhausted, you must not leave it unexamined.

Make a list of the cattle employed in cultivation [to distribute the cattle to best advantage during the seasons of the year], both the royal and the private, and take the utmost care that the offspring of the royal cattle, when old enough to eat hay, be consigned to...

Take care also that the prescribed supplies of corn, of which I send you a list, are brought down to Alexandria punctually, not only correct in amount but also tested and fit for use.

Also visit the weaving establishments in which the linen is woven, and do your utmost to have the largest possible number of looms in operation, the weavers supplying the full amount of embroidered stuffs prescribed for the district. If any of them are in arrears with the pieces ordered, let the prices fixed by the ordinance for each kind of stuff be exacted from them. Take special care, too, that the linen is good and has the prescribed number of weft threads...

Since the revenue from the pasturage dues, too, is one of the most important, it will most readily be increased if you carry out the registration [for taxation purposes] of cattle in the best possible way. The most favorable season for one so engaged is about the month of Mesore [July/August], for the whole country in this month, being covered with water, it happens that cattle breeders send their flocks to the highest places, being unable to scatter them on other places.

See to it, too, that the goods for sale be not sold at prices higher than those prescribed. Make also a careful investigation of those goods which have no fixed prices and on which the dealers may put what prices they like.

Source: *Select Papyri: Non-Literary Papyri. Public Documents.* Volume II. Translated by A. S. Hunt and C. C. Edgar. Cambridge and London: Loeb Classical Library, 1934.

GREECE

5. A New King Comes to Power

In Antigone, *a play by the fifth-century* B.C. *Athenian playwright Sophocles,* Creon *has assumed the kingship of Thebes. In this excerpt, he announces to an assemblage of elders his governing philosophies.*

Gentlemen: I have the honor to inform you that our Ship of State, which recent storms have threatened to destroy, has come safely to harbor at last, guided by the merciful wisdom of Heaven. I have summoned you here this morning because I know that I can depend on you. Your devotion to King Laius [an earlier king of Thebes] was absolute; you never hesitated in your duty to our later ruler Oedipus, and when Oedipus died, your loyalty was transferred to his children. Unfortunately, as you know, his two sons, the princes Eteocles and Polyneices, have killed each other in battle. And I, as the next in blood, have succeeded to the full power of the throne.

I am aware, of course, that no ruler can expect complete loyalty from his subjects until he has been tested in office. Nevertheless, I say to you at the very outset that I have nothing but contempt for the kind of governor who is afraid, for whatever reason, to follow the course that he knows is best for the state. And as for the man who sets private friendship above the public welfare, I have no use for him, either. I call the gods to witness that if I saw my country headed for ruin, I would not be afraid to speak out plainly, and I need hardly remind you that I would never have any dealings with an enemy of the people. No one values friendship more highly than I do, but we must remember that friends made at the risk of wrecking out Ship of State are not real friends at all.

These are my principles.

Source: *Greek and Roman Writers*. Compiled by Reverend William T. McNiff, O.S.C. ["Antigone" from THE ANTIGONE OF SOPHOCLES, AN ENGLISH VERSION by Dudley Fitts and Robert Fitzgerald, copyright 1939 by Houghton Mifflin Harcourt Publishing Company and renewed 1967 by Dudley Fitts and Robert Fitzgerald, reprinted by permission of the publisher. CAUTION: All rights, including professional, amateur, motion picture, recitation, lecturing, performance, public reading, radio broadcasting, and television are strictly reserved. Inquiries on all rights should be addressed to Harcourt, Inc., Permissions Department, Orlando, FL 32887-6777].

6. A Critic's View of the Athenian Democracy

The Athenian democracy came to full flower in the fifth century B.C., *but not all Athenians were enamored of this form of government, including an anonymous critic known as the Old Oligarch.*

And as for the fact that the Athenians have chosen the kind of constitution that they have, I do not think well of their doing this, inasmuch as in making their choice, they have chosen to let the worst people be better off than the good. Therefore, on this account, I do not think well of their constitution. But since they have decided to have it so, I intend to point out how well they preserve their constitution, and accomplish those other things for which the rest of the Greeks criticize them.

First, I want to say this: there the poor and the people generally are right to have more than the highborn and the wealthy, for the reason that it is the people who man the ships and impart strength to the city. The steersmen, the boatswains, the sub-boatswains, the look-out officers and the shipwrights—these are the ones who impart strength to the city far more than the hoplites, the highborn, and the good men. This being the case, it seems right for everyone to have a share in the magistracies, both allotted and elective, for anyone to be able to speak his mind if he wants to. Then there are those magistracies which bring safety or danger to the people as a whole, depending on whether or not they are well managed. Of these, the people claim no share...

Someone might say that they ought not to let everyone speak on equal terms and serve on the council, but rather just the cleverest and finest. Yet their policy is also excellent in this very point of allowing even the worst to speak. For if the good men were to speak and make policy, it would be splendid for the likes of themselves, but not so for the men of the people. But, as things are, any wretch who wants to can stand up and obtain what is good for him and the likes of himself...

Further, for oligarchic cities it is necessary to keep alliances and oaths. If they do not abide by agreements, or if injustice is done, there are the names of the few who made the agreement. But whatever agreements the populace makes can be repudiated by referring the blame to the one who spoke or took the vote, while the others declare that they were absent or did not approve of the agreement made in the full assembly. If it seems advisable for their decisions not to be effective, they invent myriad excuses for not doing what they do not want to do. And if there are any bad results from the people's plans, they charge that a few persons, working against them, ruined their plans. But if there is a good result, they take the credit for themselves...

I pardon the people themselves for their democracy. One must forgive everyone for looking after his own interests. But whoever is not a man of the people and yet prefers to live in a democratic city rather than in an oligarchic one has readied himself to do wrong and has realized that it is easier for an evil man to escape notice in a democratic city than in an oligarchic.

As for the constitution of the Athenians, I do not praise its form, but since they have decided to have a democracy, I think they have preserved the democracy well by the means which I have indicated.

Source: *Xenophon: Scripta Minora*, Volume VII. Translated by E. C. Marchant. London and Cambridge: Loeb Classical Library, 1925.

7. A Proponent's View of the Athenian Democracy: Pericles's Funeral Oration

At the outset of the Peloponnesian War in 430 B.C., the famed Athenian politician and statesman Pericles (c. 495–429 B.C.) was selected to make a speech. The circumstances of the speech, and the following excerpts from it content, are reported by the historian Thucydides (c. 460-c. 400 B.C.), in his book on the war.

When [funerals for the war dead have been held], a man chosen by the city for his intellectual gifts and for his general reputation makes an appropriate speech in praise of the dead, and after the speech, all depart...Now, at the burial of those who were the first to fall in the war, Pericles, the son of Xanthippus, was chosen to make the speech...

"I have no wish to make a long speech on subjects familiar to you all...What I want to do is, in the first place, to discuss the spirit in which we faced our trials, and also our constitution and the way of life which has made us great...

An engraving of Lucian, ancient Greek rhetorician, pamphleteer, and satirist. Library of Congress.

"Let me say that our system of government does not copy the institutions of our neighbors. It is more the case of our being a model to others, than of our imitating anyone else. Our constitution is called a democracy because power is in the hands not of a minority, but of the whole people. When it is a question of settling private disputes, everyone is equal before the law. When it is a question of putting one person before another in positions of public responsibility, what counts is not membership of a particular [social] class, but the actual ability which the person possesses. No one, so long as he has it in him to be of service to the state, is kept in political obscurity because of poverty. And, just as our political life is free and open, so is our day-to-day life in our relations with each other. We do not get angry with our next door neighbor if he enjoys himself in his own way, nor do we give him the kind of hateful looks which, though they do no real harm, still do hurt people's feelings. We are free and tolerant in our private lives, but in public affairs, we keep to the law. This is because it commands our deep respect.

"We obey those whom we put in positions of authority, and we obey the laws themselves, especially those which are for the protection of the oppressed, and those unwritten laws which it is an acknowledged shame to break...

"Then there is a great difference between us and our opponents [especially the Spartans], in our attitude towards military security. Here are some examples: Our city is open to the world, and we have no periodical deportations in order to prevent people from observing or finding out secrets which might be of military advantage to the enemy. This is because we rely, not on secret weapons, but on our own real courage and loyalty. There is a difference, too, in our educational systems. The Spartans, from their earliest boyhood, are submitted to the most laborious training in courage. We pass our lives without all these restrictions, and yet are just as ready to face the same dangers as they are...

"We regard wealth as something to be properly used, rather than as something to boast about. As for poverty, no one need be ashamed to admit it. The real shame is in not taking practical measures to escape from it. Here, each individual is interested not only in his own affairs, but in the affairs of the government as well. Even those who are mostly occupied with their own business are extremely well-informed on general politics. This is a peculiarity of ours: we do not say that a person who takes no interest in politics is someone who minds his own business; we say that he has no business here at all...

"Taking everything together, then, I declare that our city is the school of Greece, and I declare that in my opinion, each single one of our citizens, in all the manifold aspects of life, is able to show himself the rightful lord and owner of his own person, and so this, moreover, with exceptional grace and exceptional versatility... Mighty indeed are the marks and monuments of our empire which we have left. Future ages will wonder at us, as the present age wonders at us now."

Source: *History of the Peloponnesian War by Thucydides,* translated by Rex Warner, with an introduction and notes by M. I. Finley. Penguin Classics 1954, revised edition 1972. Translation copyright © Rex Warner, 1954. Introduction and Appendices copyright © M. I. Finley, 1972. Reproduced by permission of Penguin Books Ltd. and Curtis Brown Group, Ltd., London, on behalf of the Estate of Rex Warner.

ROME

8. The Best of All Political Systems

In this excerpt from his Histories, *the Greek historian Polybius (c. 205–c. 123* B.C.*) discusses the workings of the Roman Republic.*

The three kinds of government I spoke of [monarchy, aristocracy, democracy] above all shared in the control of the Roman state. And such fairness and propriety in all respects was shown in the use of these three elements for drawing up the constitution and in its subsequent administration that it was impossible for even a native to pronounce with certainty whether the whole system was aristocratic, democratic, or monarchical. This was indeed only natural. For if one fixed one's eyes on the power of the consuls, the constitution seemed completely monarchical and royal; if on that of the senate, it seemed to be aristocratic; and when one looked at the power of the masses, it seemed clearly to be a democracy. The parts of the state falling under the control of each element were, and with a few modifications, still are as follows:

The consuls, previous to leading out their legions, exercise authority in Rome over all public affairs, since all the other magistrates except the tribunes are under them and bound to obey them, and it is they who introduce embassies to the senate. Besides this, it is they who consult the senate on matters of urgency, they who carry out in detail the provisions of its decrees. Again, as concerns all affairs of state administered by the people, it is their duty to take these under their charge, to summon assemblies, to introduce measures, and to preside over the execution of popular decrees. As for preparation for war and the general conduct of operations in the field, here their power is almost uncontrolled, for they are empowered to make what demands they choose on the allies, to appoint military tribunes, to levy soldiers and select those who are fittest for service. They also have the right of inflicting, when on active service, punishment on anyone under their command. And they are authorized to spend any sum they decide upon from the public funds, being accompanied by a quaestor [financial official] who faithfully executes their instructions. So that if one looks at this part of the administration alone, one may reasonably pronounce the constitution to be a pure monarchy or kingship. I may remark that any changes in these matters or in others of which I am about to speak that may be made in present or future times do not in any way affect the truth of the views I state here.

To pass to the senate: In the first place, it has control of the treasury, all revenue and expenditure being regulated by it. For with the exception of payments made to the consuls, the quaestors are not allowed to disburse for any particular object without a decree of the senate. And even the item of expenditure which is far heavier and more important than any other—the outlay every five years by the censors on public works, whether constructions or repairs—is under the control of the senate, which makes a grant to the censors for the purpose. Similarly, crimes committed in Italy which require a public investigation, such as treason, conspiracy, poisoning, and assassination, are under the jurisdiction of the senate. Also, if any private person or community in Italy is in need of arbitration or indeed claims damages or requires help or protection, the senate attends to all such matters. It also occupies itself with the dispatch of all embassies sent to countries outside of Italy for the purpose of either settling differences, or of offering friendly advice, or indeed imposing demands, or of receiving submission, or of declaring war. And in like manner with respect to embassies arriving in Rome, it decides what reception and what answer should be given to them. All these matters are in the hands of the senate, nor have the people anything whatever to do with them. So that again to one residing in Rome during the absence of the consuls, the constitution appears to be entirely aristocratic. And this is the conviction of many Greek states and many of the kings, as the senate manages all business connected with them.

After this, we are naturally inclined to ask what part in the constitution is left for the people, considering that the senate controls all the particular matters I mentioned, and, what it most important, manages all matters of revenue and expenditure, and considering that the consuls again have uncontrolled authority as regards armaments and operations in the field. But nevertheless there is a part and a very important part left for the people. For it is the people which alone has the right to confer honors and inflict punishment, the only bonds by which kingdoms and states and, in a word, human society in general are held together. For where the distinction between these is overlooked or is observed but ill applied, no affairs can be properly administered. How is this possible when good and evil men are held in equal estimation? It is by the people, then, in many cases that offenses punishable by a fine are tried when the accused have held the highest office. And they are the only court which may try on capital charges. As regards the latter, they have a practice which is praiseworthy and should be mentioned. Their usage allows those on trial for their lives, when found guilty, the liberty to depart openly, thus inflicting voluntary exile on themselves...

It is the people who bestow office on the deserving, the noblest reward of virtue in a state; the people have the power of approving or rejecting laws, and what is most important of all, they deliberate on the question of war and peace. Further, in the case of alliances, terms of peace, and treaties, it is the people who ratify all these, or the reverse. Thus, here again, one might plausibly say that the people's share in the government is the greatest, and that the constitution is a democratic one.

Having stated how political power is distributed among the different parts of the state, I will now explain how each of the three parts is enabled, if they wish, to counteract or cooperate with the others. The consul, when he leaves with his army,...appears indeed to have absolute authority in all matters necessary for carrying out his purpose. But in fact, he requires the support of the people and the senate, and is not able to bring his operations to a conclusion without them...It also depends on the senate whether or not a general can carry out completely his conceptions and plans, since it has the right of either superseding him when his year's term of office has expired, or of retaining him in command...As for the people, it is most indispensable for the consuls to be on good terms with them, however far away from home they may be. For, as I said, it is the people which ratifies or annuls terms of peace and treaties, and what is most important, on laying down office, the consuls are obliged to account for their actions to the people. So in no respect is it safe for the consuls to neglect keeping in favor with both the senate and the people.

The senate, which possesses such great power, is obligated in the first place to pay attention to the commons in public affairs and respect the wishes of the people, and it cannot carry out inquiries into the most grave and important offenses against the state, punishable with death, and their correction, unless their decrees are confirmed by the people…If anyone introduces a law meant to deprive the senate of some of its traditional authority, or to abolish the precedence and other distinctions of the senators, or even to curtail them of their private fortunes, it is the people alone which has the power of passing or rejecting any such measure…Therefore, for these reasons the senate is afraid of the masses, and must pay due attention to the popular will.

Similarly, the people must be submissive to the senate and respect its members both in public and in private. Through the whole of Italy, a vast number of contracts, which it would not be easy to enumerate, are given out…for the construction and repair of public buildings, and besides this there are many things which are farmed, such as navigable rivers, harbors, gardens, mines, lands, in fact everything that forms part of the Roman dominion…Now in all these matters, the senate is supreme. It can grant extension of time; it can relieve the contractor if any accident occurs; and if the work proves to be absolutely impossible to carry out, it can liberate him from his contract. There are, in fact, many ways in which the senate can either benefit or injure those who manage public property, as all these matters are referred to it. What is even more important is that the judges in most civil trials, whether public or private, are appointed from its members, where the action involves large interests. So that all citizens, being at the mercy of the senate, and looking forward with alarm to the uncertainty of litigation, are very hesitant to obstruct or resist its decisions…

Such being the power that each part has of hampering the others or cooperating with them, their union is adequate to all emergencies, so that it is impossible to find a better political system than this.

Source: *Polybius: The Histories*. Volume III. Translated by W. R. Paton. London and New York: Loeb Classical Library, 1923.

Justice and Legal Systems

Written law codes were prominent in many ancient civilizations, especially Sumeria (Document 9), Israel (Document 10), and Rome (Document 19). Respect for the law was emphasized, as illustrated by Documents 12 and 13. Laws, obviously, do not happen without legislators, and in Document 16, the careers of two noted Athenian legislators are featured. The administration of justice is described in Documents 11 and 15.

The system of ostracism, whereby a corrupt or dangerous politician could be exiled for 10 years, seems to have been unique to Athens. The process is explained in Document 17. Women seldom played a leading role in law or politics, but that was not always the case, as Document 20 indicates.

No judicial system could function without judges. The standards for judges in Egypt are contained in Document 14, while Documents 21 and 22 delineate the actions of two specific judges. Possibly the most famous trial in all of ancient history occurred in 399 B.C., when the famous philosopher *Socrates* was prosecuted in Athens for sophistry, advocating new systems of education, and undermining the state by leading the youth of Athens astray. Socrates's defense of his actions has been preserved in one of Plato's most well known writings, *Apology*, excerpts of which appear in Document 18.

Socrates was condemned by a large margin of the jurors' votes, and eventually forced to commit suicide. Had the Roman orator Cicero lived in that day and age, perhaps the jurors could have learned something from his writings on the importance of being just (Document 23).

SUMERIA

9. Selections from the Code of Hammurabi

Reproduced here is a selection of laws and regulations from the Code of Hammurabi, which was promulgated in Babylon in the eighteenth century B.C.:

226. If a barber, without the knowledge of his master, cuts the sign of a slave on a slave not to be sold, the hands of this barber shall be cut off.

228. If a builder builds a house for someone and completes it, he shall give him a fee of two shekels in money...

229. If a builder builds a house for someone, and does not construct it properly, and the house which he built falls in and kills its owner, then that builder shall be put to death.

230. If the house kills the son of the owner, the son of that builder shall be put to death.

232. If the house ruins goods, he shall make compensation for all that has been ruined, and inasmuch as he did not construct this house properly, which he built and it fell, he shall rebuild the house at his own expense.

233. If a builder builds a house for someone, even though he has not yet completed it, if then the walls seem to be toppling, the builder must make the walls solid at his own expense.

235. If a shipbuilder builds a boat for someone, and does not make it water-tight, if during that same year that boat is sent away and suffers injury, the shipbuilder shall take the boat apart and put back together, water-tight, at his own expense. The water-tight boat he shall give to the boat owner.

236. If a man rents his boat to a sailor, and the sailor is careless, and the boat is wrecked or goes aground, the sailor shall give the owner of the boat another boat as compensation.

253. If anyone agrees with another to tend his field, gives him seed, entrusts a yoke of oxen to him, and binds him to cultivate the field, if he steals the corn or plants, and takes them for himself, his hands shall be cut off.

265. If a herdsman, to whose care cattle or sheep have been entrusted, is guilty of fraud and makes false returns of the natural increase, or sells them for money, then he shall be convicted, and pay the owner ten times the loss.

282. If a slave says to a master: "You are not my master," if they convict him, his master shall cut off his ear.

Source: *The Code of Hammurabi.* Translated by L. W. King. The Avalon Project at Yale Law School: http://www.yale.edu/lawweb/avalon/medieval/hamcode.htm.

ISRAEL

10. Moses's Augmentation of the Ten Commandments

In this passage from his Jewish Antiquities, *the first-century* A.D. *Jewish historian Josephus summarizes the Ten Commandments, and then recounts how, in response to the request of the people, Moses procured a more detailed code of laws and the administration of justice.*

The first word teaches us that God is one and that He only must be worshipped. The second commands us to make no image of any living creature for adoration, the third not to swear by God on any frivolous matter, the fourth to keep every seventh day by resting from all work, the fifth to honor our parents, the sixth to refrain from murder, the seventh not to commit adultery, the eighth not to steal, the ninth not to bear false witness, the tenth to covet nothing that belongs to another.

The people, having thus heard from the very mouth of God that of which Moses had told them, rejoicing in these commandments, dispersed from the assembly. But on the following days, often visiting their leader's tent, they requested him to bring them laws also from God. And he both established these laws and in later times, indicated how they should act in all circumstances...

As rulers, let each city have seven men long exercised in virtue and in the pursuit of justice...Let those to whom it shall fall to administer justice in the cities be held in all honor, none being permitted to be abusive or insolent in their presence. For a respect for human dignitaries will make people too reverential to be ever contemptuous of God. Let the judges have the power to pronounce whatever sentence they think fit, always provided that no one denounce them for having received a bribe to pervert justice or bring forward some other charge to convict them of not having pronounced correctly. For they must be influenced neither by money nor by rank in declaring judgment, but must set justice above all. Otherwise, God would appear to be disrespected, and considered weaker than those to whom, from fear of their strength, the judge accords his vote. For God's strength is justice; and one who gives this away out of favor to persons of rank makes them more powerful than God. But if the judges do not see how to pronounce upon the matters set before them—and with people, such things often happen—let them send up the entire case to the holy city and let the high priest and the prophet and the council of elders meet and pronounce as they see fit.

Do not place trust in a single witness, but let there be three or at the least two, whose evidence shall be accredited by their past lives. From women, let no evidence be accepted, because of the levity and temerity of their sex. Do not let slaves bear witness, because of the baseness of their soul, since whether from greed or from fear, it is likely that they will not be truthful. If anyone is thought to have borne false witness, let him on conviction suffer the penalty which would have been incurred by him against whom he has borne witness.

If a murder has been done in any place and the doer of the deed is not found, nor is anyone suspected of having killed the victim from hatred, let them make a diligent search for the culprit, offering rewards for information. But if no informer appears, let the magistrates of the towns adjacent to the spot where the murder was done, along

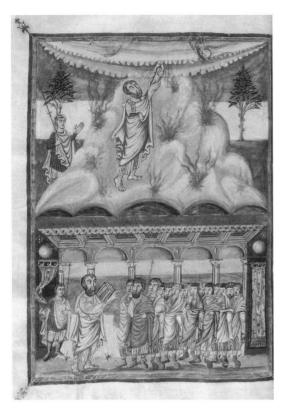

Moses receives tablets of the law from Heaven on Mount Sinai, from Moutier-Grandval bible, A.D. 800–900. The Art Archive/British Library.

with the council of elders, assemble and measure the ground from the place were the body lies. And whichever town is the nearest, let the public officers purchase a heifer and, conducting it to a ravine, to a spot unfitted for plowing or plantation, let them cut the sinews of the creature's neck. Then, after washing their hands in holy water over the head of the animal, let the priests, the Levites, and the council of that city proclaim that their hands are pure of this murder, that they neither did it, nor saw it done, and that they implore God to be gracious and that so dire a calamity may no more befall the land. . . .

Let it not be permitted to displace boundary markers, whether of your own land or of the land of others with whom you are at peace. Beware of uprooting, as it were, a stone by God's decree. For from this come wars and rebellions, from that desire of the covetous to overstep their boundaries. In truth, those who displace boundary markers are not far from transgressing the laws. . .

When reaping and gathering in the crops, you shall not glean, but shall even leave some of the sheaves for the destitute, to come as a godsend for their sustenance. Likewise, at the vintage, leave the little bunches for the poor, and pass over somewhat of the fruit of the olive yards, to be gathered by those who have none of their own of which to partake. For that minute care in garnering will not bring the owners wealth so great as the gratitude which would so come to them from the needy. God, too, will render the earth more eager to foster its fruits for those who look not only to their own interests, but also have regard to the support of others. Nor must you muzzle the oxen when they crush the ears of corn on the threshing-floor, for it is not just to exclude from the fruit your fellow laborers who have toiled to produce it. Nor yet, when autumn fruits are at their prime, must you forbid wayfarers to touch them, but let them take their fill, as if they were their own, be they natives or strangers, rejoicing at thus affording them a share in the fruits of the season. . . For one must not account as expenditure that which out of liberality one lets people take, since God bestows this abundance of good things not for our enjoyment alone, but that we may also share them generously with others, and He is desirous that by these means the special favor that He bears to the people of Israel and the bounty of his gifts may be manifested to others also, when out of all that superabundance of ours, they too receive their share from us. . .

For the stealing of a person, the penalty shall be death. The purloiner of gold or silver shall pay double the sum. He that kills another while engaged in burglary shall be innocent, even if the thief were still in the process of breaking through the wall. He that steals a head of cattle shall pay fourfold as penalty, except in the case of an ox, for which he shall be fined fivefold. He who does not have the means to pay the fine shall become the slave of those who have had him condemned. . .

If anyone finds gold or silver on the road, after a diligent search for the loser and public proclamation of the place where he found it, let him duly restore it, reckoning it dishonest to profit by another's loss. Similarly in the case of beasts which one meets straying in a desert place. But if the owner is not found immediately, let him keep them at his home, calling God to witness that he has not stolen the goods of another.

It is not permissible to pass by unheeding, when a man's beasts of burden, buffeted by a storm, have fallen in the mud. One must help to rescue them and lend aid as though one labored for oneself.

One must point out the road to those who are ignorant of it, and not, for the pleasure of laughing about it, impede another's business by misleading him.

Similarly, no one must curse the sightless or the mute...

Poison, whether deadly or of those designed for other injurious ends, let no Israelite possess. If one be caught in possession of it, let him die, undergoing the fate that he would have inflicted on the intended victims of the drug.

He that maims another shall undergo the like, being deprived of that limb which he deprived the other, unless the maimed person is willing to accept money. For the law empowers the victim himself to assess the damage that has befallen him and makes this concession, unless he would show himself too severe [i.e., ask for too much money].

An ox that gores with its horns shall be slaughtered by its owner. If on the threshing floor it kills any man by goring him, it shall itself be stoned to death and rejected as unfit even for eating. But if the owner himself be convicted of having known of its nature beforehand, and taken no precautions, he also shall die, as answerable for the death of the beast's victim...

Do not punish children for the wrongdoing of their parents, but by reason of their own virtue deem them deserving rather of pity for having been born of depraved parents than of hatred for their base lineage. One must not impute to the fathers the sin of the sons, for the young permit themselves much that is contrary to our instruction, in their disdain of discipline...

Such, then, is the constitution that Moses left.

Source: *Josephus: Jewish Antiquities*. Volume IV. Translated by H. St. J. Thackeray. Cambridge and London: Loeb Classical Library, 1930.

11. The Administration of Justice in Ancient Israel

In another passage from his Jewish Antiquities *(see also Document 10), the Jewish historian Josephus relates that judges are to be respected but are also to adhere to strict codes of ethics in the way in which they administer justice.*

Let those to whom it shall fall to administer justice in the cities be held in all honor, none being permitted to be abusive or insolent in their presence. A respect for human dignitaries will make people too reverential to be ever contemptuous of God. Let the judges have power to pronounce whatever sentence they think appropriate, always provided that no one denounces them for having received a bribe to pervert justice or bring forward some other charge to convict them of not having pronounced correctly.

They must not be influenced by money nor by rank in declaring judgment, but must set justice above all. Otherwise, God would appear to be condemned and considered weaker than those to whom, from fear of their strength, the judge accords his vote. For God's strength is justice, and one who gives this away out of favor to persons of ranks makes them more powerful than God. But if the judges do not see how to pronounce upon the matters set before them—and with human beings, such things often happen— let them send up the entire case to the holy city and let the high priest and the prophet and the council of elders meet and pronounce as they think appropriate.

Do not put trust in a single witness, but let there be three or at least two, whose evidence will be accredited by their past lives. No evidence should be accepted from women, because of the levity and temerity of their sex. Neither let slaves bear witness, because of the baseness of their souls, since whether from greed or fear, it is likely that they will not be truthful. If anyone is believed to have borne false witness, let him on conviction suffer the penalty which would have been incurred by him against whom he has borne witness.

Source: *Josephus: Jewish Antiquities*. Volume IV. Translated by H. St. J. Thackeray. Cambridge and London: Loeb Classical Library, 1930.

CHINA

12. The Right Laws for Directing the People

The Book of Lord Shang, *written by Lord Shang, a fourth-century* B.C. *government official, contains information about legal systems and legal reform in ancient China.*

Duke Xiao discussed his policy. The three Great Officers, Gongsun Yang (Shang Yang), Gan Long, and Du Zhi, were in attendance on the ruler. Their thoughts dwelt on the vicissitudes of the world's affairs; they discussed the principles of rectifying the law, and they sought for the way of directing the people. The ruler said, "Not to forget, at his succession, the tutelary spirits of the soil and of grain, is the way of a ruler; to shape the laws and to see to it that an intelligent ruler reigns are the tasks of a minister. I intend, now, to alter the laws, so as to obtain orderly government, and to reform the rites, so as to teach the people, but I am afraid that all-under-Heaven will criticize me."

Gongsun Yang said, "I have heard it said, that he who hesitates in action does not accomplish anything, and that he who hesitates in affairs gains no merit. Let your highness settle your thoughts quickly about altering the laws and perhaps not heed the criticism of all-under-Heaven. Moreover, he who surpasses others is, as a matter of course, disapproved of by the world; he who has thoughts of independent knowledge is certainly despised by the world. The saying runs, 'The stupid do not even understand an affair when it has been completed, but the wise see it even before it has sprouted...'

"Ordinary people abide by old practices, and scholars are immersed in the study of what is reported from antiquity. These two kinds of men are all right for filling offices and for maintaining the law, but they are not the kind who can take part in a discussion that goes beyond the law. The Three Dynasties have attained supremacy by different rites, and the five Lords Protector have attained their protectorships by different laws. Therefore, a wise man creates laws, but a foolish man is controlled by them. A man of talent reforms rites, but a worthless man is enslaved by them...

"The way to administer a state well is for the laws regulating officials to be clear; one does not rely on men to be intelligent and thoughtful. The ruler makes the people single-minded so they will not scheme for selfish profit. Then the strength of the state will be consolidated, and a state whose strength has been consolidated is powerful, but a country that loves talking is dismembered...

"It is the nature of people to be orderly, but it is circumstances that cause disorder. Therefore, in the application of punishments, light offenses should be regarded as serious; if light offenses do not occur, serious ones have no chance of coming. This is said to be 'ruling the people while in a state of law and order.'

"If in the application of punishments, serious offenses are regarded as serious, and light offenses as light, light offenses will not cease and, in consequence, there will be no means of stopping the serious ones. This is said to be 'ruling the people while in a state of lawlessness.' So if light offenses are regarded as serious, punishments will be abolished, affairs will succeed, and the state will be strong. But if serious offenses are regarded as serious, and light ones as light, then punishments will appear. Moreover, trouble will arise and the state will be dismembered...

"Punishments should know no degree or grade, but from ministers of state and generals down to great officers and ordinary people, whoever does not obey the king's commands, violates the interdicts of the state, or rebels against the statutes fixed by the ruler should be guilty of death and should not be pardoned. Merit acquired in the past should not cause a decrease in the punishment for demerit later, nor should good behavior in the past cause any derogation of the law for wrong done later. If loyal ministers and filial sons do wrong, they should be judged according to the full measure of their guilt, and if among officials who have to maintain the law and to uphold an office, there are those who do not carry out the king's law, they are guilty of death and should not be pardoned, but their punishment should be extended to their family for three generations."

Source: From *Sources of Chinese Tradition*. Volume I. Second edition. Compiled by William Theodore de Bary and Irene Bloom. Copyright © 1999 Columbia University Press. Reprinted with permission of the publisher.

INDIA

13. Making One's Thought Like the Law

The following statement on the primacy of law is to be found in the Dharmasangiti Sutra, *which dates from the era of Mahayana Buddhism in the first and second centuries* A.D.

The blessed Buddhas, of virtues endless and limitless, are born of the Law of Righteousness. They dwell in the Law, are fashioned by the Law, they have the Law as their master, the Law as their light, the Law as their field of action, the Law as their refuge. They are produced by the Law...and all the joys in this world and the next are born of the Law and produced by the Law...

The Law is equal, equal for all beings. For low or middle or high, the Law cares nothing.
So must I make my thought like the Law.

The Law has no regard for the pleasant. Impartial is the Law.
So must I make my thought like the Law.

The Law is not dependant on time. Timeless is the Law…
So must I make my thought like the Law.

The Law is not in the lofty without being in the low. Neither up nor down will the Law bend.
So must I make my thought like the Law.

The Law is not in that which is whole without being, in that which is broken. Devoid of all superiority or inferiority is the Law.
So must I make my thought like the Law.

The Law is not in the noble with being in the humble. No care for fields of activity has the Law.
So must I make my thought like the Law.

The Law is not in the day without being in the night…Ever firm is the Law.
So must I make my thought like the Law.

The Law does not lose the occasion of conversion. There is never delay with the Law.
So must I make my thought like the Law.

The Law has neither shortage nor abundance. Immeasurable, innumerable is the Law. Like space, it ever lessens or grows.
So must I make my thought like the Law.

The Law is not guarded by beings. Beings are protected by the Law.
So must I make my thought like the Law.

The Law does not seek refuge. The refuge of all the world is the Law.
So must I make my thought like the Law.

The Law has none who can resist it. Irresistible is the Law.
So must I make my thought like the Law.

The Law has no preferences. Without preference is the Law.
So must I make my thought like the Law.

The Law has no fear of the terrors of birth-and-death, nor is it lured by Nirvana. Ever without misgiving is the Law.
So must I make my thought like the Law.

Source: From *Sources of Indian Tradition*. Volume I. Edited by William Theodore de Bary. Copyright © 1958 Columbia University Press. Reprinted with permission of the publisher.

EGYPT

14. Proper Judicial Conduct

This excerpt from the maxims of Ptah-hotep, a twenty-fourth-century B.C. *Egyptian vizier, focuses on serving as a judge.*

If you should function as a noble official of the court,
Appointed to settle disputes among the populace,
Nurture (in yourself) ignorance of partiality.
When you speak, do not incline toward one side.
Be careful, in case someone voices his opinion

(To) the magistrates: "He turns the matter upside down."
Then your action will turn into censure (of yourself).
If you feel merciful concerning a misdeed which has happened
And feel favorable toward someone because of his honesty,
Pass over it and do not recall it,
Since he was silent before you from the very first.

Source: *The Literature of Ancient Egypt.* Edited by William Kelly Simpson. New Haven, CT: Yale University Press, 2003. Copyright © 2003 by Yale University Press. All rights reserved. Reprinted with permission of the publisher.

15. Crime and Punishment in Alexandria

This passage from a third-century B.C. papyrus prescribes the punishments for various kinds of crimes committed in Alexandria.

Threatening with iron. If a freeman threatens a freeman with iron or copper or stone . . . or wood, he shall forfeit 100 drachmas, if he loses the case. But if a male or female slave does any of these things to a freeman or a freewoman, they shall receive not less than 100 stripes, or else the master of the offender, if he is defeated in the suit, shall forfeit to the injured party twice the amount of the penalty which is prescribed for a freeman.

Injuries done in drunkenness. Whoever commits a person injury in a drunken state or by night or in a temple or in the marketplace shall forfeit twice the amount of the prescribed penalty.

For a slave striking a freeman. If a male slave or a female slave strikes a freeman or a freewoman, they shall receive not less than 100 stripes, or else the master, if he acknowledges the fact, shall pay on behalf of his slave twice the amount of the penalty which is prescribed for a freeman. But if he disputes it, the plaintiff shall indict him, claiming for one blow 100 drachmas, and if the master is condemned, he shall forfeit three times that amount without assessment. And for a greater number of blows, the plaintiff shall himself assess the injury when he brings the suit, and whatever assessment is fixed by the court, the master shall forfeit three times that amount.

Blows between freemen. If a freeman or a freewoman, making an unjust attack, strikes a freeman or a freewoman, they shall forfeit 100 drachmas without assessment, if they are defeated in the suit. But if they strike more than one blow, the plaintiff in bringing the suit shall himself assess the damage caused by the blows, and whatever assessment is fixed by the court, the accused shall forfeit twice that amount. And if anyone strikes one of the magistrates while executing the administrative duties prescribed to the magistracy, he shall pay the penalties tripled, if he is defeated in the suit.

Outrage. If any person commits against another an outrage not provided for in the code, the injured party shall himself assess the damage in bringing his suit, but he shall further state specifically in what manner he claims to have been outraged and the date on which he was outraged. And the offender, if condemned, shall pay twice the amount of the assessment fixed by the court.

Source: *Select Papyri: Non-Literary Papyri. Public Documents.* Volume II. Translated by A. S. Hunt and C. C. Edgar. Cambridge and London: Loeb Classical Library, 1934.

GREECE

16. A Comparison of Two Famous Athenian Legislators

In this excerpt from his Attic Nights, *the Roman writer Aulus Gellius (A.D. c. 125–c. 180) offers a brief comparison of* Draco *and* Solon, *two of the most famous Athenian lawgivers, of the seventh and sixth centuries B.C., respectively.*

Draco the Athenian was considered a good man and of great wisdom, and he was skilled in law, human and divine. This Draco was the first of all to make laws for the use of the Athenians. In those laws, he decreed and enacted that one guilty of any theft whatsoever should be punished with death, and added many other statutes that were excessively severe [hence the modern word *Draconian*].

Therefore his laws, since they seemed very much too harsh, were abolished, not by order and decree, but by the tacit, unwritten consent of the Athenians. After that, they made use of other, milder laws, compiled by Solon. This Solon was one of the famous seven wise men. He thought it proper by his law to punish thieves not with death, as Draco had formerly done, but by a fine of twice the value of the stolen goods.

But the same author also notes that things were a little different in Egypt and Sparta.

I recall that I read in the work of the jurist Aristo, a man of no slight learning, that among the ancient Egyptians, a race of people known to have been ingenious in inventions and skilled in getting to the bottom of things, thefts of all kinds were lawful and went unpunished. Among the Spartans, too, those serious and vigorous people, a matter for which the evidence is not as remote as in the case of the Egyptians, many famous writers, who have composed records of their laws and customs, affirm that thieving was lawful and customary, and that it was practiced by their young men, not for base gain or to furnish the means for indulgence or amassing wealth, but as an exercise and training in the art of war, for dexterity and practice in thieving made the minds of the young men sharp and strong for clever ambuscades, and for endurance in watching, and for the swiftness of surprise.

Source: *The Attic Nights of Aulus Gellius.* Volume II. Translated by John C. Rolfe. Cambridge and London: Loeb Classical Library, 1927.

17. A Unique Method for Banishing an Unpopular or Corrupt Politician

The ancient Athenians had an interesting and mostly effective mechanism for banishing from Athens politicians who became corrupt, dishonest, or overly ambitious, as the Greek biographer Plutarch (A.D. c. 45–c. 120) relates in this passage from his biography of the fifth-century B.C. politician Aristides.

The sentence of ostracism was not in itself a punishment for wrongdoing. It was described for the sake of appearances as a measure to curtail and humble a man's power and prestige in cases where these had grown oppressive. But in reality, it was a humane device for appeasing the people's jealousy, which could thus vent its desire to do harm, not by inflicting some irreparable injury, but by a sentence of ten years' banishment . . . The procedure, to give a general account of it, was as follows: Each voter took an *ostrakon*, or broken piece of pottery, wrote on it the name of the citizen he wished to be banished and carried it to [the polling place]. Then the archons [city officials] first counted the total number of votes cast, for if there were less than 6,000, the ostracism was void. After this, they sorted [and tallied] the votes, and the man who had the most recorded against his name was proclaimed to be exiled for ten years, with the right, however, to receive the income from his estate.

Source: *The Rise and Fall of Athens: Nine Greek Lives by Plutarch.* Translated by Ian Scott-Kilvert. New York: Penguin Books, 1960. Reproduced by permission of Penguin Books Ltd.

18. The Trial of Socrates

In 399 B.C., the famous Athenian philosopher Socrates (469–399 B.C.) was put on trial in Athens. He was charged with various crimes, including undermining the state and misleading the youth of Athens. He spoke in his own defense at his trial; these, according to Plato (428–347 B.C.), were some of his words. Despite his eloquence, Socrates was convicted by the jury and condemned to death.

I do not know what effect my accusers have had upon you, gentlemen [of the jury], but for my own part, I was almost carried away by them, so convincing were their arguments. On the other hand, scarcely a word of what they said was true. I was especially astonished at one of their many misrepresentations. I mean when they told you that you must be careful not to let me deceive you, the implication being that I am a skillful speaker. I thought that it was particularly brazen of them to tell you this without a blush, since they must know that they will soon be effectively confuted, when it becomes obvious that I have not the slightest skill as a speaker, unless, of course, by a skillful speaker, they mean one who speaks the truth. If that is what they mean, I would agree that I am an orator, though not after their pattern. My accusers, then, as I maintain, have said little or nothing that is true, but from me, you will hear the whole truth . . .

What did my critics say in attacking my character? I must read out their affidavit, so to speak, as though they were my legal accusers. "Socrates is guilty of criminal meddling, in that he inquires into things below the earth and in the sky, and makes the weaker argument defeat the stronger, and teaches others to follow his example." . . . The fact is that there is nothing in any of these charges, and if you have heard anyone say that I try to educate people and charge a fee, there is no truth in that, either . . .

There is another reason for my being unpopular. A number of young men with wealthy fathers and plenty of free time have deliberately attached themselves to me because they enjoy hearing other people cross-questioned. These often take me as their model, and go on to try to question others, whereupon, I suppose, they find an unlimited number of people who think that they know something, but really know little or nothing. Consequently, their victims become annoyed, not with themselves, but with me, and they complain that there is a pestilential busybody called Socrates who fills young people's heads with wrong ideas. If you ask them what he does, and what he teaches that has this effect, they have no answer, not knowing what to say. But since they do not want to admit their confusion, they fall back on the stock charges against any philosopher: that he teaches his students about things in the heavens and below the earth, and to disbelieve in gods, and to make the weaker argument defeat the stronger. They would be very reluctant, I imagine, to admit the truth, which is that they are being convicted of pretending to have knowledge, when they are entirely ignorant...

I do not think that it is right for a man to appeal to the jury or to get himself acquitted by doing so. He ought to inform them of the facts and convince them by argument. The jury does not sit to dispense justice as a favor, but to decide where justice lies, and the oath which they have sworn is not to show favor at their own discretion, but to return a just and lawful verdict. It follows that we must not develop in you, nor you allow to grow in yourselves, the habit of perjury. That would be sinful for us both... Surely it is obvious that if I tried to persuade you and prevail upon you by my entreaties to go against your solemn oath, I would be teaching you contempt for religion, and by my very defense, I would be accusing myself of having no religious belief. But that is very far from the truth. I have a more sincere belief, gentlemen, than any of my accusers, and I leave it to you and to the gods to judge me.

Source: *Plato: The Last Days of Socrates.* Translated by Hugh Tredennick. Baltimore: Penguin Books, 1954. Reproduced by permission of Penguin Books Ltd.

ROME

19. Ancient Rome's Earliest Written Laws

Reproduced below are some of the provisions of the Twelve Tables, *the oldest surviving law code in the history of Roman jurisprudence; it was published around 450* B.C.

Table I. Trial procedures.

If plaintiff summons defendant to court, he shall go. If he does not go, plaintiff shall call witness thereto. Then only shall he take defendant by force.

If defendant shirks or takes to his heels, plaintiff shall lay hands on him.

If disease or old age is an impediment, he [who summons defendant to court] shall grant him a team; he shall not spread with cushions the covered carriage if he does not so desire.

For a landowner, a landowner shall be surety; but for a proletarian person, let anyone who is willing be his protector.

There shall be the same right of bond and conveyance with the Roman people for a person restored to allegiance [i.e., a rebellious person] as for a loyal person [one who had never rebelled].

When parties make a settlement of the case, the judge shall announce it. If they do not reach a settlement, they shall state the outline of their case in the meeting place or Forum before noon.

They shall plead it out together in person. After noon, the judge shall adjudge the case to the party present. If both be present, sunset shall be the time limit [of proceedings]...

Table III. Debt.

When a debt has been acknowledged, or judgment about the matter has been pronounced in court, thirty days must be the legitimate time of grace. After that, the debtor may be arrested by laying on of hands. Bring him into court. If he does not satisfy the judgment, or no one in court offers himself as surety in his behalf, the creditor may take the defaulter with him. He may bind him with a weight no more than 15 pounds, or with less if he shall so desire. The debtor, if he wishes, may live on his own.

Table VII. Rights concerning land.

Ownership within a five-foot strip [between two pieces of land] shall not be acquired by long usage.

The width of a road [extends] to eight feet where it runs straight ahead, 16 around a corner...

Persons shall mend roadways. If they do not keep them laid with stone, a person may drive his beasts where he wishes...

If a water course directed through a public place shall do damage to a private person, he shall have the right of suit to the effect that damage shall be repaired for the owner.

Branches of a tree may be lopped off all around to a height of more than 15 feet...Should a tree on a neighbor's farm be bent crooked by a wind and lean over your farm, action may be taken for the removal of that tree.

It is permitted to gather up fruit falling down on another man's farm.

Table VIII. Torts or delicts.

If any person has sung or composed against another person a song such as was causing slander or insult to another, he shall be clubbed to death.

If a person has maimed another's limb, let there be retaliation in kind unless he makes agreement for settlement with him.

If he has broken or bruised a freeman's bone with his hand or a club, he shall undergo penalty of 300 *as* pieces; if a slave's, 150...

If a four-footed animal shall be said to have caused loss, legal action...shall be either the surrender of the thing which damaged, or else the offer of assessment for the damage.

For pasturing on, or cutting secretly by night, another's crops acquired by tillage, there shall be capital punishment in the case of an adult malefactor...he shall be hanged and put to death as a sacrifice to [the goddess] Ceres. In the case of a person under the age of puberty,

Ovid, one of the most prolific poets of Rome's Golden Age. Library of Congress.

at the discretion of the judge, either he shall be scourged, or settlement shall be made for the harm done by paying double damages.

Any person who destroys by burning any building or heap of corn deposited alongside a house shall be bound, scourged, and put to death by burning at the stake, provided that he has committed the said misdeed with malice aforethought; but if he shall have committed it by accident, that is, by negligence, it is ordained that he repair the damage, or, if he be too poor to be competent for such punishment, he shall receive a lighter chastisement...

If a theft has been done by night, if the owner kill the thief, the thief shall be held lawfully killed.

It is forbidden that a thief be killed by day...unless he defend himself with a weapon; even though he has come with a weapon, unless he use his weapon and fight back, you shall not kill him. And even if he resists, first call out.

In the case of all other thieves caught in the act, if they are freemen, they should be flogged and adjudged to the person against whom the theft has been committed, provided that the malefactors have committed it by day and have not defended themselves with a weapon. Slaves caught in the act of theft should be flogged and executed. Boys under the age of puberty should, at the judge's discretion, be flogged, and the damage done by them should be repaired.

Source: From *Roman Civilization Sourcebook II: The Empire*, by Naphtali Lewis and Meyer Reinhold. Copyright © 1955 Columbia University Press. Reprinted with permission of the publisher.

20. Uppity Women

In 215 B.C., a law was passed—the Lex Oppia—which placed restrictions on the amount of gold that a woman could possess, or the kinds of colored clothing she could wear. In addition, no women could ever travel in a horse-drawn wagon in a city or a town unless participating in a religious ceremony. A few years later, in 195 B.C., some thought was given to repealing the Lex Oppia, but many politicians were opposed to this proposal, including the crusty, austere Cato the Elder (234–149 B.C.). Below are excerpts from Cato's public speech in opposition to repeal as recorded by the historian Livy (59 B.C.–A.D. 17). Despite Cato's opposition, the law was repealed.

Citizens of Rome, if each one of us had set himself to retain the rights and the dignity of a husband over his own wife, we should have less trouble with women as a whole sex. As things are, our liberty, overthrown in the home by female inattention to discipline, is now being crushed and trodden underfoot here too, in the Forum. [According to Livy, "the matrons could not be confined within doors on the advice of their husbands...nor by their husbands' command; they flooded onto all the streets of the city and all the approaches to the Forum, and as the men came down to the Forum they accosted them...to allow the women the restoration of their former luxuries. The number of women increased daily."] It is because we have not kept them under control individually that we are now terrorized by them collectively...There is the greatest danger from any class of people, once you allow meetings and conferences and secret consultations. For myself, indeed, I find it hard to decide in my own mind which is worse: the activities themselves, or the precedents which they set. The activities concern us consuls and the other magistrates; the precedent, citizens, concerns you. For the question of whether the proposal brought before you is in the public interest or not, is a question to be decided by you, who are soon to vote upon it. But this female tumult... is, beyond doubt, something to the discredit of the magistrates...

For myself, it was with something like a blush of shame that I made my way just now to the Forum through the midst of an army of women. Had I not been restrained by my respect for the dignity and modesty of some individual women, rather than that of the female sex as a whole, if I had not feared that it might appear that such women had been rebuked by a consul, I would have said: "What sort of behavior is this? Are you in the habit of running out into the streets, blocking the roads, and addressing other women's husbands? Couldn't you have made the very same request of your own husbands at home? Or are you more alluring in the street than in the home, more attractive to other women's husbands than to your own?" And yet, even at home, if modesty restrained women within the limits of their own rights, it would not be appropriate for you to be concerned about the question of what laws should be passed or repealed...

Indeed, if they get their way on this matter, what will they not attempt? Run over all the laws relating to women whereby your ancestors curbed their freedom and brought them into subjection to their husbands. Even with all these restraints, you can hardly hold them back. And what will happen if you allow them to... wrest these restraints from your hands one by one, and finally to attain equality with their husbands? Do you imagine that you will find them endurable? The very moment they begin to be your equals, they will be your superiors. Good heavens! They object to the passing of a new measure against them. They complain that this is not law but rank injustice. In fact, their aim is that you should repeal a law which you have approved and sanctioned by your votes, whose worth you have tested in the practical experience of all these years. They intend, in other words, that by the abolition of this one law you should weaken the force of all the others. If every individual is to destroy and demolish any law which hinders him in his particular interests, what use will it be for the whole citizen body to pass measures which will soon be repealed by those whom they directed?

Source: *Livy: Rome and the Mediterranean*, Books XXXI–XLV of *The History of Rome from its Foundation*. Translated by Henry Bettenson. Baltimore: Penguin Books, 1976. Reproduced by permission of Penguin Books Ltd.

21. Augustus as Judge

As the following passage from the writings of the Roman biographer Suetonius (A.D. c. 70–c. 140) indicates, the emperor Augustus (reigned 27 B.C.–A.D. 14) was personally involved in the administration of Roman justice.

He himself administered justice regularly, and sometimes up to nightfall, having a litter placed on the tribunal, if he was indisposed, or even lying down at home. In his administration of justice, he was both highly conscientious and very lenient. For to save a man clearly guilty of parricide from being executed, a punishment which was inflicted only on those who pleaded guilty, he is said to have put the question to him in this form: "You surely did not kill your father, did you?" Again, in a case concerning a forged will, in which all the signers were liable to punishment...he distributed to the jury not merely the two tablets for condemnation or acquittal, but a third as well, for the pardon of those who were shown to have been induced to sign by misrepresentation or misunderstanding. Each year he referred appeals of cases involving citizens to the city judge, but those between foreigners, to ex-consuls, of whom he had put one in charge of the business affairs of each province.

He revised existing laws and enacted new ones, for example, on extravagance, on adultery and chastity, on bribery, and on the encouragement of marriage among the various classes of citizens. Having made somewhat more stringent changes in the last of these than in the others, he was unable to carry it out because of an open revolt against its provisions, until he had abolished or mitigated a part of the penalties, besides increasing the rewards and allowing a three years' exemption from the obligation to marry after the death of a husband or wife...And on finding that the spirit of the law was being evaded by betrothal with immature girls and by frequent changes of wives, he shortened the duration of betrothals and set a limit on divorce.

Source: *Suetonius*. Volume I. Translated by J. C. Rolfe. Cambridge and London: Loeb Classical Library, 1913.

22. Aulus Gellius as Judge

The essayist Aulus Gellius (A.D. c. 125–c. 180) had once been asked to serve as a judge in a case involving a dispute over the payment of some money. Gellius was not quite certain about the proper way to adjudicate the case, so he first "hunted up books written in both languages [i.e., Greek and Latin] on the duty of a judge" but soon discovered that "such books gave [him] no aid at all." So he decided to consult his learned friend, the philosopher Favorinus, on the best way to proceed. The following is an excerpt from the reply of Favorinus.

The question which you are now considering may seem to be of a trifling and insignificant character. But if you wish me to instruct you as to the full duties of a judge, this is by no means a fit place or time; for such a discussion involves many intricate questions and requires long and anxious attention and consideration. For—to touch at once upon a few leading questions for your benefit—the first query relating to the duty of a judge is this: If a judge happens to have knowledge of a matter which is brought to trial before him, and the matter is clearly known to him alone from some external circumstance or event, before it has begun to be argued or brought into court, but nevertheless the same thing is not proved in the course of the trial, ought he to decide in accordance with what he knew beforehand, or according to the evidence in the case?

This question also, said he, is often raised, whether it is fitting and proper for a judge, after a case has been heard, if there seems to be an opportunity for compromising the dispute, to postpone the duty of a judge for a time and take the part of a common friend and peacemaker, as it were. And I know that this is further a matter of doubt and inquiry, whether a judge, when hearing a suit, ought to mention and ask about the things which it is for the interest of one of the parties to the suit to mention and inquire, even if the party in question neither mentions nor calls for them. For they say that this is in fact to play the part of an advocate, not of a judge.

Besides these questions, there is disagreement also on this point, whether it is consistent with the practice and office of a judge by his occasional remarks so to explain and set forth the matter and the case which is being tried, that before the time of his decision, as the result of statements which at the time are made before him in a confused and doubtful form, he gives signs and indications of the emotions and feelings by which he is affected on each occasion and at every time. For those judges who give the impression of being keen and quick to think that the matter in dispute cannot be examined and understood, unless the judge by frequent questions and necessary interruptions makes his own opinion clear and grasps that of the litigants. But on the other hand, those who have a reputation for calmness and dignity maintain that the judge ought not, before giving his decision and while the case is being pleaded by both parties, to indicate his opinion whenever he is influenced by some argument that is brought forward. For they say that the result will be, since one emotion of the mind after another must be excited by the variety of points and arguments, that such judges will seem to feel and speak differently about the same case and almost at the same time...

In this case about which you are in doubt, the claimant is a person of the highest character and the one on whom the claim is made is the worst of men, and there are no witnesses to the transaction between the two. So then go and give credit to the claimant and condemn the one on whom the claim is made, since, as you say, the two are not equal and the claimant is the better man.

Source: *The Attic Nights of Aulus Gellius*. Volume III. Translated by John C. Rolfe. Cambridge and London: Loeb Classical Library, 1927.

23. The Importance of Being Just

In this excerpt from his treatise entitled "On Duties," the Roman orator Cicero (106–43 B.C.) states that Rome's earliest kings were chosen in part on their ability to administer justice.

Now it seems to me, at least, that...among our own ancestors, men of high moral character were made kings in order that the people might enjoy justice. For, as the masses in their helplessness were oppressed by the strong, they appealed for protection to some one man who was conspicuous for his virtue. And, as he shielded the weaker classes from wrong, he managed by establishing equitable conditions to hold the higher and the lower classes in an equality of right. The reason for making constitutional laws was the same as that for making kings. For what people have always sought is equality of rights before the law. For rights that were not open to all alike would be no rights. If the people secured their end at the hands of the one just and good man, they were satisfied with that. But when such was not their good fortune, laws were invented, to speak to all people at all times in one and the same voice.

This, then, is obvious: nations used to select for their rulers those men whose reputation for justice was high in the eyes of the people. If in addition they were also thought wise, there was nothing that men did not think they could secure under such leadership. Justice is, therefore, in every way to be cultivated and maintained, both for its own sake (for otherwise it would not be justice) and for the enhancement of personal honor and glory.

Source: *Cicero: De Officiis*. Translated by Walter Miller. Cambridge and London: Loeb Classical Library, 1913.

Warfare

Source material on warfare in the ancient world is a mixture of businesslike manuals on tactics and strategy, such as the one penned by the Roman engineer Frontinus (Document 36); treatises on the precepts and rules of warfare (Documents 24, 25, 38); and stories of the pleasant and not so pleasant moments in the lives of individual soldiers (Documents 29, 30, 39). Weaponry is the subject of Document 27.

Several of the documents defy easy classification. For example, in Document 32, tales are recounted of Alexander the Great's noted warhorse, *Bucephalus*. The Spartan king *Agesilaus* had some unique methods of motivating and training his soldiers, including organizing various kinds of martial competitions, with prizes for the winners (Document 33).

Accounts of crucial battles often attracted the attention of ancient historians. One of the most famous of these battles occurred in 480 B.C., at the mountain pass of Thermopylae in Greece, where Leonidas and his 300 Spartans held off the advancing Persian army just long enough for the Athenian general Themistocles to organize the defenses in and around Athens, and ultimately to turn the Persians away (Document 31). The mercenary general *Pyrrhus* fought a number of battles against the Romans in the third century B.C. After one such battle, technically a victory for Pyrrhus's forces, but at a great loss of life, he is said to have remarked: "If we are victorious in one more battle with the Romans, we will be utterly ruined." It was history's first Pyrrhic victory (Document 37).

The antithesis of warfare, peace, was not ignored by ancient historians, politicians, and philosophers (Documents 26, 28, 35). In Document 34, the Greek writer Xenophon noted that in times of peace, the state treasury was flush with money, but that "the whole of it was spent in time of war."

ISRAEL

24. Rules of War in Ancient Israel

In this passage from his Jewish Antiquities, *the first-century* A.D. *Jewish historian Josephus enunciates the rules of engagement for Israelite armies.*

When you are on the verge of war, send an embassy with heralds to your aggressive enemy. For, before taking up arms, it is proper to speak with them and to represent that, though you have a large army, horses and munitions, and above all are blessed with God's gracious favor and support, nevertheless you desire not to be forced to make war on them and, in robbing them of what is theirs, to gain for yourselves unwanted profit. If, then, they yield to those arguments, it obligates you to keep the peace. But if, confident of their superior strength, they wish to do you wrong, lead out an army against them, taking God for your supreme commander and electing as His lieutenant the one man who is preeminent in bravery. For divided control, besides being a hindrance to those for whom prompt action is imperative, is apt to injure those who practice it. The army under him must be immaculate, made up of all who excel in vigor of body and hardihood of soul, after rejection of the cowardly, for fear that they might flee during the battle, to the advantage of the enemy. Those too who have lately built themselves houses and have not yet had a year to enjoy them, with those who have planted and have not harvested the fruits, must be left on the land, as also the betrothed and recently married, because in their sadness over leaving behind their possessions or their spouses, they may deliberately shirk danger in their desire to return to them.

Once encamped, take heed to refrain from any of the more outrageous actions. When you are engaged in a siege and lack timber for the construction of your engines, do not shear the ground by cutting down the cultivated trees. Spare them, reflecting that they were created for the service of people, and that, were they gifted with a voice, they would plead with you and say that they were in no way responsible for the war, that they were being maltreated unjustly, and that, had they the power, they would have migrated and moved to another country. Having won the battle, kill those that have resisted you, but leave the rest alive to pay you tribute, except for the race of the Canaanites; for them, you must exterminate wholesale.

Josephus also recounts an amazing stratagem employed by Moses to drive off poisonous snakes from a route that the army must traverse.

Moses, summoned both by Thermuthis and by the [Egyptian] king, gladly accepted the task [of leading the Egyptian army], to the delight of the sacred scribes of both nations. For the Egyptians hoped through his valor both to defeat their enemies and at the same time to make away with Moses by guile, while the Hebrew hierarchy foresaw the possibility of escape from the Egyptians with Moses as their general. Thereupon, to surprise the enemy before they had even learned of his approach, he mustered and marched off his army, taking the route not by the way of the river, but through the interior. There he gave a wonderful proof of his sagacity. For the route is rendered difficult for a march by reason of a multitude of serpents, which the region produces in abundant varieties, insomuch that there are some found nowhere else and bred here alone, remarkable for their power, their malignity, and their strange appearance. And among them are some which are actually winged, so that they can attack one from their hiding place in the ground or inflict unforeseen injury by rising into the air. Moses, then, to provide security and a safe passage for his troops, devised a marvelous stratagem: he had baskets, resembling chests, made of the bark of papyrus, and took these with him full of ibises. This animal is the serpents' deadliest enemy. They flee before its attack and in making off are caught, just as they are by stags, and swallowed up. The ibis is otherwise a tame creature and ferocious only to the serpent tribe... When, therefore, he entered the infested region, he by means of these birds drove off the vermin, letting them loose upon them, and using these auxiliaries to clear the ground.

Source: *Josephus*, Volume IV. Translated by H. St. J. Thackeray. Cambridge and London: Loeb Classical Library, 1930.

CHINA

25. Sunzi's Precepts on Warfare

Below are excerpts from the classic Chinese text on military matters, which is still much studied today, The Art of War, *authored by Sunzi, a military leader who was born in the sixth century* B.C.

The military is a great matter of the state. It is the ground of life and death, the Way of survival or extinction. One cannot but investigate it. Thus, base it in the five. Compare by means of the appraisals, and so seek out its nature.

The first is the Way, the second is Heaven, the third is Earth, the fourth is the general, the fifth is method.

The Way is what orders the people to have the same purpose as their superior. Thus they can die with him, live with him, and not harbor deceit.

Heaven is yin and yang, cold and hot, the order of the seasons. Going with it, going against it—this is military victory.

Earth is high and low, broad and narrow, far and near, steep and level, death and life.

The general is wisdom, trustworthiness, courage, and strictness.

Method is ordering divisions, the way of ranking, and principal supply.

The military is a Way of deception.

Thus when able, manifest inability. When active, manifest inactivity.

When near, manifest as far. When far, manifest as near.

When he seeks advantage, lure him.

When he is in chaos, take him.

When he is substantial, prepare against him.

When he is strong, avoid him.

Attack where he is unprepared. Emerge where he does not expect.

These are the victories of the military lineage. They cannot be transmitted in advance...

In general, the method of employing the military:

Taking a state whole is superior. Destroying it is inferior to this.

Taking a division whole is superior. Destroying it is inferior to this.

Taking a battalion whole is superior. Destroying it is inferior to this.

Taking a company whole is superior. Destroying it is inferior to this.

Taking a squad whole is superior. Destroying it is inferior to this.

Therefore, one hundred victories in one hundred battles is not skillful. Subduing the other's military without battle is skillful.

Thus the superior military cuts down strategy. Its inferior cuts down alliances. Its inferior cuts down the military. The worst attacks cities.

Knowing victory has five aspects.

Knowing when one can and cannot do battle is victory.

Discerning the use of the many and the few is victory.

Superior and inferior desiring the same is victory.

Using preparation to await the unprepared is victory.

The general being capable and the ruler not interfering is victory.

These five are a Way of knowing victory. Thus it is said:

Knowing the other and knowing oneself,

In one hundred battles no danger.

Not knowing the other and knowing oneself,

One victory for one defeat.

Not knowing the other and not knowing oneself,

In every battle certain danger.

In the past, the skillful first made themselves invincible to await the enemy's vincibility.

Invincibility lies in oneself. Vincibility lies in the enemy.

Thus the skilled can make themselves invincible. They cannot cause the enemy's vincibility. Thus it is said, 'Victory can be known but cannot be made.'

Invincibility is defense. Vincibilty is attack.

Defend and one has a surplus. Attack and one is insufficient.

One skilled at defense hides below the nine earths and moves above the nine heavens. Thus one can preserve oneself and be all-victorious...

In general when in battle:

Use the orthodox to engage. Use the extraordinary to attain victory.

Thus one skilled at giving rise to the extraordinary is as boundless as Heaven and Earth, as inexhaustible as the Yellow River and the ocean.

Ending and beginning again, like the sun and the moon. Dying and then being born, like the four seasons...

One who takes position first at the battleground and awaits the enemy is at ease.

One who takes position later at the battleground and hastens to do battle is at labor.

Thus one skilled at battle summons others and is not summoned by them.

How one can make the enemy arrive of their own accord is through benefit. How one can prevent the enemy from arriving is through harm.

Thus one can make the enemy labor when at ease and starve them when full. It is a matter of emerging where they must hasten.

To go a thousand *li* [about 330 miles] without fear is to go through unpeopled ground.

To attack and surely take it is to attack where they do not defend. To defend and surely hold firm, defend where they will surely attack.

Thus, with one skilled at attack the enemy does not know where to defend. With one skilled at defense the enemy does not know where to attack...

The ultimate is giving form to the military is to arrive at formlessness. When one is formless, deep spies cannot catch a glimpse and the wise cannot strategize.

Rely on form to bring about victory over the multitude, and the multitude cannot understand. People all know the form by which I am victorious, but no one knows how I determine form.

Do not repeat the means of victory, but respond to form from the inexhaustible.

Now, the form of the military is like water. Water in its movement avoids the high and hastens to the low. The military in its victory avoids the solid and strikes the empty.

Thus water determines its movement in accordance with the earth. The military determines victory in accordance with the enemy.

Source: From *Sources of Chinese Tradition*. Volume I. Second edition. Compiled by William Theodore de Bary and Irene Bloom. Copyright © 1999 Columbia University Press. Reprinted with permission of the publisher.

INDIA

26. Peace Is Superior to War

Jainism is a religion and philosophy that originated in ancient India. The pages of Jain literature are filled with essays and poems about politics, war, and peace issues, as the following excerpt illustrates.

The force of arms cannot do what peace does. If you can gain your desired end with sugar, why use poison?...

What sensible man would abandon his bale [of merchandise] for fear of having to pay a toll on it?

For when the water is drained from the lake, the crocodile grows thin as a snake.

A lion, when he leaves the forest, is no more than a jackal.

And a snake whose fangs are drawn is a mere rope.

In union is strength. Even a mad elephant will trip on a twisted clump of grass. And the [mythical, divine] elephants of the quarters are held by ropes of twisted fibers.

But what is the use of other means when the enemy can only be put down by force? Such expedients are like a libation of ghee [clarified butter] poured on the fire [which makes it burn more fiercely].

Source: From *Sources of Indian Tradition*. Volume I. Edited by William Theodore de Bary. Copyright © 1958 Columbia University Press. Reprinted with permission of the publisher.

27. Indian Military Ordnance

Not all Indians subscribed to the Jainist philosophies (see Document 26, above), as the second-century A.D. Greek historian Arrian indicates in the following description of Indian war equipment.

Indian war equipment is not all the same. The infantry have a bow as tall as the archer, which they base on the ground, and set their left foot on it before shooting, drawing the bowstring a very long way back; for their arrows are little short of three cubits, and an arrow shot by an Indian archer penetrates anything, shield or breastplate or any armor, however strong. In their left hands, they carry small shields of rawhide, narrower than their bodies, but not much shorter. Others have javelins in place of bows. All carry a broad sword, not less than three cubits long, and when they have a hand-to-hand fight—and Indians do not readily fight in this way among themselves—they bring it down with both hands in smiting, so as to make the stroke heavy. Their horsemen have two javelins, like lances, and a small shield, smaller than the infantry. Their horses are not saddled nor do they use bits like the Greek or Celtic, but a band of stitched rawhide is fitted around the muzzle of the horse, with bronze or iron goads, not very sharp, turned inwards. The rich use goads of ivory. Inside their mouths, their horses have a piece of iron like a spit, to which the reins are attached. And so when the rein is pulled, the spit controls the horse and, since the goads are attached to it, they prick the horse and compel him to obey the rein.

Source: *Arrian.* Volume II. Translated by P. A. Brunt. Cambridge and London: Loeb Classical Library, 1933.

28. The Benefits of Peace

This excerpt from the Suvarnaprabhasottama Sutra, *which dates from the third or fourth century* A.D., *praises the benefits of peace.*

Protect all those royal families, cities, lands, and provinces, save them, cherish them, guard them, ward off invasion from them, give peace and prosperity. Keep them free from all fear, calamity, and evil portent. Turn back the troops of their enemies, and create in all the earthly kings of India a desire to avoid fighting, attacking, quarrelling, or disputing with their neighbors...When the eighty-four thousand kings of the eighty-four thousand cities of India are contented with their own territories, and with their own kingly state and their own hordes of treasure, they will not attack one another, or raise mutual strife. They will gain their thrones by the due accumulation of the merit of former deeds; they will be satisfied with their own kingly state, and will not destroy one another, nor show their mettle by laying waste whole provinces. When all the eighty-four thousand kings of the eighty-four thousand capital cities of India think of their mutual welfare and feel mutual affection and joy,...contented in their own domains...India will be prosperous, well-fed, pleasant, and populous. The earth will be fertile, and the months and seasons and years will all occur at the proper time. Planets and stars, moon and sun, will duly bring on the days and nights. Rain will fall upon earth at the proper time. And all living beings in India will be rich with all manner of riches and corn, very prosperous but not greedy.

Source: From *Sources of Indian Tradition.* Volume I. Edited by William Theodore de Bary. Copyright © 1958 Columbia University Press. Reprinted with permission of the publisher.

EGYPT

29. A Noted Egyptian's Military Career

Weni the Elder, an Old Kingdom general, judge, and palace overseer wrote an interesting inscriptional autobiography. In the passage below, he describes his military career.

It was after he had formed an army of many ten thousands of the southland in its entirety that His Majesty took action against the sand-dwellers of the Aamu [Asiatic people living in Upper Egypt]...

His Majesty sent me at the head of this army, there being counts, there being royal sealbearers, there being sole companions of the Great Estate, there being chieftains and estate rulers of the southland and northland, companions, overseers of foreign tongue speakers, overseers of priests of the southland and northland, and overseers of the work centers at the head of the troop of the southland and northland and the estates and towns which they governed...I used to effectuate (military) plans for them, my office being (only) that of overseer of the officials of the palace, through the rectitude of my position, so that not one of them struck his fellow, so that not one of them took away a loaf of bread or a pair of sandals from a wayfarer, so that not one of them seized a bolt of cloth from any town, so that not one of them took away a goat from anyone. I led them from the northern island...

> Having hacked up the land of the sand-dwellers,
> this army (of mine) returned safely.
> Having trounced the land of the sand-dwellers,
> this army (of mine) returned safely.
> Having overturned its walled settlements,
> this army (of mine) returned safely.
> Having cut down its figs and its vines,
> this army (of mine) returned safely.
> Having set fire to (the crops) of all its people,
> this army (of mine) returned safely.
> Having slain the troops therein by many ten thousands,
> this army (of mine) returned safely.
> [Having brought back the troops] therein very greatly as captives,
> this army (of mine) returned safely.

[With the result that] His Majesty praised me on account of it more than anything.

His Majesty sent me to lead [the army] on five occasions to crush the land of the sand-dwellers each time they rebelled, with these troops of mine. I acted so that His Majesty [praised me].

I was told that there were rebels because of a dispute among these foreigners [living near Mount Carmel]. I crossed over with rafts together with these troops of mine...It was (only) after I had captured them in their entirety and (only) after I had slain every rebel among them that I returned.

Source: *The Literature of Ancient Egypt.* Edited by William Kelly Simpson. New Haven, CT: Yale University Press, 2003. Copyright © 2003 by Yale University Press. All rights reserved. Reprinted with permission of the publisher.

30. The Soldierly Life in Ancient Egypt

The following passage from a description of the soldier's life comes from an Egyptian scribal manuscript of the thirteenth century B.C.

What is it that you say they relate, that the soldier's is more pleasant than the scribe's (profession)? Come, let me tell you the condition of the soldier, that much castigated one. He is brought while a child to be confined in the camp. A searing beating is given his body, an open wound inflicted on his eyebrows. His head is split open with a wound. He is laid down and he is beaten like papyrus. He is struck with torments. Come, [let me relate] to you his journey to Khor [Palestine] and his marching upon the hills. His rations and his water are upon his shoulder like the load of an ass, while his neck has been made a backbone like that of an ass. The vertebrae of his back are broken, while he drinks of foul water. He stops work (only) to keep watch. He reaches the battle, and he is like a plucked fowl. He proceeds to return to Egypt, and he is like a stick which the worm has devoured. He is sick, prostration overtakes him. He is brought back upon an ass, his clothes taken away by theft, his henchmen fled...Turn back from the saying that the soldier's is more pleasant than the scribe's (profession).

Source: *The Literature of Ancient Egypt.* Edited by William Kelly Simpson. New Haven, CT: Yale University Press, 2003. Copyright © 2003 by Yale University Press. All rights reserved. Reprinted with permission of the publisher.

GREECE

31. The Persian Invasion of Greece

In 480 B.C.*, the Persians and their allies, under the leadership of King Xerxes, attempted to invade Greece with a huge navy and army. In the following passages from Book Seven of his* Histories, *the fifth-century* B.C. *Greek historian Herodotus provides the statistics of the campaign and the details of the Greek defense of the mountain pass at Thermopylae.*

I find by calculation that their numbers [in the fleet] up to this stage were as follows: first there was the fleet of 1207 ships belonging to the various nations which sailed from Asia, with it original complement of 241,000 men...Each of these vessels carried...30 fighting men...making an additional 36,210. Add to these the crews of the penteconters (50-oared galleys), carrying roughly 80 men apiece; there were...3000 penteconters, so this will make another 240,000. This was the naval force brought by Xerxes from Asia...

As to the army, the infantry was 1,700,000 strong and the cavalry 80,000. Then there were the Arabian camel corps, which I reckon as a further 20,000. The grand total, therefore, of land and sea forces brought over from Asia was 2,317,610. To this, moreover, must be added the troops which were collected as Xerxes passed through Europe. Here I must be content with a rough estimate. [Herodotus then enumerates and itemizes the numbers of soldiers and ships gathered from Europe.]...thus [I] arrive at my final estimate which is, that Xerxes...reached [Greece] at the head of an army consisting, in all, of 5,283,320 men.

Herodotus next describes the Persian march toward the Greek peninsula, and how Xerxes's huge army—5,283,320 is probably an exaggeration, but it certainly was very large—was delayed for a time at the pass of Thermopylae, by a much smaller Greek army, the core of which was a force of 300 Spartans under King Leonidas of Sparta.

The Persian army was now close to the pass, and the Greeks, suddenly doubting their power to resist, held a conference to consider the advisability of retreat. It was proposed by the Peloponnesians generally that the army should fall back...[but] Leonidas [the Spartan king] gave his voice for staying where they were and sending, at the same time, an appeal for reinforcements...During the conference, Xerxes sent a man on horseback to ascertain the strength of the Greek force and to observe what the troops were doing...At that moment, these happened to be the Spartans, and some of them were stripped for exercise, while others were combing their hair. The Persian spy watched them in astonishment...Back in his own camp, he told Xerxes what he had seen. Xerxes was bewildered; the truth, namely that the Spartans were preparing themselves to die and deal death with all their strength, was beyond his comprehension, and what they were doing seemed to him merely absurd.

For four days, Xerxes waited, in constant expectation that the Greeks would make good their escape; then, on the fifth, when still they had made no move and their continued presence seemed mere impudent and reckless folly, he was seized with rage and sent forward [his best troops], with orders to take them alive and bring them into his presence...All day the battle continued;...[ultimately, Xerxes sent] his picked Persian troops—the King's Immortals—who advanced to the attack in full confidence of bringing the business to a quick and easy end. But, once engaged, they were no more successful than the [others] had been...

On the Spartan side, it was a memorable fight; they were men who understood war, pitted against an inexperienced enemy, and among the feints they employed was to turn their backs on a body and pretend to be retreating in confusion, whereupon the enemy would pursue them with a great clatter and roar. But the Spartans, just as the Persians were on them, would wheel and face them, and inflict in the new struggle innumerable casualties. The Spartans had their losses, too, but not many.

Herodotus then recounts that Xerxes, with the aid of an informant, learned more about the geography of the mountain pass the Greeks were defending. Meanwhile, most of the Greek force fled, but King Leonidas and his 300 Spartans felt that retreat was dishonorable, so they remained to defend the pass against the overwhelming numbers of the Persian army. Xerxes's new knowledge about the geography of the place, combined with his numerical advantage, spelled doom for the waiting Spartans.

In the morning, Xerxes poured a libation to the rising sun, and then waited till [the sun] was well up before he began to move forward...As the Persian army advanced to the assault, the Greeks under Leonidas, knowing that they were going to their deaths, went out into the wider part of the pass much further than they had done before; in the previous days' fighting, they had been holding the wall and making sorties from behind it into the narrow neck, but now they fought outside the narrows. Many of the invaders fell; behind them, the company commanders plied their whips indiscriminately, driving the men on. Many fell into the sea and were drowned, and still more were trampled to death by their friends. No one could count the number of the dead. The Spartans, who knew that the enemy were on their way around the mountain track and that death was inevitable, put forth all their strength and fought with fury and desperation. By this time, most of their spears were broken, and they were killing Persians with their swords.

In the course of that fight, Leonidas fell, having fought most gallantly, and many distinguished Spartans with him—their names I have learned, as those of men who deserve to be remembered. Indeed, I have learned the names of all the three hundred...

Of all the Greeks who fought so valiantly, the most signal proof of courage was given by the Spartan Dieneces. It is said that before the battle, he was told...that, when the Persians shot their arrows, there were so many of them that they hid the sun. Dieneces, however, quite unmoved by the thought of the strength of the Persian army, merely remarked: "This is pleasant news...If the Persians hide the sun, we will have our battle in the shade."

Source: *Herodotus: The Histories*. Translated by Aubrey de Selincourt. Baltimore: Penguin Books, 1954. Reproduced by permission of Penguin Books Ltd.

32. Alexander the Great's Warhorse

As this excerpt from the Attic Nights *of Aulus Gellius (A.D. c. 125–c. 180) records, Bucephalus, the warhorse of Alexander the Great (356–323 B.C.), became almost as famous as its owner.*

The horse of king Alexander was called *Bucephalus*, because of the shape of his head [in Greek, *bucephalus* means "ox-headed"]. [The historian] Chares wrote that he was bought for 13 talents [perhaps equivalent to four million dollars] and given to King Philip [Alexander's father]...It seemed a noteworthy characteristic of this horse that when he was armed and equipped for battle, he would never allow himself to be mounted by any other than the king. It is also related that Alexander in the war against India, mounted upon that horse and doing brave deeds, had driven him, with disregard of his own safety, too far into the enemies' ranks. The horse had suffered deep wounds in his neck and side from the weapons hurled from every hand at Alexander, but although dying and almost

Alexander the Great charging the Persian king Darius in his chariot, from amphora of the Greek painter, Darius, c. 330–20 B.C. The Art Archive/Musée Archéologique Naples/Alfredo Dagli Orti.

exhausted from loss of blood, yet he speedily bore the king from the midst of the enemy soldiers. But when he had taken him out of the range of the weapons, the horse at once fell, and satisfied with having saved his master, he breathed his last, with indications of relief that were almost human. Then the king Alexander, after winning the victory in that war, founded a city in that region and in honor of his horse called it Bucephalon.

Source: *The Attic Nights of Aulus Gellius.* Volume I. Translated by John C. Rolfe. Cambridge and London: Loeb Classical Library, 1927.

33. Agesilaus's War Machine

According to this excerpt from the Greek writer Xenophon (c. 430–c. 354 B.C.), the Spartan general Agesilaus (444–360 B.C.) had unique methods of training and preparing his troops for battle.

When spring was just coming on [in 395 B.C.], he gathered his whole army at Ephesus. And desiring to train the army, he offered prizes both to the heavily-armed divisions, for the division which turned out to be in the best physical condition, and to the cavalry divisions, for the one which displayed the best horsemanship. And he also offered prizes to light infantrymen and archers, for all who should prove themselves best in their respective duties. So one might have seen all the gymnasiums full of men exercising, the hippodrome full of riders, and the javelin throwers and bowmen practicing. In fact, he made the entire city where he was staying a sight worth seeing, for the central part of the city was full of all sorts of horses and weapons, offered for sale, and the copper workers, carpenters, smiths, leather cutters, and painters were all engaged in making military weaponry, so that one might have thought that the city was really a workshop of war.

And one would have been encouraged at another sight also: Agesilaus in the forefront, and after him the rest of the soldiers, returning garlanded from the gymnasiums and dedicating their garlands to Artemis. For where people reverence the gods, train themselves in deeds of war, and practice obedience to authority, may we not reasonably suppose that such a place abounds in high hopes?

Source: *Xenophon: Hellenica.* Volume I. Translated by Carleton L. Brownson. Cambridge and London: Loeb Classical Library, 1918.

34. Is War Ever Profitable?

In this additional passage from his writings (see also Document 33, above), the fourth-century B.C. Greek writer Xenophon considers the question of the profitability of warfare.

If anyone supposes that financially war is more profitable to the state than peace, I really do not know how the truth of this can be tested better than by considering once more what has been the experience of our state in the past. He will find that in the old days, a very great amount of money was paid into the treasury in time of peace, and that the whole of it was spent in time of war. He will conclude on consideration that in our own time, the effect of the late war [against the Persians] on our revenues was that many of them ceased, while those that came in were exhausted by the multitude of expenses, whereas the end of war by sea has been followed by a rise in revenues, and has allowed the citizens to devote them to any purpose they choose.

But someone may ask me: "Do you mean to say that, even if the state is wronged, it should remain at peace with the offender?" No, certainly not. But I do say that our vengeance would follow far more swiftly on our enemies if we provoked nobody by warlike behavior, for then they would look in vain for an ally.

Source: *Xenophon: Scripta Minora.* Volume VII. Translated by E. C. Marchant. London and Cambridge: Loeb Classical Library, 1925.

ROME

35. An Early Version of a Pax Romana

As described in the following passage from the writings of the Greek biographer Plutarch (A.D. c. 45–c. 120), Numa, one of Rome's earliest kings (reigned 715–673 B.C.), presided over an era of peace and prosperity, a sort of preview of the Pax Romana (Roman Peace) that Roman rule later brought to the Mediterranean world during the reign of Augustus (27 B.C.–A.D. 14).

He has a temple at Rome with double doors, which they call the gates of war. For the temple always stands open in time of war, but is closed when peace has come. The latter was a difficult matter, and it rarely happened, since the realm was always engaged in some war, as its increasing size brought it into collision with the barbarous nations around it. But in the time of Augustus Caesar [ruled 27 B.C.–A.D. 14], it was closed, after he had overthrown Antony. And before that, when Marcus Atilius and Titus Manlius were consuls, it was closed a short time. Then war broke out again at once, and it was opened.

During the reign of Numa, however, it was not seen open for a single day, but remained shut for the space of 43 years together, so complete and universal was the cessation of war. For not only was the Roman people softened and charmed by the righteousness and mildness of their king, but also the surrounding cities, as if some cooling breeze or healthy wind were wafted upon them from Rome, began to experience a change of temper, and all of them were filled with longing desire to have good government, to be at peace, to till the earth, to raise their children in quiet, and to worship the gods. Festivals and feasts, hospitalities and friendly conversation between people who visited one another without fear—these prevailed throughout Italy, while honor and justice flowed into all hearts from the wisdom of Numa, as from a fountain, and the calm serenity of his spirit diffused itself abroad. Thus even the exaggerations of the poets fall short of picturing the state of man in those days: "And on the iron-bound shield handles lie the tawny spider's webs," and, "rust now subdues the sharp-pointed spears and two-edged swords; no longer is the blast of brazen trumpets heard, nor are the eyelids robbed of delicious sleep." For there is no record either of war, or faction, or political revolution while Numa was king.

Source: *Plutarch's Lives.* Volume I. Translated by Bernadotte Perrin. London and Cambridge: Loeb Classical Library, 1914.

36. Military Strategies

The first-century A.D. *Roman architect and engineer Sextus Julius Frontinus wrote a book about military strategies, entitled, appropriately,* Stratagems. *Frontinus also wrote a book about the Roman aqueducts; its pages are mostly filled with technical information about flow rates, pipe sizes and specifications, laws governing aqueduct usage, and the like; it is a very factual and detail-oriented monograph. But at one point, Frontinus seems overcome with emotion as he considers the sheer genius of the Roman aqueduct system: "With such an array of indispensable structures carrying so many waters, compare, if you will, the idle pyramids, or the useless, though famous, works of the Greeks!"* (Frontinus: The Stratagems and The Aqueducts of Rome. *Translated by Clemens Herschel. London and New York: Loeb Classical Library, 1925.) Below are excerpts from* Stratagems.

Since I alone of those interested in military science have undertaken to reduce its rules to a system [referring to a now-lost book which he wrote on warfare], and since I seem to have fulfilled that purpose...I still feel obligated, in order to complete the task I have begun, to summarize in convenient sketches the adroit operations of generals, which the Greeks embrace under the one name *strategemata*. For in this way, commanders will be furnished with specimens of wisdom and foresight, which will serve to foster their own power of conceiving and executing similar deeds. There will result the added advantage that a general will not fear the issue of his own stratagem, if he compares it with experiments already successfully made...

Types of stratagems for the guidance of a commander in matters to be attended to before battle:

     I. On concealing one's plans.
    II. On finding out the enemy's plans.
   III. On determining the character of the war.
   IV. On leading an army through places infested by the enemy.
    V. On escaping from difficult situations.
   VI. On laying and meeting ambushes while on the march.
  VII. How to conceal the absence of the things we lack, or to supply substitutes for them.
 VIII. On distracting the attention of the enemy.
   IX. On quelling a mutiny of soldiers.
    X. How to check an unseasonable demand for battle.
   XI. How to arouse an army's enthusiasm for battle.
  XII. On dispelling the fears inspired in soldiers by adverse omens.

Following is one example from each of Frontinus's twelve categories:

I. On concealing one's plans: Gaius [Julius] Caesar, distrusting the loyalty of the Egyptians, and wishing to give the appearance of indifference, indulged in riotous banqueting, while devoting himself to an inspection of the city [Alexandria] and its defenses, pretending to be captivated by the charm of the place and to be succumbing to the customs and life of the Egyptians. Having made ready his reserves while he thus dissembled, he seized Egypt [in 48 B.C.].

II. On finding out the enemy's plans: In the Etruscan war (third century B.C.), the consul Aemilius Paulus was on the point of sending his army down into the plain near the town of Vetulonia, when he saw from far off a flock of birds rise in somewhat startled flight from a forest, and realized that some treachery was lurking there, both because the birds had risen in alarm and at the same time, in great numbers. He therefore sent some scouts ahead and discovered that 10,000 Boii were lying in wait at that point to meet the Roman army. These he overwhelmed by sending his legions against them at a different point from that at which they were expected.

III. On determining the character of the war: When Hannibal was lingering in Italy, Scipio sent an army into Africa, and so forced the Carthaginians to recall Hannibal. In this way, he transferred the war from his own country to that of the enemy.

IV. On leading an army through places infested by the enemy: When the [fourth-century B.C.] Athenian general Iphicrates was engaged in a campaign against the Spartan Anaxibius on the Hellespont...he had to lead his army on one occasion through places occupied by enemy patrols, hemmed in on the one side by steep mountains, and on the other washed by the sea. For some time, he delayed, and then on an unusually cold day, when no one suspected such a move, he selected his most rugged men, rubbed them down with oil and warmed them up with wine, and then ordered them to skirt the very edge of the sea, swimming across the places that were too steep to pass. Thus by an unexpected attack from the rear, he overwhelmed the guards of the path.

V. On escaping from difficult situations: When Gnaeus Pompey [the Great] at Brundisium had planned to leave Italy and to transfer the war to another field, since Caesar was heavy on his heels, just as he was on the point of embarking, he placed obstacles in some roads; others he blocked by constructing walls across them; others he intersected with trenches, setting sharp stakes in the latter, and laying hurdles covered with earth across the openings. Some of the roads leading to the harbor he guarded by throwing beams across and piling them one upon another in a huge heap. After consummating these arrangements, wishing to produce the appearance of intending to retain possession of the city, he left a few archers as a guard on the walls. He led out the remainder of his troops to the ships. Then, when he was underway, the archers also withdrew by familiar roads, and caught up to him in small boats.

VI. On laying and meeting ambushes while on the march: When our army was about to pass through the Litana Forest, the Boii cut into the trees at the base, leaving them only a slender support by which to stand, until they should be pushed over. Then the Boii hid at the further edge of the woods and by toppling over the nearest trees, caused the fall of those more distant, as soon as our men entered the forest. In that way they spread general disaster among the Romans, and destroyed a large force [216 B.C.].

VII. How to conceal the absence of the things we lack, or to supply substitutes for them: This place, I think, is not inappropriate for recounting that famous deed of Alexander of Macedon. Marching along the desert roads of Africa, and suffering in common with his men from most distressing thirst, when some water was brought him in a helmet by a soldier, he poured it out on the ground in the sight of all, in this way serving his soldiers better by his example of restraint than if he had been able to share the water with the rest.

VIII. On distracting the attention of the enemy: Titus Didius at one time [in Spain, early first century B.C.] lacked confidence because of the small number of his troops, but continued the war in hopes of the arrival of certain legions which he was awaiting. On hearing that the enemy planned to attack these legions, he called an assembly of the soldiers and ordered them to get ready for battle, and purposely to exercise a careless supervision over their prisoners. As a result, a few of the latter escaped and reported to their people that battle was imminent. The enemy, to avoid dividing their strength when expecting battle, abandoned their plan of attacking those for whom they were lying in wait, so that the legions arrived without hindrance and in perfect safety at the camp of Didius.

IX. On quelling a mutiny of soldiers: When on one occasion legions of Roman soldiers had broken out in a dangerous mutiny, Lucius Sulla shrewdly restored sanity to the frenzied troops. For he ordered a sudden announcement to be made that the enemy was at hand, bidding a shout to be raised by those summoning the men to arms, and the trumpets to be sounded. Thus the mutiny was broken up by the union of all forces against the foe.

X. How to check an unseasonable demand for battle: When Agesilaus, the Spartan, was fighting against the Thebans and had encamped on the bank of a stream, being aware that the forces of the enemy far outnumbered his own, and wishing therefore to keep his men from the desire of fighting, he announced that he had been ordered by a response of the gods to fight on high ground. Accordingly, posting a small guard on the bank, he withdrew to the hills. The Thebans, interpreting this as a mark of fear, crossed the stream, easily dislodged the defending troops and, following the rest too eagerly, were defeated by a smaller force, owing to the difficulties of the terrain [369 B.C.].

XI. How to arouse an army's enthusiasm for battle: Gaius [Julius] Caesar, when about to fight the Germans and their king, Ariovistus, at a time when his own men had been thrown into a panic, called his soldiers together and declared to the assembly that on that day, he proposed to employ the services of the tenth legion alone. In this way, he caused the soldiers of this legion to be stirred by his tribute to their unique heroism, while the rest were overwhelmed with mortification to think that reputation for courage should rest with others [58 B.C.].

XII. On dispelling the fears inspired in soldiers by adverse omens: When Agathocles the Syracusan was fighting against the Carthaginians, and his soldiers on the eve of battle were thrown into panic by an eclipse of the moon, which they interpreted as a bad omen, he explained the reason why this happened, and showed them that, whatever it was, it had to do with nature, and not with their own purposes [310 B.C.].

Frontinus's manual on stratagems is divided into four books. The other three books, which all contain short examples similar to those above, include these topics:

Book Two: *I. On choosing the time for battle; II. On choosing the place for battle; III. On the disposition of troops for battle; IV. On creating panic in the enemy's ranks; V. On ambushes; VI. On letting the enemy escape, so that he does not in desperation renew the battle; VII. On concealing reverses; VIII. On restoring morale by firmness; IX. On bringing the war to a close after a successful engagement; X. On repairing one's losses after a reverse; XI. On ensuring the loyalty of those whom one mistrusts; XII. What to do for the defense of the camp, in case a commander lacks confidence in his present forces; XIII. On retreating.*

Book Three: *I. On surprise attacks; II. On deceiving the besieged; III. On inducing treachery; IV. By what means the enemy may be reduced to want; V. How to persuade the enemy that the siege will be maintained; VI. On distracting the attention of a hostile garrison; VII. On diverting streams and contaminating waters; VIII. On terrorizing the besieged; IX. On attacks from an unexpected quarter; X. On setting traps to draw out the besieged; XI. On pretended withdrawals. Stratagems for protecting the besieged: XII. On stimulating the vigilance of one's own troops; XIII. On sending and receiving messages; XIV. On introducing reinforcements and supplying provisions; XV. How to produce the impression of abundance of what is lacking; XVI. How to meet the menace of treason and desertion; XVII. On sorties. XVIII. Concerning steadfastness on the part of the besieged.*

Book Four: *I. On discipline; II. On the effect of discipline; III. On restraint and disinterestedness; IV. On justice; V. On determination; VI. On good will and moderation; VII. On sundry maxims and devices.*

Source: *Frontinus: The Stratagems.* Translated by Charles E. Bennett. London and New York: Loeb Classical Library, 1925.

37. The First Pyrrhic Victory

The famous third-century B.C. *Greek general* Pyrrhus *tangled with the Romans, almost to his undoing, as the Greek biographer Plutarch (*A.D. *c. 45–c. 120) recounts in this passage from his biography of Pyrrhus.*

After recuperating his army [from a previous battle], he marched to the city of Asculum, where he engaged the Romans. Here, however, he was forced into regions where his cavalry could not operate, and upon a river with swift current and wooded banks, so that his elephants could not charge and engage the enemy's phalanx. Therefore, after many had been wounded and slain, for the time being the struggle was ended by the coming of night. But on the next day, designing to fight the battle on level ground, and to bring his elephants to bear upon the ranks of the enemy, Pyrrhus occupied the unfavorable parts of the field with a detachment of his troops. Then he put great numbers of slingers and archers in the spaces between the elephants and led his forces to the attack in dense array and with a mighty impetus. So the Romans, having no opportunity for sidelong shifts and counter moves...were obliged to engage on level ground and front to front. And being anxious to repulse the enemy soldiers before their elephants came up, they fought fiercely with their swords against the enemy's spears, reckless of their lives, and thinking only of wounding and slaying, while caring not at all for what they suffered. After a long time, however, . . . they began to be driven back at the point where Pyrrhus himself was pressing hard upon his opponents. But the greatest havoc was wrought by the furious strength of the elephants, since the courage of the Romans was of no use in fighting them, but they felt that they must yield before them as before an onrushing billow or a crashing earthquake, and not stand their ground only to die in vain, or suffer all that is most grievous without doing any good at all.

After a short flight, the Romans reached their camp, with a loss of 6,000 men . . . on the side of Pyrrhus, according to the king's own commentaries, 3,505 were killed . . . The two armies separated, and we are told that Pyrrhus said to one who was congratulating him on his victory, "If we are victorious in one more battle with the Romans, we will be utterly ruined." [This is source of the modern phrase *Pyrrhic victory*, a battle won at too great a cost to the victors.] For he had lost a great part of the forces with which he came, and all his friends and generals except a few. Moreover, he had no others whom he could summon from home, and he saw that his allies in Italy were becoming indifferent, while the army of the Romans, as if from a fountain gushing forth indoors, was easily and speedily filled up again, and they did not lose courage in defeat. In fact, their anger gave them all the more vigor and determination for the war.

Source: *Plutarch's Lives*. Volume IX. Translated by Bernadotte Perrin. Cambridge and London: Loeb Classical Library, 1920.

Cicero, widely considered one of Rome's greatest orators and prose stylists. © (2008) Jupiterimages Corporation.

38. Rules of War According to Cicero

The first-century B.C. Roman orator Cicero, in this excerpt from his treatise "On Duties," discusses the various justifications for, and circumstances of, warfare and rules of engagement.

Then, too, in the case of a state in its external relations, the rights of war must be strictly observed. For since there are two ways of settling a dispute—first, by discussion, second, by physical force—and since the former is characteristic of human beings, the latter of animals, we must resort to force only in case we may not avail ourselves of discussion. The only excuse, therefore, for going to war is that we may live in peace unharmed; and when the victory is won, we should spare those who have not been bloodthirsty and barbarous in their warfare . . . In my opinion, at least, we should always strive to secure a peace that shall not admit of guile. And if my advice had been heeded on this point, we should still have at least some sort of constitutional government, if not the best in the world, whereas, as it is, we have none at all.

Not only must we show consideration for those whom we have conquered by force of arms, but we must also ensure protection to those who lay down their arms and throw themselves upon the mercy of our generals, even though the battering ram has hammered at their walls. And among our countrymen, justice has been observed so conscientiously in this direction, that those who have given promise of protection to states or nations subdued in war become, after the custom of our forefathers, the patrons of those states.

As for war, humane laws touching it are drawn up in the fetial code of the Roman People under all the guarantees of religion. And from this it may be gathered that no war is just, unless it is entered upon after an official demand for satisfaction has been submitted or warning has been given and a formal declaration made...But when a war is fought out for supremacy and when glory is the object of war, it must still not fail to start from the same motives which I said a moment ago were the only righteous grounds for going to war. But those wars which have glory for their end must be carried on with less bitterness.

Source: *Cicero: De Officiis.* Translated by Walter Miller. Cambridge and London: Loeb Classical Library, 1913.

39. A Soldier's Perks

In this excerpt from his sixteenth Satire, *the Roman poet Juvenal, who wrote in the early second century* A.D., *enumerates some of the advantages of soldiering.*

Who, Gallius, can count the benefits of serving a term
In the fortunate army? If I could enter a camp of affirmed
Prosperity under a lucky star, I myself would enlist
As a trembling recruit...
Let's first consider advantages all our soldiers now share.
Not the least of these is this, that no civilian would dare
To beat you up. If *he* [a civilian] gets beaten [by a soldier], he'd better not breathe
A word, or run to the praetor [judge], showing his knocked-out teeth,
His swollen face, black and blue, and the one eye left, so mangled
The doctor despairs of saving it. If he'd sue, he's entangled
With rough courts martial, a judge in hobnailed infantry boots
And a jury of brawny legs called up to hear the dispute
At the solemn bench, according to old army rules and the law
Of Camillus, forbidding that any soldier should be brought
To court outside the camp and away from his battle corps...
The whole battalion will be in cahoots
Against you, each squad to a man will agree to give you a cure
That will make your damages won in court far worse to endure
Than those you complained of...
Now let's note some other rewards and perquisites of the pledge
To serve in the army. Should some conniving neighbor allege
That a grove or field of my forbears' estate is his...[or]
Should a debtor refuse to repay his loan and claim the seal
Is faked, the signatures forged, the documents null and void,
I must wait for the regular session of court, to be annoyed
By everyone else with lawsuits on the docket and face
Even then, a thousand tiresome postponements, a thousand delays.

This happens so often...
But those privileged fellows [Roman soldiers] with buckled belts and a fine array
Of weapons get their cases scheduled whenever they please,
And their funds aren't erased by endless chains of legalities.
Moreover, only a soldier is given the right to make
A will while his father lives; for whatever a soldier may take
As pay for his army service is held under law not to be
Part of the estate that the father controls [contrary to the usual custom].

Source: *The Satires of Juvenal.* Translated by Hubert Creekmore. New York: The New American Library, 1963.

Part VII

RECREATIONAL LIFE

Sports and Games

Organized athletic competition, especially among the Greeks and Romans, always excited the interest of spectators and writers alike. References to sporting events in ancient literature are numerous, even in the writings of authors who were decidedly non-athletic.

One could begin with the Greek poet Homer, who described athletic competitions in both his classic epic poems, *Iliad* and *Odyssey*. In the former, the funeral games in honor of Patroclus occupy most of Book 22, including a stirring account of a chariot race (Document 3). In the *Odyssey*, Odysseus is offered an opportunity to compete at various events with a group of younger athletes, who think that he will be easily defeated because of his age. But he turns the tables on them by hurling a discus farther than any of them (Document 4). Following in Homer's poetic footsteps, the Roman epic poet Virgil, in his epic masterpiece *Aeneid*, included an account of the funeral games for Anchises; his description of a boxing match is the subject of Document 15.

Playwrights also provided coverage of sporting events (Documents 5 and 6, where a foot race and a chariot race are described, respectively). However, probably the most famous organized athletic competition was the *Olympic Games*, traditionally said to have been founded in 776 B.C. (Document 7). A number of athletes gained Olympic fame (Documents 10, 11, and 12), but the most successful of all was undoubtedly the wrestler *Milo of Croton* (Document 9). As athletic competition became more specialized and more sophisticated, training manuals came into vogue; these included information on the requisite physical attributes for athletes competing in the various events. One of the most popular of these events was wrestling; whether it was the oldest sport is the topic of Document 13.

Philosophers and other social critics often debate the importance of athletic competition in the larger scheme of things, and such debates often occurred in both ancient Greece and Rome (Documents 14, 16, and 18). Chariot racing was one of the most popular spectator sports in ancient Rome. Documents 17 and 19 reflect this passion. But the Romans did not confine their interests to spectacularly big events.

They also enjoyed more cerebral games, including an ancient version of chess (Documents 20 and 21).

EGYPT

1. An Athletic Egyptian King

According to the following inscription from a stele, the Eighteenth Dynasty Egyptian king Amenhotep II (reigned 1427–1400 B.C.) excelled in many athletic activities.

Now, further, his majesty appeared as a king as a goodly youth. When he had matured and completed 18 years on his thighs in valor, he was one who knew every task of Montu [an ancient Egyptian god of war]. There was no one like him on the field of battle. He was one who knew horses; there was not his like in this numerous army. There was not one therein who could draw his bow. He could not be approached in running.

Strong of arms, one who did not weary when he took the oar, he rowed at the stern of his falcon boat as the stroke for 200 men. When there was a pause, after they had attained half an *iter's* course, they were weak, their bodies were limp, they could not draw a breath, whereas his majesty was still strong under his oar of 20 cubits in its length. He left off and moored his falcon boat only after he had attained three *iters* in rowing, without letting down in pulling. Faces were bright at the sight of him, when he did this.

He drew 300 stiff bows in comparing the work of the craftsmen of them, in order to distinguish the ignorant from the wise. When he had just come from doing this which I have called to your attention, he entered into his northern garden and found that there had been set up for him four targets of Asiatic copper of one palm in their thickness, with 20 cubits between one post and another. Then his majesty appeared in a chariot like Montu in his power. He grasped his bow and gripped four arrows at the same time. So he rode northward, shooting at them like Montu in his regalia. His arrows had come out on the back thereof while he was attacking another post. It was really a deed which had never been done nor heard of by report: shooting at a target of copper an arrow which came out of it and dropped to the ground—except for the king, rich in glory, whom Amon made strong, the king of Upper and Lower Egypt...

Now when he was still a lad, he loved his horses and rejoiced in them. It was a strengthening of the heart to work them, to learn their natures, to be skilled in training them, and to enter into their ways. When it was heard in the palace by his father, the Horus, Mighty Bull, Appearing in Thebes, the heart of his majesty was glad when he heard it, rejoicing at what was said about his eldest son... Then his majesty said to those who were at his side: "Let there be given to him the very best horses in my majesty's stable which is in Memphis and tell him: 'Take care of them, instill fear in them, make them gallop, and handle them if there be resistance to you!'" Now after it had been entrusted to the King's Son to take care of the horses of the king's stable, well then, he did that which had been entrusted to him. Rashap and Astarte were rejoicing in him for doing all that his heart desired.

He trained horses without their equal. They would not grow tired when he took the reins, nor would they sweat even at a high gallop. He would harness with the bit in Memphis and stop at the rest house of Harmakhis, so that he might spend a moment there, going around and around it and seeing the charm of this rest house.

Source: *Stele of Amenhotep II.* Translated by J. A. Wilson. Translation appearing in William C. McDermott and Wallace E. Caldwell, eds. *Readings in the History of the Ancient World.* New York: Rinehart and Company Inc., 1951.

2. An Athlete's Pension

In this excerpt from a papyrus from A.D. 276, an Egyptian Olympic athlete applies for a pension payment.

To their excellencies the senate of Hermopolis, the great, ancient, most august, and most illustrious city, from Aurelius Leucadius, Hermopolitan, victor in the sacred games, pankratiast [the pankration was an event that featured a combination of boxing and wrestling]...I request that an order be given to pay me from the municipal account as my pension for the victory for which I was crowned at the sacred triumphal games for the 48 months...at the rate of 180 drachmas per month, one talent, 2640 drachmas...and for the first victory for which I was crowned at the sacred triumphal universal juvenile contest, held also at Olympia, for 35 months...at the rate of 180 drachmas per month, one talent, 450 drachmas, making the total of the claim two talents, 3090 drachmas, without prejudice to any rights possessed by the city and the senate.

Source: *Select Papyri.* Volume II. Translated by A. S. Hunt and C. C. Edgar. Cambridge and London: Loeb Classical Library, 1934.

GREECE

3. An Epic Chariot Race

In the Iliad, *the legendary Greek poet Homer describes the athletic contests held in honor of the recently deceased Patroclus. Achilles, as sponsor of the games, presides over the running of the various events. The first of these was a chariot race, which is described in the passage reproduced below.*

First, for the fastest charioteers he set out glittering prizes:
a woman to lead away, flawless, skilled in crafts,
and a two-eared tripod, twenty-two measures deep—
all that for the first prize.
Then for the runner-up he brought forth a mare,
unbroken, six years old...
For the third he produced a fine four-measure cauldron
never scorched by flames, its sheen as bright as new.
For the fourth he set out two gold bars, for the fifth,

untouched by fire as well, a good two-handled jar.
[Achilles then stood up and asked for contestants to come forward.]

Achilles' call rang out,
and it brought the fastest drivers crowding forward.
The first by far, Eumelus…who excelled in horsemanship
and following him powerful Diomedes…
Then Atreus' son, Menelaus…
And the fourth to yoke his full-maned team was Antilochus…
Now after Meriones yoked his sleek horses fifth,
they boarded their chariots…
Ready, whips raised high, at the signal all together
lashed their horses' backs and shouted, urging them on.
They broke in a burst of speed, in no time swept the plain,
leaving the ships behind and lifting under their chests,
the dust clung to the teams like clouds or swirling gales
as their manes went streaming back in the gusty tearing wind.
The chariots shot on, now jouncing along the earth that rears us all,
now bounding clear in the air, but the drivers kept erect
in the lurching chariots and the heart of each man raced,
straining for victory—each man yelled at his horses
as they flew across the plain in a whirl of dust.
But just out of the turn,
starting the homestretch back to sunlit sea,
the horses lunged, each driver showed his form,
the whole field went racing full tilt and at once
the fast mares of Eumelus surged far out in front.
And after him came Diomedes' team [not far behind].
And at any moment it seemed they'd mount Eumelus' chariot,
their hot breath steaming his back and broad shoulders,
their heads hovering over him, breakneck on they flew.
And now he'd have passed him or forced a dead heat
if Apollo all of a sudden raging at Diomedes
had not knocked the shining whip from his fist.
Tears of rage came streaming down his cheeks
as he watched Eumelus' mares pulling farther ahead
and his team losing pace, no whip to lash them on.
But Athena, missing nothing of Apollo's foul play
that robbed Diomedes, sped to the gallant captain,
handed him back his whip, primed his team with power,
and flying after Eumelus in full immortal fury
the goddess smashed his yoke. His mares bolted apart,
careening off the track and his pole plowed the ground
and Eumelus hurled from the chariot, tumbling over the wheel,
the skin was ripped from his elbows, mouth and nostrils,
his forehead battered in, scraped raw at the brows,
tears filling his eyes, his booming voice choked.
But veering around the wreck, Diomedes steered his racers
shooting far ahead of the rest, leaving them in the dust
as Athena fired his team and gave the man his glory.
And after him came the son of Atreus, red-haired Menelaus,
next Antilochus, urging his father's horses:

"Drive, the two of you—full stretch and fast!
I don't tell you to match the leader's speed,
skilled Diomedes' team...
But catch Menelaus' pair—fast—and don't get left behind!"...
Whipped with fear by their master's threats, they put on a fresh burst
for a length or two but suddenly brave Antilochus
saw the narrow place where the road washed out—
a sharp dip in the land where massing winter rains
broke off the edge, making it all one sunken rut.
There Menelaus was heading—no room for two abreast—
but Antilochus swerved to pass him, lashing his horses
off the track, then swerving into him neck-and-neck
and Menelaus, frightened, yelled out at the man,
"Antilochus, you drive like a maniac! Hold your horses!
The track's too narrow here—it widens soon for passing–
Watch out; you'll crash your chariot, wreck us both!"
So he cried out, but Antilochus drove on all the wilder,
cracking his lash for more speed like a man stone deaf.
As far as a full-shoulder throw of a whirling discus
hurled by a young contender testing out his strength,
so far they raced dead even. But then Menelaus' pair
dropped back as he yielded, cut the pace on purpose.
He feared the massive teams would collide on the track
and the tight-strung chariots capsize, the men themselves
go sprawling into the dust, striving, wild for triumph.
As his rival passed, the red-haired captain cursed him:
"Antilochus—no one alive more treacherous than you!
Away with you, madman! Damn you!
How wrong we were when we said you had good sense.
You'll never take the prize unless you take the oath!"
Turning back to his team, calling, shouting them on:
"Don't hold back, don't stop now—galled as you are—
that team in the lead will sag in the leg before you.
Robbed of their prime, their racing days are done!"
And lashed with fear by their master's angry voice
they put on a surge, closing on them fast. And all the while
the armies tense in a broad circle watched for horses
flying back on the plain in a rising whirl of dust...
[Two of the spectators, Idomeneus and Ajax, got into an argument over which chariot was
in the lead. Achilles had to intervene.]

"Enough! No more trading your stinging insults now.
Ajax, Idomeneus! It's offensive; this is not the time.
You'd be the first to blame a man who railed this way.
Sit down in the ring, you two, and watch the horses.
They'll be home in a moment, racing hard to win.
Then each can see for himself who comes in second,
who takes off first prize." In the same breath,
Diomedes came on storming toward them. Closer, look,
closing, lashing his team nonstop, full-shoulder strokes,
making them kick high as they hurtled toward the goal.
Constant sprays of dust kept pelting back on the driver,

the chariot sheathed in gold and tin careening on
in the plunging stallions' wake, its spinning rims
hardly leaving a rut behind in the thin dust
as the team thundered in, a whirlwind finish!
He reined them back in the ring with drenching sweat,
lather streaming down to the ground from necks and chests.
Their master leapt down from the bright burnished chariot,
propped his whip on the yoke. His [friend and] aide lost no time—
the hardy Sthenelus rushed to collect the prizes,
gave their proud troops the woman to lead away
and they carried off the handsome two-eared tripod
as he was loosing the horses from the harness.
Antilochus next, the son of Nestor, drove in second,
beating Menelaus not by speed but cunning,
but still Menelaus kept his racers close behind,
tight as the closing gap between the wheel and horse...that much, no more
Menelaus trailed Antilochus, dauntless driver...
And now, if the two teams had a longer course to run,
Menelaus would have passed him, no dead heat about it.
Then...Meriones came in fourth,
trailing the famed Menelaus by a spear-throw.
His team had sleek manes but the slowest pace on the field,
and the man himself was the poorest racing driver.
But Admetus' son Eumelus came in last of all,
dragging his fine chariot, flogging his team before him.
Seeing him there, the swift Achilles filled with pity,
rose in their midst and said these winging words:
"The best man drives his purebred team home last!
Come, let's give him a prize, it's only right,
but second prize, of course.
Diomedes, the son of Tydeus, must carry off the first." So he spoke,
and the armies assented to what he urged...
Achilles was just about to give the man the mare
when Antilochus, son of magnanimous old Nestor,
leapt to his feet and lodged a formal protest:
"Achilles, I'll be furious if you carry out that plan!
Do you really mean to strip me of my prize?...
I won't give up the mare! The one who wants her,
step this way, and try.
He'll have to fight me for her with his fists!"
He flared up and the swift runner Achilles smiled,
delighting in Antilochus; he liked the man immensely.
He answered him warmly, winged words: "Antilochus,
you want me to fetch an extra gift from my tents,
a consolation prize for Eumelus? I'm glad to do it."

Menelaus became angry at this compromise, and demanded the mare for himself, as compensation for Antilochus' unethical racing tactics. Antilochus yielded and apologized. Not only did Menelaus accept the apology, but gave him the mare as a gift. Five more events followed: boxing, wrestling, a foot race, sword fighting, and archery.

Source: *Homer: The Iliad.* Translated by W.H.D. Rouse. Originally published by Thomas Nelson and Sons, Ltd., 1938. Reprinted by The New American Library of World Literature.

4. An Old Athlete Holds His Own

The Homeric hero Odysseus may not have been the prototypical athlete, and after many years of fighting in the Trojan War, he probably was not in the prime physical condition necessary for success in athletic competition, especially when matched against younger, stronger opponents. But when he was shipwrecked in the land of the Phaeacians, and their young men challenged him to compete in their athletic contests, his competitive spirit was aroused. Homer describes the context of the competition in this passage from the eighth book of The Odyssey.

Odysseus frowned, and eyed him coldly, saying:
"That was uncalled for, friend, you talk like a fool.
The gods deal out no gift, this one or any—
birth, brains, or speech—to every man alike.
In looks a man may be a shade, a specter,
and yet be master of speech so crowned with beauty
that people gaze at him with pleasure. Courteous,
sure of himself, he can command assemblies,
and when he comes to town, the crowds gather.
A handsome man, contrariwise, may lack
grace and good sense in everything he says.
You now, for instance, with your fine physique—
a god's indeed—you have an empty noddle.
I find my heart inside my ribs aroused
by your impertinence. I am no stranger
to contests, as you fancy. I rated well
when I could count on youth and my two hands.
Now pain has cramped me, and my years of combat
hacking through ranks in war, and the bitter sea.
Aye. Even so I'll give your games a trial.
You spoke heart-wounding words. You shall be answered."
He leapt out, cloaded as he was, and picked a discus,
a rounded stone, more ponderous than those
already used by the Phaiákian throwers,
and, whirling, let it fly from his great hand
with a low hum. The crowd went flat on the ground—
all those oar-pulling, seafaring Phaiákians—
under the rushing noise. The spinning disk
soared out, light as a bird, beyond all others.
Disguised now as a Phaiákain, Athena
staked it and called out:
                              "Even a blind man,
friend, could judge this, finding with his fingers
one discus, quite alone, beyond the cluster.
Congratulations; this event is yours;
not a man here can beat you or come near you."
That was a cheering hail, Odysseus thought,
seeing one friend there on the emulous field,
so, in relief, he turned among the Phaiákians
and said:
                    "Now come alongside that one, lads.

The next I'll send as far, I think, or farther.
Anyone else on edge for competion
try me now. By heaven, you angered me.
Racing, wrestling, boxing—I bar nothing
with any man except Laódamas,
for he's my host. Who quarrels with his host?
Only a madman—or no man at all—
would challenge his protector among strangers,
cutting the ground away under his feet.
Here are no others I will not engage,
none but I hope to know what he is made of.
Inept at combat, am I? Not entirely.
Give me a smooth bow; I can handle it,
and I might well be first to hit my man
amid a swarm of enemies, though archers
in company around me drew together.
Philoktêtês alone, at Troy, when we
Akhaians took the bow, used to outshoot me.
Of men who now eat bread upon the earth
I hold myself the best hand with a bow—
conceding mastery to the men of old,
Heraklês, or Eurytos of Oikhalía,
heroes who vied with gods in bowmanship.
Eurytos came to grief, it's true; old age
never crept over him in his long hall;
Apollo took his challenge ill, and killed him.
What then, the spear? I'll plant it like an arrow.
Only in sprinting, I'm afraid, I may
be passed by someone.

Source: Excerpts from THE ODYSSEY by Homer, translated by Robert Fitzgerald. Copyright © 1961, 1963 by Robert Fitzgerald. Copyright renewed 1989 by Benedict R. C. Fitzgerald, on behalf of the Fitzgerald children. Reprinted by permission of Farrar, Straus and Giroux, LLC.

5. Orestes the Runner

In this excerpt from the play Electra, *a work of the Athenian playwright Sophocles (c. 496–406 B.C.), another legendary figure,* Orestes, *son of Agamemnon and Clytemnestra, journeys to Delphi to compete in the quadrennial Pythian Games in honor of Apollo. His first event, as described below, is the foot race.*

He came to Delphi for the Pythian Games,
That pride and glory of the land of Greece.
So, when he heard the herald's voice proclaim
The foot race, which was first to be contested,
He stepped into the course, admired by all.
And soon he showed that he was swift and strong
No less than beautiful, for he returned
Crowned with the glory of a victory.
But though there's much to tell, I will be brief.
That man was never known who did the like.

Of every contest in the Festival
He won the prize, triumphantly. His name
Time and again was heard proclaimed: "Winner:
Orestes, citizen of Argos, son
Of Agamemnon, who commanded all
The Greeks at Troy," And so far, all was well.

Source: *Sophocles. Three Tragedies: Antigone; Oedipus the King; Electra.* Translated by H.D.F. Kitto, 1962. By permission of Oxford University Press.

6. Orestes the Charioteer

In the following two passages from Sophocles's play Electra *(see also Document 5, above,), Orestes, after glorying in his victorious efforts in all the other contests, prepares for the last competition, the chariot race.*

But when the gods are adverse, human strength
Cannot prevail, and so it was with him.
For when upon another day, at dawn,
There was to be a contest of swift chariots,
He took his place, and he was one of many:
One from Achaea, one from Sparta, two
From Libya, charioteers of skill. Orestes
Was next—the fifth—driving Thessalian mares.
Then an Aetolian with a team of chestnut horses.
The seventh was from Magnesia, the eighth
From Aenia. He was driving bays.
The ninth was from that ancient city Athens.
The tenth and last was a Boeotian.
They drew their places. Then the umpire set them
Each at the station that had been allotted.
The brazen trumpet sounded. They were off.
They shouted to their horses, shook the reins.
You could hear nothing but the rattling din
Of chariots. Clouds of dust arose; they all
Were bunched together. Every driver
Goaded his horses, hoping so to pass
His rival's wheels and then his panting horses.
Foam from the horses' mouths was everywhere,
On one man's wheels, upon another's back.
So far, no chariot had been overturned.

Possibly one of the most dangerous moments in ancient chariot racing occurred when one of the chariots overturned. If the race was closely bunched, the other drivers would need to rely on all their strength and skill to avoid colliding with the overturned chariot, and suffering a similar setback themselves. The excerpt from Electra *reproduced below describes what happens when this occurs to Orestes.*

But now, the sixth lap finished and the seventh
Begun, the Aenian driver lost control.

Sophocles, one of the great playwrights of the golden age of Greek drama. © (2008) Jupiterimages Corporation.

His horses, hard of mouth, swerved suddenly
And dashed against a Libyan team. From this
Single mishap there followed crash upon crash.
The course was full of wreckage. Seeing this,
The Athenian—a clever charioteer—
Drew out and waited, till the struggling mass
Had passed him by. Orestes was behind,
Relying on the finish. When he saw
That only the Athenian was left
He gave his team a ringing cry, and they
Responded. Now the two of them raced level.
First one, and then the other, gained the lead,
But only by a head. And as he drove,
Each time he turned the pillar at the end,
Checking the inside horse, he gave full rein
To the outer one, and so he almost grazed
The stone [which served as the turning post]. Eleven circuits now he had
Safely accomplished. Still he stood erect,
And still the chariot ran. But then, as he
Came to the turn, slackening the left-hand rein
Too soon, he struck the pillar. The axle shaft
Was snapped in two, and he was flung headlong,
Entangled in the reins. The horses ran
Amok into mid-course and dragged Orestes
Along the ground. Oh, what a cry arose
From all the company when they saw him thrown!
That he, who had achieved so much, should meet
With such disaster, dashed to the ground, and now
Tossed high, until the other charioteers,
After a struggle with the horses, checked them
And loosed him, torn and bleeding, from the reins,
So mangled that his friends would not have known him...
Such is my tale, painful enough to hear.
For those of us who saw it, how much worse!
For worse than anything I yet have seen.

Source: *Sophocles. Three Tragedies: Antigone; Oedipus the King; Electra.* Translated by H.D.F. Kitto, 1962. By permission of Oxford University Press.

7. The Founding of the Olympics

According to tradition, the ancient Olympic games were founded in 776 B.C., and for that Olympiad, as well as the next 13, the only event was a stade race, a distance of 220 yards. Eventually, other events were added, as the second-century A.D. Greek travel writer Pausanias reveals in the following excerpt from his Guide to Greece.

In the period when the Olympic games have been continuously remembered [starting in 776 B.C.], the prize was first of all for a foot race, and Coroebus of Elis won it...At the 14th Olympics, they added the two-lap race, and a man from Pisa called Hypenos won the wild olive for it, and the next time [the 15th Olympics, 720 B.C.], Acanthos the Laconian won the long distance race. At the 18th Olympics, they added the pentathlon and wrestling, and two more Laconians won, Lampis in the pentathlon and Eurybatos in wrestling. At the 23rd Olympics, they gave prizes for boxing; the winner was Onomastos of Smyrna...At the 25th, they added the race for fully grown horses, and Pagondas of Thebes and his team were proclaimed winners.

In the seventh game after those, they added the pankration [a combination of boxing and wrestling], and ridden horses. Crauxidas of Crannons' horse came in first, and Lygdamis of Syracuse beat the others who entered the pankration...

The boys' running and wrestling prizes [separate contests for athletes under the age of 18] were first offered at the 37th Olympics; Hipposthenes of Laconia won the wrestling, and Polynices of Elis won the running. Boy boxers were invited to the 41st Olympics, and Philytas of Sybaris beat the other boys who entered. The race in armor was tried at the 65th Olympics, I suppose for the sake of military training. The first winner among the armored runners was Damaretos of Heraea. [Various other kinds of horse and chariot races are next mentioned.]

Some contests at Olympia have been abolished, when the Eleans [the administrators of the games] decided to stop holding them. For example, there was a boys' pentathlon at the 38th Olympics—Eutelidas of Laconia won it—but the Eleans felt that it was better from then on for boys not to enter the pentathlon...

There are a lot of truly wonderful things you can see and hear about in Greece, but there is a unique divinity of disposition about...the games at Olympia.

Source: *Pausanias: Guide to Greece. Volume 2: Southern Greece.* Translated by Peter Levi. New York: Penguin Books, 1971. Reproduced by permission of Penguin Books Ltd.

8. Requisite Physical Attributes for Athletes

A third-century A.D. treatise attributed to an author named Philostratus (there were three such authors bearing that name, and it is uncertain which one of the three authored the text below) describes the various physical qualities required for pentathletes, boxers, wrestlers, pankratiasts, and runners.

The contestant in the pentathlon [the five events were javelin and discus throwing, long jumping, wrestling, and racing] should be heavy rather than light, slender, of good build, tall, not excessively muscular, but not light, either. He should have long legs, rather than in proportion to his body, and hips that are flexible and limber, on account of bending backward in throwing the javelin, and the discus, as well as on account of the jump. He will jump with less jolting, and will break nothing in his body, if he gains a firm footing, letting his hips down gradually. His hands should be long and his fingers also, for he will throw the discus far better if the discus rim is sped upwards from the hollow of his hand because of the length of his fingers. And he will throw the javelin with less trouble if his fingers do not barely reach the strap, as will be the case if they are short.

The best candidate for the long distance race should have a powerful neck and shoulders just as for the pentathlon, but he should have light, slender legs just like the runners in the stade [220 yards] race. The latter, with the help of their hands, stir their legs into the quick run as if their hands were wings. The runners in the long distance race do this near the goal but the rest of the time they move almost as if they were walking, holding up their hands in front of them, with the result that they need stronger shoulders.

No one any longer makes any distinction between the contestants for the hoplite [in which the racers wore armor and carried a shield], stade, and double-stade races, since Leonidas of Rhodes won the three of them [beginning in 164 B.C.] for four Olympiads. Still, we should distinguish between those entering for just one of these, and those who do so for all of them. The athlete in the hoplite race should have a long waist, well-developed shoulders, and a knee tilted upwards, in order that the shield can be carried easily, with these parts holding it up.

Of the runners in the stade race—the least strenuous of the events—those of symmetrical build are very good, but better than these are those who are not too tall but yet a bit too tall for their proportion; excessive height lacks firmness, just like plants which have shot up high. They should be solidly built, because the fundamental thing in running well is to stand well. Their proportions should be as follows: the legs should balance with the shoulders; the chest should be smaller than normal and should contain sound inner organs; the knee must be limber, the shank straight, hands above average in size; the muscles should be only medium, for oversize muscles inhibit speed.

Candidates for the double-stade race should be stronger than those for the stade, but lighter than those in the hoplite race. Those who compete in all three of the races should be assembled from the best and should possess a combination of all the qualifications which are needed in each single race. Do not consider that this is impossible, because there have been runners such as these even in our day.

The boxer should have a long hand, strong forearm, and upper arm not weak, powerful shoulders, and a long neck. As for the wrists, thick ones deal heavier blows, whereas those less thick are flexible and strike with ease. Well-built hips should support him, for the forward thrust of the hands throws the body out of balance, unless it is held steady by firm hips. Thick calves, in my opinion, are not adapted to any of the events, and least of all to boxing, chiefly because they are especially slow in footwork against their opponent's legs and are easily caught off guard by the opponent's footwork. The boxer should have straight shins of proportionate size, while the thighs should be well-separated and set wide apart, because the figure of the boxer is better adapted for attack if the thighs do not come together. The best kind of a belly is one which recedes, for such men are nimble and have good wind. Still, a boxer derives some advantage from a belly, for it wards off blows from the face when it projects into the path of the opponent's punch.

Let us proceed to those aspiring to wrestle. The regulation wrestler should be tall rather than in proportion, but built like those in proportion, with neither a long neck, nor yet one set down on the shoulders. The latter type of neck is not ill-adapted but looks rather deformed than athletic, and to anyone who is familiar with the two kinds of statues of Hercules, ever so much more pleasing and godlike are the high-born types and those without short necks. The neck should stand straight as in a handsome horse that is conscious of its own worth, and the throat should extend down to each collar bone. The shoulder blades should be drawn together, and the tips of the shoulders erect, thus lending to the wrestler size, nobility of aspect, force, and superiority in wrestling. A well-marked arm [i.e., with broad veins] is an advantage in wrestling…It is better to have a chest which is prominent and curved outward, for the organs rest in it as though in a firm, well-shaped room…In my opinion, persons with hollow, sunken chests should neither strip nor engage in exercises, for they suffer from stomach trouble, and they have unsound organs, and are short-winded.

The belly should be drawn back in its lowest part—for this is a useless burden to the wrestler—and it should be carried upon groins that are not hollow but well-rounded, for such groins in every move which wrestling presents are adapted to press together, and being pressed together, will cause pain to the opponent rather than suffer pain.

A back is suitable if it is straight, but the slightly curved one is [better]…because it is more naturally adapted to the position in the ring…The hip, placed as an axis for the members above and below it, should be supple, easy to turn and to rotate…A well-built thigh turned outwards combines strength with beauty and gives good support, and even better if the leg which supports it does not bow outward, and the thigh rests on a straight knee. Ankles which are not straight, but slanting inward, trip a person up, just as bases which are not straight spoil the balance of firmly fixed columns.

Such is the wrestler and such a man will be able to compete in the pankration, although he will do less well in the hand-holds. Perfect competitors for the pankration are those who are more adapted to wrestling than boxers, and more adapted to boxing than wrestlers.

Source: Philostratus Gymnastics. Translated by Rachel Sargent Robinson, in *Sources for the History of Greek Athletics.* Urbana: University of Illinois Press, 1927.

9. The (Ancient) World's Greatest Athlete

Possibly the most famous Greek athlete of all time was the sixth-century B.C. *wrestler Milo of Croton, winner of the wrestling matches in six consecutive Olympiads. Stories about his prowess, like the ones excerpted here from the writings of the second-century* A.D. *travel writer Pausanias, abounded.*

Milo, the son of Diotomos, [was]…from Croton. Milo won six times in the wrestling at Olympia, once as a boy [there were separate competitions for those under the age of 18], and six times as a man and once as a boy at Delphi [at the quadrennial Pythian Games in honor of Apollo]. He came to wrestle at Olympia a seventh time, but he was not able to out-wrestle his fellow citizen Timasitheos, who was still young…Milo is supposed to have carried his own statue into the stadium, and there are other stories about Milo…He could hold a pomegranate so that no one could force him to release it, and yet the pressure of his hand did it no damage. And he could stand on a greased discus and laugh at people flinging themselves at him and trying to shove him off.

And there were other spectacular things he did. He tied a string around his brows like a ribbon or a wreath, and by holding his breath and filling the veins of his head with blood, he snapped the string with the power of his veins. He is supposed to have kept his right elbow by his side and held out his forearm straight to the front with the hand turned thumb uppermost and fingers flat, yet no one could pull down his little finger.

They say he was killed by wild beasts. Somewhere in the Crotonian territory, he came across a tree of dry wood split open, and held with wedges. It came into Milo's head to put his hands inside the tree; the wedges slipped, and Milo was held in the tree, and the wolves found him [and devoured him].

Source: *Pausanias: Guide to Greece. Volume 2: Southern Greece.* Translated by Peter Levi. New York: Penguin Books, 1971. Reproduced by permission of Penguin Books Ltd.

10. Glaucos the Boxer

In this further excerpt from his Guide to Greece *(see also Documents 7 and 9), Pausanias also recounts the exploits of a famed Olympic boxer, Glaucos of Carystos.*

His father was named Demylos, and they say that he [Glaucos] began as a laborer on the land. [One day], when the ploughshare fell out of the plough, he stuck it in again using his hand for a hammer. Demylos happened to see what the boy had done, so he took him along to Olympia to box. Glaucos had no experience as a boxer and his opponents hurt him, and when he was boxing with the last one, people thought that he was too badly hurt to carry on. And then they say that his father shouted out to him: "Come on, son, remember the plough!," and he hit his opponent a harder punch, and suddenly found that he had won. They say he won other championships as well: twice at the Pythian Games, and eight times each at Nemea and the Isthmian Games [the latter three were all prestigious athletic festivals]...Glaucos had the best natural hand movement in his generation.

Source: *Pausanias: Guide to Greece. Volume 2: Southern Greece.* Translated by Peter Levi. New York: Penguin Books, 1971. Reproduced by permission of Penguin Books Ltd.

11. A Very Noteworthy Greek Athlete

The ancient Greeks knew and recounted many fabulous stories about famous athletes; some of these tales may have contained a grain or two of truth, while others might have been strictly legends. In this passage from his Description of Greece, *(see also Documents 7, 9, and 10), Pausanias profiles one of these athletes.*

This man, Polydamus, the son of Nicias, is the tallest man of our own era...Others have won glorious victories in the pankration, but Polydamus, besides his prizes for the pankration, has to his credit the following exploits of a different kind. The mountainous part of Thrace...breeds among other wild beasts lions...These lions often roam right into the land around Mount Olympus...Here on Mount Olympus, Polydamus slew a lion, a huge and powerful beast, without the help of any weapon...

In addition to this, Polydamus is remembered for another wonderful deed. He went among a herd of cattle and seized the biggest and fiercest bull by one of its hind feet, holding the hoof tightly in spite of the bull's leaps and struggles, until at last it put forth all its strength and escaped, leaving the hoof in Polydamus' grasp. It is also said of him that he stopped a charioteer who was driving his chariot at a high rate of speed. Seizing with one hand the back of the chariot, he kept a tight hold on both horses and driver [until the chariot ground to a halt].

Dareius...learning when he was king [of the Persians] of the exploits of Polydamus, sent messengers [to him], with the promise of gifts, and persuaded him to come into his presence at Susa. There he challenged three of the Persians called Immortals [the Persian king's best soldiers] to fight him—one against three—and Polydamus killed them.

But the prophecy...respecting those who take too much pride in their strength was to be fulfilled in the case of Polydamus, and he too was fated to perish through his own might. For Polydamus entered a cave with the rest of his good friends. It was in the summer, and, as bad luck would have it, the roof of the cave began to crack. It was obvious that it would quickly fall in, and could not hold out much longer. Realizing the impending disaster, the others turned and ran away, but Polydamus resolved to remain, holding up his hands in the belief that he could prevent the falling of the cave and would not be crushed by the mountain. Here Polydamus met his end.

Source: *Pausanias: Description of Greece*. Volume III. Translated by W.H.S. Jones. Cambridge and London: Loeb Classical Library, 1933.

12. A Boxer Who Was Wronged

In this further passage from his Description of Greece *(see also Documents 7, 9, 10, and 11), Pausanias relates some interesting facts about the career of the boxer Euthymus, winner of the boxing crown in the 74th Olympiad in 484 B.C.*

It would not be right for me to pass over the boxer Euthymus, his victories and his other glories...who, although he won the prize for boxing at the 74th Olympic festival, was not to be so successful at the next. Theagenes of Thasos, trying to win the prizes for boxing and for the pankration at the same festival, defeated Euthymus at boxing, although he did not have the strength to win the pankration, because he was already exhausted from his fight with Euthymus. Thereupon the umpires fined Theagenes a talent, to be sacred to the god, and a talent for the harm done to Euthymus, ruling that it was merely to spite him that he entered the boxing competitions. For this reason they ordered him to pay an extra fine privately to Euthymus. At the 76th festival, Theagenes paid in full the money owed to the god...and as compensation to Euthymus, he did not enter the boxing match. At this Olympiad, and also the next one, Euthymus won the crown for boxing. His statue is the handiwork of Pythagoras, and is very well worth seeing. [Statues of champion athletes were erected in the environs of Olympia, a sort of hall of fame of famous athletes.]

Source: *Pausanias: Description of Greece.* Volume III. Translated by W. H. S. Jones. Cambridge and London: Loeb Classical Library, 1933.

13. Is Wrestling the Oldest Sport?

In this passage from his Moralia, *the second-century* A.D. *Greek biographer Plutarch creates a banquet scene in which he and three guests—Lysimachus, Sosicles, and Philinus— discuss whether wrestling is the oldest sport.*

The gymnastic contests being near, most of the conversation concerned the wrestlers, for it so happened that many famous ones had come. And Lysimachus . . . said that he had recently heard a grammarian show that wrestling, on the evidence even of the word, was the oldest of all sports, for it is reasonable to assume, he said, that the more recent institutions makes use of terms established for the older . . . And so one calls *palaestra* [a building where wrestlers trained and practiced] the place in which all athletes exercise, the inference being that wrestling—*pale*—occupied it first before sharing it with sports subsequently invented.

I said that this was not strong evidence, since the *palaestra,* I continued, is not named for wrestling because this is the oldest of the sports, but because it alone of the forms of gymnastic contests happens to require clay, dusting pit, and ring. It is not at running nor boxing that one trains for in the *palaestra,* but wrestling, and the rolling and tumbling of the pankration, which is clearly indeed a combination of boxing and wrestling. "And besides," I said, "how does it make sense that wrestling, which is the most skillful and strategic of sports, is at the same time the oldest too? For necessity produces first what is simple, artless, and accomplished by force rather than systematic skill." When I had spoken, Sosicles said, "You are right, and I'll offer you confirmation with an etymology: 'wrestling,' *pale,* seems to me to be derived from *paleuein,* which means 'to trick,' or 'to overthrow by deception.'"

And Philinus said, "It seems to me to be derived from *palaiste,* 'palm,' for it is principally with this part of the hand that wrestlers operate as, on the contrary, boxers do with the fist, *pugme.* So the one activity is called 'boxing,' *pugme,* the other 'wrestling,' *pale.* And there is another possibility. Since poets say 'sprinkle,' *palunai,* for 'dusting' and 'powdering,' of which we see wrestlers, *palaistai,* make much used, it is possible also in this way to derive the true meaning of the word.

"Consider again," he said, "is it not the goal of runners to distance each other as much as possible, to put the maximum amount of space between each other? And boxers are not allowed by referees to clinch, however aggressive they may be. It is only the wrestlers we see grabbing hold of each other and grappling; most parts of the contest, frontal and lateral attacks, frontal and lateral stances, bring them together and mix them up with each other. Clearly the inference is that wrestling, *pale*, got its name from 'draw near,' *plesiazein*, and 'be close,' *pelas*."

Source: *Plutarch's Moralia*. Volume VIII. Translated by Paul A. Clement and Herbert B. Hoffleit. London and Cambridge: Loeb Classical Library, 1969.

14. Anacharsis Quizzes Solon on the Value of Sports and Athletic Training

In this excerpt from the writings of the second-century A.D. satirist Lucian, the itinerant Scythian (Scythia was in southern Russia) philosopher Anacharsis pays a visit to Athens, where he has several animated conversations with Solon about various Athenian customs, including athletics. In the dialogue that follows, Anacharsis has been observing boxers and wrestlers in training, and he has some questions for Solon.

[Anacharsis asks:] And why are your young men doing all this, Solon? Some of them, locked in each other's arms, are tripping one another up, while others are choking and twisting each other and groveling together in the mud, wallowing like pigs. Yet in the beginning, as soon as they had taken their clothes off, they put oil on themselves... very peacefully. I saw it. Since then, I do not know what got into them that they push one another about with lowered heads and butt their foreheads together like rams. And see there! That man picked the other one up by the legs and threw him to the ground, and then fell down upon him and will not let him get up, shoving him all down into the mud. And now, after winding his legs around his middle and putting his forearm underneath his throat, he is choking the poor man, who is slapping him sideways on the shoulder... so that he may not be strangled completely.

Even out of consideration for the oil, they do not avoid getting dirty. They rub off the ointment, plaster themselves with mud, mixed with streams of sweat, and make themselves a laughing stock, to me at least, by slipping through each other's hands like eels.

Another group is doing the same in the uncovered part of the gym, although not in mud. They have a layer of deep sand under them in the pit, as you see, and not only sprinkle one another, but of their free will, they heap the dust on themselves like so many young roosters, in order that it may be harder to break away in the clinches, I suppose, because the sand takes off the slipperiness and gives them a firmer grip on a dry surface.

Others, standing upright, covered with dust, are attacking each other with blows and kicks. This one here looks as if he were going to spit out his teeth, unlucky man, his mouth is so full of blood and sand. He has sustained a blow on the jaw, as you see. But even the official there does not separate them and break up the fight—I assume from his purple cloak that he is one of the officials—but on the contrary, he eggs them on and praises the one who struck the blow.

Others in other places are all exerting themselves. They jump up and down as if they were running, but they stay in the same place, and they spring high up and kick the air.

I want to know, therefore, what good it can be to do all this, because to me at least the thing looks more like insanity than anything else, and nobody can easily convince me that men who act in that way are not out of their minds.

[Solon replies:] It is only natural, Anacharsis, that what they are doing should have that appearance to you, since it is unfamiliar and very much different from Scythian customs. In a similar way, you yourselves probably have much in your education and training which would appear strange to us Greeks if one of us should look in upon it as you are doing now. But have no fear. It is not insanity, and it is not out of brutality that they strike one another and tumble each other in the mud, or sprinkle each other with dust. The thing has a certain usefulness, not unattended by enjoyment, and it gives much strength to their bodies. As a matter of fact, if you stop for some time, as I think you will, in Greece, before long you yourself will be one of the muddy or dusty group, so delightful and profitable will the thing seem to you.

[Anacharsis's retort:] Get out of town, Solon! You Greeks may have those benefits and pleasures, but as for me, if one of you were to treat me like that, he would find out that we do not carry these daggers at our belts for nothing! But tell me, what name do you give to these performances? What are we to say they are doing?

[Solon:] The place itself, Anacharsis, we call a gymnasium, and it is consecrated to [the god] Apollo. You see his statue . . . As for these forms of athletics, that one over there in the mud is called wrestling, and the men in the dust are wrestling, too. When they stand up straight and hit each other, we call it the pankration [combination of boxing and wrestling]. We have other such athletic exercises, too: boxing, throwing the discus, and jumping, in all of which we hold contests, and the winner is considered best in his class, and carries off the prizes.

[Anacharsis:] And these prizes of yours. What are they?

[Solon:] At the Olympic Games, a wreath made of wild olive, at the Isthmian one of pine, and at the Nemean one of parsley, at the Pythian some of the apples sacred to Apollo, and with us at our Panathenaic Games, the oil from the holy olive. What made you laugh, Anacharsis? Because you think that these are trivial prizes?

[Anacharsis:] No, the prizes that you have described are absolutely overwhelming, Solon. They may well cause those who have offered them to brag about their generosity, and the athletes themselves to be tremendously eager to carry off such trophies, so that they will go through all these preliminary hardships and risks, getting choked and broken in half by each other, for apples and parsley, as if it were not possible for anyone who wants them to get plenty of apples without any trouble, or to wear a wreath of parsley or of pine without having his face splattered with mud or letting himself be kicked in the belly by his opponent!

[Solon:] But it is not the mere prizes that we consider. They are merely tokens of the victory, and marks to identify the winners. But the reputation that goes with them is worth everything to the winners, and to get it, even to be kicked, is nothing to athletes who seek to gain fame through hardships. It cannot be acquired without hard work. The athlete who really wants it must put up with many difficulties in the beginning, before at last he can expect the profitable and rewarding outcome of his exertions.

[Anacharsis:] By this profitable and rewarding outcome, Solon, you mean that everybody will see them wearing wreaths and will applaud them for their victory after having pitied them a long time beforehand for their hard knocks, and that they will be overjoyed to have apples and parsley in compensation for their hard work!

[Solon:] You still don't understand our ways, I tell you. After a little while, you will think differently about them, when you go to the games and see that huge crowd of spectators gathering to watch the athletic events, and amphitheaters filling that will hold thousands, and the athletes applauded, and the one among them who succeeds in winning considered equal to the gods.

[Anacharsis:] That is precisely the most pitiful part of it, Solon. If they undergo this treatment not just in front of a few, but in the presence of so many spectators and witnesses of the brutality, who no doubt congratulate them on seeing them streaming with blood or getting strangled by their opponents...I am absolutely amazed at the spectators, the prominent people who come, you say, from all corners of the world to view the games, if they neglect their urgent business and fritter their time away in such ways. I cannot conceive of what enjoyment it is to them to see men struck, pummeled, dashed on the ground, and crushed by each other.

Source: *Lucian.* Volume IV. Translated by A. M. Harmon. London and New York: Loeb Classical Library, 1925.

ROME

15. An Epic Boxing Match

In the Aeneid, *the first-century* B.C. *Roman poet Virgil describes the funeral games held in honor and memory of Aeneas's father, Anchises. The account of these games recalls Homer's description of funeral games for Patroclus in the* Iliad *(see Document 3, above). The events include a boat race, a foot race, boxing, and archery. Following is the account of the boxing match, featuring the young braggart Dares against the grizzled veteran Entellus.*

Next is a boxing bout. "Whoever has the courage
And fighting spirit in his heart, step forward
And put the gloves on!" There are double prizes:
For the winner, a bullock, decked with gold and ribbons,
A sword and shining helmet for the loser.
Without delay, Dares gets up. A murmur
Runs through the crowd as this big man comes forward...
Now Dares holds his head up for the battle,
Shakes his broad shoulders loose, warms up a little,
A left, a right, a left, in shadow boxing.
Who will oppose him? No one puts the gloves on,
No one, from all that throng, is in a hurry
To take on Dares. So, exultant, thinking
Himself a winner by default, he grabs
The bullock by one horn, says to Aeneas:
"If no man is taking chances,
How long must I keep standing here? How long
Hang around waiting? Give the order, let me

Lead home my prize!" The Trojans all applaud him.
But King Acestes [king of the Sicilians, where the games are taking place], sprawling on the
   greensward,
Beside Entellus, nudges him a little.
"What was the use, Entellus, of being a hero,
Of having been our bravest, after Eryx [a noted Sicilian boxer]?...
Does Dares get away with this, no contest,
And all those prizes, and you sit here tamely?"
Entellus answers: "Oh, I still love glory
And praise. There's nothing the matter with my courage,
But I'm too old, the blood is slow and colder,
The strength not what it used to be. That bragger
Has one thing, youth, and how he revels in it!
If I had what he has, I'd not need prizes,
Bullocks or helmets either, to get me fighting."
From somewhere he produced the gloves of Eryx
And tossed them into the ring, all stiff and heavy,
Seven layers of hide, and insewn lead and iron.
The spectators stand amazed, and Dares shudders,
Wanting no part of gloves like these. Aeneas
Inspects them, turning them slowly, over and over,
And old Entellus adds a word of comment:
"Why, these are nothing! What if you had seen
The gloves of Hercules? He used to fight here.
These are the gloves that Eryx wore against him.
You can still see the blood and a splash of brains
That stained them long ago. I used to wear them
Myself when I was younger, and unchallenged
By Time, that envious rival. But if Dares
Declines these arms, all right, make matters equal,
Don't be afraid. I waive the gloves of Eryx,
You put the Trojan gloves aside. Aeneas
Will see fair play...
He throws the double cloak from off his shoulders,
Strips down to the great limbs, great bones, great muscles,
A giant in the ring. Aeneas brings them
Matched pairs of gloves. They take their stand, each rising
On the balls of his feet, their arms upraised, and rolling
Their heads back from the punch. They spar, they lead,
They watch for openings. Dares, much the younger,
Is much the better in footwork. Old Entellus
Has to rely on strength. His knees are shaky,
His wind not what it was. They throw their punches,
And many miss. And some, with a solid thump,
Land on the ribs or chest. Temples and ears
Feel the wind of a miss, or the jaws rattle
When a punch lands. Entellus stands flat-footed,
Wasting no motion, just a slip of the body,
The watchful eyes alert. And Dares, feinting,
Like one who artfully attacks a city,
Tries this approach, then that, dancing around him
In varied vain attack. Entellus, rising,

Draws back his right (in fact, he telegraphs it),
And Dares, seeing it coming, slips aside.
Entellus lands on nothing but the wind
And, thrown off balance, heavily comes down
Flat on his face...
Roaring, the Trojans and Sicilians both
Rise to their feet. The noise goes up to heaven.
Acestes rushes in, to raise his comrade
In pity and sorrow. But that old-time fighter
Is not slowed down a bit, nor made more wary.
His rage is terrible, and his shame awakens
A consciousness of strength. He chases Dares
All over the ring, left, right, left, right, the punches
Rattle like hailstones on a roof. He batters Dares,
Spins him halfway around with one hand, clouts him
Straight with the other again. At last Aeneas
Steps in and stops it, with a word of comfort
For the exhausted Dares. "Unlucky man,
Yield to the god! What madness blinds your vision
To strength beyond your own?" They rescue Dares,
And drag him to the ships, with his knees caving,
Head rolling side to side, spitting out blood
And teeth. He hardly sees the sword and helmet.
They leave the palm and bullock for Entellus,
Who, in the pride of victory, cries aloud:
"Look, goddess-born [Aeneas]! Watch, Trojans, and discover
Two things: how strong I was when I was younger,
And what a death you've kept away from Dares!"
And, with the word, he faced his prize, the bullock,
Drew back his right hand, poised it, sent it smashing
Between the horns, shattering the skull, and splashing
Brains on the bones, as the great beast came down, lifeless.
"This life, a better one than Dares', Eryx,
I vow as sacrifice, and so, victorious,
Retire, and lay aside the gloves forever."

Virgil, one of the most influential Roman authors throughout history. © (2008) Jupiterimages Corporation.

16. Not Interested in Chariot Races

The second-century A.D. writer and government official Pliny the Younger was one Roman who could do without the delights of the race track, as the following excerpt from his letters indicates.

I have been spending all the last few days among my notes and papers in most welcome peace. How could I do so in the city? The chariot races were on, a type of spectacle which has never had the slightest attraction for me. I can find nothing new or different in them. Once seen is enough, so it surprises me all the more that so many thousands of adult men should have such a childish passion for watching galloping horses and drivers standing in chariots, over and over again. If they were attracted by the speed of the horses or the drivers' skill, one could account for it, but in fact it is the racing colors [i.e., the factions, or racing teams] they really support and care about. And if the colors were to be exchanged in mid-course during a race, they would transfer their favor and enthusiasm, and rapidly desert the famous drivers and horses whose names they shout as they recognize them from a distance. Such is the popularity and importance of a worthless shirt. I don't mean with the crowd, which is worth less than the shirt, but with certain serious individuals. When I think how this futile, tedious, monotonous business can keep them sitting endlessly in their seats, I take pleasure in the fact that their pleasure is not mine. And I have been very glad to make good use of my idle hours with literary work during these days which others have wasted in the idlest of occupations.

Source: *Pliny: Letters and Panegyricus*. Volume II. Translated by Betty Radice. Cambridge and London: Loeb Classical Library, 1969.

17. The (Ancient) World's Best Charioteer

Pliny (see Document 16, above) probably would not have been overly impressed with the statistics amassed by one of the most famous and successful charioteers in Roman history, Appuleius Diocles, who survived for 24 years in his high-risk profession. Upon his retirement, at age 42, the following long inscription was carved to detail his career highlights.

Appuleius Diocles, a driver of the Red faction [charioteers were grouped into four teams, or factions, designated by colors: Red, Green, Blue, White], from Lusitania in Spain, aged 42 years, seven months, 23 days. He first drove for the White faction, during the consulship of Acilius Aviola and Corellius Pansa [A.D. 122]. He first won in the same faction, during the consulship of Manlius Acilius Glabrio and Caius Bellicius Torquatus [A.D. 124]. He first drove for the Green faction during the consulship of Torquatus Asprens and Annius Libo [A.D. 128]. He first won for the Red faction during the consulship of Laenus Pontianus and Antonius Rufinus. Summary [of his career]: he drove chariots for 24 years, having been sent from the gate 4257 times [that is, he competed in 4,257 races]. He won 1462: from the procession [the first race of the day], 110 wins. Singles races [where he competed on his own, instead of cooperatively with other faction teammates]: 1064 wins. Of these, he won the major prize 92 times: 30,000 sesterces 32 times, including three times with a six-horse team [four horses was the standard number]; 40,000 sesterces 28 times. He won 50,000 sesterces 29 times; of these, one was with a seven-horse team. He won 60,000 sesterces three times. He won 347 doubles races, and 51 triples races. In the three-horse chariots, he won the 15,000 sesterces prize four times. He placed [that is, finished first, second, or third] 2900 times.

He finished second 861 times, third 576 times. He failed to place 1351 times. He won ten times for the Blue faction, 91 times for the White faction, including two wins worth 30,000 sesterces each. He won 35,863,120 sesterces [overall in his career]. Furthermore, he won three races in two-horse chariots. He won once for the Whites and twice for the Greens in three-horse chariots. He won by taking the lead at the start

815 times. He won by coming from behind 67 times. He won after deliberately falling behind 36 times. He won using various other strategies 42 times. He won on the stretch run 502 times, including 216 wins over the Green faction, 205 against the Blue faction, and 81 against the White faction. He gained the 100th wins for nine horses, and the 200th win for one horse.

Source: *Corpus Inscriptionum Latinarum (Collection of Latin Inscriptions)* 6.10048. Translated by David Matz.

18. Attitudes Towards Charioteers and Gladiators

The ambivalent attitude of so-called polite society towards charioteers and gladiators is outlined by the early Christian apologist Tertullian (A.D. c. 160–c. 225) in this excerpt from his treatise De Spectaculis.

Consider those who produce and administer the spectacles [chariot races; gladiatorial shows; theatrical productions]. Look at their attitude to the charioteers, players, athletes, gladiators, most loving of men, to whom men surrender their souls, and women their bodies, for whose sake they commit the sins they blame. On one and the same account they glorify them and they degrade and diminish them. Yes, further, they openly condemn them to disgrace and civil degradation. They keep them religiously excluded from council chamber, rostrum, senate, knighthood, and every other kind of office and a good many distinctions. The perversity of it! They love whom they lower; they despise whom they approve; the art they glorify, the artist they disgrace. What sort of judgment is this: that a man should be denounced for what he shines in?

Source: *Tertullian: Apology; De Spectaculis.* Translated by T. R. Glover. Cambridge and London: Loeb Classical Library, 1931.

19. The Circus Maximus: A Great Place to Meet People

The bleacher seats of the Circus Maximus—*the huge racetrack in Rome that could accommodate 250,000 spectators—offered many opportunities for sitting at close quarters, a situation that could be used to advantage by an amorous young man trying to make contact with a young lady, as the Roman poet Ovid (43 B.C.–A.D. 17) relates below in one of his love poems.*

I'm no great student of horse-racing myself, but if you're a fan of one of the drivers, then he's my man, too. I've come here so as to be able to sit by you and talk, and let you know how I feel about you. You look at the races. I'll look at you. Then we will both be looking at what we like!

Whoever your favorite charioteer may be, what a lucky man he is! He's the one you care about. How I wish I were that man! As soon as my horses shot out of the traps, I would urge them on regardless. One moment, I'd give them free rein, the next I would ply the whip furiously, then graze the turning post with my near-side wheel. If I saw you among the crowd as I flashed past, I would pull back, and the reins would fall slack in my hands…

Why are you edging away from me? It's no use. We must keep inside our lines on the seats. That's the best part of being in the Circus.

You, there, on the lady's right! Be careful! You're hurting her with your pushing. And you behind, keep your feet to yourself and don't poke your knee into her back.

Now your dress is trailing in the dust. Pick it up—or rather, let me. I can brush the dirt off it. It was too bad of that dress to hide such great looking legs. The longer I look, the lovelier they are…

Would you like me to fan you with my race card? Or maybe it's my love that is so warm, not the day…

But look, your legs are dangling, with nothing to rest them on. I'm sorry I forgot to bring a stool. If you like, you can poke your toes through the holes in the railings in front. Let me straighten your seat cushion.

Now the track is clear for the big race…The starter has given the signal. I can see your man. With you as his supporter, he's sure to win. Even his horses seem to know what you want.

But look! He has swung wide round the turn. What are you doing? The man just behind is coming up inside you. What are you doing, you fool? You're really letting my lady down. For Heaven's sake, throw your weight into those left-hand reins…

Come on, boys, demand a re-run [apparently, the finish was too close to determine a winner, so an additional lap would have to be run]. Toss up your cloaks, and show the starter what you want.

Yes, it's a re-run. But all those waving cloaks are spoiling your hair-do. Snuggle up to me and let me protect you.

Now it's a fresh start, and the drivers' colors are flashing onto the track again. Do better this time. Make the pace right from the start, and make my lady friend's prayers come true—and mine.

Well, my lady's prayers have been granted, and her charioteer has won; mine remain to be gratified. He has his palm of victory. I have still to ask for mine…She smiled, and her bright eyes flashed a promise. That is enough in the Circus; the rest awaits another place.

Source: *Ovid: Amores.* Translated by H. A. Harris. In Harris, H. A. *Sport in Greece and Rome.* Ithaca, NY: Cornell University Press, 1972.

20. A Game of Chance

In this passage, the Roman biographer Suetonius (A.D. c. 70–c. 140) relates that the emperor Augustus (reigned 27 B.C.–A.D. 14) enjoyed games of chance, particularly dice games.

He did not in the least shrink from a reputation for gaming, and played earnestly and openly for recreation, even when he was well on in years, not only in the month of December [during the Saturnalia, probably the most raucous holiday of the Roman year], but on other holidays as well, and on working days, too. There is no question about this, for in a letter in his own handwriting, he says: "Dear Tiberius: I dined with the same company of people. We also had as guests Vicinius and the elder Silius. We gambled like old men during the meal both yesterday and today. When the dice were thrown, whoever turned up the 'dog' [when only ones appeared] or the six, put a coin in the pool for each one of the dice, and the whole pot was taken by anyone who threw the 'Venus' [when all different numbers turned up]." And in another letter: "Dear Tiberius: We spent the Quinquatria [a five-day festival held each March] very happily, for we played all day long and kept the gaming board warm. Your brother made a great outcry about his luck, but when all was said and done, he did not come out far behind in the long run. After losing heavily, he unexpectedly, and little by little, got back a good deal. For my part, I lost 20,000 sesterces, but because I was extravagantly generous in my play, as usual. If I had demanded of everyone the stakes which I let go, and had kept everything that I gave away, I would have won at least 50,000. But I like that better, because my generosity will exalt me to immortal glory." To his daughter, he writes: "I sent you 250 denarii, the sum which I gave to each of my guests, in case they wanted to play at dice or at odd and even during the dinner."

Suetonius, Roman scholar and official, best-known as the author of the *Lives of the Twelve Caesars*. Library of Congress.

Source: *Suetonius*. Volume I. Translated by John C. Rolfe. Cambridge and London: Loeb Classical Library, 1913.

21. A Roman Chess Game

A very popular board game among the Romans was Latrunculi, or "Robbers." The game was apparently similar to chess, in that the capture of an opponent's game pieces played a major role in determining the outcome. The most complete description of the game's strategies and moves is provided in the passage below by the unknown author of the first-century A.D. Panegyric on Piso.

[I]n more cunning fashion, a piece is moved into different positions and the contest is waged to a finish with glass soldiers, so that white checks the black pieces, and black checks white. But what player has not retreated before you? What piece is lost when you are its player? Or what piece before capture has not reduced the enemy? In a thousand ways, your army fights: one piece, as it retreats, itself captures its pursuer; a reserve piece, standing on the alert, comes from its distant retreat—this one dares to join the fray and cheats the enemy coming for his spoil. Another piece submits to risky delays and, seemingly checked, itself checks two more. This one moves toward higher results so that, quickly played and breaking the opponent's defensive line, it may burst out on his forces and, when the rampart is down, devastate the enclosed city…You win with your phalanx intact or deprived of only a few men, and both your hands rattle with the crowd of pieces you have taken.

Source: *Panegyric on Piso* (in *Minor Latin Poets*). Translated by J. Wight Duff. Cambridge and London: Loeb Classical Library, 1934.

Fishing and Hunting

All kinds of creatures were hunted in the ancient world: elephants (Document 22); tigers (Document 23); turtles (Document 24); rabbits (Documents 25 and 31); foxes (Document 25); boars (Document 29); hedgehogs (Document 40); and lions (Document 38). Then as now, hunting dogs were often employed in the hunts (Documents 28 and 30), and, in at least one case, an unfortunate hunter was devoured by his own hounds (Document 28). Some creative hunters even used music as a way to lure unwary prey (Document 39). Hunting licenses were sometimes required (Document 27), and hunting and fishing regulations had to be observed and obeyed (Documents 27 and 35). Game refuges were established (Document 34), and, in some areas, the equivalent of "No Hunting" signs were posted (Document 26).

Fishing was also very popular, and many methods of catching fish were employed (Documents 32 and 41), including enlisting the aid of dolphins (Document 36). The ancient Greeks knew about fly-fishing, as Document 33 reveals. Sometimes, as Document 37 indicates, overeager fishermen could be taken advantage of.

INDIA

22. Hunting Elephants in India

The ancient Indians had a unique method of hunting elephants, as described by in this passage from the writings of the second-century A.D. *Greek historian Arrian.*

The Indians hunt wild animals in general in the same way as the Greeks, but their way of hunting elephants is unique, like the animals themselves. They choose a level place, open to the sun's heat, and dig a ditch in a circle, large enough for a great army to camp in, about 30 feet wide and 24 feet deep. The earth thrown out of the ditch is heaped on either side, and used as a wall. Then they make dugout shelters for themselves beneath the mound on the outside lip of the ditch, and leave small windows in them through which the light reaches them, and they can see the animals coming up to and charging up to the enclosure. Within the enclosure, they put three or four of the tamest females and leave only one entrance in the ditch by making a bridge over it, where they heap a great deal of earth and grass so that the animals cannot distinguish the bridge, in case they might suspect a trap. The hunters themselves keep out of the way, hiding in the shelters under the ditch.

The wild elephants do not approach inhabited places by daylight, but at night they wander everywhere and feed in herds, following the largest and finest of their number, as cows follow bulls. When they get near the enclosure and hear the voice of the females and scent their presence, they charge to the enclosed place and, working around the outside edge of the ditch, find the bridge and shove their way over it into the enclosure. The hunters observe the entry of the wild elephants. Some smartly remove the bridge, others run off to the neighboring villages and report that the elephants are caught in the enclosure, and the inhabitants, on hearing the news, mount the most spirited and manageable elephants and drive them towards the enclosure, but on arrival they do not at once join battle, but let the wild elephants grow distressed by hunger and mastered by thirst. Only when they think that they are in a bad way, do they erect the bridge again, and drive into the enclosure.

At first there is a fierce battle between the tame elephants and the captives, and then, as one would expect, the wild elephants are overcome, distressed as they are by sinking of their spirits and hunger. Then the men dismount from their elephants, tie together the feet of the wild elephants, which are now exhausted, and then order the tame elephants to punish the rest by repeated blows, till in their distress they fall to the ground. They then stand by them, throw nooses around their necks and climb on them as they lie there. To prevent them tossing their drivers or doing them an injury, they make an incision around their necks with a sharp knife, and bind the noose around the cut, so that the sore makes them keep their head and neck still. If they were to turn around to do mischief, the wound beneath the rope would chafe them. So they keep quiet and, knowing themselves beaten, they are roped to the tame elephants and led away.

Akbar inspecting a wild elephant captured near Malwa. From the Akbarnama, Moghul dynasty, c. 1590. Victoria & Albert Museum, London/Art Resource, NY.

Elephants not yet full grown or not worth acquiring because of a defect are released to their own haunts. The captives are led off to the villages, and first of all are given green stalks and grass to eat. From want of spirit, they are not willing to eat anything, so the Indians arrange themselves around them and lull them to sleep with songs, drums, and cymbals, beating and singing. For if there is an intelligent animal, it is the elephant. Some elephants, when their drivers have died in battle, have actually caught them up and carried them to burial. Others have protected them where they lay or risked their own lives for the fallen. One indeed, who in a passion killed his driver, died from remorse and grief.

Source: *Arrian: History of Alexander and Indica.* Volume II. Translated by E. Iliff Robson, with revisions by P. A. Brunt. Cambridge and London: Loeb Classical Library, 1933.

23. Hunting Tigers in India

The first-century A.D. *Roman writer Pliny the Elder describes the Indian method of hunting and capturing tigers in the following passage from his* Natural History.

India produces the tiger, an animal of terrific speed, which is most noticeable when the whole of its litter, which is always numerous, is being captured. The litter is taken by a man lying in wait with the swiftest horse obtainable, and is transferred successively to fresh horses. But when the mother tiger finds the lair empty (for the males do not look after their young) she rushes off at headlong speed, tracking them by scent. The captor, when her roar approaches, throws away one of the cubs. She snatches it up in her mouth, and returns and resumes the pursuit at even a faster pace owing to her burden, and so on in succession until the hunter has regained the ship and her ferocity rages vainly on the shore.

Source: *Pliny: Natural History.* Volume III. Translated by H. Rackham. London and Cambridge: Loeb Classical Library, 1940.

24. Hunting Turtles in India

In this further excerpt from his Natural History *(see also Document 23, above), Pliny the Elder also states that the Indian Ocean abounds in turtles, which were hunted and caught.*

The Indian Ocean produces turtles of such size that the natives roof houses with the expanse of a single shell, and use them as boats in sailing…They are caught in a number of ways, but chiefly as they rise to the surface of the sea when the weather in the morning attracts them, and float across the calm waters with the whole of their backs projecting, and this pleasure of breathing freely cheats them into self-forgetfulness so much that their hide gets dried up by the heat and they are unable to dive, and go on floating against their will, an opportune prey for their hunters. They also say that turtles come ashore at night to graze and after gorging greedily grow languid, and when they have gone back in the morning, doze off to sleep on the surface of the water. They say that this is disclosed by the noise of their snoring, and that then the natives swim quietly up to them, three men to one turtle, and two turn it over on its back while the third throws a noose over it as it lies, and so it is dragged ashore by more men hauling from the beach.

Source: *Pliny: Natural History.* Volume III. Translated by H. Rackham. London and Cambridge: Loeb Classical Library, 1940.

25. Hunting Rabbits and Foxes in India

In this passage from his On the Characteristics of Animals, *the Roman writer Aelian* (A.D. *c. 170–235) describes the Indian method of hunting rabbits and foxes.*

This is the way in which Indians hunt rabbits and foxes. They have no need of hounds for the hunt, but they catch the young of eagles, ravens, and kites also, rear them, and teach them how to hunt. This is their method of instruction: to a tame rabbit or to a domesticated fox, they attach a piece of meat, and then let them run. And having sent the birds in pursuit, they allow them to pick off the meat. The birds give chase at full speed, and if they catch the rabbit or the fox, they have the meat as a reward for the capture. It is for them a highly attractive bait.

When, therefore, they have perfected the birds' skill at hunting, the Indians let them loose after mountain rabbits and wild foxes. And the birds, in expectation of their accustomed feed, whenever one of these animals appears, fly after it, quickly seize it, and bring it back to their masters, as [the historian and diplomat] Ctesias tell us. And from the same source, we also learn that in place of the meat which has before this been attached, the entrails of the animals they have caught provide a meal.

Source: *Aelian: On the Characteristics of Animals.* Volume I. Translated by A. F. Scholfield. London and Cambridge: Loeb Classical Library, 1958.

26. Off-Limits to Hunters

In another excerpt from On the Characteristics of Animals *(see also Document 25, above), Aelian describes other species of birds that are not hunted but are raised in parks and other protected areas.*

In the royal residences of India where the greatest of the kings of that country lives, there are so many objects for admiration that neither Memnon's city of Susa with all its extravagance, nor the magnificence of Ecbatana is to be compared with them. These places appear to be the pride of Persia, if there is to be any comparison between the two countries... [I]n the parks, tame peacocks and pheasants are kept, and they live in the cultivated shrubs to which the royal gardeners pay due attention. Moreover, there are shady groves and foliage growing among them, and the boughs are interwoven by the woodman's art. And what is more remarkable about the climate of the country, the actual trees are of the evergreen type, and their leaves never grow old and fall... And these... are an ornament to the place and enhance its beauty.

There are other birds besides, free and unenslaved, which come of their own accord, and make their nests and resting places in these trees. There, too, parrots are kept and crowd around the king. But no Indian eats a parrot in spite of their great numbers, the reason being that the Brahmins regard them as sacred and even place them above all other birds. And they add that they are justified in so doing, because the parrot is the only bird that gives the most convincing imitation of human speech.

There are also in these royal domains beautiful lakes, the work of human hands, which contain tame fish, of immense size. And nobody hunts them, only the king's sons during their childhood.

Source: *Aelian: On the Characteristics of Animals.* Volume III. Translated by A. F. Scholfield. London and Cambridge: Loeb Classical Library, 1958.

EGYPT

27. Hunting Licenses

Hunting licenses are not a modern phenomenon, as the following excerpt from a second-century A.D. Egyptian papyrus indicates.

To Philippus…and his fellow superintendents of pastures in the marshland of the village of Theadelphia, from Heron, son of Apollonius…hunter…I desire to be granted a permit by you for hunting and catching in the aforesaid marshland every bird in the locality, for the present 18th year only of Antoninus Caesar the lord [A.D. 154–155], at a total rent of 40 silver drachmas which I will pay in the month of Pharmouthi [March] of the said present year, and I will have with me two assistants, if you agree to give the concession.

Source: *Select Papyri: Non-Literary Papyri. Public Documents.* Volume II. Translated by A. S. Hunt and C. C. Edgar. Cambridge and London: Loeb Classical Library, 1934.

GREECE

28. A Hunter Devoured by His Own Hunting Dogs

In his Metamorphoses, *the Roman poet Ovid (43 B.C.–A.D. 17) recounts the following story from Greek mythology about* Actaeon, *a hunter devoured by his own hunting dogs.*

One of the grandsons [of the Theban king Cadmus] was the lad Actaeon,
First cause of Cadmus' sorrow. On his forehead
Horns sprouted, and his hound dogs came to drink
The blood of their young master. In the story,
You will find Actaeon guiltless; put the blame
On luck, not crime. What crime is there in error?
There was a mountain, on whose slopes had fallen
The blood of many kinds of game; high noon,
Short shadows, and Actaeon, at ease, and friendly
Telling his company: "Our nets and spears
Drip with the blood of our successful hunting.
Today has brought us luck enough; tomorrow
We try again. The Sun-god, hot and burning,
Is halfway up his course. Give up the labor,
Bring home the nets." And they obeyed his orders.
There was a valley there, all dark and shaded
With pine and cypress, sacred to [the goddess] Diana,
Gargaphie, its name was, and it held
Deep in it inner shade a secret grotto
Made by no art, unless you think of Nature
As being as artist. Out of rock and tufa
She had formed an archway, where the shining water
Made slender watery sound, and soon subsided
Into a pool, and grassy banks around it.
The goddess of the woods, when tired from hunting,
Came her to bathe her limbs in the cool crystal.
She gave her armor-bearer spear and quiver
And loosened bow; another's arm received
The robe, laid off; two nymphs unbound her sandals…
But look! While she was bathing there, all naked,
Actaeon came, with no more thought of hunting

Till the next day, wandering, far from certain,
Through unfamiliar woodland till he entered
Diana's grove, as fate seemed bound to have it.
And when he entered the cool dripping grotto,
The nymphs, all naked, saw him, saw a man,
And beat their breasts and screamed, and all together
Gathered around their goddess, tried to hide her
With their own bodies, but she stood above them,
Taller by head and shoulders...
Diana blushed at being seen, and turned
Aside a little from her close companions,
Looked quickly for her arrows, found no weapon
Except the water, but scooped up a handful
And flung it in the young man's face, and over
The young man's hair. Those drops had vengeance in them.
She told him so: "Tell people you have seen me,
Diana, naked! Tell them if you can!"
She said no more, but on the sprinkled forehead
Horns of the long-lived stag began to sprout,
The neck stretched out, the ears were long and pointed,
The arms were legs, the hands were feet, the skin
A dappled hide, and the hunter's heart was fearful.
Away in flight he goes and, going, marvels
At his own speed, and finally sees, reflected,
His features in a quiet pool. "Alas!"
He tries to say, but has no words. He groans,
The only speech he has, and the tears run down
Cheeks that are not his own. There is one thing only
Left him, his former mind. What should he do?
Where should he go? Back to the royal palace
Or find some place of refuge in the forest?
Fear argues against one, and shame the other.
And while he hesitates, he sees his hounds,
Blackfoot, Trailchaser, Hungry, Hurricane,
Gazelle and Mountain-Ranger, Spot and Sylvan,
Swift Wingfoot, Glen, wolf-sired, and the bitch Harpy
With her two pups, half-grown, ranging beside her,
Tigress, another bitch, Hunter, and Lanky,
Chop-jaws, and Soot, and Wolf, with the white marking
On his black muzzle, Mountaineer, and Power,
The Killer, Whirlwind, Whitey, Blackskin, Grabber,
And others it would take too long to mention,
Arcadian hounds, and Cretan-bred, and Spartan.
The whole pack, with the lust of blood upon them,
Come baying over cliffs and crags and ledges
Where no trail runs. Actaeon, once pursuer
Over this very ground, is now pursued,
Fleeing his old companions. He would cry
"I am Actaeon! Recognize your master!"
But the words fail, and nobody could hear him,
So full the air of baying. First of all
The Killer fastens on him, then the Grabber,

Then Mountaineer gets hold of him by a shoulder.
These three had started last, but beat the others
By a short-cut through the mountains. So they run him
To stand at bay until the whole pack gathers
And all together nip and slash and fasten
Till there is no more room for wounds...
Actaeon goes to his knees, like a man praying,
Faces them all in silence, with his eyes
In mute appeal, having no arms to plead with,
To stretch to them for mercy...
He would rather see and hear the dogs than feel them.
They circle him, dash in, and nip, and mangle
And lacerate and tear their prey, not master,
No master whom they know, only a deer.
And so he died, and so Diana's anger
Was satisfied at last.

Source: *Ovid: Metamorphoses*. Translated by Rolfe Humphries. Bloomington: Indiana University Press, 1957. Reprinted with permission of Indiana University Press.

29. The Hunt for the Calydonian Boar

In another passage from the poem Metamorphoses *(see also Document 28, above), Ovid also describes the hunt for the fearsome Calydonian Boar, one of the most famous stories of Greek mythology.*

King Oeneus, in giving thanks for a rich harvest...
...paid his due homage also
To all the gods of heaven, but Diana,
Somehow or other, slipped his mind; her altar
Received no incense. But the gods are subject
To anger, even as humans. "They will pay for this,"
Diana said. "We may be without honor,
But without vengeance, never!" And the goddess
Set loose over Calydon a great avenger,
A boar as big as a bull, with blood-shot eyes,
A high stiff neck, and the bristles rising from it
Like spears along a wall, and hot foam flecking
The shoulders, dripping from the jaws that opened
With terrible grunting sounds; his tusks were long
As an Indian elephant's, and lightning flashed
Out of his mouth, and his breath would burn the grasses.
He would trample down the corn in blade or ear,
So that the threshing floor, the storage bin, stood empty
Waiting in vain for harvest...
The people fled behind walls, their only hope of safety.
Then Meleager, and young men, spurred by glory,
Began to come together...[Many noted legendary heroes are named.]
And there came the pride of the Arcadian woodlands, Atalanta.

A buckle, polished, clasped her robe at her neck.
One knot held back her hair; from her left shoulder,
An ivory quiver hung, and with her motion
Resounded, and her left hand carried a bow.
You would call her features girlish in a boy,
Or boyish in a girl. As soon as he saw her,
The Calydonian hero longed for her,
Though the gods willed it otherwise. He felt
The flame in his heart. "O happy man," he thought,
"If she ever loves a man." But neither the time
Nor his own sense of self-restraint would let him
Go any further. The greater task was waiting.
There was a forest, virgin and primeval,
Rising above the plain and looking down
Over the spreading ploughland, and the heroes
Came here, and spread the nets, and set free the hounds,
Keen on the trail. And there was a deep valley,
Draining the rainy rivulets from the mountains…
And out of this, like lightning out of cloud,
The boar came charging, and the weight of his onrush
Laid low the grove, and the great trees came down crashing.
The young men shouted, but with steady hands
Kept the broad iron of the spearheads level.
The boar came rushing on, scattered the pack,
Thrusting and slashing. The first spear, Echion's,
Went wide, glanced off a maple tree. The next one,
Jason's, was thrown too far. Then Mopsus cried:
"If I have been your worshipper, Apollo,
As I am still, grant me good aim!" The god
Granted his prayer, in part at least. The spear
Did strike the beast, but did him little damage,
For, as the weapon flew, Diana twisted
The iron from the shaft, and only the wood
With no barb in it, found the mark and, raging,
With hotter fire than lightning, the boar's eyes
Burned, and the breath of the throat was hot. As a rock
Flies from the catapult at walls, at towers,
At soldiers, so the beast came rushing on,
Death-dealing, irresistible. Two men,
Eupalamus and Pelagaon, went down,
And their companions dragged them out of danger.
They could not save Enaesimus, who turned
To run, was caught by a slash of the tusks, and hamstrung.
And Nestor came near missing the Trojan War,
But used his spear to vault with, and went flying
Into the branches of a tree. From there,
He watched the boar, using an oak to sharpen
The edge of his tusks, and then, with one stroke, gashing
Hippasus' thigh wide open. Castor and Pollux
Came riding up, showy above the others
On horses white as snow. They poised their spears,

Rifled them, quivering, through the air. These would have
Ended the hunt, but the boar turned suddenly cunning,
Took to the woods where neither spear nor charger
Could follow…
Atalanta sent her arrow flying.
It grazed the back of the boar, struck under the ear,
Staining the bristles red. And Meleager
Was happier than Atalanta even
At her good luck. He was the first to see
The blood, to point it out to his companions,
To offer praise: "All honor to your prowess!"
The men, ashamed, urged on each other, gaining
Courage from their own cries, flinging the spears
With no particular aim, so many missiles
That none of them were any use. Ancaeus,
A man from Arcas, grabbed an axe and shouted:
"The weapons of a man are always better
Than any girl's. Make room for me! Diana
Can shield the brute from arrows, but the axe
And my right hand will fix him!" Swollen with pride,
The bragger heaved his two-edged axe on high,
Reared to full height to strike, but the boar got him
Between the legs, first one tusk, then the other,
And Ancaeus fell, and the ground was soaked in blood,
Smeared with his entrails. Then Ixion's son,
Pirithous, came forward, brandishing
His hunting spear, with Theseus, frightened, calling,
"Stay out of it, keep far away, my friend…
Brave men can fight long range, with no disgrace. Ancaeus
Brought himself hurt with his excess of daring."
As he spoke, he hurled his spear, bronze-tipped and heavy,
And well-aimed, too, but an oak tree's leafy branch
Made it glance off, and the spear…
Had bad luck also, as it struck and wounded
One of the hounds, and pinned him to the ground.
Meleager flung two spears: one missed, and one
Struck in the monster's back, and he whirled around
In circles, spouting blood and foam, and the huntsman
Closed in, and drove a spear straight through the shoulder,
And all the hunters cheered, seeking the hand
That won the victory, and stood in wonder
Watching the boar brought low, and covering acres,
And though they thought it hardly safe to touch him,
All dipped their spears in his blood.
And Meleager, his foot upon that deadly head, was speaking
To Atalanta: "O Arcadian maiden,
The prize is yours. I share my glory with you."
He gave the spoils to her, the bristling hide,
The long-tusked head, and she was very happy
In both the gift and the giver.

Source: *Ovid: Metamorphoses*. Translated by Rolfe Humphries. Bloomington: Indiana University Press, 1957. Reprinted with permission of Indiana University Press.

30. *The Ideal Hunting Hound*

In the following excerpt from his writings, the fourth-century B.C. *Greek historian Xenophon gives advice on the characteristics of the ideal hunting hound.*

First, then, they should be big. Next, the head should be light, flat [in profile], and muscular. The lower parts of the forehead should be sinewy; the eyes prominent, black, and sparkling; the forehead broad, with a deep dividing line; the ears small and thin with little hair behind. The neck should be long, loose, and round; the chest broad and fleshy; the shoulder blades slightly outstanding from the shoulders; the forelegs short, straight, round and firm; the elbows straight. The ribs should be not low down on the ground, but sloping in an oblique line. The loins should be fleshy, of medium length, and neither too loose nor too hard; the flanks of medium size; the hips round and fleshy at the back, not close at the top, and smooth on the inside. The under part of the belly, and the belly itself, should be slim; the tail long, straight, and thin; the thighs hard; the shanks long, round, and solid; the hind legs much longer than the forelegs and slightly bent; the feet round. Hounds like these will be strong in appearance, agile, well-proportioned, and speedy, and they will have a jaunty expression and a good mouth.

When tracking, they should get out of the game paths quickly, hold their heads well down and aslant, smiling when they find the scent, and lowering their ears. Then they should all go forward together along the trail... with eyes continually on the move and tails wagging. As soon as they are close to the rabbit, they should let the hunter know, quickening the pace and showing more emphatic signs by their excitement, movements of the head and eyes, changes of attitude, by looking up and looking into the covert and returning again and again to the rabbit's form, by leaps forward, backward, and to the side, displays of unaffected agitation and overpowering delight at being near the quarry.

They should pursue with endless energy,... barking freely, dogging the rabbit's steps wherever she goes. They should be fast and brilliant in the chase... and they should not leave the track and go back to the hunter.

Along with this appearance and behavior, they should be enthusiastic, and have keen noses, sound feet, and good coats. They will be enthusiastic if they do not leave the hunting ground when the heat is oppressive; keen-nosed if they smell the game on bare, parched, and sunny ground;... sound in the feet if at the same season their feet are not torn to bits during a run in the mountains; they will have a good coat if the hair is fine, thick, and soft.

The color of the hounds should be not entirely tawny, black, or white, for this is not a sign of good breeding. On the contrary, unbroken color indicates a wild strain. So the tawny and the black hounds should show a patch of white about the face, and the white hounds a tawny patch. At the top of the thighs, the hair should be straight and thick, and on the loins and at the lower end of the tail, but it should be moderately thick higher up.

A later engraving of Xenophon. Library of Congress.

It is advisable to take the hounds to the mountains often, but less frequently to cultivated land. In the mountains, it is possible to track and follow a rabbit without hindrance, whereas it is impossible to do either in cultivated land...It is also well to take the hounds out into rough ground, whether they find a rabbit or not, for they get healthy in the feet, and hard work in such country is good for their bodies. In summer, they should be out till midday; in winter, at any hour of the day, in autumn, at any time except midday, and before evening during the spring, for at these times, the temperature is mild...

The equipment of hounds are collars, leashes, and harnesses. The collars should be soft and broad, so as not to chafe the hound's coat. The leashes should have a noose for the hand, and nothing else, for if the collar is made in one piece with the leash, perfect control of the hounds is impossible. The harness straps should be broad, so as not to rub the flanks, and they should have little spurs sewed on to them, to keep the breed pure.

Hounds should not be taken out hunting when off their feed, since this is a proof that they are ailing; nor when a strong wind is blowing, since it scatters the scent and they cannot smell [nor will the snares stay in position]. But when neither of these hindrances prevents it, have the hounds out every other day. Do not let them take to pursuing foxes, for it is utter ruin, and they are never at hand when wanted. Vary the hunting ground frequently, so that the hounds may be familiar with the hunting grounds and the master with the country. Start early, and so give the hounds a fair chance of following the scent. A late start robs the hounds of the find and the hunters of the prize, for the scent is by its nature too thin to last all day.

Source: *Xenophon: Scripta Minora.* Volume VII. Translated by E. C. Marchant. London and Cambridge: Loeb Classical Library, 1925.

31. Hunting Rabbits in Greece

In this excerpt from his treatise on hunting, the Greek writer Xenophon (see also Document 30, above) describes methods and tracking for hunting rabbits.

Track the hare when it snows so hard that the ground is covered, but if there are black spaces, it will be hard to find. When it is cloudy and the wind is from the north, the tracks lie plain on the surface for a long time, because the snow melts slowly, but only for a short time if the wind is from the south and the sun shines, since the snow soon melts.

When it snows without stopping, don't try rabbit hunting, because the tracks are covered, nor when there is a strong wind, since they are buried in the snowdrifts it causes. On no account have the dogs out with you for this kind of hunting, because the snow freezes their noses and feet, and destroys the scent of the rabbit...But take the hunting nets, and go with a friend to the mountains, passing over the cultivated land, and as soon as the tracks are found, follow them. If they are complicated, go back from the same ones to the same place and work in circles and examine them, trying to find where they lead. Rabbits roam about, uncertain where to rest, and moreover, it is their habit to be tricky in their movements, because they are constantly being pursued in this manner.

As soon as the track is clear, push straight ahead. It will lead either to a thickly wooded spot, or to a steep downward slope. The gusts of wind carry the snow over such places; consequently, many resting places are created, and the rabbit looks for one of these. As soon as the tracks lead to such a place, don't go near, or the rabbit will run off, but walk around and explore [to determine if the tracks really end there]. But it is probably there, and there will be no doubt about the matter, since nowhere will the tracks run out from such places. As soon as it is evident that the rabbit is there, leave it—for it will not move—and look for another before the tracks become obscure, and take care, in case you find others, that you will have enough daylight left to surround them with the nets.

When the time has come, stretch the nets around each of them in the same way as in places where there is no snow, enclosing anything that the rabbit may be near, and as soon as the nets are set, approach the rabbit and startle it. If it wiggles out of the hunting nets, run after it along the tracks. It will make for other places of the same sort, unless it squeezes itself into the snow. Wherever it may be, mark the place and surround it, or, if it doesn't wait, continue the pursuit. The rabbit will be caught even without the nets, for it soon tires because of the depth of the snow, and because large lumps of it cling to the bottom of its hairy feet.

Source: *Xenophon: Scripta Minora.* Volume VII. Translated by E. C. Marchant. London and Cambridge: Loeb Classical Library, 1925.

32. Four Ways to Catch Fish

In this passage from his On the Characteristics of Animals *(see also Documents 25 and 26, above), Aelian (A.D. c. 170–235) describes four methods of fishing.*

There are, they say, four different methods of fishing: with nets, with a pole, with a trap, and with a hook. Netting fish brings wealth, and may be compared to the capture of a camp and the taking of prisoners. It requires a variety of gear, for instance, rope, fishing line white and black, cord…corks, lead, pine timber…a six-oared ship…And there fall into the nets fish of different kinds, varied droves in their multitude.

Fishing with a pole is the most manly form and needs a fisherman of very great strength. He must have a straight pole of pine wood, ropes, and firesticks of thoroughly sappy pine. He also needs a small boat and vigorous oarsmen with strong arms.

Fishing with a trap is a pursuit that calls for much craft and deep design, and seems highly unbecoming to free men. The essentials are club rushes…a large stone, anchors, sea weed, leaves of rushes and cypress, corks, pieces of wood, a bait, and a small skiff.

Fishing with a hook is the most accomplished form and the most suitable for free men. One needs horse hair, white, black, red, and gray in color. If the hairs are dyed, fishermen select only those colored blue-gray, and sea purple. All the rest, they say, are bad. Fishermen also use the straight bristles of wild boars and flax also [for fish lines], and a quantity of bronze, lead, cords of esparto, feathers [for fly fishing], especially white, black, and multi-colored. And anglers also use crimson and sea-purple wool, corks, and pieces of wood. Iron and other materials are needed, among them reeds of straight growth and unsoaked, club-rushes that have been soaked, stalks of fennel rubbed smooth, a fishing rod of cornel wood, the horns and hide of a goat. Some fish are caught by one device, others by another.

Source: *Aelian: On the Characteristics of Animals.* Volume III. Translated by A. F. Scholfield. London and Cambridge: Loeb Classical Library, 1959.

33. Fly-Fishing

Fly-fishing was practiced by the ancient Greeks. In this further excerpt from his On the Characteristics of Animals *(see also Documents 25, 26, and 32), Aelian describes the method they used.*

I have heard and can tell of a way of catching fish in Macedonia [in Greece], and it is this... Now there are in [Macedonian rivers] fishes of a speckled color... These fish feed upon the flies of the country which flit about the surface of the river, and are very unlike flies elsewhere. They do not look like wasps... nor bumblebees, although they possess a distinctive feature of both of those insects... You might say they are the size of a bumblebee but their color is similar to that of the wasp, and they buzz like a honeybee. All the natives call them *hippurus*.

These flies settle on the stream and seek the food that they like. They cannot, however, escape the notice of the fishes that swim below. So when a fish observes a *hippurus* on the surface, it swims up noiselessly under water for fear of disturbing the surface and to avoid scaring its prey. Then, when close at hand in the fly's shadow, it opens its jaws and swallows the fly.

Although fishermen know of these happenings, they do not use these flies as fish bait, because if the human hand touches them, it destroys the natural bloom. Their wings wither, and the fish refuse to eat them... And so with angling skill, the fishermen circumvent the fish with the following clever trick. They wrap the hook in scarlet wool, and to the wool they attach two feathers that grow beneath a rooster's wattles, and are the color of wax. The fishing rod is six feet long, and so is the line. So they let down this lure, and the fish, attracted and excited by the color, comes to meet it, and believing from the beauty of the sight that he is going to have a wonderful banquet, opens wide his mouth, is entangled with the hook, and gains a bitter feast, for he is caught.

Source: *Aelian: On the Characteristics of Animals.* Volume I. Translated by A. F. Scholfield. London and Cambridge: Loeb Classical Library, 1959.

34. Game Refuges

As recounted below by Aelian in his On the Characteristics of Animals *(see also Documents 25, 26, 32, and 33), game refuges were established in both ancient Greece and Cyprus.*

In Arcadian territory, there is a shrine of [the god] Pan; Aule is the name of the place. Any animals that take refuge there, the god respects as suppliants and protects in complete safety. Wolves in pursuit are afraid to enter it and are checked at the mere sight of the place of refuge. So there is private property for these animals, too, to enable them to survive.

In Cyprus, when the deer (of which there are a great number and many hunters keen in pursuit of them) take refuge in the temple of Apollo there—the precinct is of very wide extent—the hounds bay at them but do not dare to approach. But the deer in a body graze undeterred and without fear and by some mysterious instinct trust to the god for their safety.

Source: *Aelian: On the Characteristics of Animals.* Volume III. Translated by A. F. Scholfield. London and Cambridge: Loeb Classical Library, 1959.

35. Hunting and Fishing Regulations

Hunting and fishing regulations are by no means a phenomenon of the modern world, as the fourth-century B.C. Greek philosopher Plato reminds us in this passage from The Laws.

Hunting is a large and complex matter, all of which is now generally embraced under this single name. Of the hunting of water animals, there are many varieties, and many of the hunting of fowls. And very many varieties of hunts of land animals, not of beasts only, but also, of men, both in war and often too, in friendship, a kind of hunt that is partly approved, and partly disapproved. And then there are robberies and hunts carried on by pirates and by gangs.

When the lawgiver is making laws about hunting, he is necessarily bound to make this point clear, and to lay down directions by imposing regulations and penalties for all these kinds. When, then, ought to be done about these matters? The lawgiver, for his part, will be right in praising or blaming hunting with an eye to the toils and pursuits of the young. And the young person will be right in listening and obeying, and in allowing neither pleasure nor toil to hinder him, and in holding in greater respect the orders that are sanctioned by praise, and carrying them out, rather than those which are enacted by law under threat of penalties.

After these prefatory observations, there will follow adequate praise and blame of hunting: praise of the kind which renders the souls of the young better, and blame of the kind which does the opposite. Our next step will be to address the young people with prayer: "O friends, would that you might never be seized with any desire or craving for hunting by sea, or for angling, or for ever pursuing water animals with creels that do your lazy hunting for you, whether you sleep or wake. And may no longing for man hunting by sea and piracy overtake you, and render you cruel and lawless hunters. And may the thought of committing robbery in country or city not so much as cross your minds. Neither may there seize upon any of the young the crafty craving for snaring birds, not a very gentlemanly pursuit! Thus there is left for our athletes only the hunting and capture of land animals. Of this branch of hunting, the kind called night stalking, in which the work is intermittent, being the job of lazy men who take turns sleeping, is one that deserves no praise. Nor does that kind deserve praise in which there are intervals of rest from toil, when hunters master the wild force of beasts by nets and traps instead of doing so by the victorious might of a toil-loving soul. Accordingly, the only kind left for all, and the best kind, is the hunting of quadrupeds with horses and dogs and the hunter's own limbs, when men hunt in person, and subdue all the creatures by means of their own running, striking, and shooting. All the hunters, that is to say, who cultivate the courage that is divine."

Concerning the whole of this subject, the exposition we have now given will serve as the praise and blame. And the law will run thus: "None shall hinder these truly sacred hunters from hunting wheresoever and howsoever they wish. But the night trapper who trusts to nets and snares, no one shall ever allow to hunt anywhere. No man shall hinder the fowler on fallow land or mountain. But he that finds him on tilled fields or on sacred lands shall drive him off. The fisherman shall be allowed to fish in all waters except havens and sacred rivers and pools and lakes, but only on the condition that he makes no use of muddying juices [poisons to kill the fish]."

Source: *Plato: Laws.* Volume II. Translated by R. G. Bury. London and Cambridge: Loeb Classical Library, 1926.

ROME

36. Dolphins That Helped Fishermen

There were many stories and legends in the ancient Greek and Roman world about interactions between humans and dolphins. One of these tales, recounted in Pliny the Elder's (A.D. 23–79) Natural History, *concerned dolphins helping fishermen.*

In the region of Nismes in the province of Narbonne [France], there is a marsh named Latera, where dolphins catch fish in partnership with a human fisherman. At a regular season, a countless shoal of mullet rushes out of the narrow mouth of the marsh into the sea, after watching for the turn of the tide, which makes it impossible for nets to be spread across the channel—indeed, the nets would be equally incapable of withstanding the mass of the weight even if the craft of the fish did not watch for the opportunity. For a similar reason, they make straight out into the deep water produced by the neighboring eddies, and hasten to escape from the only place suitable for setting nets. When this is observed by the fishermen—and a crowd collects at the place, because they know the time, and even more because of their enthusiasm for this sport—and when the entire population from the shore shouts as loud as it can, calling for "Snubnose" for the conclusion of the show, the dolphins quickly hear their wishes if a northerly breeze carries the shout to sea, although if the wind is from the south, against the sound, it carries it more slowly. But then they hasten to the spot, to offer their assistance.

Their line of battle comes into view, and at once deploys in the place where they are to join in battle. They bar the passage on the side of the sea and drive the scared mullet into the shallows. Then the fishermen put their nets around them and lift them out of the water with forks. Nonetheless, the pace of some mullets enables them to leap over obstacles, but these are caught by the dolphins, which are satisfied for the time being with merely having killed them, postponing a meal until victory is won. The action is hotly contested, and the dolphins pressing on with the greatest bravery are delighted to be caught in the nets, and for fear that this itself may hasten the enemy's flight, they glide out between the boats and the nets or the swimming fishermen so gradually as not to open ways of escape. None of them try to get away by jumping out of the water, which otherwise they are very fond of doing, unless the nets are put below them ...

When in this way the catch has been completed, they tear in pieces the fish they have killed. But since they know that they have had too strenuous a task for only a single day's pay, they wait there until the following day, when they are given a feed of bread mash dipped in wine, in addition to the fish.

Source: *Pliny: Natural History.* Volume III. Translated by H. Rackham. London and Cambridge: Loeb Classical Library, 1940.

37. Scamming the Fisherman

In this excerpt from his essay "On Duties," the first-century B.C. *Roman orator Cicero relates the story of a Roman knight by the name of Gaius Canius, who bought some waterfront property in the erroneous belief that good fishing was available. Unfortunately, he had been duped.*

Gaius Canius, a Roman knight, a man of considerable wit and literary culture, once went to Syracuse for a vacation, as he himself used to say, and not for business. He gave out that he had a mind to purchase a little country house, where he could invite his friends and enjoy himself, uninterrupted by troublesome visitors. When this fact was made known, one Pythius, a banker of Syracuse, informed him that he had such an estate, and that it was not for sale. However, Canius might make himself at home there, if he pleased, and at the same time, he invited him to the estate for dinner the next day. Canius accepted.

Then Pythius, who, as might be expected of a money lender, could command favors of all classes, called the fishermen together and asked them to do their fishing the next day out in front of his villa, and he told them what he wanted them to do. Canius came to dinner at the appointed hour. Pythius had a sumptuous banquet prepared. There was a whole fleet of boats before their eyes. Each fisherman brought in, in turn, the catch that he had made, and the fish were deposited at the feet of Pythius.

"Tell me, Pythius," said Canius, "what does this mean? All these fish? All these boats?"

"No wonder," answered Pythius. "This is where all the fish in Syracuse are. Here is where the fresh water comes from. The fishermen cannot get along without this estate."

Inflamed with desire for it, Canius insisted on Pythius's selling it to him. At first, he hesitated. To make a long story short, Canius won out. The man was rich and, in his desire to own the country house, he paid for it all that Pythius asked, and he bought all the furniture, too. Pythius entered the amount in his ledger and completed the transfer.

The next day, Canius invited his friends, and he himself came early. Not so much as an oar was in sight. He asked his next door neighbor whether it was a fisherman's holiday, for not a sign of any fisherman did he see.

"Not so far as I know," he said, "but none are in the habit of fishing here. And so I couldn't figure out what was happening yesterday!"

Canius was furious, but what could he do?

Source: *Cicero: De Officiis*. Translated by Walter Miller. Cambridge and London: Loeb Classical Library, 1913.

38. Hunting and Capturing Lions

In another excerpt from his Natural History *(see also Document 36, above), the first-century* A.D. *writer Pliny the Elder explains how the Romans hunted and captured lions.*

Capturing lions was once a difficult task, chiefly accomplished by means of pitfalls. In the principate of Claudius [A.D. 41–54], chance taught a shepherd a method that was almost one to be ashamed of in the case of a wild animal of this nature. When it charged, he flung a cloak against its attack—a feat that was immediately transferred to the arena as a show—the creature's great ferocity abating in an almost incredible manner when its head is covered with even a light wrap, with the result that it is vanquished without showing fight. The fact is that all its strength is concentrated in its eyes.

Source: *Pliny: Natural History*. Volume III. Translated by H. Rackham. London and Cambridge: Loeb Classical Library, 1940.

39. Using Music in Hunting

In this passage from On the Characteristics of Animals *(see also Documents 25, 26, 32, 33, and 34), Aelian describes an Etruscan method of hunting and capturing animals with music. The Etuscans lived in Etruria, a region just north of Rome.*

There is an Etruscan story current which says that the wild boars and the stags in that country are caught by using nets and hounds, as is the usual manner of hunting, but that music plays a part, and even the larger part, in the struggle.

And how this happens I will now relate. They set the nets and other hunting gear that ensnare the animals in a circle, and a man proficient on the pipes stands there and tries his utmost to play a rather soft tune, avoiding any shriller note, but playing the sweetest melodies possible. The quiet and the stillness easily carry [the sound] abroad, and the music streams up to the heights and into ravines and thickets; in a word, every lair and resting place of these animals. At first, when the sound penetrates to their ears, it strikes them with terror and fills them with dread, and then an unalloyed and irresistible delight in the music takes hold of them, and they are so beguiled as to forget about their offspring and their homes. And yet wild beasts do not care to wander away from their native haunts. But little by little these creatures in Etruria are attracted as though by some persuasive spell, and beneath the wizardry of the music they come and fall into the snares, overpowered by the melody.

Source: *Aelian: On the Characteristics of Animals.* Volume III. Translated by A. F. Scholfield. London and Cambridge: Loeb Classical Library, 1959.

40. Hunting Hedgehogs

Pliny the Elder describes the method of hunting hedgehogs in this passage from his Natural History *(see also Documents 36 and 38).*

Hedgehogs prepare food for winter, and fixing fallen apples on their spines by rolling on them and holding one more in their mouth, they carry them to hollow trees. The same animals foretell a change in wind direction from north to south by holing up in their den. But when they perceive someone hunting them, they draw together their mouth and feet and all their lower part, which has thin and harmless down on it, and roll up into the shape of a ball, so that it would not be possible to take hold of any part of them except by the prickly spines...Afterwards, the ball into which they roll up can be made to unroll by a sprinkle of hot water, and to fasten them up by one of their hind feet kills them through starvation when hanging. It is not possible to kill them in any other way and avoid damaging the hide,...[which] is used in dressing cloth for garments.

Source: *Pliny: Natural History.* Volume III. Translated by H. Rackham. London and Cambridge: Loeb Classical Library, 1940.

41. Catching the Big Ones

In another excerpt from On the Characteristics of Animals *(see also Documents 25, 26, 32, 33, 34, and 39), Aelian describes the methods employed in catching large ocean-dwelling fish.*

Those who are in the habit of fishing around the Tyrrhenian Islands [off the northern coast of Sicily] go after a gigantic fish which they call the *aulopias*...In the matter of size, the largest *aulopias* is smaller than the largest tunas, but if matched against them it would take the prize for strength and courage. True, the tuna is also a powerful species of fish, but after its first encounter with its adversary and vigorous opponent [i.e., the fisherman] it loses its strength, and as its blood congeals, it very soon surrenders, and then is caught. The *aulopias*, on the other hand, carries on the fight for a long time...and withstands the fisherman...and on most occasions, gets the better of him by gathering itself together, bowing its head, and thrusting down into the depths. It has a forceful jaw and a powerful neck, and is very strong. But when it is captured, it is a most beautiful sight. It has wide open eyes, round and large...And the jaw, although powerful, as I remarked, contributes to its beauty...A stripe of a golden color starts at the head and descending to the region of the tail, ends in a circle.

I wish also to speak of the methods employed in catching it which I remember to have heard. The fishermen previously select spots from a large area where they think that the *aulopiae* might be congregating, and after catching a number of crowfish [species uncertain], they anchor their boat and create continuous noise; meanwhile, they bind up the crowfish with nooses, and let them out on a line. The *aulopiae*, hearing the noise and seeing the bait, come swimming up from all sides and congregate and circle around the boat. And the noise and the quantity of food have such a soothing effect on them that, even though the fishermen reach out their hands, they remain and submit to the human touch because, in my opinion, they are slaves to food and in fact, as their pursuers maintain, because their strength gives them confidence. There are also tame ones among them, which the fishermen recognize as their benefactors,…so with them they maintain a truce. And other strange fish follow them like leaders, and these aliens, as one might call them, the fishermen hunt and kill, but they do not hunt the tame fish, which may be compared to decoy doves, but they spare them, nor would any prudent fisherman ever be reduced to such a condition as to catch a tame *aulopias* deliberately, for if by some accident one happens to be caught, it brings trouble. The [non-tame] fish is captured either by being pierced with a hook or by being mortally wounded.

We see bird hunters also refraining from killing birds that decoy others, whether for sale or for the table.

Source: *Aelian: On the Characteristics of Animals.* Volume III. Translated by A. F. Scholfield. London and Cambridge: Loeb Classical Library, 1959.

Vacations, Celebrations, and Festivals

Everyone needs some time off now and then, and this was certainly true in the ancient world. National holidays dotted the calendars of the ancient Greeks and Romans (Documents 42 and 45). Sometimes, celebrations were declared to commemorate a major military triumph (Document 43). But, undoubtedly, most people enjoyed most of all the private family vacations (Document 44), and some expressed their longing for such a vacation when work schedules became too oppressive (Document 46).

GREECE

42. A Celebration of Freedom

In this passage, the Greek biographer Plutarch (A.D. c. 45–c. 120) describes the annual festivities held in the town of Plataea to commemorate the Battle of Plataea, a victory over the mighty Persian army fought in 478 B.C.

At a general assembly of the Greeks, Aristides moved a resolution that delegates and religious representatives from all the Greek states should meet every year at Plataea, and that every four years the Eleutheria, or festival games in honor of freedom, should be celebrated…

The Plataeans undertook to offer up a sacrifice to the dead every year in honor of those Greeks who had fallen in battle and were buried in the field, and this ceremony they still carry out to this day in the following manner...They conduct a procession; this is led forth at daybreak by a trumpeter who sounds the charge. After him come wagons full of myrtle leaves and garlands, and then a black bull. These are followed by young men of free birth who carry libations of wine and milk in jars and pitchers of olive oil and myrrh, and no slave is allowed to play any part in the ceremony, since the men who are being honored gave their lives for freedom. Last of all comes the chief magistrate of Plataea, who for the rest of his term of office is forbidden to touch iron or to wear clothes of any color but white, but on this occasion is dressed in a scarlet tunic. He carries aloft an urn from the public record office and proceeds, sword in hand, through the middle of the city to the tombs. There with his own hands he takes water from the sacred spring, washes the gravestones, and anoints them with myrrh. Then he slaughters the bull by the funeral pyre, offers prayers to Zeus and Hermes of the Underworld, and calls upon the brave men who died for Greece to come to the banquet and drink the libations of blood. After this, he mixes a bowl of wine and water, drinks and pours a libation from it, saying these words: "I drink to the men who died for the freedom of Greece." These rites have been observed by the Plataeans down to the present day.

Source: *The Rise and Fall of Athens: Nine Greek Lives by Plutarch.* Translated by Ian Scott-Kilvert. New York: Penguin Books, 1960. Reproduced by permission of Penguin Books Ltd.

ROME

43. Festivities in Honor of a Roman General

In this passage from his writings, the historian Livy (59 B.C.–A.D. 17) describes the festivities held in Greece in 167 B.C. in honor of the Roman general Lucius Aemilius Paulus and his various military conquests in Greece.

The serious business was followed by an entertainment, a most elaborate affair staged at Amphipolis [in Greece]. This had been under preparation for a considerable time, and Paulus had sent messengers to the cities and kings of Asia to give notice of the event, while he had announced it in person to the leading citizens in the course of his tour of the Greek states. A large number of skilled performers of all kinds in the sphere of entertainment assembled from all over the world, besides athletes and famous horses, and official representatives with sacrificial victims. And all the other usual ingredients of the great games of Greece, provided for the sake of gods and men, were supplied on such a scale as to excite admiration not merely for the splendor of the display, but also for the well-organized showmanship in a field where the Romans were at that time mere beginners. Banquets for the official delegations were put on, equally sumptuous and arranged with equal care. A remark of Paulus himself was commonly quoted, to the effect that a man who knew how to conquer in war was also a man who would know how to arrange a banquet and to organize a show...

The stage show, the contests between men, the horse races, were not the only sights to interest the crowds which had come to Amphipolis. They were equally attracted by all the booty from Macedonia. There were statues, pictures, textiles, vessels of gold, silver, bronze, and ivory, fashioned with immense pains in the king's palace, not for temporary display, like the objects with which the palace at Alexandria was crammed, but for lasting use.

Source: *Livy: Rome and the Mediterranean: Books XXXI–XLV of The History of Rome from its Foundation.* Translated by Henry Bettenson. Baltimore: Penguin Books, 1977. Reproduced by permission of Penguin Books Ltd.

44. Cicero's Vacation in Antium

Around the year 59 B.C., the Roman orator Cicero (106–43 B.C.) took a vacation in Antium, a seacoast town about 30 miles south of Rome. He wrote the following letter to his friend Atticus about his experiences there.

I am not so certain now about fulfilling the promises that I made in former letters to produce some work during my vacation tour, because I have fallen so in love with idleness that I can't tear myself from it. So I either enjoy myself with my books, of which I have a pleasant abundance here at Antium, or else I count the sea waves. The rough weather won't allow me to catch shads. My soul utterly rebels against writing. The geographical work I had planned is a big undertaking... The subject is frustratingly hard to explain, and it is boring, nor does it give one as many opportunities for flowers of fancy as I imagined. Besides—and this is the main point—I find any excuse for laziness good enough. I am even debating settling down at Antium and spending the rest of my life here. I really wish I had been a magistrate here instead of in Rome... To think of there being a place so close to Rome where there are lots of people who have never seen Vatinius [a rival politician], where there is not a single soul except for me who cares whether any of our new commissioners are alive or dead, where no one bothers me, although everyone likes me. This, this is the very place for me to play the politician.

Source: *Cicero: Letters to Atticus.* Volume I. Translated by E. O. Winstedt. Cambridge and London: Loeb Classical Library, 1912.

45. Roman Holidays

According to the following excerpt from the Saturnalia *of the early fifth-century A.D. writer Macrobius, there were four kinds of vacation days permissible and celebrated during the Roman year (see* Saturnalian Festival *in Glossary).*

The celebration of a religious festival consists of the offering of sacrifices to the gods or the marking of the day by a ritual banquet, or the holding of public games in honor of a god, or the observance of rest days. Public rest days are of four kinds: they are either fixed, movable, extraordinary, or market days. In the fixed rest days, all the people share. They are held on set and appointed days, in set and appointed months. They are noted in the calendar, and the observances are defined...

Movable rest days are those which are proclaimed yearly by the magistrates or the priests, to be held on days which may or may not be set days...Extraordinary rest days are those which are promulgated by the consuls or the praetors by virtue of their discretionary powers. Market days are the concern of the villagers and country people, who assemble on these days to attend to their private affairs and to market their wares.

Besides the public rest days, there are those which belong exclusively to certain families…Rest days are also kept by individuals; for example, on the occasion of a birthday, the fall of a thunderbolt, a funeral, or an act of atonement…

The priests used to maintain that a rest day was desecrated if, after it had been duly promulgated and proclaimed, any work was done on it. Furthermore, the [priests] might not see work in progress on a rest day, and for this reason, they would give public warning by a herald that nothing of the sort should be done. Neglect of this command was punished by a fine, and it was said that one who had inadvertently done any work on such days had, in addition to the fine, to make atonement by the sacrifice of a pig…[The pontiff] Scaevola, when asked what might be done on a rest day replied that anything might be done which it would be harmful to have left undone. And so a head of a household who, on a rest day, collected his laborers and freed an ox from a pit into which it had fallen was not thought to have desecrated the day, nor a man who propped up a broken roof beam to save it from a threatening collapse. And that is why Vergil, who is an authority in every branch of learning, knowing that sheep are washed either to clean the wool or to cure mange, declared that a sheep might be dipped on a rest day, if the intention was to effect some cure, as appears from the line:

"To dip the bleating flock into the health-giving stream."

The use of the adjective "health-giving" makes it clear that the action is permissible only if its aim is to prevent disease and if there is no ulterior motive of cleaning the wool to make a profit.

Source: From *Macrobius: The Saturnalia.* Translated by Percival Vaughn Davies. Copyright © 1969 Columbia University Press. Reprinted with permission of the publisher.

46. Oh, for a Vacation!

Pliny the Younger's (A.D. 62–114) heavy work schedule in Rome kept him from enjoying a greatly needed vacation, as he relates in this letter to his friend Caninius Rufus.

Are you reading, fishing, or hunting, or doing all three? You can do all together on the shores of Lake Como, for there are plenty of fish in the lake, game to hunt in the woods around, and every opportunity to study in the depths of your retreat. Whether it is everything or only one thing, I can't say that I begrudge you your pleasures. I am only annoyed at being denied them myself, for I hanker after them like a sick man does for wine, baths, and cool springs. I wonder if I will ever be able to shake off these constricting chains if I am not allowed to undo them, and I doubt if I ever will. New business piles up on the old before the old is finished, and as more and more links are added to the chain, I see my work stretching out farther and farther every day.

Source: *Pliny: Letters and Panegyricus.* Volume I. Translated by Betty Radice. Cambridge and London: Loeb Classical Library, 1969.

Part VIII
RELIGIOUS LIFE

Deities

The origin of the gods was a matter of curiosity and speculation (Document 8); there seemed to have been some thought that the gods originated in Egypt (Document 5). The Egyptian goddess *Isis* was known to the Romans, and one Roman author, Apuleius, even claimed to have seen Isis in a dream (Document 4). There was also a tradition of animal worship in Egypt (Documents 6 and 7).

The Greeks and the Romans both felt a healthy measure of respect for their deities (Documents 9 and 10), and had fixed ideas on how best to worship them (Document 11). But in India, there was at least one school of thought that subscribed to the belief that there was no divine input into the creation of the world (Document 3).

The Greeks and Romans were adept at the construction of large, ornate, and imposing temples in honor of their gods and goddesses, but it is doubtful that any of those structures could rival the magnificent temple built by Solomon in honor of the Hebrew God (Document 2).

The Romans never seemed to know exactly how to deal with the growing influence of Christianity. Pliny the Younger, normally a gentle man not prone to violence, had no apparent problem with ordering the execution of Christians in his capacity as the governor of Bithynia in the early second century A.D. It may have been easier for him to order the executions knowing that he enjoyed the support of the emperor *Trajan* for his actions (Document 12).

SUMERIA

1. A Prayer to Shamash

The Babylonian sun-god, Shamash, was one of the most powerful gods in the pantheon, as the following prayer, from the early part of the second millennium B.C., indicates.

Shamash, at your arising mankind bows down...
Illuminator, dispeller of darkness of the vault of the heavens,
Who sets aglow the beard of light, the corn field, the life of the land.

Your splendor covers the vast mountains,
Your fierce light fills the lands to their limits.
You climb to the mountains surveying the earth,
You suspend from the heavens the circle of the lands.
You care for all the peoples of the lands,
And everything that Ea [god of wisdom], king of the counselors, had created is entrusted to you.
Whatever has breath you shepherd without exception,
You are their keeper in upper and lower regions.
Regularly and without cease you traverse the heavens,
Every day you pass over the broad earth…
In the underworld, you care for the counselors of Kusu, the Anunnaki [underworld judges],
Above, you direct all the affairs of mankind,
Shepherd of that beneath, keeper of that above,
You, Shamash, direct, you are the light of everything…
There is none who is supreme like you in the whole pantheon of gods.
At your rising, the gods of the land assemble;
Your fierce glare covers the land.
Of all the lands of varied speech,
You know their plans, you scan their way.
The whole of mankind bows to you,
Shamash, the universe longs for your light…
You stand by the traveler whose road is difficult,
To the seafarer in dread of the waves…
It is you who patrol the unseen routes,
You constantly tread paths which confront Shamash alone.
You save from the storm the merchant carrying his capital,
The […] who goes down to the ocean you equip with wings.
You point out settling places to refugees and fugitives,
To the captive, you point out routes that only Shamash knows…
A man who covets his neighbor's wife
Will […] before his appointed day.
A nasty snare is prepared for him […]
Your weapon will strike at him, and there will be none to save him…
You give the unscrupulous judge experience of fetters,
Him who accepts a present and yet lets justice miscarry, you make bear his punishment.
As for him who declines a present, but nevertheless takes the part of the weak,
It is pleasing to Shamash, and he will prolong his life.
The merchant who practices trickery as he holds the balances,
Who uses two sets of weights, thus lowering the […]
He is disappointed in the matter of profit and loses his capital.
The honest merchant who holds the balances and gives good weight—
Everything is presented to him in good measure […]
The merchant who practices trickery as he holds the corn measure,
Who weighs out loans of corn by the minimum standard, but requires a large quantity in
    repayment,
The curse of the people will overtake him before his time,
If he demanded repayment before the agreed date, there will be guilt upon him…
The honest merchant who weighs out loans of corn by the maximum standard, thus
    multiplying kindness,
It is pleasing to Shamash, and he will prolong his life.
He will enlarge his family, gain wealth,
And like the water of a never failing spring, his descendants will never fail…

The progeny of evil-doers will fail.
Those whose mouth says "No"—their case is before you.
In a moment you discern what they say.
You hear and examine them; you determine the lawsuit of the wronged.
Every single person is entrusted to your hands.
You manage their omens; that which is perplexing, you make plain.
You observe, Shamash, prayer, supplication, and benediction,
Obeisance, kneeling, ritual murmurs, and prostration.
The feeble man calls you form the hollow of his mouth,
The humble, the weak, the afflicted, the poor,
She whose son is captive constantly and unceasingly confronts you...
Which are the mountains not clothed with your beams?
Which are the regions not warmed by the brightness of your light?
Brightener of gloom, illuminator of darkness,
Dispeller of darkness, illuminator of the broad earth.

Source: *Readings in Ancient History. From Gilgamesh to Diocletian.* Bailkey, Nels, *Readings in Ancient History.* Copyright © 1969 by Houghton Mifflin Company. Reprinted with permission.

ISRAEL

2. Solomon Constructs God's Temple

The construction of the Temple of Solomon in Jerusalem is described in First and Second Chronicles in the Bible. Fundraising is described in the first excerpt and the preparations for building the temple in the second.

David told the crowd: "God chose my son Solomon to build the temple, but Solomon is young and has no experience. This is not just any building—this is the temple for the LORD God! That's why I have done my best to get everything Solomon will need to build it: gold, silver, bronze, iron, wood, onyx, turquoise, colored gems, all kinds of precious stones, and marble.

"Besides doing all that, I have promised to give part of my own gold and silver as a way of showing my love for God's temple. Almost one hundred twenty tons of my finest gold and over two hundred fifty tons of my silver will be used to decorate its walls and to make gold and silver objects. Now, who else will show their dedication to the LORD by giving gifts for building his temple?"

After David finished speaking, the family leaders, the tribal leaders, the army commanders, and the government officials voluntarily gave gifts for the temple. These gifts included almost two hundred tons of gold, three hundred eighty tons of silver, almost seven hundred tons of bronze, and three thousand seven hundred fifty tons of iron. Everyone who owned precious stones also donated them to the temple treasury...David and the people were very happy that so much had been given to the LORD, and they all celebrated.

Next described are the preparations for building the temple.

Solomon decided to build a temple where the LORD would be worshiped, and also to build a palace for himself. He assigned seventy thousand men to carry building supplies and eighty thousand to cut stone from the hills. And he chose three thousand six hundred men to supervise these workers.

Solomon sent the following message to King Hiram of Tyre:

"Years ago, when my father David was building his palace, you supplied him with cedar logs. Now will you send me supplies? I am building a temple where the LORD my God will be worshiped…Send me a worker who can not only carve, but who can work with gold, silver, bronze, and iron, as well as make brightly-colored cloth. The person you send will work here in Judah and Jerusalem with the skilled workers that my father has already hired.

"I know that you have workers who are experts at cutting timber in Lebanon. So would you please send me some cedar, pine, and juniper logs? My workers will be there to help them, because I'll need a lot of lumber to build such a large and glorious temple. I will pay your woodcutters one hundred twenty-five thousand bushels of wheat, the same amount of barley, one hundred fifteen thousand gallons of wine, and that same amount of olive oil."

Hiram sent his answer back to Solomon:

"I know that the LORD must love his people, because he has chosen you to be their king…I am sending Huram Abi to you. He is very bright…Not only is Huram an expert at working with gold, silver, bronze, iron, stone, and wood, but he can also make colored cloth and fine linen. And he can carve anything if you give him a pattern to follow. He can help your workers and those hired by your father, King David.

"Go ahead and send the wheat, barley, olive oil, and wine you promised to pay my workers. I will tell them to start cutting down trees in Lebanon. They will cut as many as you need, then tie them together into rafts, and float them down along the coast to Joppa. Your workers can take them to Jerusalem from there."…

Solomon's workers began building the temple in Jerusalem…The inside of the temple was ninety feet long and thirty feet wide…Across the front of the temple was a porch thirty feet high. The inside walls of the porch were covered with pure gold. Solomon had the inside walls of the temple's main room paneled first with pine and then with a layer of gold, and he had them decorated with carvings of palm trees and designs that looked like chains…Solomon also had the workers carve designs of winged creatures into the walls.

The most holy place was thirty feet square, and its walls were covered with almost twenty-five tons of fine gold. More than a pound of gold was used to cover the heads of the nails. The walls of the small storage rooms were also covered with gold…

A curtain was made of fine linen woven with blue, purple, and red wool, and embroidered with designs of winged creatures.

Two columns were made for the entrance to the temple. Each one was fifty-two feet tall and had a cap on top that was seven and a half feet high…

After the LORD'S temple was finished, Solomon put in its storage rooms everything that his father David had dedicated to the LORD, including the gold and silver, and the objects used in worship.

Source: *The Holy Bible: Contemporary English Version.* Translator(s) not stated. New York: American Bible Society, 1995.

INDIA

3. God Did Not Create the World

The ninth-century B.C. authors of this passage from the literature of ancient India took a skeptical point of view about the existence of God, and the need for divine input for the creation of the world.

Some foolish men declare that Creator made the world,
The doctrine that the world was created is ill-advised, and should be rejected.
If God created the world, where was he before creation?
If you say he was transcendent then, and needed no support, where is he now?
No single being had the skill to make this world—
For how can an immaterial god create that which is material?
How could God have made the world without any raw material?
If you say he made this first, and then the world, you are faced with an endless
    regression.
If you declare that this raw material arose naturally, you fall into another fallacy,
For the whole universe might thus have been its own creator, and have arisen equally
    naturally.
If God created the world by an act of his own will, without any raw material,
Then it is just his will and nothing else—and who will believe this silly stuff?
If he is ever perfect and complete, how could the will to create have arisen in him?
If, on the other hand, he is not perfect, he could no more create the universe than
    a potter could.
If he is formless, actionless, and all-embracing, how could he have created the world?
Such a soul, devoid of all modality, would have no desire to create anything.
If he is perfect, he does not strive for the three aims of man [righteousness, profit, and
    pleasure],
So what advantage would he gain by creating the universe?
If you say that he created to no purpose, because it was his nature to do so, then God is
    pointless.
If he created in some kind of sport, it was the sport of a foolish child, leading to trouble.
If he created because of the karma of embodied beings [acquired in a previous creation],
He is not the Almighty Lord, but subordinate to something else . . .
If out of love for living things and need of them he made the world,
Why did he not make creation wholly blissful, free from misfortune?
If he were transcendent he would not create, for he would be free;
Nor if involved in transmigration, for then he would not be almighty.
Thus the doctrine that the world was created by God makes no sense at all.
And God commits great sin in slaying the children whom he himself created.
If you say that he slays only to destroy evil beings, why did he create such beings in the first
    place . . . ?
Good men should combat the believer in divine creation, maddened by an evil doctrine.
Know that the world is uncreated, as time itself is, without beginning and end,
And is based on the principles, life and the rest.
Uncreated and indestructible, it endures under the compulsion of its own nature,
Divided into three sections—hell, earth and heaven.

Source: From *Sources of Indian Tradition.* Volume I. Edited by William Theodore de Bary. Copyright © 1958
    Columbia University Press. Reprinted with permission of the publisher.

EGYPT

4. Apuleius Sees the Goddess Isis in a Dream

In this passage from his Latin novel The Metamorphoses *(also known as* The Golden Ass*), the second-century* A.D. *Roman author Apuleius describes a dream in which a vision of the Egyptian goddess Isis appeared to him.*

[As I was sleeping, there] appeared to me from the midst of the sea a divine and venerable face, worshipped even by the gods themselves. Then, little by little, I seemed to see the whole figure of her body, bright and mounting out of the sea and standing before me. Therefore, I propose to describe her divine appearance if the poverty of my human speech will allow me, or her divine power gives me a power of eloquence rich enough to express it.

First, she had a great abundance of hair, flowing and curling, dispersed and scattered about her divine neck. On the crown of her head, she bore many garlands interlaced with flowers, and in the middle of her forehead was a plain circlet in the fashion of a mirror, or rather resembling the moon by the light that it gave forth. And this was borne up on either side by serpents that seemed to rise from the furrows of the earth, and above it were blades of corn set out. Her vestment was of the finest linen, yielding diverse colors, somewhere white and shining, somewhere yellow like the crocus flower, somewhere rosy red, somewhere flaming. And (which very much troubled my sight and spirit) her cloak was utterly dark and obscure, covered with shining black, and being wrapped around her from under her left arm to her right shoulder in the manner of a shield. Part of it fell down, pleated in most subtle fashion, to the skirts of her garment, so that the welts appeared attractive. Here and there upon its edge and throughout its surface, the stars glittered, and in the middle of them was placed the moon in mid-month, which shone like a flame of fire. And round about the whole length of the border of that fine robe was a crown or garland with an unbroken wreath, made with all flowers and all fruits. She bore many diverse things: in her right hand, she had a timbrel of brass, a flat piece of metal curved in the manner of a girdle, wherein passed not many rods through the periphery of it. And when with her arm she moved these triple chords, they gave forth a shrill and clear sound. In her left hand, she bore a cup of gold like a boat; upon its handle, in the upper part which is best seen, an asp lifted up its head with a wide-swelling throat. Her pleasant feet were covered with shoes interlaced and crafted with victorious palm. Thus the divine shape, breathing out the pleasant spice of fertile Arabia, did not disdain to speak to me with her holy voice.

Source: *Apuleius: The Golden Ass, Being the Metamorphoses of Lucius Apuleius.* Translated by W. Adlington, with revisions by S. Gaselee. Cambridge and London: Loeb Classical Library, 1915.

5. The Gods Originated in Egypt

In the following excerpt from his writings, the first-century B.C. *Greek historian Diodorus Siculus puts forward the idea that Egypt was the birthplace of the gods.*

Since Egypt is the country where mythology places the origin of the gods, where the earliest observations of the stars are said to have been made, and where, furthermore, many noteworthy deeds of great men are recorded, we will begin our history with the events connected with Egypt.

The Egyptians have an account like this: When in the beginning the universe came into being, humans first came into existence in Egypt, both because of the favorable climate of the land and because of the nature of the Nile. For this stream, since it produces much life and provides a spontaneous supply of food, easily supports whatever living things have been engendered... It is manifest that, when the world was first taking shape, the land of Egypt could better than any other have been the place where mankind came into being because of the well-tempered nature of its soil...

The people of Egypt, they say, when ages ago they came into existence, as they looked up at the firmament and were struck with both awe and wonder at the nature of the universe, conceived that two gods were both eternal and first, namely, the sun and the moon, whom they called respectively Osiris and Isis, these appellations having in each case been based upon a certain meaning in them. For when the names are translated into Greek, Osiris means "many-eyed," and properly so; for in shedding his rays in every direction he surveys with many eyes, as it were, all land and sea. And the words of the poet [i.e., Homer] are also in agreement with this conception, when he says:

"The sun, who sees all things and hears all things."

And of the ancient Greek writers of mythology, some give to Osiris the name Dionysus... Some say that Osiris is also represented with the cloak of fawn skin about his shoulders, as imitating the sky when spangled with the stars. As for Isis, when translated the word means "ancient," the name having been given to her because her birth was from everlasting and ancient. And they put horns on her head both because of the appearance which she has to the eye when the moon is crescent-shaped, and because among the Egyptians a cow is held sacred to her.

These two gods, they believe, regulate the entire universe, giving both nourishment and increase to all things by means of a system of three seasons which complete the full cycle through an unobservable movement, these being spring and summer and winter... Moreover, practically all the physical matter which is essential to the generation of all things is furnished by these gods, the sun contributing the fiery element and the spirit, the moon the wet and the dry, and both together, the air. And it is through these elements that all things are engendered and nourished. And so it is out of the sun and the moon that the whole physical body of the universe is made complete.

Source: *Diodorus of Sicily*. Volume I. Translated by C. H. Oldfather. London and Cambridge: Loeb Classical Library, 1933.

6. Animal Worship in Egypt: Plutarch

The following anecdote, recorded in Plutarch's Moralia, *pertains to the Egyptian worship of various kinds of animals. Plutarch was a Greek biographer and essayist who wrote in the second century A.D.*

Detail of the Book of the Dead showing the deceased laying an offering on a table with two god-desses behind, one lion-headed and the other snake-headed, both holding a long black snake. The Art Archive/Egyptian Museum Cairo/Alfredo Dagli Orti.

Granted that [pigs are] ugly and dirty, still they are no more absurd in appearance or crude in disposition than dung beetle, field mouse, crocodile, or cat, each of which is treated as sacred by a different group of Egyptian priests... The field mouse is said to have been deified among the Egyptians because of its blindness, since they regarded darkness as superior to light. And they thought that the field mouse was born of ordinary mice every fifth generation at the new moon, and also that its liver was reduced in size at the dark of the moon.

They associate the lion with the sun because it, alone of quadrupeds that have claws, bears young that can see at birth, sleeps only for a moment, and has eyes that gleam in sleep. Egyptian fountains pour forth their water through lion mouths, because the Nile brings new water to the fields of Egypt.

Source: *Plutarch's Moralia.* Volume VIII. Translated by Paul A. Clement. Cambridge and London: Loeb Classical Library, 1969.

7. Animal Worship in Egypt: Pliny the Elder

In this excerpt from his Natural History, *the first-century* A.D. *writer Pliny the Elder reports that in Egypt a sacred ox called Apis was the object of veneration.*

In Egypt an ox is even worshipped in place of a god; its name is Apis. Its distinguishing mark is a bright white spot in the shape of a crescent on the right flank, and it has a knob under the tongue which they call a beetle. It is not lawful for it to exceed a certain number of years of life, and they kill it by drowning it in the fountain of the priests, proceeding with lamentation to look for another to put in its place, and they go on mourning until they have found one, actually shaving the hair off their heads. Nevertheless, the search never continues long.

When the successor is found, it is led by 100 priests to Memphis. It has a pair of shrines, which they call its bedchambers...When it enters one, this is a joyful sign, but in the other one, it portends terrible events. It gives answers to private individuals by taking food out of the hand of those who consult it...Usually living in retirement, when it comes out into assemblies, it proceeds with bodyguards to clear the way, and companies of boys escort it singing a song in its honor. It seems to understand, and to desire to be worshipped. These companies are suddenly seized with frenzy and chant prophecies of future events. Once a year, a cow is displayed to it, she too with her decorations, although they are not the same as his. And it is traditional for her always to be found and put to death on the same day.

At Memphis, there is a place in the Nile which from its shape they call the Goblet. Every year they throw into the river there a gold and silver cup on the days which they keep at the birthdays of Apis. These are seven, and it is a remarkable fact that during these days, nobody is attacked by crocodiles, but that after midday on the eighth day, the creature's savagery returns.

Source: *Pliny: Natural History.* Volume III. Translated by H. Rackham. London and Cambridge: Loeb Classical Library, 1940.

GREECE

8. The Birth of the God Zeus

The eighth-century B.C. *Greek poet Hesiod, in this excerpt from his lengthy poem "Theogony," tells the tale of the birth of the god Zeus.*

Rhea, overpowered by Cronus, bore him splendid children: Hestia, Demeter, and golden-sandaled Hera, and powerful Hades, who dwells in mansions beneath the earth and has a pitiless heart, and the loud-sounding Earthshaker [Poseidon], and the counselor Zeus, the father of gods and of humankind, by whose thunder the broad earth is shaken. Great Cronus would swallow these down as each one came from his mother's holy womb to her knees, mindful that no one else of Sky's illustrious children should have the honor of kingship among the immortals. For he had heard from Earth and starry Sky that, mighty though he was, he was destined to be overpowered by a child of his, through the plans of great Zeus. For this reason, then, he held no unseeing watch, but observed closely, and swallowed down his children, and unremitting grief gripped Rhea. But when she was about to bear Zeus, the father of gods and of humankind, she begged her own dear parents, Earth and starry Sky, to contrive some scheme so that she could bear her dear son without being noticed, and take retribution for the avenging deities of her father and of her children, whom great crooked-counseled Cronus had swallowed down.

They listened well to their dear daughter and obeyed her, and they revealed to her everything that was fated to come about concerning Cronus the king and his strong-spirited son. They told her to go to Lyctus, to the rich land of Crete, when she was about to bear the youngest of her children, great Zeus. And huge Earth received him in broad Crete, to nurse him and rear him up. There she came first to Lyctus, carrying him through the swift black night. Taking him in her hands, she concealed him in a deep cave, under the hidden places of the holy earth, in the Aegean mountain, abounding with forests. And she wrapped a large stone in swaddling clothes and put it into the hand of Sky's son, the great ruler, the king of the earlier gods [the Titans]. He seized this with his hands and put it down into his belly—cruel one, nor did he know in his spirit that in place of the stone, his son remained hereafter, unconquered and untroubled, who would overpower him with force and his own hands, and would soon drive him out from his honor and be king among the immortals.

Swiftly, then, the king's strength and his splendid limbs grew. And when a year had revolved, great crooked-counseled Cronus, deceived by Earth's very clever suggestions, brought his offspring up again, overcome by his son's devices and force. First, he vomited up the stone, since he had swallowed it down last of all. Zeus set it fast in the broad-pathed earth...to be a sign thereafter, a marvel for mortal human beings.

And he freed from their deadly bonds his father's brothers, Sky's sons [the Cyclopes], whom their father had bound in his folly. And they repaid him in gratitude for his kind deed, giving him the thunder and the blazing thunderbolt and the lightning, which huge Earth had concealed before. Relying on these, he rules over mortals and immortals.

Source: *Hesiod: Theogony; Works and Days; Testimonia.* Translated by Glenn W. Most. Cambridge and London: Loeb Classical Library, 2006.

9. Divine Omnipotence

In this passage from his Moralia *(see also Document 6, above), the second-century A.D. Greek biographer Plutarch recounts the thoughts of the philosopher* Anacharsis *on the role and power of the divine in the natural world.*

Anacharsis said that as Thales had set forth the excellent hypothesis that soul exists in all the most dominant and most important parts of the universe, there is no proper ground for wonder that the most excellent things are brought to pass by the will of God. "For the body," he continued, "is the soul's instrument, and the soul is God's instrument. And just as the body has many movements of its own, but the most, and most excellent, from the soul, so the soul performs some actions by its own instinct, but in others it yields itself to God's use for Him to direct it and turn it in whatsoever course He may desire, since it is the most adaptable of all instruments. For it is a dreadful mistake to assume that, on the one hand, fire is God's instrument, and wind and water also, and clouds and rain, by means of which He preserves and fosters many things, and ruins and destroys many others, but that, on the other hand, He never as yet makes any use whatever of living creatures to accomplish any one of his purposes. It is far more likely that the living, being dependant on God's power, serve Him and are responsive to His movements even more than bows are responsive to the Scythians, or lyres and flutes to the Greeks."

Source: *Plutarch's Moralia.* Volume II. Translated by Frank Cole Babbitt. London and New York: Loeb Classical Library, 1928.

ROME

10. Definitions of the Gods and Their Power

In this passage from his philosophical essay "On the Nature of the Gods," the first-century B.C. *Roman orator Cicero discusses the variety of opinions about the gods.*

There are a number of branches of philosophy that have not as yet been by any means adequately explored. But the inquiry into the nature of the gods, which is both highly interesting in relation to the theory of the soul, and fundamentally important for the regulation of religion, is one of special difficulty and obscurity...

As regards the present subject, most thinkers have affirmed that the gods exist, and this is the most probable view and the one to which we are all led by nature's guidance...The upholders of the divine existence differ and disagree so widely, that it would be a troublesome task to recount their opinions. Many views are put forward about the outward form of the gods, their dwelling places and abodes, and mode of life, and these topics are debated with the widest variety of opinion among philosophers. But as to the question upon which the whole issue of the dispute principally turns, whether the gods are entirely idle and inactive, taking no part at all in the direction and government of the world, or whether on the contrary all things both were created and ordered by them in the beginning and are controlled and kept in motion by them throughout eternity, here there is the greatest disagreement of all. And until this issue is decided, mankind must continue to labor under the profoundest uncertainty, and to be in ignorance about matters of the highest moment.

For there are and have been philosophers who hold that the gods exercise no control over human affairs whatever. But if their opinion is the true one, how can piety, reverence or religion exist? For all these are tributes which it is our duty to render in purity and holiness to the divine powers solely on the assumption that they take notice of them, and that some service has been rendered by the immortal gods to the human race. But if on the contrary, the gods have neither the power nor the will to aid us, if they pay no heed to us at all and take no notice of our actions, if they can exert no possible influence upon the life of humans, what ground have we for rendering any sort of worship, honor, or prayer to the immortal gods? Piety, however, like the rest of the virtues, cannot exist in mere outward show and pretense, and with piety, reverence and religion must likewise disappear. And when these are gone, life soon becomes a welter of disorder and confusion. And in all probability, the disappearance of piety towards the gods will entail the disappearance of loyalty and social union among people as well, and of justice itself, the queen of all the virtues.

Later in the same treatise, Cicero discusses various proofs for the existence of the gods:

When we gaze upward to the sky and contemplate the heavenly bodies, what can be so obvious and so manifest as that there must exist some power possessing transcendent intelligence by whom these things are ruled? Were it not so, how comes it that the words of [the poet] Ennius carry conviction to all readers:

"Behold this dazzling vault of heaven, which all mankind as Jove invoke" and not only as Jove, but as sovereign of the world, ruling all things with his nod, and as Ennius likewise says, "father of gods and mankind" a deity omnipresent and omnipotent? If anyone doubts this, I really cannot see why he should not also be capable of doubting the existence of the sun. How is the latter fact more evident than the former? Nothing but the presence in our minds of a firmly grasped concept of the deity could account for the stability and permanence of our belief in him, a belief which is only strengthened by the passage of the ages and grows more deeply rooted with each successive generation of mankind. In every other case, we see that fictitious and unfounded opinions have dwindled away with the lapse of time...

Hence both in our own nation and among all others reverence for the gods and respect for religion grow continually stronger and more profound. Nor is this unaccountable or accidental. It is the result, first, of the fact that the gods often manifest their power in bodily presence... Prophecies and premonitions of future events must be understood as proofs that the future may appear or be foretold as a warning or portended or predicted to mankind... Our empire was won by those commanders who obeyed the dictates of religion. Moreover, if we care to compare our national characteristics with those of foreign peoples, we will find that, while in all other respects we are only the equals or even the inferiors of others, yet in the sense of religion, that is, in reverence for the gods, we are far superior.

Source: *Cicero: De Natura Deorum.* Translated by H. Rackham. Cambridge and London: Loeb Classical Library, 1933.

11. Some Advice on How to Worship the Gods

In this excerpt from his 95th Epistle, the first-century A.D. Roman philosopher Seneca offers some advice about the proper way to worship the gods.

Precepts are commonly given as to how the gods should be worshipped. But let us forbid lamps to be lighted..., since the gods do not need light, nor do humans take pleasure in soot. Let us forbid the practice of offering morning salutation and to throng the doors of the temples; mortal ambitions are attracted by such ceremonies, but the gods are worshipped by those who truly know them. Let us forbid bringing towels and

Seneca, Roman Stoic philosopher, statesman, dramatist, tutor, and later advisor to emperor Nero. Library of Congress.

flesh-scrapers [i.e., athletic supplies, most likely offered by men] to Jupiter, and offering mirrors [i.e., most like offered by women] to Juno, for the gods do not seek servants. Of course not. Jupiter himself does service to mankind; everywhere and to all he is at hand to help. Although a suppliant hears what limit he should observe in sacrifice, and how far he should recoil from burdensome superstitions, he will never made sufficient progress until he has conceived a right idea of the gods—regarding them as beings who possess all things, and who bestow them without price. And what reason do the gods have for doing deeds of kindness? It is their nature. One who thinks that they are unwilling to do harm is wrong; they *cannot* do harm. They cannot receive or inflict injury; for doing harm is in the same category as suffering harm. The universal nature, all-glorious and all-beautiful, has rendered incapable of inflicting ill those whom it has removed from the danger of ill.

The first way to worship the gods is to believe in the gods; the next, to acknowledge their majesty, to acknowledge their goodness, without which there is no majesty. Also, to know that they are supreme commanders in the universe, controlling all things by their power and acting as guardians of the human race, even though they are sometimes unmindful of the individual. They neither give nor have evil, but they do chasten and restrain certain persons, and impose penalties, and sometimes punish by giving that which seems good outwardly. Do you want to win over the gods? Then be a good person. Whoever imitates them is worshipping them sufficiently.

Source: *Seneca: Ad Lucilium Epistulae Morales*. Volume III. Translated by Richard M. Gummere. Cambridge and London: Loeb Classical Library, 1925.

12. When Romans Come into Contact with Christians

Reproduced below is one of the most famous of the many letters of Pliny the Younger (A.D. 62–114). In about A.D. 111, when Pliny was governor of the province of Bithynia in Asia Minor, he wrote to the emperor Trajan to ask how best to deal persons accused of being Christians. The letter is thus one of the earliest non-Christian accounts of early Christian worship and of the official reasons for punishing Christians. Also given below is Trajan's letter of reply.

It is my custom to refer all my difficulties to you, Sir, for no one is better able to resolve my doubts and to inform my ignorance.

I have never been present at an examination of Christians. Consequently, I do not know the nature or the extent of the punishments usually meted out to them, nor the grounds for starting an investigation and how far it should be pressed. Nor am I at all sure whether any distinction should be made between them on the grounds of age, or if young people and adults should be treated alike; whether a pardon ought to be granted to anyone retracting his beliefs, or if he has once professed Christianity, he will gain nothing by renouncing it, and whether it is the mere name of Christian which is punishable, even if innocent of crime, or rather the crimes associated with the name.

For the moment, this is the course of action I have taken with all persons brought before me on the charge of being Christians. I have asked them in person if they are Christians, and if they admit it, I repeat the question a second and third time, with a warning of the punishment awaiting them. If they persist, I order them to be led away for execution; for, whatever the nature of their admission, I am convinced that their stubbornness and unshakeable obstinacy ought not to go unpunished. There have been others similarly fanatical who are Roman citizens. I have entered them on the list of persons to be sent to Rome for trial.

Now that I have begun to deal with this problem, as so often happens, the charges are becoming more widespread and increasing in variety. An anonymous pamphlet has been circulated which contains the names of a number of accused persons. Among these I considered that I should dismiss any who denied that they were or ever had been Christians when they had repeated after me a formula of invocation to the gods and had made offerings of wine and incense to your statue, which I had ordered to be brought into court for this purpose along with the images of the gods, and furthermore had reviled the name of Christ. None of these things, I understand, can any genuine Christian be induced to do.

Others, whose names were given to me by an informer, first admitted the charge and then denied it. They said that they had ceased to be Christians two or more years previously, and some of them even 20 years ago. They all did reverence to your statue and the images of the gods in the same way as the others, and reviled the name of Christ. They also declared that the sum total of their guilt or error amounted to no more than this: they had met regularly before dawn on a fixed day to chant verses alternately among themselves in honor of Christ as if to a god, and also to bind themselves by oath, not for any criminal purpose, but to abstain from theft, robbery and adultery, to commit no breach of trust and not to deny a deposit when called upon to restore it.

After this ceremony, it had been their custom to disperse and reassemble later to take food of an ordinary, harmless kind. But they had in fact given up this practice since my edict, issued on your instructions, which banned all political societies. This made me decide it was all the more necessary to extract the truth by torture from two slave women, whom they call deaconesses. I found nothing but a degenerate sort of cult carried to extravagant lengths.

I have therefore postponed any further examination and hastened to consult you. The question seems to me to be worthy of your consideration, especially in view of the number of persons endangered. A great many individuals of every age and class, both men and women, and being brought to trial, and this is likely to continue. It is not only the towns, but villages and rural districts too which are infected through contact with this wretched cult. I think, though, that it is still possible for it to be checked and directed to better ends, for there is no doubt that people have begun to throng the temples which had been almost entirely deserted for a long time. The sacred rites which had been allowed to lapse are being performed again, and flesh of sacrificial victims is on sale everywhere, though up till recently scarcely anyone could be found to buy it. It is easy to infer from this that a great many people could be reformed if they were given an opportunity to repent.

Trajan's reply:

You have followed the right course of procedure, my friend, in your examination of the cases of persons charged with being Christians, for it is impossible to lay down a general rule to a fixed formula. These people must not be hunted out; if they are brought before you and the charge against them is proved, they must be punished, but in the case of anyone who denies that he is a Christian, and makes it clear that he is not, by offering prayers to our gods, he is to be pardoned as a result of his repentance, however suspect his past conduct may be. But pamphlets circulated anonymously must play no part in any accusation. They create the worst sort of precedent and are quite out of keeping with the spirit of our age.

Source: *Pliny: Letters and Panegyricus.* Volume II. Translated by Betty Radice. Cambridge and London: Loeb Classical Library, 1915.

Priests and Religious Rituals

Priests in all the ancient cultures had to fulfill the expectations of the faithful to maintain their credibility. Standards of behavior were strict, as in Egypt, where priests were expected to be fair, honest, and trustworthy, and to live lives that were free of sin (Document 15). In Rome, the priests and priestesses who presided over the worship of the god Jupiter had to be fully versed in all the details of the ceremonial rituals pertaining to that god. They faced odd prohibitions, such as not being allowed to ride a horse, nor to walk under an arbor of vines, nor to touch yeast-fermented bread (Document 19). Although priests were generally well respected, the same was not always true of soothsayers (Document 23).

The Romans observed and obeyed many rituals in connection with deity worship (Document 20). Sometimes, specific events would cause an outpouring of religious veneration; for example, whenever the Romans "felt an earthquake or received report of one," they immediately declared a holy day of prayer and repentance (Document 21).

Not only were the gods thought to have originated in Egypt, but so too were many often well-attended rituals and ceremonies. The fifth-century B.C. Greek historian Herodotus claimed that at one particular annual religious festival as many as 700,000 people might appear (Document 14). And it was an Egyptian priest who foretold the birth and eventual power of Moses (Document 13). Under certain circumstances, priestly offices in Egypt could be bought and sold (Document 16). In Rome, the rules for the selection of the priestesses of the goddess Vesta were strict and prescriptive (Document 24). Sometimes, kings did not wish to hear advice from priests, but failure to heed these messages could result in disaster, as *Agamemnon* (Document 18) and *Pentheus* (Document 17) learned to their dismay.

ISRAEL/EGYPT

13. The Birth of Moses

As recounted by the first-century A.D. *Jewish historian Josephus in this excerpt from his* Jewish Antiquities, *an Egyptian priest foretold the birth of Moses.*

One of the [Egyptian] sacred scribal priests—persons with considerable skill in accurately predicting the future—announced to the king that there would be born to the Israelites at that time one who would abase the sovereignty of the Egyptians and exalt the Israelites, were he reared to manhood, and would surpass all people in virtue and win everlasting renown. Alarmed, the king, on this sage's advice, ordered that every male child born to the Israelites should be destroyed by being cast into the river, and that the labors of pregnant Hebrew women should be observed and watch kept for their delivery by the Egyptian midwives. For this duty was, by his orders, to be performed by women who, as compatriots of the king, were not likely to transgress his will. Those who defied this decree and stealthily ventured to save their offspring, he ordered to be put to death, along with their progeny. So the calamity confronting the victims was terrible: not only were they to be bereft of their children, not only must the parents themselves be accessories to the destruction of their offspring, but the plan to extinguish their race by the massacre of the infants and their own approaching dissolution rendered their lot cruel and inconsolable. Such was their miserable situation.

But no one can defeat the will of God, whatever countless devices he may contrive to that end. For this child, whose birth the sacred scribe had foretold, was reared, eluding the king's vigilance, and the prophet's words concerning all that was to be done through him proved true.

Source: Josephus: Jewish Antiquities. Volume IV. Translated by H. St. J. Thackeray. Cambridge and London: Loeb Classical Library, 1930.

EGYPT

14. *Egyptian Religious Rituals*

In this passage from his Histories, *the fifth-century* B.C. *historian Herodotus provides an extensive account of Egyptian religious rituals.*

It was the Egyptians who originated and taught the Greeks to use ceremonial meetings, processions, and liturgies, a fact which can be inferred from the obvious antiquity of such ceremonies in Egypt, compared with Greece, where they have been only recently introduced. The Egyptians meet in solemn assembly not once a year only, but on a number of occasions, the most important and best attended being the festival of Artemis at Bubastis. Second in importance is the assembly at Busiris—a city in the middle of the Delta, containing a vast temple dedicated to Isis, the Egyptian equivalent to Demeter, in whose honor the meeting is held...

The procedure at Bubastis is this: They come in barges, men and women together, a great number in each boat. On the way, some of the women keep up a continual clatter with castanets and some of the men play flutes, while the rest, both men and women, sing and clap their hands. Whenever they pass a town on the river bank, they bring the barge close to the shore, some of the women continuing to act as I have said, while others shout abuse at the women of the place, or start dancing, or stand up and hitch up their skirts. When they reach Bubastis, they celebrate the festival with elaborate sacrifices, and more wine is consumed than during all the rest of the year. The numbers that meet there are, according to native report, as many as 700,000 men and women, excluding children.

[As for] the festival of Isis at Busiris: it is here that everybody—tens of thousands of men and women—when the sacrifice is over, beat their breasts...Any Carians who happen to live in Egypt go even further and cut their foreheads with knives, thus proving that they are foreigners and not Egyptians. At Sais, on the night of the sacrifices, everybody burns a great number of lights in the open air around the houses; the lamps they use are flat dishes filled with oil and salt, with a floating wick which keeps burning throughout the night. The festival is called the Festival of Lamps, and even the Egyptians who cannot attend it mark the night of the sacrifice by lighting lamps, so that on that night lamps are burning not only in Sais, but throughout the country. There is a sacred tradition which accounts both for the date and for the manner of these observances.

Source: *Herodotus: The Histories*. Translated by Aubrey de Selincourt, with revisions by R. Burn. Baltimore: Penguin Books, 1954. Reproduced by permission of Penguin Books Ltd.

15. A Job Description for Priests

The following inscribed text from a Ptolemaic temple provides information about expectations of priests (Ptolemaic Egypt lasted from 305–30 B.C.).

O you prophets, great pure priests, guardians of what is secret, pure priests of the god, all you who enter into the presence of the gods, ritual priests who are in the temple! Oh all of you, judges, administrators of the domain, intendants who are in your mouth...turn your face toward this domain in which His Majesty has placed you! When he sails across the sky, he looks below, and he is satisfied if his law is observed! Do not present yourselves in a state of sin! Do not enter in a state of filth! Do not tell lies in his house! Divert none of the provisions. Do not levy taxes injuring the little person in favor of the powerful! Do not add to the weight and the measure, but lessen them! Do not set to pillaging with the bushel...Do not reveal what you see in any secret matter of the sanctuary! Do not stretch out your hand over anything in his home, and do not go as far as to steal before the lord, bearing a sacrilegious thought in your heart! One lives on the provisions of the gods, but one calls "provision" that which leave the altar after the god has satisfied himself with it!

Source: Dunand, Francoise, and Christiane Zivie-Coche. *Gods and Men in Egypt: 3000 B.C.E. to 395 C.E.* Translated from the French by David Lorton. Ithaca, NY: Cornell University Press, 2004. Courtesy of Cornell University Press and Armand Colin. © Armand Colin, 2001.

16. Office of Prophet for Sale!

An Egyptian papyrus dated A.D. 146 contains the following account of a certain Pakebis and his attempt to buy a priestly office.

To Tiberius Claudius Justus, administrator of the private account, from Pakebis...

I wish to purchase the office of prophet in the aforesaid temple [of Soknebtunis, a crocodile god], which has been offered for sale for a long time, on the understanding that I shall...carry the palm branches and perform the other functions of the office of prophet, and receive in accordance with the orders the fifth part of all the revenue which falls to the temple, at the total price of 2200 drachmas...which sum I will pay if my appointment is ratified, into the local bank at the customary dates. And I and my descendants and successors shall have the permanent ownership and possession of this office forever with all the same privileges and rights, on payment by each one of 200 drachmas for admission.

If therefore it seems good to you, my lord, you will ratify my appointment here in the city [Alexandria] upon these terms and write to the strategus of the nome about this matter, in order that the due services of the gods who love you may be performed. The 5th share of the proceeds of the revenues which falls to me, as aforesaid, after deducting expenses is 50 measures of wheat, nine and five-eighths of lentils, 60 drachmas of silver. Farewell.

Source: *Select Papyri: Non-Literary Papyri. Public Documents.* Volume II. Translated by A. S. Hunt and C. C. Edgar. Cambridge and London: Loeb Classical Library, 1934.

GREECE

17. Some Priestly Advice for King Pentheus

One of the most famous soothsayers in Greek literature and mythology was the blind prophet Tiresias. In this excerpt from the play Bacchae *by the Athenian playwright Euripides (c. 480–406 B.C.), the elderly Tiresias chides the Theban king Pentheus for refusing to pay homage to the god Dionysus.*

When a clever man has a plausible theme to argue, to be eloquent is no great feat. But though you seem, by your glib tongue, to be intelligent, yet your words are foolish. Power and eloquence in a headstrong man can only lead to folly; and such a man is a danger to the state.

This new divinity [Dionysus] whom you ridicule—no words of mine could adequately express the ascendancy he is destined to achieve through the length and breadth of Greece. There are two powers, young man, which are supreme in human affairs: first, the goddess Demeter; she is the Earth—call her by what name you will—and she supplies mankind with solid food. Second, Dionysus, the son of Semele; the blessing he provides is the counterpart to the blessing of bread. He discovered and bestowed on humankind the service of drink, the juice that streams from the vine-clusters. People have but to take their fill of wine, and the sufferings of an unhappy race are banished, each day's troubles are forgotten in sleep. Indeed, this is our only cure for the weariness of life. Dionysus, himself a god, is poured out in offering to the gods, so that through him, mankind receives blessing.

Now, for the legend that he was sewn up in Zeus's thigh— do you mock it? Then I will explain to you the truth that lies in the legend. When Zeus snatched the infant Dionysus away

Euripides, ancient Greek dramatist. Library of Congress.

from the fire of the lightning, and brought him to Olympus as a god, Hera wanted to cast him out of heaven. So, to prevent her, Zeus, as you would expect, devised a plan. He broke off a piece of the sky that envelopes the earth, made it into the likeness of a child, and gave it to Hera as a pledge, to soothe her jealousy. He entrusted the true Dionysus to others to bring up...

And this god is a prophet. For the Bacchic [i.e., Dionysian] ecstasy and frenzy contain a strong element of prophecy. When Dionysus enters in power into a human body, he endows the possessed person with power to foretell the future. He also in some degree shares the function of Ares, god of war. It has happened that an army, equipped and stationed for battle, has fled in panic before a spear has been raised. This, too, is a madness sent by Dionysus...

Come, Pentheus, listen to me. You rely on force, but it is not force that governs human affairs. If you think otherwise, beware of mistaking your perverse opinion for wisdom. Welcome Dionysus to Thebes; pour libations to him, garland your head and celebrate his rites. Dionysus will not compel women to control their lusts. Self-control in all things depends on our own natures. This is a fact you should consider... And think of this too: when crowds stand at the city gates, and the people glorify the name of Pentheus, you are filled with pleasure. So, I think, Dionysus is glad to receive honor.

So then I, and Cadmus [grandfather of Pentheus], whom you mock, will wear the ivy wreath and join in the dancing. We are both old men, but this is our duty. And no words of yours will persuade me to fight against the gods. For your mind is most pitifully diseased, and there is no medicine that can heal you.

Source: *Euripides: The Bacchae and Other Plays.* Translated by Philip Vellacott. Baltimore: Penguin Books, 1954. Reproduced by permission of Penguin Books Ltd.

18. Shooting, or at Least Upbraiding, the Messenger

When prophets and soothsayers in ancient Greece bore bad news, the recipients of that news often reacted angrily. As related in this passage from Homer's Iliad, the soothsayer Calchas found this out during the darkest days of the Trojan War, when he reported to Agamemnon, king of the Greeks, that the plague sweeping through the Greek army was Agamemnon's fault.

Calchas rose among them,
Thestor's son, the clearest by far of all the seers
who scan the flight of birds. He knew all things that are,
all things that are past and all that are to come,
the seer who had led the Greek ships to Troy
with the second sight that god Apollo gave him.
For the armies' good, the seer began to speak:
"Achilles, dear to Zeus...
you order me to explain Apollo's anger,
the distant deadly archer? I will tell it all.
But strike a pact with me, swear you will defend me
with all your heart, with words and strength of hand.

For there is a man I will enrage—I see it now—
a powerful man who lords it over all the Greeks,
one the Greeks must obey. A mighty king,
raging against an inferior, is too strong.
Even if he can swallow down his anger today,
still he will nurse the burning in his chest
until, sooner or later, he sends it bursting forth.
Consider it closely, Achilles. Will you protect me?"
And the matchless runner reassured him: "Courage!
Out with it now, Calchas. Reveal the will of god,
whatever you may know. And I swear by Apollo
dear to Zeus, the power you pray to, Calchas,
when you reveal the god's will to the Greeks, no one,
not while I am alive and see the light on earth, no one
will lay his heavy hands on you by the hollow ships.
None among all the armies. Not even if you mean
Agamemnon here, who now claims to be, by far,
the best of the Greeks."
The seer took heart
and this time he spoke out, bravely: "Beware,
the god [Apollo] casts no blame for a vow we failed, a sacrifice.
The god's enraged because Agamemnon spurned his priest,
he refused to free his daughter, he refused the ransom.
That's why the Archer-god sends us pains and he will send us more
and never drive this shameful destruction from the Greeks,
not till we give back the girl with sparkling eyes
to her loving father—no price, no ransom paid—
and carry a sacred hundred bulls to Chryse's town [the priest whom Agamemnon had
    offended].
Then we can calm the god, and only then appease him."
So he declared, and sat down. But among them rose
the fighting son of Atreus, lord of the far-flung kingdoms,
Agamemnon—furious, his dark heart filled to the brim,
blazing with anger now, his eyes like searing fire.
With a sudden, killing look, he wheeled on Calchas first:
"Seer of misery! Never a word that works to my advantage!
Always misery warms you heart, your prophecies.
Never a word of profit said or brought to pass.
Now, again, you predict god's will for the armies,
spread the rumor around as fact, why the deadly Archer
multiplies our pains, because I, I refused
[to return the priest's kidnapped daughter to him]."

Source: "The Rage of Achilles" by Homer, from THE ILIAD by Homer, translated by Robert Fagles, copyright
© 1990 by Robert Fagles. Used by permission of Viking Penguin, a division of Penguin Group (USA) Inc.

ROME

---

19. A Job Description for Priests

In this excerpt from his Attic Nights, *the Latin writer Aulus Gellius* (A.D. c. 125–c. 180)
describes the rituals and duties of the priest and priestess of Jupiter.

Ceremonies in great number are imposed upon the priest of Jupiter and also many abstentions of which we read in the books written *On Public Priests*...Of these, the following are in general what I remember:

It is unlawful for the priest of Jupiter to ride upon a horse. It is also unlawful for him to see the classes arrayed outside the religious boundaries of the city, that is, the army in battle array. Hence the priest of Jupiter is rarely made consul, since wars were entrusted to the consuls. Also, it is always unlawful for the priest to take an oath, and likewise to wear a ring, unless it be perforated and without a gem. It is against the law for fire to be taken from the *flaminia,* that is, from the home of the flamen Dialis [priest of Jupiter], except for a sacred rite. If a person in chains enters his house, he must be freed, the bonds must be drawn up through a skylight in the ceiling to the roof and from there let down into the street. He has no knot in his head-dress, girdle, or any other part of his clothing. If anyone is being taken to be flogged, and falls at his feet as a suppliant, it is unlawful for the man to be flogged on that day. Only a free man may cut the hair of the priest. It is not customary for the priest to touch, or even name, a she-goat, raw flesh, ivy, and beans.

The priest of Jupiter must not pass under an arbor of vines. The feet of the couch on which he sleeps must be smeared with a thin coating of clay, and he must not sleep away from this bed for three nights in succession, and no other person must sleep in that bed. At the foot of his bed, there should be a box with sacrificial cakes. The cuttings of the nails and hair of the priest must be buried in the earth under a fruitful tree. Every day is a holy day for the priest. He must not be in the open air without his cap; that he may go without it in the house only recently has been decided by the pontiffs...and it is said that some other ceremonies have been remitted, and he has been excused from observing them.

The priest of Jupiter must not touch any bread fermented with yeast. He does not remove his inner tunic except under cover, in order that he may not be naked in the open air, as it were under the eye of Jupiter. No other person has a place at the table above the priest of Jupiter, except for the priest who presides over sacrifices. If the priest has lost his wife, he abdicates his office. The marriage of the priest cannot be dissolved except by death. He never enters a place of burial, he never touches a dead body, but he is not forbidden to attend a funeral.

The ceremonies of the priestess of Jupiter are about the same. They say that she observes other separate ones. For example, she wears a dyed robe, that she has a twig from a fruitful tree in her head-dress, that it is forbidden for her to go up more than three rounds of a ladder. Also, when she goes to a chapel, that she neither combs her head nor dresses her hair.

I have added the words of the praetor in his standing edict concerning the priest of Jupiter and the priestess of [the goddess] Vesta: "In the whole of my jurisdiction, I will not compel the priest of Jupiter or a priestess of Vesta to take an oath." The words of Marcus Varro about the priest of Jupiter...: "He alone has a white cap, either because he is the greatest of priests, or because a white victim should be sacrificed to Jupiter."

Source: *The Attic Nights of Aulus Gellius.* Volume II. Translated by John C. Rolfe. Cambridge and London: Loeb Classical Library, 1927.

20. Religious Rules, Regulations, and Rituals

In this passage from his book entitled Laws, *the first-century* B.C. *Roman orator Cicero provides information on various religious rituals.*

They shall approach the gods in purity, bringing piety, and leaving riches behind. Whoever shall do otherwise, God Himself will deal out punishment to him.

No one shall have gods to himself, either new gods or alien gods, unless recognized by the state. Privately they shall worship those gods whose worship they have duly received from their ancestors.

In cities they shall have shrines; they shall have groves in the country and homes for the Lares [household gods].

They shall preserve the rites of their families and their ancestors.

They shall worship as gods both those who have always been regarded as dwellers in heaven, and also those whose merits have admitted them to heaven... They shall perform the established rites.

On holidays they shall refrain from lawsuits. Holidays they shall celebrate together with their slaves, after their tasks are done. Let holidays be so arranged as to fall at regularly recurring breaks in the year. The priest shall offer on behalf of the State the prescribed grains and the prescribed fruits. This shall be done according to prescribed rites and on prescribed days... And so that no violation of these customs shall take place, the priests shall determine the mode and the annual circuit of such offerings. And they shall prescribe the victims which are proper and pleasing to each of the gods.

The several gods shall have their several priests, the gods all together their pontiffs, and the individual gods their priests. The Vestal Virgins shall guard the eternal fire on the public hearth of the city.

Those who are ignorant as to the methods and rites suitable to these public and private sacrifices shall seek instruction from the public priests. Of them, there shall be three kinds: one to have charge of ceremonies and sacred rites; another to interpret those obscure sayings of soothsayers and prophets which shall be recognized by the senate and the people; and the interpreters of Jupiter the Best and the Greatest, namely the public augurs, shall foretell the future from portents and auspices, and maintain their art. And the priests shall observe the omens in regard to vineyards and orchards and the safety of the people; those who carry on war or affairs of state shall be informed by them beforehand of the auspices, and shall obey them. The priests shall foresee the wrath of the gods and yield to it. They shall observe flashes of lightning in fixed regions of the sky, and shall keep free and unobstructed the city and fields and their places of observation. Whatever an augur shall declare to be unjust, unholy, pernicious, or ill-omened, shall be null and void. And whosoever does not obey shall be put to death.

The fetial priests [priests involved with solemnizing treaties, truces, and other international matters; see the following selection for a description of their rituals] shall be judges and messengers for treaties, peace and war, truces, and embassies. They shall make the decisions in regard to war.

Prodigies and portents shall be referred to the Etruscan soothsayers, if the senate so decree... They shall make expiatory offerings to whatever gods they decide upon, and shall perform expiations for flashes of lightning and for whatever shall be struck by lightning...

Sacrilege which cannot be expiated shall be held to be impiously committed. That which can be expiated shall be atoned for by the public priests.

At the public games which are held without chariot races or athletic contests, the public pleasure shall be provided for with moderation by song to the music of harp and flute, and this shall be combined with honor to the gods...

Whoever steals or carries off what is sacred or anything entrusted to what is sacred shall be considered as equal in guilt to a parricide.

For the perjurer, the punishment from the gods is destruction. The human punishment shall be disgrace.

The pontiffs shall inflict capital punishment on those guilty of incest.

No wicked man shall dare to appease the wrath of the gods with gifts.

Vows shall be scrupulously performed. There shall be a penalty for the violation of the law.

No one shall consecrate a field. The consecration of gold, silver, and ivory shall be confined to reasonable limits.

The sacred rites of families shall remain forever.

The rights of the gods of the lower world shall be sacred. Kinsfolk who are dead shall be considered gods. The expenditure and mourning for them shall be limited.

Source: *Cicero: De Re Publica; De Legibus.* Translated by Clinton Walker Keyes. Cambridge and London: Loeb Classical Library, 1928.

21. Religious Rituals in Case of an Earthquake

The causes of earthquakes were not well known in the ancient world, but just in case some god happened to be responsible, the Romans believed that religious expiation was in order, as the Latin author Aulus Gellius (A.D. c. 125–c. 180) explains in this passage from his Attic Nights (see also Document 19, above).

What is to be regarded as the cause of earthquakes is not only not obvious to the ordinary understanding and thought of mankind, but it is not agreed upon even among the natural philosophers whether they are due to the mighty winds that gather in the caverns and hollow places of the earth, or to the ebb and flow of subterranean waters in its hollows, as seems to have been the view of the earliest Greeks, who called Neptune "the Earth Shaker," or whether they are due to the divine power of some other god—all this, I say, is not yet a matter of certain knowledge. For that reason, the Romans of long ago, who were not only exceedingly scrupulous and careful in discharging all the other obligations of life, but also in fulfilling religious duties and venerating the immortal gods, whenever they felt an earthquake or received report of one, decreed a holy day on that account, but refused to declare and specify in the decree, as is commonly done, the name of the god in whose honor the holy day was to be observed, for fear that by naming one god instead of another, they might involve the people in a false observance. If anyone had desecrated that festival, and expiation was therefore necessary, they used to offer a victim "to either the god or goddess" …and this usage was established by a decree of the pontiffs, since it was uncertain what force, and which of the gods or goddesses, had caused the earthquake.

Source: *The Attic Nights of Aulus Gellius*. Volume I. Translated by John C. Rolfe. Cambridge and London: Loeb Classical Library, 1927.

22. Marcus Valerius and the Solemnizing of a Treaty

The fetial priests, who solemnized treaties, followed prescribed formulaic rituals in the execution of their duties. In this excerpt from his writings, the Roman historian Livy (59 B.C.–A.D. 17) describes a seventh-century B.C. consummation of a treaty between the Romans and the nearby Albans, which was presided over by the fetial priests.

The fetial was Marcus Valerius. He appointed Spurius Fusius to be *pater patratus* [spokesman for the fetials], touching his head and hair with the sacred sprig. The *pater patratus* is appointed to pronounce the oath, that is, to solemnize the pact. And this he accomplishes with many words, expressed in a long metrical formula which it is not worthwhile to quote. The conditions then being recited, he cries: "Hear, Jupiter, hear *pater patratus* of the Alban people; hear ye, People of Alba. From these terms, as they have been publicly rehearsed from beginning to end, without fraud, from these tablets, or this wax, and as they have been this day clearly understood, the Roman People will not be the first to depart. If it shall first depart from them, by general consent, with malice aforethought, then on that day do thou, great Jupiter, so smite the Roman People as I shall here today smite this pig. And so much the harder smite them as your power and your strength are greater." When Spurius had said these words, he struck the pig with a flint. In like manner, the Albans pronounced their own forms and their own oath, by the mouth of their own dictator and priests.

Source: *Livy*. Volume I. Translated by B. O. Foster. Cambridge and London: Loeb Classical Library, 1919.

23. Skepticism of Soothsayers

Although the Roman orator Cicero (106–43 B.C.) apparently had a healthy respect for the gods and for priests, he seemed a bit more skeptical about soothsayers, as reflected in the following dialogue from his treatise On Divination.

But indeed, that was quite a clever remark which Cato made many years ago: "I wonder," said he, "that a soothsayer doesn't laugh when he sees another soothsayer." How many things predicted by them really come true? If any do come true, then what reason can be advanced why the agreement of the event with the prophecy was not due to chance? While Hannibal was in exile at the court of King Prusias, he advised the king to go to war, but the king replied, "I do not dare, because the entrails forbid it." "And do you," said Hannibal, "put more faith in pieces of ox meat than you do in a veteran commander?"

Again, when Julius Caesar himself was warned by a most eminent soothsayer not to cross over to Africa before the winter solstice, did he cross? If he had not done so, all the forces opposed to him would have joined together. Why need I give instances—and, in fact, I could give countless ones—where the prophecies of soothsayers either were without result or the issue was directly the reverse of the prophecy? How many times they were mistaken in the recent civil war! [49–45 B.C.] What oracular messages the soothsayers sent from Rome to our Pompeian party then in Greece! What assurances they gave to [the commander] Pompey! For he placed great reliance in divination by means of entrails and portents. I have no wish to call these instances to mind, and indeed it is unnecessary—especially to you, since you had personal knowledge of them. Still, you are aware that the result was nearly always contrary to the prophecy.

Source: *Cicero: De Senectute; De Amicitia; De Divinatione.* Translated by William Armistead Falconer. Cambridge and London: Loeb Classical Library, 1923.

24. Selecting Vestal Virgins

As described in this passage from the Attic Nights *of Latin writer Aulus Gellius (A.D. c. 125–c. 180), the priestesses of the goddess Vesta, the Vestal Virgins, underwent a rigorous selection process (see also Documents 19 and 21).*

Those who have written about taking a Vestal Virgin... have stated that it is unlawful for a girl to be chosen who is less than six, or more than ten, years old. She must also have both father and mother living. She must be free, too, from any impediment in her speech, must not have impaired hearing, or be marked by any other bodily defect. She must not herself have been freed from paternal control, nor her father before her, even if her father is still living and she is under the control of her grandfather. Neither one nor both of her parents may have been slaves or engaged in mean occupations. But they say that one whose sister has been chosen to that priesthood acquires exemption, as well as one whose father is a priest or an augur... The daughter of a man without residence in Italy must not be chosen, and that the daughter of one who has three children must be excused.

Now, as soon as the Vestal Virgin is chosen, escorted to the house of Vesta and delivered to the pontiffs, she immediately passes from the control of her father without the ceremony of emancipation or loss of civil rights, and acquires the right to make a will.

But as to the method and ritual for choosing a Vestal, there are, it is true, no ancient written records, except that the first to be appointed was chosen by [Rome's second king], Numa...

Now, many think that the term "taken" ought to be used only of a Vestal. But, as a matter of fact, the priests of Jupiter also, as well as the augurs, were said to be "taken"... The Vestal is called "Amata" when taken by the chief pontiff, because there is a tradition that the first one who was chosen bore that name.

Source: *The Attic Nights of Aulus Gellius.* Volume I. Translated by John C. Rolfe. Cambridge and London: Loeb Classical Library, 1927.

Death and the Afterlife

Thoughts about death, and reactions to it, could vary from the pompous last will and testament of a rich man like *Trimalchio* (Document 38), to the simple but poignant sentiments carved on the tombstones of everyday people (Document 39). Not surprisingly, funeral rites and customs also varied from place to place. Kings and notable citizens often received lavish funerals (Documents 30, 34, and 37). Thirty days of mourning were decreed by the Israelites when Moses died (Document 25). In Egypt, ornate tombs were constructed for kings and pharaohs (Document 31). In Greece, some attempts were made to regulate wills and funerals through the use of legislation (Document 35).

Suicide is always a tragic way to bring an end to life, whether done privately (Document 28), or in the form of a mass suicide (Document 26). Imaginary travels through the afterlife were a staple of ancient literature (Documents 32 and 33).

An interesting story is told of the Greek actor Polus, whose acting skills were known far and wide. He was scheduled to act in a play in which he had to carry an urn containing the ashes of the deceased *Orestes*, and put on convincing expression of grief. It so happened that Polus's own son had recently died, so when it came time for him to act his part in the play, he substituted the urn containing the ashes of his son, "and filled the whole place, not with the appearance and imitation of sorrow, but with genuine grief and unfeigned lamentation" (Document 36).

ISRAEL

25. The Death of Moses

In this passage from his Jewish Antiquities, *the first-century* A.D. *Jewish historian Josephus recounts the final days of Moses.*

On advancing to the place where he was destined to disappear, they all followed him, bathed in tears. Thereupon Moses, by a signal of his hand, ordered those in the distance to remain still, while by word of mouth he exhorted those nearer to him not to make his passing a tearful one by following him. And they, deciding to honor his wishes in this matter, that is, to leave him to depart according to his own desire, held back, weeping with one another. Only the elders escorted him, with Eleazar the high priest, and Joshua the general. But when he arrived on the mountain called Abaris—a lofty eminence situated above Jericho and affording to those on its summit a wide view beneath of the best of the land of the Canaanites—he dismissed the elders. And as he was bidding farewell to Eleazar and Joshua and talking with them, a cloud suddenly descended upon him and he disappeared in a ravine...

He lived in all 120 years... having surpassed in understanding all people that ever lived and put to noblest use the results of his reflections. In speech and in addresses to a crowd, he found favor in every way, but chiefly through his thorough command of his emotions... As general he had few to equal him, and as prophet none, insomuch that in all his utterances, one seemed to hear the voice and word of God Himself. So the people mourned for him for 30 days, and never were Hebrews oppressed by grief so profound as that which filled them then on the death of Moses. Nor was he missed only by those who had known him personally, but the readers of his laws have sadly felt his loss, deducing from these the superlative quality of his virtue.

Such, then, be our description of the end of Moses.

Source: *Josephus: Jewish Antiquities.* Volume IV. Translated by H. St. J. Thackeray. Cambridge and London: Loeb Classical Library, 1930.

26. A Rebellion's Tragic Conclusion

In the early A.D. 70s, a small band of Jewish rebels held out against the Roman army for several years in a mountain-top fortress called Masada. *The contemporary Jewish historian Josephus, writing only a few years after the end of the Jewish rebellion against Rome, recounts the terrifying outcome of this action in the following passage from his Jewish War.*

Masada stood on a high rock, which was surrounded by deep ravines. It could be reached by only two narrow and difficult paths... The fortress was well-stocked with provisions—enough grain, wine, oil, legumes, and dates to last for years—and enough arms for 10,000 men, along with unwrought iron, brass, and lead...

[The Roman commander Flavius Silva] brought up a battering ram, which hammered against the wall until it made a breach. But in the meantime, the *sicarii* ["daggermen"] had erected another wall inside built of wood and earth which, being soft, cushioned the blows of the ram and even became firmer from the blows. Silva then ordered his soldiers to throw burning torches on it, and the wood soon caught fire. But before long, a north wind blew the flames in the faces of the Romans, and they were afraid that their siege engines would be burned. Yet suddenly the wind shifted and blew fiercely from the south, driving the flames against the wall and setting it ablaze from top to bottom. The Romans returned rejoicing to their camp, intending to attack the enemy on the following day. During the night, they kept a tighter watch, to prevent any of besieged to escape.

Eleazar [the Jewish leader], however, did not intend to flee, nor would he allow anyone else to do so. When he saw the wall in flames, he thought it would be nobler for all to die than fall into Roman hands, and so he assembled his bravest comrades. "Long ago, we decided to serve neither Roman nor anyone else except God," he said, "and now the time has come to verify that resolution by action. We, who were the first to revolt and are the last in arms against the Romans, must not disgrace ourselves by letting our wives die dishonored and our children enslaved. We still have the free choice of a noble death with those we hold dear. When they are gone, let us render a generous service to each other. But first we must destroy our property and the fortress by fire, sparing only our provisions, so that the Romans will know it was not hunger that subdued us, but that we preferred death to slavery."

Some of his hearers were eager to respond, but others could not bear the thought of putting their wives and children to death, and tears stole down their cheeks. Seeing them wavering, Eleazar addressed them again, asserting that "life, not death, is man's misfortune, for death liberates the soul from its imprisonment in a mortal body. Why, then, should we fear death, we who welcome the calm of sleep?" Indian philosophers happily greeted the purifying flames, he added, and then told of the tortures they could expect from the Romans, who would also violate their wives. "Let us die as free men with our wives and children," he concluded, "and deny the Romans their joy of victory! Let us rather strike them with amazement at our brave death!"

While Eleazar was still speaking, he was cut short by his hearers, who were filled with zeal to comply. They rushed away like possessed men, and began the bloody work. While they embraced their wives and took their children in their arms, clinging in tears to their parting kisses, they killed them.

When all were put to death, they gathered together their effects and set fire to them. Then they chose by lot ten of their number to kill the rest. They lay down beside their dead wives and children and, flinging their arms around them, offered their throats to those who slaughtered them all. The ten then cast lots, and he on whom it fell killed the other nine. He then looked about to see that all were dead, set fire to the place, and finally drove his sword through his body, falling beside his family. Two women and five children, however, escaped by hiding in an underground aqueduct during the massacre. The victims numbered 960, and the tragedy occurred [on May 2, A.D. 73].

Early the next morning, the Romans advanced to the wall over gangways, expecting fierce resistance. But no enemy appeared, and an awful silence hung over the place. They finally shouted in their perplexity, to arouse anyone. Hearing the noise, the two women who had saved themselves came out of hiding and informed the Romans of what had happened, one of the two lucidly reporting Eleazar's speech. At first they could hardly believe the story until, putting out the flames, they cut their way into the place and there found the mass of bodies. Instead of rejoicing over their enemies, the Romans admired the nobility of their determination.

The general left a garrison at Masada and departed with his army for Caesarea. Not an enemy remained in the country, all of it now subdued by this protracted war.

Source: *Josephus: The Essential Writings. A Condensation of* Jewish Antiquities *and* The Jewish War. Translated and edited by Paul L. Maier. Grand Rapids, MI: Kregel Publications, 1988.

CHINA

27. Heaven, According to Master Mo

The philosopher Mozi, or Master Mo (c. 470–c. 390 B.C.), provides in the following excerpt from his writings a description of Heaven.

Now what does Heaven desire, and what does it hate? Heaven desires rightness, and hates what is not right. Thus if I lead the people of the world to devote themselves to rightness, then I am doing what Heaven desires. If I do what Heaven desires, then Heaven will do what I desire. Now what do I desire, and what do I hate? I desire good fortune and prosperity, and I hate misfortune and calamity. If I do not do what Heaven desires and instead do what Heaven does not desire, then I will be leading the people of the world to devote themselves to what will bring misfortune and calamity.

How do I know that Heaven desires rightness and hates what is not right? In the world, where there is rightness, there is life; where there is no rightness, there is death. Where there is rightness, there is wealth; where there is no rightness, there is poverty. Where there is rightness, there is order; where there is no rightness, there is disorder. Now Heaven desires life and hates death, desires wealth and hates poverty, desires order and hates disorder. So I know that Heaven desires rightness and hates what is not right...

How do we know that Heaven loves the people of the world? Because it enlightens them universally. How do we know that it enlightens them universally? Because it possesses them universally. How do we know that it possesses them universally? Because it accepts sacrifices from them universally. Because within the four seas, among all the people who live on grain [i.e., the Chinese people], there are none who do not feed their sacrificial oxen and sheep, fatten their dogs and pigs, prepare clean offerings of millet and wine, and sacrifice to the Lord-on-High and the spirits. Since Heaven possesses all the cities and people, how could it fail to love them?

Moreover, I say that he who kills one innocent person will invariably suffer one misfortune. Who is it that kills the innocent person? It is man. And who is it that sends down the misfortune? It is Heaven. If Heaven did not love the people of the world, then why would it send down misfortune simply because one man kills another? Thus I know that Heaven loves the people of the world.

Source: From *Sources of Chinese Tradition*. Volume I. Second edition. Compiled by William Theodore de Bary and Irene Bloom. Copyright © 1999 Columbia University Press. Reprinted with permission of the publisher.

INDIA

28. A Monk Commits Suicide

Suicide by monks was generally frowned upon by the authors of Jain literature *in ancient India, but exceptions occurred, as the following excerpt from the* Acaranga Sutra *suggests.*

If a monk feels sick, and is unable duly to mortify the flesh, he should regularly diminish his food. Mindful of his body, immovable as a beam, the monk should strive to waste his body away. He should enter a village or town...and beg for straw. Then he should take it and go to an out-of-the-way place. He should carefully inspect and sweep the ground, so that there are no eggs, living beings, sprouts, dew, water, ants, mildew, drops of water, mud, or cobwebs left on it. Thereupon he carries out the final fast...Speaking the truth, the saint who has crossed the stream of transmigration, doing away with all hesitation, knowing all things but himself unknown, leaves his frail body. Overcoming manifold hardships and troubles, with trust in his religion, he performs this terrible penance. Thus in due time he puts an end to his existence. This is done by those who have no delusions. This is good; this is joyful and proper. This leads to salvation. This should be followed.

Source: From *Sources of Indian Tradition*. Volume I. Edited by William Theodore de Bary. Copyright © 1958 Columbia University Press. Reprinted with permission of the publisher.

EGYPT

29. Defending His Life

In one of the most famous sections of the Egyptian Book of the Dead, *the deceased defends his life in front of a tribunal of no fewer than 42 gods.*

Hail to you, great god, Lord of the Two Truths! I have come before you, my lord, just so that you might bring me so that I might see your beauty. I know you and I know your name and the names of the 42 gods who are with you in this Hall of the Two Truths, who live on those who preserve evil, who swallow their blood on that day of the reckoning of characters in the presence of Wennefer [an epithet of the god Osiris]... Behold, I have come before you bringing to you Truth, having repelled for you falsehood.

I have not committed wrongdoing against anyone.
I have not mistreated cattle.
I have not done injustice in the place of Truth.
I do not know that which should not be.
I have not done evil.
I have not daily made labors in excess of what should be done for me.
My name has not reached the bark of the Governor [the god Re].
I have not debased a god.
I have not deprived an orphan.
I have not done that which the gods abominate.
I have not slandered a servant to his superior.
I have not caused pain.
I have not caused weeping.
I have not killed.
I have not commanded to kill.
I have not made suffering for anyone.
I have not diminished the offering loaves in the temples.
I have not damaged the offering cakes of the gods.
I have not stolen the cakes of the blessed dead.
I have not copulated.
I have not been lascivious.
I have not added to nor have I subtracted from the offering measure...
I have not encroached upon fields.
I have not added to the weight of the balance.
I have not tampered with the plummet of the scales.
I have not taken milk from the mouths of children.
I have not deprived the flocks of their pasturage.
I have not snared birds of the branches of the gods.
I have not trapped fish in their marshes.
I have not diverted water in its season.
I have not erected a dam against flowing water.
I have not extinguished a fire at its critical moment.
I have not neglected the days concerning their meat offerings.
I have not driven away the cattle of a god's property.
I have not stopped a god in his procession.
I am pure, I am pure, I am pure, I am pure!

My purity is the purity of that great phoenix that is in Heracleopolis, because I am indeed that nose of the Lord of breath, who vivifies all the subjects on that day of filling the Eye of Horus in Heliopolis in the second month of winter, last day, in the presence of the Lord of this land. I am one who has seen the filling of the Eye of Horus in Heliopolis. Evil shall not happen against me in this land or in this Hall of the Two Truths because I know the names of the gods who are in it, the followers of the great god.

Source: *The Literature of Ancient Egypt.* Edited by William Kelly Simpson. New Haven, CT: Yale University Press, 2003. Copyright © 2003 by Yale University Press. All rights reserved. Reprinted with permission of the publisher.

30. A King Is Laid to Rest

Below are two excerpts from the writings of the first-century B.C. *Greek historian Diodorus Siculus. The first gives an account of the mourning customs and funeral rites accorded a deceased Egyptian king, and the second provides an example of two kings who were not revered after their deaths.*

The Egyptian ceremonies which followed upon the death of a king afforded no small proof of the good will of the people towards their rulers. The fact is that the honor which they paid was to one who was insensible of it, and this constituted an authentic testimony to its sincerity. For when any king died, all the inhabitants of Egypt united in mourning for him, tearing their clothing, closing the temples, stopping the sacrifices, and celebrating no festivals for 72 days, and plastering their heads with mud and wrapping strips of linen cloth below their breasts. Women as well as men went about in groups of two or three hundred, and twice each day, reciting the dirge in a rhythmic chant. They sang the praises of the deceased, recalling his virtues, nor would they eat the flesh of any living thing, or food prepared from wheat, and they abstained from wine and luxury of any sort. And no one would ever have seen fit to make use of baths or unguents or soft bedding; they would not even have dared to indulge in sexual pleasures, but every Egyptian grieved and mourned during those 72 days as if it were his own beloved child that had died.

But during this interval, they made splendid preparations for the burial, and on the last day, placing the coffin containing the body before the entrance to the tomb, they set up, as custom prescribed, a tribunal to sit in judgment upon the deeds done by the deceased during his life. And when permission had been given to anyone who so wished to lay a complaint against him, the priests praised all his noble deeds one after another, and the common people, who had gathered in myriads to the funeral, listening to them, shouted their approval if the king had led a worthy life, but if he had not, they raised a clamor of protest. And in fact many kings have been deprived of the public burial customarily accorded them because of the opposition of the people. The result was, consequently, that the successive kings practiced justice, not merely for the reasons just mentioned, but also because of their fear of the spite which would be shown their body after death, and of eternal harsh criticism...

The following selection gives an example of people's displeasure with two deceased kings:

Upon the death of this king [Chemmis], his brother Cephren succeeded to the throne, and ruled 56 years. But some say that it was not the brother of Chemmis, but his son, named Chabryes, who took the throne. All writers, however, agree that it was the next ruler who, emulating the example of his predecessor, built the second pyramid, which was the equal of the [first] in the skill displayed in its execution, but far behind it in size...And an inscription on the larger pyramid gives the sum of money expended on it...The smaller has no inscription, but has steps cut into one side. And although the two kings built the pyramids to serve as their tombs, neither of them was buried in them, for the people, because of the hardships which they had endured in the building of them and the many cruel and violent acts of these kings, were filled with anger against those who had caused their sufferings and openly threatened to tear their bodies apart and throw them out of the tombs. Consequently, each ruler, when dying, requested his kinsmen to bury his body secretly in an unmarked place.

Source: *Diodorus of Sicily.* Volume I. Translated by C. H. Oldfather. London and Cambridge: Loeb Classical Library, 1933.

31. Building a Pyramid

The fifth-century B.C. Greek historian Herodotus provides below an account of the construction of one of the famous Egyptian pyramids.

Up to the time of Rhampsinitus, Egypt was excellently governed and very prosperous. But his successor Cheops, to continue the account which the priests gave me, wrought the country into all sorts of misery. He closed all the temples, then, not content with excluding his subjects from the practice of their religion, compelled them without exception to labor as slaves for his own advantage. Some were forced to drag blocks of stone from the quarries in the Arabian hills to the Nile, where they were ferried across and taken over by others, who hauled them to the Libyan hills. The work went on in three-monthly shifts, a hundred thousand men in a shift. It took ten years of this oppressive slave labor to build the track along which the blocks were hauled—a work, in my opinion, of hardly less magnitude than the pyramid itself, for it is five furlongs in length, 60 feet wide, 48 feet high at its highest point, and constructed of polished stone blocks decorated with carvings of animals. To build it took, as I said, ten years—including the underground sepulchral chambers on the hill where the pyramids stand. A cut was made from the Nile, so that the water from it turned the site of these into an island.

To build the pyramid itself took 20 years. It is square at the base, its height, 800 feet, equal to the length of each side. It is of polished stone blocks beautifully fitted, none of the blocks being less than 30 feet long. The method employed was to build it in steps, or, as some call them, tiers or terraces. When the base was complete, the blocks for the first tier above it were lifted from ground level by contrivances made of short timbers. On this first tier there was another, which raised the blocks a stage higher, then yet another which raised them higher still. Each tier, or story, had its set of levers, or it may be that they used the same one, which, being easy to carry, they shifted up from stage to stage as soon as its load was dropped into place. Both methods are mentioned, so I give them both here.

The finishing off of the pyramid was begun at the top and continued downwards, ending with the lowest parts nearest the ground. An inscription is cut upon it in Egyptian characters recording the amount spent on radishes, onions, and leeks for the laborers, and I remember distinctly that the interpreter who read me the inscription said the sum was 1,600 talents of silver. If this is true, how much must have been spent in addition on bread and clothing for the laborers during all those years the building was going on, not to mention the time it took (not a little, I should think) to quarry and haul the stone, and to construct the underground chamber?

Source: *Herodotus: The Histories.* Translated by Aubrey de Selincourt, with revisions by A. R. Burn. Baltimore: Penguin Books, 1954. Reproduced by permission of Penguin Books Ltd.

32. Setne's Travels Through the Afterlife

This excerpt from a first-century A.D. papyrus provides information on the Egyptian view of the afterlife as seen through the eyes of a recently deceased individual named Setne.

[They entered the fourth hall, and Setne saw] people who were [plaiting ropes, while donkeys were chewing them up]. There were others whose provisions of water and bread were hung above them, and while they scrambled to bring them down, other people were digging pits at their feet, to prevent them from getting at them.

They entered the fifth hall, and Setne saw the noble spirits standing in their ranks. But those who were accused of crimes were standing at the door pleading, and the pivot of the door of the fifth hall was fixed in the right eye of a man who was pleading and lamenting loudly.

…They entered the seventh hall, and Setne saw the mysterious form of Osiris, the great god, seated on his throne of fine gold…Anubis, the great god, was on his left, the great god Thoth was on his right, and the gods of the tribunal of the inhabitants of the netherworld stood on his left and right. The balance stood in the center before them, and they weighed the good deeds against the misdeeds, Thoth, the great god, writing, while Anubis gave the information to his colleague.

Source: Dunand, Francoise, and Christiane Zivie-Coche. *Gods and Men in Egypt: 3000 B.C.E. to 395 C.E.* Translated from the French by David Lorton. Ithaca, NY: Cornell University Press, 2004.

GREECE

33. Odysseus's Travels Through the Afterlife

In Book XI of Homer's Odyssey, *Odysseus makes a fearsome voyage to the Underworld, where he encounters the spirits of relatives and friends. The following is excerpted from the account of his meeting with his deceased mother.*

          …I answered her:
'Mother, I came here, driven to the land of death
in want of prophecy from Teirêsias' shade;
nor have I yet coasted Akhaia's hills
nor touched my own land, but have had hard roving
since first I joined Lord Agamémnon's host
by sea for Ilion, the wild horse country,
to fight the men of Troy.
But come now, tell me this, and tell me clearly,
what was the bane that pinned you down in Death?
some ravaging long illness, or mild arrows
a-flying down one day from Artemis?
Tell me of Father, tell me of the son
I left behind me; have they still my place,
my honors, or have other men assumed them?
do they not say that I shall come no more?
And tell me of my wife: how runs her thought,
still with her child, still keeping our domains,
or bride again to the best of the Akhaians?'
To this my noble mother quickly answered:
'Still with her child indeed she is, poor heart,
still in your palace hall. Forlorn her nights
And days go by, her life used up in weeping.
But no man takes your honored place. Telémakhos
has care of all your garden plots and fields,
and holds the public honor of a magistrate,
feasting and being feasted. But your father
is country bound and comes to town no more.
he owns no bedding, rugs, or fleecy mantles,
but lies down, winter nights, among the slaves,
rolled in old cloaks for cover, near the embers.
or when the heat comes at the end of summer,
the fallen leaves, all round his vineyard plot,
heaped into windrows, make his lowly bed.
He lies now even so, with aching heart,
and longs for your return, while age comes on him.
so I, too, pined away, so doom befell me,
not that the keen-eyed huntress with her shafts
had marked me down and shot to kill me; not
that illness overtook me—no true illness
wasting the body to undo the spirit;
only my loneliness for you, Odysseus,
for your kind heart and counsel, gentle Odysseus,
took my own life away.'
          I bit my lip,
rising perplexed, with longing to embrace her,
and tried three times, putting my arms around her,
but she went sifting through my hands, impalpable
as shadows are, and wavering like a dream.
Now this embittered all the pain I bore,
and I cried in the darkness:

A Roman copy of an early third century B.C. Hellenistic portrait of Homer. Vanni/Art Resource, NY.

'O my mother,
will you not stay, be still, here in my arms,
may we not, in this place of Death, as well,
hold one another, touch with love, and taste
salt tears relief, the twinge of welling tears?
Or is this all hallucination, sent
against me by the iron queen, Perséphonê,
to make me groan again?'

My noble mother
answered quickly:

'O my child—alas,
most sorely tried of men—great Zeus's daughter,
Perséphonê, knits no illusion for you.
all mortals meet this judgment when they die.
No flesh and bone are here, none bound by sinew,
since the bright-hearted pyre consumed them down—
the white bones long exanimate—to ash;
dreamlike the soul flies, insubstantial.
You must crave sunlight soon.
Note all things strange
seen here, to tell your lady in after days.'
So went our talk; then other shadows came…

Source: Excerpts from THE ODYSSEY by Homer, translated by Robert Fitzgerald. Copyright © 1961, 1963 by Robert Fitzgerald. Copyright renewed 1989 by Benedict R. C. Fitzgerald, on behalf of the Fitzgerald children. Reprinted by permission of Farrar, Straus and Giroux, LLC.

34. A Spartan King's Obsequies

According to this passage from The Histories *of the fifth-century* B.C. *historian Herodotus (see also Document 31, above), the death of a Spartan king was marked by elaborate ceremonies and rituals.*

Special ceremonies are observed upon a king's death. News of the death is carried by riders all over the country, and women go the rounds of the capital beating cauldrons. This is the signal for two people, one man and one woman, from every citizen's household, to put on mourning—which they are compelled to do under penalty of a heavy fine. One custom is observed on the occasion of a king's death, which is the same in Sparta as in Asia: this is, that when a death occurs, not only Spartans, but a certain number of the country people from all over Laconia [the district where Sparta was located] are forced to attend the funeral. A huge crowd assembles, consisting of many thousands of people—Spartan citizens, country people, and serfs—and men and women together strike their foreheads with every sign of grief, wailing as if they could never stop and continually declaring that the king who has just died was the best they ever had.

If a king is killed in war, they make a statue of him, and carry it to burial on a richly-draped bier. After a king's funeral, there are no public meetings or elections for ten days, all of which are spent in mourning. When a new king comes to the throne on the death of his predecessor, he follows a custom which applies in Persia on similar occasions: he remits, that is, all debts owed by Spartan citizens either to the king or to the treasury.

Source: *Herodotus: The Histories*. Translated by Aubrey de Selincourt, with revisions by A. R. Burn. Baltimore: Penguin Books, 1954. Reproduced by permission of Penguin Books Ltd.

35. Solon's Laws on Funerals and Wills

Several of the reforms of the great sixth-century B.C. Athenian lawgiver Solon pertained to funerals and wills, as related in the following excerpt from the writings of the Greek biographer and essayist Plutarch (A.D. c. 15–120).

Praise is given to that law of Solon [594 B.C.] which forbids speaking ill of the dead. For it is piety to regard the deceased as sacred, justice to spare the absent, and good policy to rob hatred of its perpetuity... He was highly esteemed also for his law concerning wills. Before his time, no will could be made, but the entire estate of the deceased must remain in his family. Whereas he, by permitting a man who had no children to give his property to whom he wished, ranked friendship above kinship, and favor above necessity, and made a man's possessions his own property. On the other hand, he did not permit all manner of gifts without restriction or restraint, but only those which were not made under the influence of sickness, or drugs, or imprisonment, or when a man was the victim of compulsion or yielded to the persuasions of his wife...

He forbade laceration of the flesh by mourners, and the use of set lamentations, and the bewailing of anyone at the funeral ceremonies of another. The sacrifice of an ox at the grave was not permitted, nor the burial with the dead of more than three changes of clothing, nor the visiting of other tombs than those of their own family, except at the time of internment.

Source: *Plutarch's Lives*. Volume I. Translated by Bernadotte Perrin. London and Cambridge: Loeb Classical Library, 1914.

36. True Grief

In this passage from his Attic Nights (see also Documents 19, 21, and 24, above), Aulus Gellius (A.D. c. 125–c. 180) relates the story of the Greek actor Polus, and how he was able to demonstrate true grief on the stage.

There was in the land of Greece an actor of wide reputation who excelled all others in his clear delivery and graceful action. They say that his name was Polus, and he often acted the tragedies of famous poets with intelligence and dignity. This Polus lost by death a son whom he dearly loved. After he felt that he had indulged his grief sufficiently, he returned to the practice of his profession.

Josephus, an invaluable source of eyewitness testimony to the development of Western civilization as well as Christianity in the first century. © (2008) Jupiterimages Corporation.

At that time, he was to act in the *Electra* of Sophocles at Athens, and it was his part to carry an urn which was supposed to contain the ashes of Orestes. The plot of the play requires that Electra, who is represented as carrying her brother's remains, should lament and bewail the fate that she believed had overtaken him. Accordingly, Polus, clad in the mourning garb of Electra, took from the tomb the ashes and urn of his son, embraced them as if they were those of Orestes, and filled the whole place, not with the appearance and imitation of sorrow, but with genuine grief and unfeigned lamentation. Therefore, while it seemed that a play was being acted, it was in fact real grief that was enacted.

Source: *The Attic Nights of Aulus Gellius*. Volume II. Translated by John C. Rolfe. Cambridge and London: Loeb Classical Library, 1927.

ROME

37. *Funeral Rites for Notable Citizens*

In the following selection, the second-century B.C. *Greek historian Polybius describes the funeral rites accorded to notable individuals.*

Whenever any illustrious man dies, he is carried at his funeral into the forum to the speaker's platform, sometimes conspicuous in an upright posture and more rarely reclined. Here with all the people standing around, an adult son, if he has one left who happens to be present, or if not, some other relative, mounts the platform and speaks about the virtues and successful achievements of the deceased. As a consequence the multitude and not only those who had a part in these achievements, but also those who had none, when the facts are recalled to their minds and brought before their eyes, are moved to such sympathy that the loss seems to be not confined to the mourners, but a public one affecting the whole people.

Next after the interment and the performance of the usual ceremonies, they place the image of the departed in the most conspicuous position in the house, enclosed in a wooden shrine. This image is a mask reproducing with remarkable accuracy both the features and the complexion of the deceased. On the occasion of public sacrifices, they display these images, and decorate them with much care, and when any distinguished member of the family dies, they take them to the funeral, putting them on men who seem to them to bear the closest resemblance to the original in stature and carriage. These representatives wear togas, with a purple border if the deceased was a consul or praetor, whole purple if he was a censor, and embroidered with gold if he had celebrated a [military] triumph or achieved anything similar. They all ride in chariots, preceded by the...insignia by which the different magistrates are customarily accompanied according to the respective dignity of the offices of state held by each during his life. And when they arrive at the speaker's platform, they all seat themselves in a row on ivory chairs.

There could not easily be a more ennobling spectacle for a young man who aspires to fame and virtue. For who would not be inspired by the sight of the images of men renowned for their excellence, all together and as if alive and breathing? What spectacle could be more glorious than this?

Besides, he who makes the oration over the man about to be buried, when he has finished speaking of him, recounts the successes and exploits of the rest whose images are present, beginning from the most ancient. By this means, by this constant renewal of the good report of brave men, the celebrity of those who performed noble deeds is rendered immortal, while at the same time, the fame of those who did good service to their country becomes known to the people, and a heritage for future generations. But the most important result is that young men are thus inspired to endure every suffering for the public welfare, in the hope of winning the glory that comes to brave men. What I say is confirmed by the facts. Many Romans have voluntarily engaged in single combat in order to decide a battle, not a few have faced certain death, some in war to save the lives of the rest, and others in peace to save the republic. Some even when in office have put their own sons to death, contrary to every law or custom, setting a higher value on the interest of their country than on the ties of nature that bound them to their nearest and dearest.

Source: *Polybius: The Histories.* Volume III. Translated by W. R. Paton. London and New York: Loeb Classical Library, 1923.

38. The Last Will and Testament of a Flamboyant Rich Man

In this passage from Petronius's (A.D. c. 27–65) novel Satyricon, *the buffoonish character* Trimalchio *throws a damper on the dinner party he is hosting when he announces to his guests, in great detail, the terms of his will.*

"I plan to free all of them [his slaves] in my will. To Philargyrus here I leave a farm and his woman, Cario, inherits a block of flats and the tax on his freedom and his bed and bedding. To my dear Fortunata [his wife], I leave everything I have, and I commend her to the kindness of my friends. But I'm telling you the contents of my will so my whole household will love me as much when I'm still alive as after I'm dead."

Once the slaves heard this, of course, they burst out with cheers and effusive thanks. But Trimalchio suddenly began to take the whole farce quite seriously and ordered his will brought out and read aloud from beginning to end while the slaves sat there groaning and moaning. At the close of the reading, he turned to Habinnas. "Well, old friend, will you make my tomb exactly as I order it? First, of course, I want a statue of myself. But carve my dog at my feet, and give me garlands of flowers, jars of perfume, and every fight in [the gladiator] Petraites' career. Then, thanks to your good offices, I'll live on long after I'm gone. In front, I want my tomb one hundred feet long, but two hundred feet deep. Around it, I want an orchard with every know variety of fruit tree. You'd better throw in a vineyard, too. For it's wrong, I think, that a man should concern himself with the house where he lives his life but give no thought to the home he'll have forever. But above all, I want you to carve this notice:

THIS MONUMENT DOES NOT PASS INTO THE POSSESSION OF MY HEIRS.

In any case, I'll see to it in my will that my grave is protected from damage after my death. I'll appoint one of my ex-slaves to act as custodian to chase off the people who might come and crap on my tomb. Also, I want you to carve me several ships with all sail crowded and a picture of myself sitting on the judge's bench in official dress with five gold rings on my fingers and handing out a sack of coins to the people. For it's a fact, and you're my witness, that I gave a free meal to the whole town and a cash handout to everyone. Also, make me a dining room, a frieze maybe, but however you like, and show the whole town celebrating at my expense. On my right, I want a statue of Fortunata with a dove in her hand. And oh yes, be sure to have her pet dog tied to her girdle. And don't forget my pet slave. Also, I'd like huge jars of wine, well stoppered so the wine won't splash out. Then sculpt me a broken vase with a little boy sobbing out his heart over it. And in the middle stick a sundial so that anyone who wants the time of day will have to read my name. And how will this do for the epitaph?

> Here lies Gaius Pompeius Trimalchio
> Maecenatianus
> Voted in absentia an official of the
> Imperial cult.
> He could have been registered
> In any category of the civil service at Rome
> But chose otherwise.
> Pious and courageous,
> A loyal friend,
> He died a millionaire,
> Though he started life with nothing.
> Let it be said to his eternal credit
> That he never listened to philosophers.
> Peace to him,
> Farewell."

At the end, he burst into tears. Then Fortunata started wailing, Habinnas began to cry, and every slave in the room burst out sobbing as though Trimalchio were dying then and there. The whole room throbbed and pulsed to the sound of mourning. I was almost in tears myself, when Trimalchio suddenly cried, "We all have to die, so let's live while we're waiting! Come on, everybody, smile, be happy."

Source: From THE SATYRICON by Petronius, translated by William Arrowsmith, copyright © 1959, renewed © 1987 by William Arrowsmith. Used by permission of Dutton Signet, a division of Penguin Group (USA) Inc.

39. Two Epitaphs

Reproduced below are two Roman funerary inscriptions from the second century B.C.

Gnaeus Cornelius Scipio Hispanus, son of Gnaeus, praetor, curule aedile, quaestor, tribune of soldiers (twice); member of the board of ten for judging lawsuits; member of the board of ten for making sacrifices.

By my good conduct I heaped virtues on the virtues of my clan. I raised a family and sought to equal the exploits of my father. I upheld the praise of my ancestors, so that they are glad I was created of their line. My honors have ennobled my stock.

Stranger, my message is short. Stand by and read it through. Here is the unlovely tomb of a lovely woman. Her parents called her Claudia by name. She loved her husband with all her heart. She bore two sons. Of these, she leaves one on earth. Under the earth she has placed the other. She was charming in conversation, yet gentle in bearing. She kept house, she made wool. That is my last word. Go your way.

Source: "Corpus Inscriptionum Latinarum (Collection of Latin Inscriptions), Volume I." From *Roman Civilization Sourcebook II: The Empire*, by Naphtali Lewis and Meyer Reinhold. Copyright © 1955 Columbia University Press. Reprinted with permission of the publisher.

GLOSSARY OF INDIVIDUALS AND TERMS

See the Appendix for biographical information on the authors of documents included in this volume.

Achilles. Achilles was the greatest Greek warrior in the Trojan War, the slayer of the Trojan hero Hector and the sponsor of the Funeral Games for his best friend Patroclus.

Acropolis. Literally, the "highest [part of the] city," the Acropolis was a high hill in Athens on which many noted buildings were constructed, including the Parthenon.

Actaeon. In Greek mythology, Actaeon was a hunter who was devoured by his own hunting dogs.

Agamemnon. Agamemnon was king of Mycenae and leader of the Greek forces during the Trojan War.

Agesilaus (444–360 B.C.). King of Sparta from about 401 B.C., Agesilaus II commanded armies against the Persians and, during the Corinthian War (395–387 B.C.), against an anti-Spartan coalition led by Thebes, the eventual success of which led to a gradual decline in Spartan power and influence during Agesilaus's long reign. Somewhat lame since birth, Agesilaus was short and unimpressive in appearance, but a brave and successful leader of men in battle.

Alexandria. Founded in about 331 B.C., by Alexander the Great, for whom it was named, the Egyptian city of Alexandria was one of the most important cultural and educational centers of the ancient world, being the home of the Lighthouse of Alexandria, one of the Seven Wonders of the Ancient World, and of the great Library of Alexandria, the largest library of the ancient world. The city was the capital of Egypt until the Arab invasion of the seventh century A.D.

Anacharsis (fl. late sixth century B.C.). Part Scythian and part Greek, Anacharsis was an itinerant philosopher who traveled, in about 589 B.C., from his Scythian homeland on the north shores of the Black Sea to Athens, where he had a number of interesting debates with the Athenian lawgiver Solon about various Athenian laws and customs.

Appian Way (Via Appia). Begun in about 312 B.C. under the direction of the Roman official Appius Claudius Caecus, the Via Appia was the first and oldest paved Roman road; it was undertaken to improve the supply of Roman armies operating in southern Italy. By 264 B.C., the Via Appia extended southeast from Rome to the port of Brundisium on the southern tip of the Italian peninsula.

Appuleius Diocles. Appuleius Diocles was a second-century A.D. Roman charioteer who, during his unusually long career won thousands of races, becoming one of the most successful charioteers on record.

Archias (c. 120–61 B.C.). Archias was a well-known Greco-Syrian poet whose disputed claim to Roman citizenship was successfully defended in court in 62 B.C. by Cicero, who argued on Archias's behalf in the speech *Pro Archia*.

Aristides the Just (530–468 B.C.). One of 10 commanders under Miltiades of the Athenian force that defeated the Persians at Marathon in 490 B.C., Aristides was a prominent fifth-century B.C. Athenian politician and soldier. In 483 B.C., he was ostracized from Athens after some voters were apparently motivated to vote against him out of personal jealousy.

Assembly (Athens). The Assembly was the chief legislative body of the Athenian democracy.

Atticus (c. 110–32 B.C.). A first-century B.C. banker and friend of the Roman orator Cicero, Atticus was the recipient of many of Cicero's surviving letters.

Augustus (63 B.C.–A.D. 14). Augustus was the title granted by the Senate in 27 B.C. to Gaius Octavius, the legal and political heir of Julius Caesar. Augustus is generally regarded as the first emperor of Rome (r. 27 B.C.–A.D. 14) and bringer of the Pax Romana, a time of peace and prosperity after decades of civil war and disorder.

Brundisium. A city in southeastern Italy, Brundisium was the terminus of the Appian Way.

Bucephalus. Bucephalus, meaning "ox head," was the name of Alexander the Great's large black warhorse and arguably the most famous horse in the ancient world. Ridden by Alexander in many battles, Bucephalus died in 326 B.C. after being wounded at the Battle of Hydaspes in modern-day Pakistan.

Calchas. Calchas was a soothsayer in Greek mythology; he appears in the *Illiad*, in which his warns that the captured Trojan girl Chryseis must be returned to her father to halt the plague sent among the Greeks by Apollo; his warning leads to the quarrel between Achilles and Agamemnon. He also appears in a play by the Athenian playwright Aeschylus, who has Calchas prophesy that Agamemnon must sacrifice his daughter to appease the goddess Artemis before the Greeks can successfully sail to Troy.

Caligula (A.D. 12–41). The third emperor of Rome, Caligula was popular with the people but is depicted in all sources of the period as an insane tyrant. After surviving various plots against him, he was assassinated by members of his Praetorian Guard.

Carthage. Carthage was a city-state in North Africa and a longstanding rival of the Romans for influence and territory in Sicily, Spain, and elsewhere in the western Mediterranean. In a series of three wars known as the First (264–241 B.C.), Second (218–201 B.C.), and Third (149–146 B.C.) Punic Wars, Rome defeated and eventually destroyed Carthage. During the long Second Punic War, the Carthaginian general Hannibal invaded Italy and defeated several Roman armies, but was never able to capture Rome itself.

Circus Maximus. The Circus Maximus was a huge chariot racetrack in Rome.

Cleisthenes. Cleisthenes was a sixth-century B.C. Athenian legislator who reformed the Athenian constitution in about 508 B.C.; his reforms and his policy of *isonomia* ("equal rights") formed the basis of the Athenian democracy that developed in the following century.

Creon. In Greek mythology, Creon was a legendary king of the Greek city of Thebes.

Demosthenes (384–322 B.C.). Demosthenes was a prominent orator and statesman of fourth-century B.C. Athens, who sought to restore his city to greatness by speaking forcefully against the threat to Greek independence from Philip II of Macedon. After Philips's death he played a leading part in the unsuccessful Athenian revolt against Philip's son, Alexander the Great.

drachma. The drachma was a basic unit of exchange in ancient Greece; its value may have been equivalent to between $50 and $100 today.

Draco. Draco was a sixth century B.C. Athenian legislator whose laws specified capital punishment as the sentence for even minor violations. According to Plutarch, Athenians of the time said that Draco's code was "written not in ink, but in blood." It is from Draco that we derive the English word *Draconian* for laws that are especially harsh or severe.

Eleazar (d. A.D. 73). Eleazar was the leader of the Jewish rebels who held the mountaintop fortress of Masada against the Romans in the early A.D. 70s; rather than surrender to the Romans, Eleazar and his people committed mass suicide.

ephod. The ephod was an embroidered cloak worn by the Jewish high priest.

Epicurus (342–271 B.C.). Epicurus was a Greek philosopher and founder of the Epicurean school of philosophy; seeing the purpose of philosophy to be the living of a happy, tranquil life, Epicurus was called the "teacher of pleasure" by the first-century A.D. Roman philosopher Seneca.

Etruscan civilization. Comprising three confederations of city-states in the region north of Rome, the vibrant and mysterious Etruscan civilization likely dominated Rome until about 400 B.C., after which the Etruscans were gradually assimilated into the Roman Republic.

Eunus. Eunus was the charismatic leader of a Sicilian slave revolt against Rome in the second century B.C.

Hippodamus of Miletus. Hippodamus of Miletus was a fifth-century B.C. city planner, who devised regular, orderly plans for Greek colonies.

Isis. In Egyptian mythology, Isis was the mother goddess, the wife of Osiris and the mother of Horus. Worship of Isis eventually spread outside Egypt and the cult became especially popular during Roman times, with temples to Isis being built throughout Europe and the Middle East.

Jain literature. The term *Jain literature* refers to ancient Indian philosophical and religious texts, the earliest of which dates to perhaps the seventh century B.C., or earlier.

Lycurgus. Lycurgus was the semi-legendary lawgiver of seventh-century B.C. Sparta, who initiated the militaristic reformation of Spartan society.

Masada. A mountain-top fortress near the Dead Sea, Masada was occupied by Jewish rebels led by Eleazar from A.D. 70-73 immediately following the Roman suppression of the Jewish Revolt and the destruction of the temple in Jerusalem. The defenders of Masada committing mass suicide to avoid capture and enslavement by a besieging Roman army.

Milo of Croton. Milo of Croton was a sixth century B.C. wrestler and one of the most successful athletes in the history of the ancient Olympics.

Nero (A.D. 37–68). Nero was the fifth emperor of Rome, reigning from A.D. 54–68. Known to history as tyrannical and dissolute, Nero initiated the first state persecution of Christians, blaming them for the fire that devastated Rome in A.D. 64. Nero committed suicide in A.D. 68 after being overthrown by the Senate.

Numa. Numa was the legendary second king of Rome; he succeeded Romulus, the city's founder, and reigned from 715–673 B.C.

Odysseus. In Greek mythology Odysseus was king of Ithaca and a Greek survivor of the Trojan War; his post-war travels and adventures are chronicled in Homer's epic poem, *Odyssey.*

Olympia; Olympic Games. Olympia was located in the southwestern Peloponnesus; it was the site of the quadrennial Olympic Games and also the site of an important shrine to the god Zeus. Prestigious international athletic games were also held at Corinth, Delphi, and Nemea.

Orestes. In Greek mythology, Orestes was the son of Agamemnon, king of Mycenae, and husband of Clytemnestra; Orestes was killed in a chariot race.

Osiris. In Egyptian mythology, Osiris was the god of life, death, and fertility. Portrayed as the husband of Isis, whose devotion to her mate after his death resulted eventually in his resurrection as god of the underworld, he was one of the oldest Egyptian gods and was worshipped in Egypt until the coming of Christianity.

ostracism. Ostracism was a practice of fifth-century B.C. Athens whereby unpopular or pompous politicians could be evicted from the city for a period of 10 years through a vote of the citizens. The well-known politician Aristides the Just was ostracized in 483 B.C.

Palimbothra. According to the second-century A.D. Greek historian Arrian, Palimbothra was the greatest of the ancient Indian cities.

Parthenon. The Parthenon was a large, ornate temple built in honor of the goddess Athena on the Acropolis in Athens in the fifth century B.C. Part of the great building program initiated by Pericles, the Parthenon was constructed under the direction of the sculptor Pheidias.

Peloponnesus. The Peloponnesus is an ancient generic place-name for the large southern peninsula of mainland Greece.

Pentheus. In Greek mythology, Pentheus was a king of Thebes who was torn apart by his mother and aunts while they were in a frenzy induced by Dionysius, the Greek god of wine.

Pericles (c. 495–429 B.C.). Pericles was an Athenian statesman, orator, and politician, and the driving force behind the so-called Periclean Age, the golden age of art and literature in fifth-century B.C. Athens.

periplous. Meaning literally "voyage-around," *periplous* was a genre of travel writings and literature.

Ph(e)idias (c. 490–430 B.C.). Pheidias was a famed fifth-century B.C. Athenian sculptor/architect, who is best known for supervising the construction of the Parthenon and for sculpting the huge statue of Athena housed within it.

Piraeus. Piraeus was the port city of Athens; during the fifth century B.C., it was connected to Athens and protected by long walls, which were razed when Athens was defeated by Sparta at the end of the Peloponnesian War.

polis. The polis was a city-state and the basic unit of political and social organization in ancient Greece and elsewhere in the ancient world.

Pyrrhus (318–272 B.C.). Pyrrhus was a third-century B.C. Greek general, who lost so many soldiers in his victory over the Romans at the Battle of Pydna (275 B.C.) that he is said to have remarked afterwards: "If we are victorious in one more battle with the Romans, we will be utterly ruined." From this battle comes the term *Pyrrhic victory,* which describes a triumph that has devastating costs for the victor.

Pythagoras (c. 580–c. 500 B.C.). Pythagoras was a sixth-century B.C. Greek philosopher who was renowned as a mathematician, mystic, and scientist. In modern mathematics, his name is recalled in the Pythagorean Theorem, which he is said to have discovered and proved; in ancient Greece he was the founder of a religious movement known as Pythagoreanism.

Romulus (r. 753–715 B.C.). Romulus was the legendary founder and first king of Rome, which, according to tradition, was established in the year 753 B.C.

Saturnalian Festival. Celebrated in December, the Saturnalia was one of the major Roman holidays; it commemorated the dedication of the temple of the god Saturn. In the fifth century A.D., the writer Macrobius wrote a work entitled *Saturnalia*, which gave an account of discussions held in the house of a prominent Roman during the week-long Saturnalia celebration. Some scholars believe that early Christians set Christmas, the birthday of Christ, in December to take advantage of the pagan holiday period, but this theory is much disputed.

Shamash. Shamash was the Babylonian sun god.

smrti. The *smrti* are texts of sacred law from ancient India.

Socrates (469–399 B.C.). Socrates was an Athenian philosopher, who was forced to commit suicide in 399 B.C. after being convicted of corrupting the youth of the city. Among his students was the famous fourth-century B.C. philosopher Plato.

Solon (c. 640–c. 560 B.C.). Solon was an Athenian statesman and politician, who reformed the laws of Athens in 594 B.C.

Sparta. Located on the Peloponnesus, the large southern peninsula of mainland Greece, Sparta was one of the most powerful city-states in ancient Greece. Sparta fought and defeated Athens during the long Peloponnesian War of the late sixth century B.C., and for a time in the early fifth century exercised political and military dominance over the Greek city-states.

sutras. The sutras were ancient Indian maxims on proper ways to live.

Thales of Miletus (c. 624–c. 546 B.C.). Regarded by many as the first philosopher in the Greek tradition, Thales of Miletus was one of the Seven Sages of Ancient Greece, the title given by Greek tradition to seven famous wise men and lawgivers that included Solon of Athens.

Tiresias. In Greek mythology, Tiresias was a blind prophet of Thebes, who features prominently in many myths and plays.

Trajan (A.D. 53–117). The second of the so-called five good emperors of Rome, Trajan ruled from A.D. 98–117. It was to Trajan that the Roman official Pliny wrote concerning the best way to deal with the people known as Christians.

Trimalchio. Trimalchio is the buffoonish, nouveau-riche protagonist in the *Cena Trimalchionis (Trimalchio's Dinner Party)*, the largest part of Petronius's fragmentary first-century A.D. Latin novel *Satyricon*.

Twelve Tables (c. 450 B.C.). The Twelve Tables constituted Rome's first written law code.

vizier. A vizier was a government official in ancient Egypt, who sometimes functioned as an advisor to the pharaoh.

Xanthippe. Xanthippe was the wife of the fifth-century B.C. Athenian philosopher Socrates.

Xerxes (r. 485–465 B.C.). Xerxes I, known as Xerxes the Great, was the Persian king who unsuccessfully attempted to conquer Greece in 480 B.C. His forces were defeated in that year at the naval battle at Salamis and in 479 B.C. at the land battle of Plataea.

Zeus. Known to the Romans as Jupiter, Zeus was king of the gods in Greek mythology.

APPENDIX: BIOGRAPHIES OF DOCUMENT AUTHORS

Listed are the ancient authors cited in the document introductions, with brief biographical information provided for each.

Aelian (c. A.D. 170–235; full Roman name: Claudius Aelianus) Aelian wrote several books, including one on the deeds of famous historical characters and one on the natural world entitled *On the Characteristics of Animals*.

Aelius Aristides (A.D. c. 117–189) Aelius Aristides was a traveling philosopher who wrote speeches and laudatory essays on the places that he visited during his travels, including Rome, Athens, and Smyrna.

Aeschylus (525–456 B.C.) One of the greatest of the Greek tragedians, Aeschylus authored around 90 plays, of which seven have survived, including his only extant trilogy (*Oresteia*), and his only surviving historical play (*Persians*). He supposedly died one day while he was out walking bare-headed on the seashore. An eagle, flying far above, mistook his bald head for solid rock, and dropped a tortoise on him, hoping to shatter the tortoise's shell, but instead killing the famous playwright.

Apicius (fl. first century A.D.; full Roman name: Marcus Gavius Apicius) Apicius was a gourmand who wrote extensively on food, cooking, and recipes. His works were collected together under the title *De Re Coquinaria (On Cooking)*, a sort of Roman cookbook.

Apuleius (fl. second century A.D.; full Roman name: Lucius Apuleius) Apuleius authored a book entitled *Metamorphoses*, a novel about the transformation of the protagonist—Apuleius—into a donkey, his adventures as a quadruped, and then his transformation once more into human form.

Aristophanes (445–380 B.C.) Aristophanes was an Athenian comic playwright whose brilliantly satirical and witty plays skewered government, public policy decisions, the court system, educational philosophies, contemporary literature, and virtually any and every other topic of public interest. Eleven of his plays are extant. One of his best-known plays, *Clouds*, ridiculed the philosopher Socrates, while three others—*Acharnians*, *Knights*, and *Lysistrata*—criticized the Peloponnesian War.

Aristotle (384–322 B.C.) One of the foremost thinkers and philosophers in the history of the Western world, the Greek philosopher Aristotle's literary output was vast and comprehensive, covering natural history, rhetoric, politics, government, economics, education, sociology, literature, logic, and ethics.

Arrian (fl. second century A.D.; full Roman name: Flavius Arrianus) Arrian was a Romanized Greek who wrote a variety of books on diverse topics, such as hunting, stoic philosophy, India, and the expeditions of Alexander the Great.

Athenaeus (fl. A.D. c. 190–200) Athenaeus's only surviving work is entitled *Deipnosophistae*, or *The Learned Banquet*, a compendium of information that might be discussed at dinner by sophisticated and knowledgeable diners. All 15 books of the work are in the form of conversations among dinner guests.

Aulus Gellius (A.D. c. 125–c.180) Aulus Gellius assembled a collection of short essays on every imaginable topic into a work called *Attic Nights*. He used that title, as he himself says, because he "began to amuse [him]self by assembling these notes [which he jotted down in random order, on anything that seemed interesting to him in his readings or in his daily life] during the long winter nights which [he] spent on a country place in the land of Attica."

Cato the Elder (234–149 B.C.; full Roman name: Marcus Porcius Cato) Called the "Elder" to distinguish him from his great-grandson of the same name, Cato was one of the most noteworthy statesmen and politicians of the ancient Roman world. An austere defender and proponent of traditional Roman values, he held most of the important elective offices of the Roman government. Of his published work, the only one that remains today is his treatise on agriculture, *De Agri Cultura*.

Celsus (fl. first century A.D.; full Roman name: Aulus Cornelius Celsus) Celsus authored an encyclopedic work covering agriculture, medicine, military affairs, oratory, and philosophy, but only the portion on medicine, *De Medicina*, survives. The treatise was so highly regarded that it earned its author laudatory epithets such as the "Roman Hippocrates" and the "Cicero of Physicians."

Cicero (106–43 B.C.; full Roman name: Marcus Tullius Cicero) Cicero is generally regarded as the most gifted orator in Roman history, as well as the finest prose author. His pre-eminence as a lawyer is unquestioned. He held many political offices during his lifetime, and he was involved in a number of highly publicized disputes and controversies with rival politicians. The transcripts of many of his court cases and speeches are still extant, as well as hundreds of his letters, and numerous philosophical essays.

Demetrius (dates uncertain) Demetrius is the name ascribed to a treatise entitled *On Style*, about the proper writing of prose. However, the date of this work, and its true authorship, are both problematical.

Diodorus (fl. first century B.C.; interchangeably surnamed Siculus, or the Sicilian) Diodorus, a Greek historian born in Sicily, wrote a comprehensive history of the ancient world in 40 books. Fifteen survive to the present day. It took him about 30 years to complete this mammoth task.

Euripides (480–406 B.C.) Euripides was one of the most accomplished Greek tragedians of the fifth century B.C. He wrote about 90 plays of which 18 survive. Euripides's best-known works include *Alcestis*, *Medea*, *Electra*, and *The Bacchae*. He is also the author of *Cyclops*, one of the few complete satyr plays—an ancient Greek form of tragicomedy similar to modern burlesque—still in existence.

Frontinus (A.D. c. 35–104; full Roman name: Sextus Julius Frontinus) Frontinus was an engineer and civil servant who wrote technical manuals on military strategies, and on the Roman aqueduct system. Although usually a very fact- and detail-oriented writer, he allowed himself an outburst of admiration in the following description of aqueducts: "With such an array of indispensable structures carrying so many waters, compare, if you will, the idle pyramids, or the useless though famous, works of the Greeks!"

Herodotus (490–425 B.C.) Sometimes called "The Father of History," the Greek historian Herodotus compiled a lengthy and entertaining account of the geography, ethnology, customs, religion, legends, and history of practically the entire Mediterranean world. His description of Persian messengers—"Nothing stays these couriers from the swift completion of their appointed rounds; neither snow, nor rain, nor heat, nor dark of night"—has become famous as the motto of the United States Postal Service.

Hesiod (fl. eighth century B.C.) Hesiod grew up on a farm in rural Greece. When his father died, he and his brother, Perses, inherited the farm. The lazy Perses soon fell into poverty, but Hesiod, a hard-working farmer, thrived, and wrote an epic poem on agriculture, *Works and Days*. *Theogony*, another epic poem, about the origins of the gods, is also attributed to Hesiod.

Hippocrates (460–377 B.C.) Antiquity's most famous physician, Hippocrates, a Greek, was the author of perhaps 60 medical treatises, although some scholars cast doubt on the proposition that Hippocrates wrote all of them, or even any of them. Some of the major topics in what might be termed the *Hippocratic corpus* include epidemics, nutrition, prognosis, fractures and dislocations, epilepsy, and the effects on health of air, wind, and water.

Homer (possibly eighth or ninth century B.C.) Homer, Western literature's first epic poet, and one of its best, wrote two classic poems about the Trojan War and its aftermath, *Iliad* and *Odyssey*. The first details the final months of the Trojan War, while the second focuses on the efforts of one of the Greek leaders, Odysseus, to return home after the war and reclaim his rightful place as king of Ithaca.

Horace (65–8 B.C.; full Roman name: Quintus Horatius Flaccus) Generally regarded as one of ancient Rome's most skilled poets, Horace is best known for his *Odes*, *Epistles*, *Epodes*, and *Satires*. He is the originator of the well-known phrase *carpe diem*, meaning "seize the day."

Isocrates (436–338 B.C.) Twenty-one speeches and nine letters survive from the writings of Isocrates, one of the finest oratorical stylists of his day. He lived to be almost 100 years of age, and he remained intellectually active well into his 90s.

Josephus (A.D. c. 37–c. 100; full Roman name: Titus Flavius Josephus). Born of an aristocratic Jewish family, Josephus eventually settled in Rome, where he was granted

Roman citizenship. He is best known for two historical works: *The Jewish War* and *Jewish Antiquities*. He wrote the former "to refute those who in their writings were doing outrage to the truth [about the war between the Jews and the Romans]". He wrote *Jewish Antiquities* "in the belief that the whole Greek-speaking world [would] find it worthy of attention; for it will embrace our entire ancient history and political constitution."

Juvenal (A.D. c. 60–c. 130; full Roman name: Decimus Junius Juvenalis) Juvenal's 16 *Satires* contain often harsh and bitter denouncements of Roman life and society. His attitude toward the city and its people is probably best summarized by his statement that deteriorating conditions in Rome made it difficult *not* to write satire: *Difficile est non scribere saturam*; "it is difficult not to write satire."

Laozi (possibly flourished in either the sixth or fourth century B.C.) Laozi is a legendary, and possibly apocryphal, figure in the history of Chinese literature. He was a Taoist philosopher and possibly a forerunner of Confucius.

Livy (59 B.C.–A.D. 17; full Roman name: Titus Livius) Livy spent most of his adult life researching and writing his massive history of Rome, *Ab Urbe Condita* (*From the Founding of the City*). As the title suggests, the work covers Roman history from its earliest beginnings up to Livy's own time. He provides an excellent rationale for the study of history: "What chiefly makes the study of history wholesome and profitable is this: you see the lessons of every kind of human experience set forth as if on a conspicuous monument; from these, you can choose for yourself and for your country what to imitate, and what to avoid."

Lucian (A.D. c. 120–c. 200) Lucian was a prolific Greek satirist and essayist, whose favorite topics for satirical ridicule included philosophy, oratory, and religious customs and beliefs.

Macrobius (fl. fifth century A.D.; full Roman name: Macrobius Ambrosius Theodosius) Macrobius's most famous work is *Saturnalia*, a series of dinner conversations about varied topics that take place during one of the most popular Roman festivals, the Saturnalia, which occurred in December. There are twelve participants in these conversations.

Oppian (fl. third century A.D.) Oppian wrote two books in Greek, one on fishing, *Halieutica*, and one on hunting, *Cynegetica*, although some historians suggest that the latter was written by a different author. Both books detail the kinds of fish and game that could be caught and hunted, and the various methods that could be employed to do so.

Ovid (43 B.C.–A.D. 17; full Roman name: Publius Ovidius Naso) Ovid, a noted Roman poet, is most famous for his *Metamorphoses*, adaptations of Greek myths that all involve some sort of change or transformation, hence the title of the work. Ovid also authored several other collections of poetry, including some racy love poems that may have been at least partially to blame for his permanent banishment from Rome in 8 A.D.

Pausanias (fl. second century A.D.) Pausanias traveled widely throughout the Greek world, and wrote a book based on those travels and the places he visited. Topics included geography, history, mythology, and monuments. Of particular interest are his descriptions of Olympia and Olympic athletes.

Petronius (A.D. c. 27–65; full Roman name: Gauis Petronius Arbiter) Petronius's most famous work is *Satyricon*, a novel about the misadventures of two vagabonds, Encolpius and Ascyltus. Their travels bring them to the mansion of the super-wealthy, and equally pompous, Trimalchio, where they enjoy the exquisite cuisine and other delights of a rich man's dinner party. Petronius was forced to commit suicide after running afoul of the emperor Nero.

Plato (428–347 B.C.) As a young man, Plato met the famous Athenian philosopher Socrates, and soon became a devoted follower. Socrates appears in many of Plato's dialogues and other writings, and it is through these writings that Socrates's thought and teachings have been preserved. Plato was a prolific writer, and unique among ancient authors in that all of his works appear to have survived.

Pliny the Elder (A.D. 23–79; full Roman name: Gaius Plinius Secundus) He is called the "Elder" to distinguish him from his nephew, Gaius Plinius Caecilius Secundus, Pliny the Younger (see below). Pliny the Elder was a soldier and lawyer as a young man, but he is best known for his monumental encyclopedic work *Natural History,* a massive compilation of facts and information on every imaginable topic pertaining to the work's title. In his preface, he notes that he gleaned information from the works of 473 different authors, and that his book contains some 20,000 facts. He was killed during the eruption of Mount Vesuvius that destroyed Pompeii.

Pliny the Younger (A.D. 62–114; full Roman name: Gaius Plinius Caecilius Secundus) As a teenager, Pliny the Younger witnessed the eruption of Mount Vesuvius, in which his uncle, Pliny the Elder, was one of the casualties (see above). He went on to enjoy a successful career in law and government. His numerous surviving letters provide a glimpse into the lifestyle of an upper-class Roman gentleman of the first and second centuries A.D.

Plutarch (A.D. c. 45–c. 120) Plutarch was born in the little town of Chaeronea, not far from Athens. He was a well-read, intelligent man, whose most famous works are probably his 50 biographies of famous Greeks and Romans. He also wrote essays on many diverse topics, collectively entitled *Moralia,* or *Moral Essays.* A recent article in *Smithsonian* (July, 2004) rightly stated that "Plutarch's voice is decent, tolerant, knowing—the voice of a grown-up."

Polybius (c. 205–123 B.C.) Polybius, a Greek historian, lived in Rome for a number of years as a hostage, the result of a war against Greece successfully carried out by the Romans. While in Rome, Polybius became a keen observer and student of Roman life and history, and eventually authored a definitive history of Rome, including a well-known laudatory defense of the Roman constitution.

Ptah-hotep (sometimes spelled Ptahhotep; fl. twenty-fourth century B.C.) Ptah-hotep was an Egyptian vizier and politician to whom is generally attributed a collection of proverbs entitled *The Maxims of Ptah-hotep*; these maxims are words of advice from a father to a son.

Quintilian (A.D. c. 35–c. 100; full Roman name: Marcus Fabius Quintilianus) Quintilian was an educator, orator, and lawyer, and the first Roman to found a public school and receive a stipend for his teaching. His treatise on education and oratory, *Institutio Oratoria*, includes information on such topics as educational principles, teaching methods, presenting a case in court, proofs and kinds of evidence, style and word usage, and intellectual and personal qualities necessary for an orator.

Seneca (4 B.C.–A.D. 65; full Roman name: Lucius Annaeus Seneca) Seneca was a Roman philosopher, playwright, and politician, and the author of numerous philosophical essays and letters. He also served for a number of years as a counselor and advisor to the emperor Nero. In A.D. 65, he was implicated in a plot to assassinate Nero and forced to commit suicide.

Sophocles (c. 496–406 B.C.) Sophocles was one of the leading fifth-century Athenian tragic playwrights. Seven of his approximately 120 plays are extant, including perhaps the most famous and finest ancient Greek play, *Oedipus the King*.

Strabo (c. 64 B.C.–A.D. 21) The widely traveled Greek geographer and historian Strabo authored a book in which he provided detailed descriptions of the topography, demographics, and history of most of the regions of the Mediterranean world, as well as India.

Suetonius (A.D. c. 70–c. 140; full Roman name: Gaius Suetonius Tranquillus) Suetonius wrote biographies of the first 12 Roman emperors, as well as biographies of noted poets, grammarians, and orators.

Sunzi (c. 544–c. 496 B.C.) Sunzi was a Chinese general and military strategist, whose book, *The Art of War*, has been widely read and studied, and is generally regarded as a classic of Chinese literature.

Tacitus (A.D. c. 55–c 117; full Roman name: Cornelius Tacitus) Although best known as a historian, Tacitus also wrote a book on oratory, a biography of his father-in-law Agricola, and a book-length description of Germany and the German people. Tacitus's two historical works, *Annals* and *Histories*, span the years A.D. 14–70.

Tertullian (A.D. c. 160–c. 225; full Roman name: Quintus Septimius Florens Tertullianus) The early Christian author Tertullian was born in Africa and wrote a number of books about various aspects of the Christian religion; over 30 of these works are extant.

Theophrastus (c. 370–287 B.C.) The most noted work of the Greek writer Theophrastus is his collection of 30 short essays entitled *Characters*, in which he delineates various human flaws, such as flattery, gossiping, stinginess, tactlessness, snobbery, and covetousness. He also authored a book on plants.

Thucydides (c. 460–c. 400 B.C.) One of the most skilled and famous historians of antiquity, Thucydides wrote a monumental book on the Peloponnesian War (431–404 B.C.), the tragic conflict between Athens and Sparta. Thucydides was a general in the Athenian army in the war's early stages; later, he served as a sort of embedded war correspondent, observing battles and battle sites, interviewing witnesses, and checking and re-checking his notes and information as carefully as possible, so that his book would be a model of accuracy and exactitude.

Varro (116–27 B.C.; full Roman name: Marcus Terentius Varro) Varro was a Roman philosopher and politician, who later devoted his life to literature, first by organizing in Rome a library of Greek and Roman works, and then by creating his own written works. He is thought to have authored over 70 books, but only two survive: *De Lingua Latina*, a book on the Latin language, and *Res Rusticae*, a treatise on farming.

Virgil (70–19 B.C.; full Roman name: Publius Vergilius Maro) Virgil (sometimes spelled Vergil) was ancient Rome's premier epic poet, the author of *Aeneid*, which is the story of the founding of the Roman race by the book's central character, Aeneas.

Vitruvius (fl. first century B.C.; full Roman name: Vitruvius Pollio) The Roman architect Vitruvius wrote the only manual on architecture surviving from the ancient world. In it, he covers such topics as construction materials and methods, city planning, temples, public buildings, private homes, house decoration, aqueduct and pipe construction, and acoustics.

Xenophon (c. 430–c. 354 B.C.) Xenophon was a Greek historian whose best known work is probably *Anabasis*, an account of the military activities and adventures of Cyrus the Younger and the Ten Thousand, a mercenary army of Greeks. He wrote several other books, including a treatise on hunting, *Cynegeticus*, and a narrative about household management, *Oeconomicus*.

Yan Zhitui (A.D. 531–590) Yan was a Chinese writer, calligrapher, lexicographer, and politician. His most noted literary work was his *Yanshi Jiaxun*, a compendium of precepts and advice to his sons on how to succeed in life.

BIBLIOGRAPHY

CONTEMPORARY TRANSLATORS, EDITORS, AND AUTHORS

Adlington, W., trans., with revisions by S. Gaselee. *Apuleius: The Golden Ass, Being the Metamorphoses of Apuleius*. Cambridge and London: Loeb Classical Library, 1915.

Armstrong, G. Cyril, trans. *Aristotle: Oeconomica and Magna Moralia*. London and Cambridge: Loeb Classical Library, 1935.

Arrowsmith, William, trans. *The Satyricon: Petronius*. New York: The New American Library, 1960.

Babbitt, Frank Cole, trans. *Plutarch's Moralia. Volume I*. London and Cambridge: Loeb Classical Library, 1927.

_____. *Plutarch's Moralia. Volume II*. London and New York: Loeb Classical Library, 1928.

_____. *Plutarch's Moralia. Volume IV*. London and Cambridge: Loeb Classical Library, 1936.

_____. *Plutarch's Moralia. Volume V*. Cambridge and London: Loeb Classical Library, 1936.

Bailkey, Nels M., ed. *Readings in Ancient History, from Gilgamesh to Diocletian*. Lexington MA: D.C. Heath and Company, 1969.

Balsdon, J.P.V.D. *Life and Leisure in Ancient Rome*. New York, St. Louis, San Francisco: Phoenix Press, 1969.

Basore, John W., trans. *Seneca: Moral Essays. Volume I*. Cambridge and London: Loeb Classical Library, 1928.

Bennett, Charles E., trans. *Frontinus: The Stratagems*. London and New York: Loeb Classical Library, 1925.

_____. *Seneca: Moral Essays. Volume II*. Cambridge and London: Loeb Classical Library, 1932.

Bettenson, Henry, trans. *Livy: Rome and the Mediterranean. Books XXXI–XLV of The History of Rome from Its Foundation*. Baltimore: Penguin Books, 1976.

Bovie, Smith Palmer, trans. *The Satires and Epistles of Horace*. Chicago: University of Chicago Press, 1959.

Brownson, Carleton L., trans. *Xenophon: Hellenica. Volume I*. Cambridge and London: Loeb Classical Library, 1918.

Brunt, P. A., trans. *Arrian. Volume II*. Cambridge and London: Loeb Classical Library, 1933.

Bury, R. G., trans. *Plato Laws. Volume II*. London and Cambridge: Loeb Classical Library, 1926.

Butler, H. E., trans. *The Institutio Oratoria of Quintilian*. Cambridge and London: Loeb Classical Library, 1920.

Clement, Paul C., and Herbert B. Hoffleit, trans. *Plutarch's Moralia*. *Volume VIII*. Cambridge and London: Loeb Classical Library, 1969.

Creekmore, Hubert, trans. *The Satires of Juvenal*. New York: The New American Library, 1963.

Davies, Percival Vaughn, trans. *Macrobius: The Saturnalia*. New York and London: Columbia University Press, 1969.

de Bary, William Theodore, ed. *Sources of Indian Tradition*. *Volume I*. New York and London: Columbia University Press, 1958.

de Bary, William Theodore, and Irene Bloom, eds. *Sources of Chinese Tradition*. *Volume I*. New York: Columbia University Press, 1999.

Duff, J. Wight, trans. *Panegyric on Piso*, in *Minor Latin Poets*. Cambridge and London: Loeb Classical Library, 1934.

Dunand, Francoise, and Christiane Zivie-Coche. *Gods and Men in Egypt: 3000 B.C.E. to 395 C.E.* Translated from the French by David Lorton. Ithaca, NY, and London: Cornell University Press, 2004.

Ebrey, Patricia Buckley, ed. *Chinese Civilization and Society: A Sourcebook*. New York: The Free Press, 1981.

Fagles, Robert, trans. *Homer: The Iliad*. New York: Penguin Books, 1990.

Fairclough, H. Rushton, trans. *Horace: Satires, Epistles, and Ars Poetica*. Cambridge and London: Loeb Classical Library, 1926.

Falconer, William Armistead, trans. *Cicero: De Senectute; De Amicitia; De Divinatione*. Cambridge and London: Loeb Classical Library, 1923.

Fitts, Dudley, and Robert Fitzgerald, trans. *Antigone*, in *Greek and Roman Writers*. Compiled by Reverend William T. McNiff, O.S.C. New York: Harcourt, Brace & World, 1939.

Fitzgerald, Robert, trans. *Homer: The Odyssey*. New York: Random House, Inc., 1961.

Foster, B. O., trans. *Livy. Volume I*. Cambridge and London: Loeb Classical Library, 1919.

Foster, John L. *Ancient Egyptian Literature: An Anthology*. Austin, TX: University of Texas Press, 2001.

Fowler, Harold North, trans. *Plato: Euthyphro, Apology, Crito, Phaedo, Phaedrus*. London and New York: Loeb Classical Library, 1914.

Freese, John Henry, trans. *Aristotle: The "Art" of Rhetoric*. London and New York: Loeb Classical Library, 1926.

Frost, Frank J. *Greek Society*. 3rd ed. Lexington, MA, and Toronto: Houghton Mifflin, 1987.

Glover, T. R., trans. *Tertullian: Apology; De Spectaculis*. Cambridge and London: Loeb Classical Library, 1931.

Granger, Frank, trans. *Vitruvius: On Architecture. Volume II*. Cambridge and London: Loeb Classical Library, 1934.

Grant, Michael, trans. *Selected Political Speeches of Cicero*. New York: Penguin Books, 1977.

Gulick, Charles Burton, trans. *Athenaeus: The Deipnosophists. Volume II*. London and New York: Loeb Classical Library, 1928.

Gummere, Richard M., trans. *Seneca: Ad Lucilium Epistulae Morales. Volume I*. Cambridge and London: Loeb Classical Library, 1917.

_____. *Seneca: Ad Lucilium Epistulae Morales. Volume III*. Cambridge and London: Loeb Classical Library, 1925.

Harmon, A. M., trans. *Lucian. Volume IV*. London and New York: Loeb Classical Library, 1925.

Harris, H. A., trans. *Ovid: Amores*, in *Sport in Greece and Rome*. Ithaca, NY: Cornell University Press, 1972.

Henderson, Jeffrey, trans. *Aristophanes: Acharnians, Knights*. Cambridge and London: Loeb Classical Library, 1998.

Herschel, Clemens, trans. *Frontinus: The Stratagems and the Aqueducts of Rome*. London and New York: Loeb Classical Library, 1925.

Hooper, William Davis, trans., with revisions by Harrison Boyd Ash. *Marcus Terentius Varro: On Agriculture*. Cambridge and London: Loeb Classical Library, 1934.

Hubbell, H. M., trans. *Cicero: De Inventione; De Optimo Genere Oratorum*. Cambridge and London: Loeb Classical Library, 1949.

Humphries, Rolfe, trans. *The Aeneid of Virgil*. New York: Macmillan Publishing Company, 1951.

_____. *Ovid: Metamorphoses*. Bloomington: Indiana University Press, 1957.

Hunt, A. S., and C. C. Edgar, trans. *Select Papyri: Non-literary papyri. Public Documents. Volume II*. Cambridge and London: Loeb Classical Library, 1934.

Ingalls, Daniel H. H., trans. *Sanskrit Poetry from Vidyakara's "Treasury."* Cambridge, MA: The Belknap Press of Harvard University, 1965.

Jones, Horace Leonard, trans. *The Geography of Strabo. Volume III*. London and New York: Loeb Classical Library, 1930.

_____. *The Geography of Strabo. Volume VIII*. London and New York: Loeb Classical Library, 1932.

Jones, W.H.S., trans. *Hippocrates*. Cambridge and London: Loeb Classical Library, 1923.

_____. *Pausanias: Description of Greece. Volume III*. Cambridge and London: Loeb Classical Library, 1933.

Keyes, Clinton Walker, trans. *Cicero: De Re Publica; De Legibus*. Cambridge and London: Loeb Classical Library, 1928.

Kitto, H.D.F., trans. *Sophocles. Three Tragedies: Antigone, Oedipus the King, Electra*. London, Oxford, New York: Oxford University Press, 1962.

Lee, H.D.P., trans. *Plato: The Republic*. Baltimore. Penguin Books, 1955.

Levi, Peter, trans. *Pausanias: Guide to Greece. Volume 2. Southern Greece*. New York: Penguin Books, 1971.

Lewis, Naphtali, and Meyer Reinhold. *Roman Civilization Sourcebook I: The Republic*. New York: Harper & Row, Publishers, 1951.

_____. *Roman Civilization Sourcebook II: The Empire*. New York: Harper & Row, Publishers, 1955.

Lichtheim, Miriam. *Ancient Egyptian Literature, Volume II: The New Kingdom*. Berkeley, Los Angeles, London: University of California Press, 1976.

Maier, Paul L., trans. *Josephus: The Essential Writings. A Condensation of Jewish Antiquities and The Jewish War*. Grand Rapids, MI: Kregel Publications, 1988.

Marchant, E. C., trans. *Xenophon: Memorabilia and Oeconomicus*. Cambridge and London: Loeb Classical Library, 1923.

_____. *Xenophon: Scripta Minora. Volume VII*. London and Cambridge: Loeb Classical Library, 1925.

May, Herbert G., and Bruce M. Metzger, eds. *The Oxford Annotated Bible with the Apocrypha*. New York: Oxford University Press, 1965.

McDermott, William C., and Wallace E. Caldwell. *Stele of Amenhotep II*, in *Readings in the History of the Ancient World*. Translated by J. A. Wilson. New York: Rinehart and Company Inc., 1951.

Melmoth, William, trans., with revisions by W.M.L. Hutchinson. *Pliny: Letters. Volume I*. Cambridge and London: Loeb Classical Library, 1915.

Miller, Walter, trans. *Cicero: De Officiis*. London and New York: Loeb Classical Library, 1913.

Most, Glenn W., trans. *Hesiod: Theogony; Works and Days; Testimonia*. Cambridge and London: Loeb Classical Library, 2006.

Norlin, George, trans. *Isocrates. Volume I*. London and New York: Loeb Classical Library, 1928.
_____. *Isocrates. Volume II*. Cambridge and London: Loeb Classical Library, 1929.
Oldfather, C. H., trans. *Diodorus of Sicily. Volume I*. London and Cambridge: Loeb Classical Library, 1933.
_____. *Diodorus of Sicily. Volume II*. London and Cambridge: Loeb Classical Library, 1935.
Paton, W. R., trans. *Polybius: The Histories. Volume III*. London and New York: Loeb Classical Library, 1923.
Perrin, Bernadotte, trans. *Plutarch's Lives. Volume I*. London and Cambridge: Loeb Classical Library, 1914.
_____. *Plutarch's Lives. Volume VII*. London and Cambridge: Loeb Classical Library, 1919.
_____. *Plutarch's Lives. Volume IX*. Cambridge and London: Loeb Classical Library, 1920.
Peterson, Sir W., with revisions by M. Winterbottom. *Tacitus: Dialogus, Agricola, Germania*. Cambridge and London: Loeb Classical Library, 1914.
_____. *Plutarch's Lives. Volume III*. Cambridge and London: Loeb Classical Library, 1916.
Rackham, H., trans. *Aristotle Politics*. London and Cambridge: Loeb Classical Library, 1932.
_____. *Cicero: De Natura Deorum*. Cambridge and London: Loeb Classical Library, 1933.
_____. *Cicero: De Oratore. Volume I*. Cambridge and London: Loeb Classical Library, 1942.
_____. *Pliny: Natural History. Volume III*. London and Cambridge: Loeb Classical Library, 1940.
_____. *Pliny: Natural History. Volume IX*. Cambridge and London: Loeb Classical Library, 1952.
Radice, Betty, trans. *Pliny: Letters and Panegyricus. Volume II*. Cambridge and London: Loeb Classical Library, 1915.
Roberts, W. Rhys, trans. *Demetrius: On Style*. London and New York: Loeb Classical Library, 1927.
Robinson, Rachel Sargent, trans. *Philostratus Gymnastics*, in *Sources for the History of Greek Athletics*. Urbana: University of Illinois Press, 1927.
Robson, E. Iliff, trans., with revisions by P. A. Brunt. *Arrian*. Cambridge and London: Loeb Classical Library, 1933.
Rolfe, John C., trans. *The Attic Nights of Aulus Gellius. Volume I*. Cambridge and London: Loeb Classical Library, 1927.
_____. *The Attic Nights of Aulus Gellius. Volume II*. Cambridge and London: Loeb Classical Library, 1927.
_____. *Suetonius. Volume I*. Cambridge and London: Loeb Classical Library, 1913.
Ross, W. D., ed. *Aristotle: Selections*. New York: Charles Scribner's Sons, 1927.
Rouse, W.H.D., trans. *Homer: The Iliad. The Story of Achilles*. Edinburgh: Thomas Nelson and Sons, 1938.
Russell, Donald A., ed. and trans. *Quintilian: The Orator's Education*. Cambridge and London: Loeb Classical Library, 2001.
Scholfield, A. F., trans. *Aelian: On the Characteristics of Animals. Volume I*. London and Cambridge: Loeb Classical Library, 1958.
_____. *Aelian: On the Characteristics of Animals. Volume III*. London and Cambridge: Loeb Classical Library, 1958.
Scott-Kilvert, Ian, trans. *The Rise and Fall of Athens: Nine Greek Lives*. New York: Penguin Books, 1960.
Selincourt, Aubrey de, trans., with revisions by A. R. Burn. *Herodotus: The Histories*. Baltimore: Penguin Books, 1954.
Shorey, Paul, trans. *Plato: The Republic*. London and New York: Loeb Classical Library, 1930.

Simpson, William Kelly, ed. *The Literature of Ancient Egypt.* 3rd ed. New Haven, CT: Yale University Press, 2003.

Smith, Charles Forster, trans. *Thucydides.* Cambridge and London: Loeb Classical Library, 1919.

Sommerstein, Alan H., trans. *Aristophanes: The Acharnians; The Clouds; Lysistrata.* New York: Penguin Books, 1973.

Spencer, W. G., trans. *Celsus: De Medicina. Volume I.* London and Cambridge; Loeb Classical Library, 1935.

Starr, Chester G. *Old Oligarch: Constitution of the Athenians,* in *The Ancient Greeks.* Translated by H. G. Dakyns. New York, London, Toronto: Oxford University Press, 1971.

Sutton, E. W., and H. Rackham, trans. *Cicero: De Oratore. Volume I.* Cambridge and London: Loeb Classical Library, 1942.

Thackeray, H. St. J., trans. *Josephus: Jewish Antiquities. Volume IV.* Cambridge and London: Loeb Classical Library, 1930.

Todd, O. J., trans. *Xenophon: Symposium and Apology.* Cambridge and London: Loeb Classical Library, 1923.

Tredennick, Hugh, trans. *The Last Days of Socrates.* Baltimore: Penguin Books, 1954.

Vehling, Joseph Dommers, trans. *Apicius: Cookery and Dining in Imperial Rome.* New York. Dover Publications, Inc., 1936.

Vellacot, Philip, trans. *Euripides: The Bacchae and Other Plays.* Baltimore: Penguin Books, 1954.

Walton, Francis R., trans. *Diodorus of Sicily. Volume XII.* London and Cambridge: Loeb Classical Library, 1967.

Warner, Rex, trans. *Fall of the Roman Republic: Six Lives by Plutarch.* Baltimore: Penguin Books, 1958.

_____. *Thucydides: History of the Peloponnesian War.* Baltimore: Penguin Books, 1954.

Winstedt, E. O., trans. *Cicero: Letters to Atticus. Volume I.* Cambridge and London: Loeb Classical Library, 1912.

SECONDARY WORKS

Avari, Burjor. *India: The Ancient Past: A History of the Indian Subcontinent from c. 7000 B.C. to A.D. 1200.* London: Routledge, 2007.

Boardman, John, Jasper Griffin, and Oswyn Murray, eds. *The Oxford History of Greece and the Hellenistic World.* Oxford: Oxford University Press, 2002.

———, eds. *The Oxford History of the Classical World.* Oxford: Oxford University Press, 1986.

———, eds. *The Oxford History of the Roman World.* Oxford: Oxford University Press, 2001.

Brewer, Douglas J., and Emily Teeter. *Egypt and the Egyptians.* Cambridge: Cambridge University Press, 1999.

Bury, J. B., and Russell Meiggs. *A History of Greece to the Death of Alexander the Great.* New York: St. Martin's Press, 1975.

Cartledge, Paul, ed. *The Cambridge Illustrated History of Ancient Greece.* Cambridge: Cambridge University Press, 2002.

Crawford, Harriet. *Sumer and the Sumerians.* 2nd ed. Cambridge: Cambridge University Press, 2004.

Ebrey, Patricia Buckley. *The Cambridge Illustrated History of China.* Cambridge: Cambridge University Press, 1999.

Grant, Michael. *From Alexander to Cleopatra: The Hellenistic World.* New York: Charles Scribner's Sons, 1982.

Grant, Michael. *History of Rome*. New York: Charles Scribner's Sons, 1978.

————. *The Classical Greeks*. New York: Charles Scribner's Sons, 1989.

————. *The History of Ancient Israel*. New York: Charles Scribner's Sons, 1984.

————. *The Jews in the Roman World*. New York: Barnes and Noble, 1995.

————. *The Rise of the Greeks*. New York: Macmillan, 1987.

Grimal, Nicolas. *A History of Ancient Egypt*. Oxford: Blackwell, 1993.

Hadas-Lebel, Mireille. *Flavius Josephus: Eyewitness to Rome's First-Century Conquest of Judea*. New York: Macmillan, 1989.

Hansen, Valerie. *The Open Empire: A History of China to 1600*. 6th ed. New York: W.W. Norton Company, 2000.

Holland, Tom. Rubicon: The Last Years of the Roman Republic. New York: Doubleday, 2003.

James, T.G.H. *A Short History of Ancient Egypt: From Predynastic to Roman Times*. Baltimore: The John Hopkins University Press, 1998.

Kramer, Samuel Noah. *The Sumerians: Their History, Culture, and Character*. Chicago: University of Chicago Press, 1971.

Loewe, Michael, and Edward L. Shaughnessy. *The Cambridge History of Ancient China: From the Origins of Civilization to 221* B.C. Cambridge: Cambridge University Press, 1999.

Mackay, Christopher S. *Ancient Rome: A Political and Military History*. Cambridge: Cambridge University Press, 2007.

Majumdar, Aoeske K. *Concise History of Ancient India*. Delhi: Munshiram Manoharlal Publishers, 1992.

Mommsen, Theodor. *The History of Rome*. 3 vols. Lenox, MA: Hard Press, 2006.

Niditch, Susan. *Ancient Israelite Religion*. New York: Oxford University Press, 1997.

Pomeroy, Sarah B., Stanley M. Burstein, Walter Donlan, and Jennifer Tolbert Roberts. *A Brief History of Ancient Greece: Politics, Society, and Culture*. Oxford: Oxford University Press, 2003.

Redford, Donald B. *Egypt, Canaan, and Israel in Ancient Times*. Princeton, NJ: Princeton University Press, 1992.

SarDesai, D. R. *India: The Definitive History*. Boulder, CO: Westview Press, 2007.

Silverman, Donal P., ed. *Ancient Egypt*. Oxford: Oxford University Press, 1997.

Ward, Allen M, Fritz M. Heichelheim, and Cedric A. Yeo. *A History of the Roman People*. 4th ed. Upper Saddle River, NJ: Prentice Hall, 2002.

White, J. E. Manchip. *Ancient Egypt: Its Culture and History*. New York: Dover Publications, 1970.

Wilson, John A. *The Culture of Ancient Egypt*. Chicago: University of Chicago Press, 1956.

Woolley, C. Leonard. *The Sumerians*. New York: W. W. Norton Company, 1965.

WEB SITES

http://www.fordham.edu/halsall/ancient/periplus.html. *Ancient History Sourcebook: The Periplus of the Erythraean Sea. Travel and Trade in the Indian Ocean by a Merchant of the First Century.* [Translator not stated.]

http://nefertiti.iwebland.com/texts/precepts_of_ptahhotep.htm

http://www.yale.edu/lawweb/avalon/medieval/hamcode.htm. The Avalon Project at Yale Law School. Translator [*Code of Hammurabi*]: L. W. King.

INDEX

ABOUT THE EDITORS

LAWRENCE MORRIS, General Editor, is Assistant Professor of English at Albright College. He received his PhD from Harvard University and has taught English literature and history at a variety of institutions including Harvard, University of Wisconsin–Green Bay, and Fitzwilliam College (Cambridge University). Morris is currently writing about the relationship between truth and literary fiction in the religious writing of the medieval British Isles.

DAVID MATZ, Volume Editor, is Professor of Classical Languages at St. Bonaventure University. His book publications include *Daily Life of the Ancient Romans* (Greenwood, 2002) and *Famous Firsts in the Greek and Roman World* (2000). He has also published numerous scholarly and popular articles.